HISTORY AND PRESENCE

HISTORY

and

PRESENCE

ROBERT A. ORSI

The Belknap Press of Harvard University Press

CAMBRIDGE, MASSACHUSETTS · LONDON, ENGLAND

First Harvard University Press paperback edition, 2018
First printing

LIBRARY OF CONGRESS CATALOGING-IN-
PUBLICATION DATA

Names: Orsi, Robert A., author.
Title: History and presence / Robert A. Orsi.
Description: Cambridge, Massachusetts : The Belknap
Press of Harvard University Press, 2016. | Includes
bibliographical references and index.
Identifiers: LCCN 2015036422 |
ISBN 9780674047891 (cloth : alk. paper)
ISBN 9780674984592 (pbk.)
Subjects: LCSH: Lord's Supper—Real presence. |
Catholic Church—Doctrines—History. | Catholic
Church—Prayers and devotions. | Catholics—Religious
life—United States—Case studies.
Classification: LCC BV825.3 .O76 2016 |
DDC 234/.163—dc23 LC record available at
http://lccn.loc.gov/2015036422

To my wife, Christine Helmer

CONTENTS

HISTORY AND PRESENCE

INTRODUCTION

Real Presence

I HAVE never known anyone with a deeper devotion to Christ in the Eucharist than my mother. Her love was so great that she simply could not understand why anyone would ever be kept from the real presence of Christ in the Host—certainly not good people, but especially not those men and women who appeared to be the least deserving, from a human perspective, of eating Christ's body and drinking his blood. In the late spring of 1998, she wrote a letter to a New York newspaper, her only published work as far as I know, sharply criticizing the city's Cardinal John O'Connor for condemning President Bill Clinton and First Lady Hillary Rodham Clinton, both non–Roman Catholics—she a Methodist, he a Southern Baptist—for receiving Communion that spring in a South African Catholic church, and the local priest for giving it to them. "The action taken by the priest in South Africa," the cardinal had said, speaking from his pulpit in Saint Patrick's Cathedral in New York City on Palm Sunday, "however well intentioned, was legally and doctrinally wrong in the eyes of Church law and Church doctrine." This is the sound of a hammer, nailing down the law.[1]

Holy Week is the time of year when Christians recall Jesus's institution of the Eucharist at the last meal he shared with his apostles. It was at this supper that Jesus, aware that his death was drawing near, spoke the words "take and eat" and "take and drink" and "do this in memory of me." Only in cases of "grave necessity," the cardinal continued, is a non-Catholic permitted to receive Communion. His Eminence reminded his listeners of the reason for this prohibition: "To receive Holy Communion in the Catholic Church means that one believes one is receiving, not a symbol of Christ, but Christ Jesus himself." The implication is clear: Protestants deal in symbols, Catholics in the really real.

From his perch on Fifth Avenue, Cardinal O'Connor was evoking and enforcing the ontological border between Catholics and others. My mother, from a less auspicious venue, protested against this, speaking out of a Southern Italian tradition of resistance to the presumptions of clerical authority. Who dares to keep anyone away from God really present in the Host? she indignantly asked the cardinal, fully ignoring his exalted status. This is the Church's problem with the real presence: controlling access to it. Such control is one of the surest grounds of ecclesiastical and political power, not only over the laity but over the rulers of nations, too. Yet presence continually exceeds the Church's efforts to contain it. In this story of the cardinal, the Clintons, and my mother, ordinary humans refused to be banned from approaching what they knew to be a powerful source of solace, hope, and companionship or to ban others from it. Everything at stake in this story—the cardinal's authority; my mother's dissent; the difference between Catholics and others, including other Christians; Catholic superiority; the distinction between the symbolic and the real; the global extension of the dispute; its implications in contemporary politics and in questions of Church-state relations—is rooted in the violent debates that exploded in sixteenth-century Europe over what Jesus meant when he said, "this is my body," "this is my blood," "take and eat," and "do this in memory of me."

* * *

Throughout the sixteenth century, Christians searched for new ways of conceiving and imagining the divine body in the Host. Or not in the Host. New knowledge about the natural world and the human body, profound changes in the arrangements of society, and the emergence of new schools of thought in philosophy all contributed to raising or reviving troubling questions about the nature of the Eucharist. Because of the momentousness of what was being debated—how the divine and human stand in relationship to each other—conflict over Christ's real presence in the consecrated Host was implicated in other exigent human concerns, such as the relationship between spirit and matter, between the past and the present, between representation and reality, between one person and another, and between political leaders and those over whom they exercised different forms of authority.

The impassioned theological debates over the divine presence coincided with early modern European global adventures. As they went out to the rest of the world on missions of conquest and conversion, Europeans brought their metaphysical differences with them. Religious distinctions and racial taxonomies went hand in hand; as much as religion was racialized, race was religionized. From early modernity forward, men and women in other parts of the world and with skin colors other than white who lived with the gods really present to them on earth were termed "savage" and "primitive." Their societies were scientifically said to be at an earlier stage on the timeline of human development and social and cultural evolution, on the basis of evidence in which religious practice loomed large. Later on in this history, people to whom the gods were really present might be institutionalized as psychotic, persecuted as socially disruptive, denigrated as feminine within the modern hierarchy of gender, or diagnosed as infantile. Neither are questions of religion absent from the domains of modern politics, psychoanalysis, developmental psychology, aesthetics, and anthropology; rather, all of these areas of knowledge, practice, and value were religionized from their foundations.

"Modernity" and "religion" as the objects of modern critical inquiry were co-constitutive, and "modernity" and "religion" have been good for each other. The result is that lived religious practices around the contemporary world inevitably become some variation of modernity, pre-, post-, anti-, proto-, or braided. This is the finger trap of the normative modern, of the modern that we may never have been, but that nonetheless retains its authority and currency. To move beyond the static paradigm of normative "modern religion" requires that we start with the Eucharistic debates of the sixteenth century, when the lineaments of the creation, "modern religion," first began to appear. What horrified the reformers who came after Martin Luther, Huldrych Zwingli principally among them, was the doctrine of the real presence of God's body; they had begun to distance themselves thoroughly from being able to conceptualize the divine in human form. "Modern religion," both as the object of theoretical study and as the authoritative assertion of what "religion" itself is, arose within an intellectual and social environment shaped by the trajectory of these theological debates, in particular by the rejection of the Catholic doctrine of the real presence and its relegation to a (Catholic) past out of step with modernity. The study of religion is or ought to be the study of what human beings do to, for, and against the gods really present—using "gods" as a synecdoche for all the special suprahuman beings with whom humans have been in relationship in different times and places—and what the gods really present do with, to, for, and against humans. Instead, modern theories of religion were written over accounts of the gods really present, submerging them in a theoretical underworld, while on the surface the gods were reborn as symbols, signs, metaphors, functions, and abstractions. One of the aims of these theories, in scholarship, law, statecraft, and aesthetics, was precisely to take hold of the disruptive, dirty, smelly, raucous, irrelevant, and otiose presence of the gods, to disperse them, or else to control them for other ends.[2]

When the rulers and bureaucrats of modernizing states, for example, set out to extend the authority of the new centers of power over the peripheries, they established governmental offices, zoning regulations, educational institutions (including medical and scientific schools), legal codes, and customary law aimed at uprooting *local* religions of the gods really present within the borders of the emergent state and enforcing their absence in favor of *national* deities. They may have mobilized some gods as allies of the state, while criminalizing or marginalizing others that could not be so mobilized; or else they transformed these others by labeling them as "culture" or "folklore" destined for the tourist itinerary or the museum. Political officials very often had the assistance of religious elites in these projects, men and women with their own reasons for wanting to see local gods corralled.

Classical theories of religion treated the gods as fairly trustworthy agents of social organization and order. But the perspective of this book is otherwise. While the gods have been agents of conformity and submission in certain contexts at particular times, they have also flouted social norms, disrupted political agendas, and disappointed the expectations of the powerful. One reason for the subversive potentiality of the gods is precisely their relative invisibility and illegibility to modern critical theory. If the gods were destined to disappear from the earth, as modern theorists anticipated, there would be increasingly little to see of them or to say about them, and so it was. This expectation gives the appearance of the gods an almost inherently subversive quality in the modern world. Presence is real, but not necessarily good, not necessarily bad, and it is rarely either good *or* bad, as these words are understood in ordinary social discourse. It is a dreadful thing to be in relationship with the gods really present. Painful and unexpected consequences may ensue. It is not safe to be so raw and vulnerable to real presences, to make desire and need so transparent. This equivocal nature of real presence is one of the governing assumptions of the book.

*　*　*

The research for the chapters ahead has spanned three decades, the earliest dating to 1988 (the story of the shrine of the dead child); the most recent is ongoing (the religious practices of survivors of clerical sexual abuse). Throughout, I also cite historical and ethnographic research I conducted in the early 2000s, primarily in rural Nebraska, southern Indiana, New Orleans, New York City, urban New Jersey, and South Phoenix, Arizona, on growing up Catholic in the mid-twentieth century. In all cases but one I have explicit permission to relate the stories my interlocutors told me about themselves and to quote them. In the one case in which I was unable, despite sustained effort, to contact relatives of the persons involved, who are now deceased, I took special care to change any details that would permit identification. I did so for all my interlocutors, with the exception of my mother and father. All persons are identified pseudonymously. Everyone I spoke with understood I was doing research that I would eventually present in written and oral forms. In the ethnographic research for this book, I adhered to the written and unwritten protocols regarding research on human subjects, first at Harvard University and then at Northwestern University. A more detailed account of my ethnographic method is given at the start of the notes.

Many of the stories I tell in this book have been foundational to how I think about religion in history and culture. I have thought about these stories for many years and I have spoken and written about some of them in other contexts. In the case of events that happened decades ago, I drew on notebooks and journals I kept at the time to refresh my memory. When possible, I consulted people involved in particular incidents to confirm what I wrote then and remember today. If I put quotation marks around a comment someone made to me, it means I am reporting *exactly* what he or she said. None of the persons that appear in these pages are a composite; there are no fictional details in any of the stories I tell, other than small changes introduced to protect anonymity.

* * *

When I have talked about this project over the years in different contexts, colleagues and friends have challenged my emphasis on the presence of the gods. They inevitably remind me that absence is also a religious category. Presence necessarily entails absence, they say. God's absence is a powerful trope of Christian theology, moreover, at once both ancient and modern. I know this. Some of the most beautiful writing in the Christian tradition has to do with the silence of God, with God's hiddenness, and with the dark nights to which humans may come in their search for this God. Absence and presence, in theory and theology, are twinned. "The same impulse that leads me to sing of God," contemporary poet Christian Wiman writes, "leads me to sing of godlessness."[3]

That said, I am inclined to believe that presence is the norm of human existence, including in religion, and absence is an authoritative imposition. Infants are oriented at birth toward faces. They grow as persons through relationships with others, who themselves carry within them, consciously and unconsciously, the histories of their relationships, along with their parents' histories, and so on and so on, into the deep past where memory exists only in genetic traces. Moreover, it is the fundamental assumption of the social sciences that humans are born into already existing social worlds. There is evidence that parental languages are recognized in the womb, so that neonates at birth have strong preferences for the surrounding linguistic group. To speak the languages they are born having already heard is as much a matter of recognition as it is of learning. And as they speak, they are situated in the way of being in the world that this language effects. There is no outside of all of this.

It is a subtle, but significant, modification of these assumptions, however, if we say that human beings are born into relationships, into relational histories, and into extensive webs of relationships, real and imagined, and that over a lifetime and beyond, into succeeding generations, human beings exist by virtue of each other. Such a perspective shifts attention away from what is already always given socially, linguistically, and historically, to what may happen in the intersubjective worlds humans are born into, then make for themselves with the tools they find and craft. It introduces creativity and unpredictability into what would otherwise be determined. Humans struggle with their languages; they reach beyond what they are able to say toward what they desire to say; they push to the edges of the sayable and the known. In relationships, they encounter what they had not expected, what they may not have wanted, what they fear. "Desire" and "fear" themselves are not singular and transparent, so that one may fear what one desires and desire what one fears.

These are questions of human development and relationality, framed in psychological language, but this does not mean they are individual matters. To say that humans are born into and live their lives within and through circles of relationship, that "we cannot exist without addressing the other and without being addressed by the other," is immediately and intimately to situate persons in the social world. So, throughout this book, I will be analytically moving among various levels and contexts of existence, from the most intimate to the most public, and I will be using different languages—historical, anthropological, psychological, and theological—to describe and analyze them. But I always understand these levels, contexts, and languages to be implicated in each other. In what social, political, and religious circumstances do relationships among humans and the gods become the motivation for particular behaviors and ways of being in the world? What is it in the gods who come and the humans who receive them that so often leads to enmity and destruction on earth, but that also may be the source of social cohesion, compassion, and generosity? Such critical reflection can take place only if the outcome is not assumed, meaning only if presence / absence are freed from the normative modern constructions of them.[4]

Absence may be imposed and enforced by authorities and powers of various sorts that are made anxious by presence. It may arise out of the quotidian doubts and anxieties of the human condition. It may open up within relationships. Sometimes humans struggle against absence; at other times they sink beneath its weight; sometimes they embrace it. Absence has had its poets and theologians, its theorists and mystics; the dark nights of the human soul have been well illuminated. I am asking readers not to make the move to absence, at least not immediately, not to surround presence with the safeguard of absence, but instead to withhold from absence the intellectual, ethical, and spiritual prestige modernity gives it, and to approach history and culture with the gods fully present to humans.

*　*　*

There is a double nomenclatural ambiguity in the term "real presence," vis-à-vis "real," and vis-à-vis "presence." The word "real" carries a heavy evaluative charge in ordinary speech as well as in Western philosophical traditions. To say that one of two or more things being compared is *real* seems to be asserting or implying that the others are not, that they are unreal, possibly deceptive, inauthentic, fake, nonexistent, and so on. Moreover, just as the word "pain" has a huge semantic range that covers everything from minor physical discomfort to excruciating agony, so, too, the word "presence" may refer, in one context, for instance, to the sense of a greater-than-human power in the awesomeness of nature and, in another, to the presence of a saint in his or her image or a chip of bone. To use the term "real presence," as I do throughout, is to court misunderstanding at best; it may also give offense because of what appears to be its presumptive claims on what is real and what is not.

As "real presence" became more sharply delineated and ever more exclusively associated with Roman Catholics following the sixteenth-century disputes among Christian theologians, the term would not be used to refer to that feeling on the beach or at the summit of a mountain, nor to the encounter with Jesus in the words of the Gospels, nor to the solitary meeting of God in the silence of human interiority. Rather, *among non-Catholics,* it meant the disgusting idea that Jesus's actual body was there to be crunched on in the Host, his blood guzzled from the chalice, and, *among Catholics,* it meant the reality of the Catholic supernatural as opposed to the empty simulacrum of the Protestant holy. Catholics became the people of real presence par excellence, in their Eucharistic theology and in their devotional practices, as I will describe in the pages ahead, practices that included eating holy cards, rubbing holy dirt on the place where the body of a loved one hurts, having the dead arrive back home, and so on. Kissing the finger-bone of a dead human (more likely a goat's bone)—how ridiculous!! Calling the Host a symbol—how empty and decadent!! So the two divisions of Western Christianity have represented and reviled each other.

Beginning in early modernity as a dispute among Christians, divergent conceptions of presence became a point of absolute division between Catholics and Protestants, and then it evolved into one of the normative categories of modernity. This was the work over time of missionaries, lawyers, explorers, colonial administrators, armies and navies, poets, theologians, and finally of scholars of religion. The internecine controversy among Christians about the nature of the Eucharist turned into the theoretical lens for the modern study of religion. Just as "masculine" and "feminine" as cultural signifiers need not (and often do not) refer to biological men and women—we say, "she is very masculine," "he has a feminine side," for example—so "presence" in the Catholic sense slipped the bounds of confessional specificity and became a category of religious analysis and religious otherness not exclusive to Catholics.

This is what I mean by "real presence." The adjective "real" allows me to make a distinction within the broad semantic field of "presence," by way of enriching the critical vocabulary for talking about "presence," and, more broadly, about religion itself in history.

* * *

Two days before Christmas in 1923 the wooden church of the Immaculate Conception in the north Bronx burned down. Ground had already been broken on a recently purchased lot across the street where a new church would rise. But the destruction of the old building was traumatic. The three-alarm fire required eight fire engines and four hook-and-ladder companies from the Bronx and Manhattan to subdue the flames. Then, while the wood of the old structure was still smoldering, three priests from nearby parishes "pressed their way through the fire lines." Firemen shouted at them that they were in danger from falling timbers, but the priests ignored the warning and rushed into the smoking ruin. A teacher from the neighborhood, Harry O'Grady, who had been the first to spot the fire, followed them. After a few minutes of tense and anxious silence, bystanders witnessed a sight that would have been strange elsewhere, but here, in this Catholic neighborhood, became the subject of local lore. O'Grady emerged from the ruins, carrying a lighted candle—had he lit it from a burning ember?—followed immediately by the three priests, walking in solemn procession, bearing the "unharmed" Blessed Sacrament. They had covered their hands with cloth so as not to touch the vessel that bore Christ's real body and blood. "Women knelt and police and firemen removed their helmets," the *New York Times* reported, as O'Grady and the priests made their way to the rectory, where the church's pastor, Father Raymond Tonnini, "a venerable [friar] with [a] long white beard," waited for them in the doorway, his face soaked "in tears." "Almost before the smoke had faded from the scene," the *Times*'s unnamed correspondent reports, "members of the congregation were told that services tomorrow would be held somewhere." A police officer suffering from "smoke and burns" was rushed to the Catholic Fordham Hospital.[5]

Stories of the rescue of the Host from disaster were a familiar genre in mid-twentieth-century Catholic children's literature, including comic books, and long before that in Catholic popular narratives of the miraculous and the holy. So this Bronx tale was an enactment in real life of what must have seemed like a memory or a dream. Not long after this, the new church rose incongruously huge above the city streets and surrounding homes, and not long after this, my mother's family, displaced from the Lower East Side by real estate development, moved into the neighborhood. The sculptor who fashioned the two marble angels that stood in the doorway of the Immaculate Conception with seashells full of holy water in their arms to greet parishioners used my mother's young body as the measure of the statues' proportions.

One

THE OBSOLESCENCE

OF THE GODS

THE 1933 novella *Tony,* written for Catholic youngsters by Father
Thomas B. Chetwood, SJ, tells the story of a deeply troubled Catholic boy in an unnamed American industrial city laid waste by the international economic crisis. Ten-year-old Tony is a tough "mick" from
the "vile and unsightly quarter of a great city." Abandoned by his parents, when we meet him, Tony is roaming the streets and gutters in filthy
clothes, cruelly abusing other children and terrorizing shopkeepers. He
is a coward and a traitor, too, who rats out his friends for money. Even
Father Chetwood seems not to care for the boy. He refers to Tony early
on as "an unregenerate bit of humanity" who "would pull the keystone
out of the arch of civilization if his small hands could reach it."[1]

One day, in the company of his pal Emmings, Tony passes by the
unfinished skeleton of a "wretched" Catholic church, a victim of the
hard times. Surreptitiously, with an air of "peculiar sullenness," Tony
doffs his ragged cap. Emmings immediately jumps on him. "Whadger
do that for, Tony?" he asks. "Sign of the tribe er somethin', ain't it?" Tony
ignores him, but Emmings continues to badger him. "They's a lot of
people that do the same. Tell me what yer do it for, will you? Somethin'
like politics, ain't it?" "Politics nuthin'," Tony says, curtly. Emmings,
"obsessed with the demon of curiosity," is unstoppable. "My ole man tole
me that youse blokes wuz brought up to figger that there was someone

livin' in the church that could look out and see yer. Zat so? Say no if it ain't so; and if yer don't say nuthin I'll take it fer yes." Tony runs off toward the city's polluted river, where the two boys are planning to go for a swim. "Yer ain't said no," Emmings, "with a shrewd look," taunts his friend, before he races after him.[2]

Horror follows. Tony ties a brick to a kitten's tail for sport and goes to the water's edge to drown the helpless animal, ignoring Emmings's pleas to stop. The narrator intrudes here to say that a year earlier, under the guidance of "an energetic young curate," Tony had made his First Communion. "Will not some fleeting memory of that holy past hold his hand now and save a bit of innocent brute life?" The narrative abruptly resumes. Tony hears a voice snarling from behind him. "Don't you drown that kitten, yer bum yer! It's mine." The speaker is Tappy Skillen, leader of a gang of Protestant boys called the Swedes. Tony glances up contemptuously, then turns back to the river and "let[s] the burden in his hands go and gloat[s] on the furious, struggling thing down below and on the bubbles as long as there [are] any to see." Retribution is quick. Laying their hands on Tony, the Swedes tie him up and hang him upside down over the greasy, rat-infested river, demanding that he declare himself "a dirty yellow-faced Dago [Tony's mother is Italian] an' a Republican an' a Protestant."[3]

But Tony cannot speak the lie "I am a Protestant," not only because he is not a Protestant, but because, as he tells his tormentors, sputtering filthy water out of his mouth, "Protestants say . . . that they ain't no one there." Whereas "I can't say Y'ere not there," Tony moans over and over, "I can't say Y'ere not there." Here is the answer to Emmings's spooked question about "someone livin' in the church that could look out and see yer." For Tony to identify himself as a Protestant would be to deny the real presence of Jesus in the Eucharist and in the reserved sacrament in the tabernacle on the altar of the unfinished church in the city. This he cannot do. So, unlike the kitten, whose death was fast by comparison, Tony dies by inches. "First came the terrible desire for air . . . it racked every inch of him up to the feet that were held above him." Over and over throughout this terrible ordeal, Tony says, "I can't say Y'ere not there." The repetition of these words, over and over, sustains and comforts him, until the moment finally comes when the boy's soul and body are filled with a "strength that was in no way his own." "All the petty sordidness . . . slipped from him—the thieving, the cowardice, the cruelty, and the scurrile vileness—as the shadows slip from the hills in the growing dawn." The tortured body of this terrible child, hanging beneath a squalid urban overpass, is transformed by his "martyrdom"—as Chetwood explicitly calls it—into a tabernacle of the real presence. The God absent from Protestant imaginations becomes present in Tony's death. On the autopsy table, Tony's dead face shines with "a pallid beauty."[4]

A native of New York City, Jesuit father Thomas B. Chetwood was a distinguished legal scholar, law school educator and administrator, novelist, and polemicist. From 1928 to 1931, immediately prior to the publication of *Tony*, Father Chetwood was regent of the Georgetown University School of Law. He presided over the significant improvement of the school's graduate curriculum, which he oriented toward the study of federal courts and legislation, to take advantage of what the law school catalog called "the great laboratory for political and social experimentation," Washington, DC. Chetwood seems an unlikely author of such a grim tale of Catholic martyrdom in a hostile Protestant land.[5]

Nor did *Tony* reflect the circumstances of American Catholicism at the time. The Catholic population of the United States had grown substantially since the turn of the century. Educational standards at all levels of Catholic schools were improving, with better-prepared instructors, many of them graduates of the Catholic normal schools founded in this era, stepping into the classrooms. Catholic churches, seminaries, schools, and hospitals were rising everywhere on the American landscape, even in the hard times, and Catholic "confidence and boosterism" were getting stronger, as one historian describes the spirit of American Catholicism at the time. Catholics were so confident of their place in American society, as well as sufficiently prosperous, to produce massive public spectacles throughout this period to mark special occasions and anniversaries. One such event was the Twenty-Eighth International Eucharistic Congress, held in Chicago in 1926, the first time this event took place in the United States. The Eucharistic Congress drew hundreds of thousands of Catholics from Chicago and around the

United States to newly built Soldier Field for the public worship and adoration of Christ really present in the sacrifice of the Mass and in the consecrated Host on the massive outdoor altar built specially for this celebration of the theology of "I can't say Y'ere not there."[6]

And yet this catalog of successes masks deeper currents of doubt and ambivalence. Within the living memory of Tony's real-world contemporaries—or if not theirs, then surely their parents' and grandparents'—was the eruption of anti-Catholic agitation across the United States in the paranoid and nativist 1920s. "Sign of the tribe?" Emmings had taunted Tony. The Ku Klux Klan, with its weird mimesis of Catholic ceremony and costume, rose to new popularity in these years, its anti-Catholicism nearly as virulent as its racism. State legislatures sought to restrict Catholic education, in some cases to prohibit it entirely. It was often said in the anxious decade after World War I—as it had been said in one way or another since the settling of New England—that Catholics did not belong in democratic, Protestant America. There were many reasons for this hostility against Catholics and Catholicism, their evident success in the nation being one of them. But tangled up with all other accusations and suspicions was Catholic metaphysics, in particular the way Catholics lived with the supernatural. This is why Tony was killed. Looked at from the perspective of the "tribal twenties," perhaps Father Chetwood was giving voice to the bitter grievances that American Catholics were harboring in this period, as well as underscoring precisely the deep ontological difference that divided Catholics from Protestants in the United States.[7]

But another reading of the story is possible, too. Tony's courageous martyrdom has an immediate and powerful effect on the non-Catholic Americans around him. Looking down on Tony's transfigured body in the city morgue, police lieutenant Lester Bradley, an Episcopalian from "a very exclusive family with influence," a graduate of "one of the most aristocratic eastern universities," and, if this were not enough, "a rattling good sportsman, too," is converted to Catholicism. By the end of the story, Bradley is worshipping in the still unfinished church before which Tony had tipped his hat. The Lutheran grocer, Gormer, whose store Tony had regularly raided, also converts, as does Emmings, who becomes a priest "and is now working in the West Indies." "The whole proletariat," not the "whole *Catholic* proletariat," "of this great republic," Father Chetwood affirms at the close of the book, gave witness to Tony's sanctity. By his death at the hands of Protestant boys, Tony has become an *American* saint.[8]

In a study of Cardinal John Henry Newman's poetics, published a few years before *Tony,* Father Chetwood writes that the courageous deaths of the ancient Christian martyrs, standing fearlessly before the "iron comb," "the white heat of the fire," or the "scalding oil of the cauldron" and calling on the name of Christ, not as "myth . . . or memory" but as a living presence among them, accounted for the triumph of Catholicism over empire and for its endurance and strength over time. From this perspective, the church in Tony's city, its construction halted midway, becomes a sign of a hopeful future for American Catholics after the Depression, a future to build toward. But it is a hope specifically premised on the faithfulness of Catholics' bold witness to the truth of the Church's sacramental theology in a Protestant land.[9]

The ambiguity of Chetwood's *Tony*—is it an expression of the most extraordinary confidence or the bitterest alienation among American Catholics?—captures the ambiguity of Catholic life in the United States at the time and more broadly in the modern world. Catholic history, locally and globally, pivots around the real presence of Christ in the Eucharist, of the holy in the material, of the supernatural in the natural, in the modern Catholic body and mind. As Chetwood says, this is the ground of both Catholic alienation and Catholic efficacy, Catholic difference and Catholic connectedness. The destiny of Catholicism in the modern world, in other words, turns on the meaning of what Jesus said to his disciples at the Last Supper.

* * *

One of the greatest sources of violence in Western history has been the question of what Jesus meant when he told his apostles to eat his body and drink his blood and to do so always in remembrance of him. Is Jesus really present in body and blood, flesh and bones, in the bread and wine?

Does Jesus become present at the moment when the priest, sealed by his ordination to this extraordinary power, lifts the Host and chalice above his head at the consecration of the Mass? What does "is" mean in the phrases "this is my body" and "this is my blood"? From Saint Paul forward, Christians have struggled to understand the meaning of God's incarnation in the human being Jesus of Nazareth, in the political, philosophical, and scientific languages available to them in their respective times. In turn, how they answered their questions about the words of institution, as they are called, had implications for these other domains of knowledge and practice. But in the sixteenth century, as the divisions within Western Christendom deepened, conflict over what Jesus meant by "take and eat" erupted with visceral force.

Catholics and the various parties of their opponents who came to be known as "Protestants" did not just debate the meaning of Jesus's words in that grim century. They tore at each other's flesh in gory "rites of violence" in what appears at this distance to be an intimate and compulsive reenactment of the dismemberment of the unity of European Christian culture taking place at the same time, largely as the result of the raging theological disputes. It was as if Catholics and their opponents were endlessly compelled to perform upon each other's bodies and blood their divergent understandings of how God became human and how Jesus remains present to his followers on earth after his death, resurrection, and ascension into heaven.[10]

The Saint Bartholomew's Day massacre in Paris in late August 1572 was one such enactment. The fury that so brutally erupted on this day had been building over a long period of time. Forty years earlier, on October 17, 1534, Catholics in Paris and other cities in France had awoken to the sight of placards posted on buildings and churches by evangelical Christians during the night, mocking the Mass as a cannibalistic ritual. The Affair of the Placards, as the event came to known, "polarized what had been a heterogeneous Christianity [in France], between two viscerally opposed understandings of Christ's presence in the Eucharist." On Saint Bartholomew's Day, Catholics took their bloody revenge for this and other outrages. Eyewitnesses report that the waters of the Seine ran red with the blood of the hacked and dismembered bodies of Protestants thrown into it. The youngest daughter of a Huguenot couple, who were among the first to be slaughtered in the streets of Paris, was dipped naked into her parents' blood in a perverse sacrament and warned not to convert to Protestantism or she would suffer the same fate.[11]

Unholy alliances between theologians and churchmen fighting over the meanings of divine presence, along with political rulers who exploited doctrinal dissent for their nationalizing purposes, generated war and destruction across Europe. Catholics suffered agonies as horrible as those they inflicted on Protestants. Among the more than 300 Catholics martyred in England between 1535 and 1679 was the Jesuit priest Father Edmund Campion. Hung from a scaffold, Campion was disemboweled—his steaming entrails, flung by the executioner into a pot, splashed the crowd crushing close with gore and blood—beheaded, and quartered, and then pieces of his body were shown at the four gates of Tyburn to warn off other Catholics. All this because of the question of what Jesus meant when he said, "this is my body," "this is my blood," "do this in memory of me."[12]

The theological destiny of the doctrine of the real presence in the sixteenth century and afterward was forged in technical language and bound up with people's changing knowledge of the world and with their new experiences of themselves as bodies, minds, and souls. The presence / absence divide was also implicated in and inflected by Christian encounters with men and women of other races and religions in the successive ages of European colonialism and imperialism. Catholic and evangelical missionaries were determined to conquer the world for what each understood to be the true meaning and authentic reenactment of Jesus's words at the Last Supper. They carried Europe's dissensions and violence with them to the rest of the world, where the question of what Jesus meant was taken up in local histories, conflicts, and cosmologies. Each act of violence, at home and in distant lands, further divided Christians over the meanings of presence. Decades of struggle among competing and irreconcilable camps of theologians "straining for ever closer definition" of what Jesus was saying to his disciples hardened divergent conceptualizations into doctrine, ecclesiology, and politics.[13]

To the great frustration and disappointment of his more radical contemporaries, Luther held fast to the doctrine of the real presence. "Who in the world ever read in the Scriptures that 'body' means 'sign of the body'?" he thundered in a 1527 polemic. "For even if we put on all the lenses in the world, we would find none of the evangelists writing, 'Take, eat, this is a sign of my body,' or 'this represents my body.'" Faithfulness to the word of God revealed in scripture required a theology that recognized Jesus's real presence in the sacrament. Luther was deeply offended by theological attempts to reimagine what took place during the Eucharist as the spiritual consumption of Jesus's body spiritually or symbolically present. By the time Luther issued the polemic quoted above, this position was associated in its most consistent and forceful expression with the Swiss reformer Huldrych Zwingli. In 1525, Zwingli published a mass based on this theology that was the sharpest break, up to that time, with the traditions of medieval Catholic liturgy, and by the time of the Marburg Colloquy of 1529, Zwingli could no longer imagine Christ to have said "this is my body" with the literal meaning Luther attributed to it. But Luther was likewise repelled, as intensely as Zwingli was, by the thought that human teeth ground up Jesus's body in the consecrated Host, causing Jesus renewed pain and suffering, or that it was Jesus's actual flesh and blood going down human gullets, into the coils of the digestive system, and out into the city's waste streams.[14]

Horror of the Eucharist as cannibalism runs forward from the origins of Christianity to the present, among dissenting groups of Christians and between Christians and others. The body and its parts and fluids are potent and versatile cultural idioms. The transgression of the body's boundaries, by breaching the wall of skin, for example, or by turning the body inside out by bleeding or cutting, has been used to articulate a range of social anxieties and distinctions. Such actions upon the body have also been effective media of religious and political control. Accusations of sacred cannibalism give the deeply felt sense of the incommensurability of divinity with corruptible matter an especially gruesome and visceral immediacy (just as, from the Catholic perspective, they give it its sublimity). Such charges have marked the border between Christianity and people of other religions, who could not fathom a community that ate the flesh and drank the blood of its god. Likewise, Christians have experienced and expressed this repulsion among themselves, at different times in history and for various reasons. Among twentieth-century Catholic adults sexually abused by priests, for example, the charge of sacramental cannibalism is a way of articulating the depth of their anger against the clerical predators who had violated their bodies and the church that protected priests but failed their victims.[15]

It was in part against the ontological squeamishness evident in anxieties about sacramental cannibalism that the Fourth Lateran Council (1215) declared as orthodox the doctrine of transubstantiation. That the Host is Jesus's actual flesh, his muscles, organs, sinews, and blood, consumed at Communion, was central to the Catholic imaginary. It was the principle of medieval Christian art and architecture. It generated the proliferation of adornments in precious stones and metals that encased the Host and the tabernacle. It underwrote the authority and status of the ordained men who alone had the power to offer the sacrifice of the Mass through which Jesus became really present. It was disclosed in miracles of the Host, when the consecrated wafer shed blood or when the Infant Jesus became visible in its elevation, as allegedly happened at various times and places. God granted saints and mystics the grace of literally experiencing Christ's nourishing body and blood without the veil of the substances of bread and wine. Jews were accused of stealing consecrated hosts and defiling them, of stabbing the Host and "the living child seen within it," of puncturing them, of killing Christian children to extract the consecrated Hosts in their bellies, of boiling Hosts, and of using the blood from bleeding Hosts in unspeakable rites. Such libelous tales contributed a powerful ontological compulsion to Catholic anti-Semitism. They were used to provoke and sanction the slaughtering of Jewish bodies and the theft of Jewish property.[16]

Christ's real presence in the consecrated Host and its formative role in the Catholic imaginary drew upon and contributed to the cult of saints that preceded and surrounded the profusion of late medieval Eucharistic visions, miracles, and devotions. The Virgin Mary and the saints were integral to Catholic Christianity, beginning with the age of the martyrs in the three centuries after Jesus's death, before Christianity became the religion of the Roman Empire. Jesus was said to be present in the flayed and scorched bodies of the martyrs, as he was in Tony's, making martyrdom a reenactment of Christ's sacrifice. The martyrs' mimesis of Jesus's Passion turned them into a privileged elite of intercessory figures between heaven and earth and an effective engine of church growth and expansion, as Father Chetwood argued. The times and places of their deaths were marked, revered, and recalled. More martyrs joined the ranks as the Catholic faith spread throughout Europe, and other figures entered the pantheon of special intercessors as well—kings and queens, monks and bishops—creating a network of relationships between heaven and earth, mirroring and inflected by the arrangements of social ties and hierarchies on earth. The bishops of early Christian Rome sent out pieces of martyrs' bodies to local rulers throughout Europe in the early Middle Ages as tokens of esteem and by way of establishing ties with them in "a world without empire." Western Christendom existed as a map of bones before it became a legal and ecclesiastical entity. Very often the figures of saints and martyrs were grafted onto local pagan supernatural beings. New shrines were built over ancient sites of power. Sometimes this interleaving occurred because a Catholic missionary was killed for his or her efforts to uproot a particular pre-Christian worship practice, object, or site that then became associated with the missionary in popular memory and church chronicles. Patronal saints, hermit saints of the forests, miraculous healers, missionary saints, and holy monks and nuns all were bound up with the pre-Christian figures they were meant to replace. The result was a densely populated world of saints and spirits, hybrid figures poised between the holy and the forbidden, orthodoxy and heterodoxy, paganism and Catholicism. The consecrated Host was the most sacred of real presences in this world, but it was not the only one.[17]

The literalness of the real presence was performed and displayed in public rituals and private devotions; in the shrines, objects, practices, prayers, and stories of the cult of saints; in church architecture and the design of altars and tombs; and in the bodies of men and women, in their desires and disciplines, in the gestures they made in church and outside, in the marking of time's passing, in the days of the month, and in the rhythms of agricultural work, when the planting of certain crops was calibrated to a particular saint's feast day. Catholics around the world adored the consecrated Host. In golden monstrances they bore the Host out into the streets of their villages and neighborhoods in great processions, well into the twenty-first century. They celebrated the presence among them of their patronal saints with public festivities and commemorative rites. The inscription on the tomb of Saint Martin of Tours read, "Here lies Martin the bishop, of holy memory, whose soul is in the hand of God; but he is fully here, present and made plain by miracles of every kind." But in the first half of the sixteenth century, the reformer closest to the Catholic understanding of the real presence declared all of this, everything except Christ present in the Eucharist, irrelevant to salvation. The world around the Eucharistic altar was changing, and with it the meaning of Jesus's words at the Last Supper, and of the consecrated Host itself, with tremendous consequences for modern Catholic life.[18]

* * *

Evangelical reformers developed many ways of understanding Jesus's continuing presence on earth after his ascension into heaven. Tony was wrong in thinking that all Protestants believe "Y'ere ain't there." Still, it is significant that Tony was made to think so, four centuries after Luther. It is also significant that Tony's erudite creator seems to be sending the message to Catholic boys and girls in the United States that the difference between Catholics and "Protestants," as Father Chetwood sets it up, remains a life-and-death matter and a potential source of sectarian violence. Father Chetwood is not completely wrong. Almost all those dissenting from Catholicism in the sixteenth and seventeenth centuries, with the exception of Luther and those of his followers who remained faithful to him, took it as a given that Jesus's actual and truly human body was in heaven and therefore could not be present on earth, because human bodies could not be in more than one place at the same time.

This was the theological problem of ubiquity. Christ's body was not in people's mouths to be chewed on and swallowed. Christ remained present on earth in various ways after the sixteenth century—in the providential order of history; in the congregation of the faithful; in the words of scripture read, spoken, and studied; in movements of the spirit; and in Christian faithfulness. But as theological debates and political conflicts dragged on and religious violence escalated across Europe, the relationship between Christ's literal body and blood and the bread and wine of the Eucharist, between flesh and sign, as Catholics and Luther intended it, began to come apart, with the result that presence in the specific Catholic sense now increasingly took on a historical trajectory different from the Protestant one.

One of the great surprises of the Council of Trent (1545–1563), according to historian Lee Palmer Wandel, was its disproportionate concern with Zwingli out of all the reformers. This made no sense from a strategic point of view. Zwingli was not the founder of a church; no movement bore his name; and by the time of the council, he was long dead. It may be, however, that the Tridentine preoccupation with the most radical theologian of the Eucharist signals the deepest Catholic anxiety of the age. A path had been entered upon, the council fathers surely knew, that, if not contested by doctrine, discipline, and force of arms, would culminate at last and inevitably in God's absence from the world. Hence the long catalog of anathemas the defenders of Catholicism issued against the Eucharistic theologies of evangelicals. Not Luther but Zwingli and John Calvin, read through a Zwinglian lens, became the voices of an emergent religious imaginary at fundamental ontological odds with the Catholic way of being in the world.[19]

With the "is" of Christ's "this is my body" interpreted as "signifies," historian G. R. Potter writes in his biography of Zwingli, "it was possible to differentiate between the bread eaten by the communicant and the Christ received by faith. All that followed was a development, elaboration, ripening, and justification of this decision." Zwingli's understanding of the Lord's Supper was profoundly influential in many regions of the emerging Protestant world, in particular among British evangelicals, in various parts of Germany, and eventually in North

America—in other words, among the once and future nations of modern global empire, the future lay with the disjuncture between sign and reality. While debates over Jesus's words did not end, by the close of the sixteenth century the difference of theological interpretation of the Eucharist between Protestants and Catholics had hardened into stark opposition. "In confessional polemics," Wandel concludes her history of the period, "[Christian] faith itself had been changed from a process to a bipolarity: presence or absence."[20]

As if to signal that Catholicism was reasserting itself at last with a renewed vigor and power and that a new age in the history of the church's engagement with the world had commenced, reports of holy monks endowed with the gifts of levitation and bilocation began to circulate around the Catholic world in the early seventeenth century. The most famous of these flying monks was Saint Joseph of Cupertino (1603–1663). (He would later be designated the patron saint of airline pilots.) On the far side of exhausted argumentation and incessant violence, the reality that human bodies, among them Jesus's human body, were capable of being in more than one place at one time was dramatically affirmed. So it would be throughout modernity. The bleeding, levitating, bilocating, elongating, incorruptible, sweetly smelling, starving-but-surviving Catholic body, male and female, became the living illustration for all to see of the reality of the intimate interpenetration of the supernatural and the natural, of heaven and earth. Catholics exalted in this. Their detractors found it risible, if not dangerous.[21]

* * *

At the very close of his interrogation, Campion's questioners wanted him to deny the real presence, just as Tony's fictional tormenters wanted centuries later and an ocean away. The modern Jesuit, Father Thomas Chetwood, never makes this connection to the early modern Jesuit, Father Edmund Campion, explicit, but the resonance across the ages is unmistakable. "I can't say Y'ere ain't there," Tony protests. With greater eloquence and theological learning, Father Campion replied to his interrogators, "What? Will you make [Christ] a prisoner now in Heaven?

Must He be bound to those properties of a natural body? Heaven is His palace and you will make it His prison." Campion, like Tony in the still hidden future, could not say that Christ was there and therefore not here, in heaven and therefore not on earth. For this they were killed, or so it is said.[22]

*   *   *

The simple equation—Catholics = presence, Protestants = absence—was a caricature and polemical overstatement already in early modernity, and it remains so in the twenty-first century. Protestantism, its Lutheran varieties certainly, but also its Anglican and Reformed, generated out of itself ways of being in the world in which not only Jesus Christ but also angels, monsters, and the souls of the dead, among other supernatural entities, were visibly and audibly present to practitioners. This was so among the different strains of pietism, including, eventually, Pentecostalism, High Church Anglicanism, and, on Protestantism's more recondite edges, in spiritualism, Mormonism, and the visualizations of New Agers. Mormon founder Joseph Smith had visions of angels in heaven, visions that occurred sometimes in the company of followers who saw what he saw. In the latter half of the twentieth century, American Pentecostal televangelists such as Oral Roberts urged viewers to put their hands against their radio consoles and later their televisions in order to bring themselves into immediate contact with the power of the Holy Spirit moving through the healer in his distant studio. The artist Warner Sallman's famous image of Jesus, which renders the Savior's gaze watchful, immediate, and penetrating, has had a unique presence and power in millions of Protestant households around the world. Sallman's Jesus is a familiar participant in the family life that takes place within sight of his loving eyes.[23]

But the taint of Catholic real presence was on these Protestant phenomena, too. Pietism and its offspring were denounced as politically destabilizing "enthusiasm," an overly exciting experience of an (un)holy intimacy with the supernatural that threatened to disrupt social order and rattle established hierarchies. The contempt of Low Church or evangelical Protestants for their High Church counterparts is often quite visceral. To give a single, but influential, example of this animus, nineteenth-century British scholar of religion and culture Edward Burnett Tylor wrote his famous book on "primitive religion" just after the heyday of the controversial Oxford Movement in the Anglican Church, which had reintroduced Roman Catholic elements into Church of England worship. Tylor was raised Quaker, but as an adult he came to see all religions as atavistic, except, perhaps, for a kind of quasi-Quaker, secular, nontheist spiritual sensibility. He made his revulsion for High Church Anglicanism evident in his theory of religious evolution. "The Anglican," he wrote, "blends gradually into the Roman scheme, a system so interesting to the ethnologist for its maintenance of rites more naturally belonging to barbaric culture." Given such ostracism, Protestants to whom Jesus or the Holy Spirit was most palpably present have also been the most fiercely anti-Catholic. This contempt served the double purpose of disciplining internal boundaries against the excesses of presence and defending the group against the charge of "popery" that fellow Protestants inevitably leveled.[24]

* * *

Such conflicts over discrepant ways of being in the world also erupted within modern Catholicism itself. At different times over the almost five centuries since the Council of Trent, Catholics who wished to bring Catholicism into a more positive and constructive relationship with the modern world than that envisioned or sanctioned in papal Rome have campaigned for it in print and in public, in the administrative offices of the Vatican, in the Catholic press, and among the faculty of Catholic universities. Such campaigns nearly always included purging, or at least thinning, the thick accretions of popular piety from the church's life and worship. Movements for purification that arose within the church often coincided with religious, political, and intellectual revolutions outside, in Europe and South America, when attacks on the entrenched power of the clergy and the alleged mystifications of devotionalism that held the populace in thrall to the Church became media for the articulation of social grievances and aspirations and sometimes the first step on the road toward coups d'état.[25]

Catholic assaults on the excesses of Catholic piety were perhaps inevitable, given that expunging "superstition" from "religion" was so crucial to the making of modernity and "modern religion," in any of its contexts, and also given that Catholic devotional practices of presence were so thoroughly identified with "superstition" in modernity. Much of this internal criticism of "superstition" had to do with the purity of the Eucharist. Catholic reformers in the twentieth century, for example, maintained that adoration of Christ present in the consecrated Host, when it took place outside the celebration of the Mass, detracted from what Jesus meant when he called on his followers to do as he did. So, too, did the clutter and disarray of devotionalism, all the saints' cults and Marian devotions, many of them historically unfounded or pagan in origin, that crowded in around the altar in such excess. These media of devotionalism appeared to Catholic moderns as aesthetically taste-less and religiously jejune. They saw them as artifacts of what one prom-inent Catholic reformer dismisses as "medieval credulity." Even those from whom greater sympathy for and understanding of ordinary people's lived devotion to the Blessed Mother and the saints might have been expected, such the Latin American liberation theologians of the late twentieth century, were deeply critical of popular practices of presence. Even when they were more sympathetic, as "second line" liberation theo-logians aimed to be, they still applied a standard of political relevance in assessing different forms of popular piety, transposing them into rec-ognizably modern idioms of protest and resistance. Only as such was the devotional imaginary tolerable. Whenever they possessed the au-thority to do so, Catholic moderns set about eliminating the abun-dance of lived devotional practices.[26]

Ordinary people tended to become aware of theological turmoil within the church when the saints disappeared from their familiar niches and supplies of holy cards, votive candles, and rosaries dwindled. At-tacks against popular piety provided emotional and religious intensity to reformers' broader ecclesiastical agendas, bringing their efforts at changing ritual practice and theological orientations close to the ground of everyday lived experience and religion. In the 1970s and 1980s, American Catholics who persisted in praying to the Virgin Mary or petitioning the saints were sometimes embarrassed, especially if they were associated with the Catholic colleges, universities, or progressive religious orders from which the new spirit of the times emanated. Shame was the devotional body's acknowledgment of, if not compliance with, emergent accounts of the faith. Others turned bitter. Some used their persistence in maligned devotional practices as a form of resentful protest against what they saw as the "Protestantization" of Catholicism and against modern life generally. Still others became creative in generating new devotions in place of the old, or variations on the old, a subject I will return to often in later chapters.[27]

The result has been a complex politics of presence within Catholicism itself from early modernity to the present. In opposition to the authority of science, to rationalism, materialism, and the nationalisms that threatened to compete with Catholics' loyalty to the universal Church, the antimodernist popes of the modern era, the curial cardinals surrounding them at the heart of the Church's bureaucracy, and sympathetic figures in the religious orders emphasized the metaphysics of real presence by encouraging new devotions to contemporary miracle-working saints and to various images and apparitions of the Blessed Mother, so long as they were approved by Rome. In this way, the supernatural was conscripted in the Church's campaigns to recapture its lost authority in the modern political order. Rome collaborated with other antimodern moderns in this global enterprise, the authoritarian rulers of Catholic empires and nation-states, the fascist regimes of the twentieth century, and anti-Communist dictators throughout the world. Political and ecclesiastical leaders alike saw in devotionalism a powerful device for ensuring popular compliance and loyalty to state and Church, maintaining order and hierarchy, and stoking hatred for enemies of the Church. Real presences would be imbued with the ethos of fascist, antidemocratic, and reactionary states, while the rulers of these nations, with the blessing of the local and universal Church, designated themselves guardians of Catholic orthodoxy. At the same time, throughout these years, the papacy sought ever-greater control over such devotions.

Subjecting claims of the miraculous to rigorous testing by Church officials and their agents, including the use of medical science to distinguish between natural and supernatural causes, Rome withheld approval of most such occurrences. The purpose was to maintain the obedience and submission of seers, stigmatics, healers, and their followers and to create a network of loyalties on earth and between heaven and earth that was centered on Rome.[28]

Yet presence was not a stable medium of ecclesiastical power and authority or of resistance to them. "This was a form of religious behavior," historian Hubert Wolf writes of ordinary Catholics' encounters with supernatural figures and the cults that developed from them, "that largely evaded the rational foundations and controls of the church." The use of science to discredit particular phenomena only had the effect of further elevating those certified as being of supernatural origin over the authority of nature's evidence; modern medicine became an ally of the holy, its guarantor as well as its guardian. Presence is a fearsome thing. Objects that hold sacred presence, such as relics or statues, may be moved, stolen, and misused. What the Virgin Mary or the saints have had to say to ordinary people has often challenged the authority, behavior, and, less often, the teachings of the Church. The fear of Church officials that lay people would somehow appropriate the consecrated wine and bread for their own perhaps nefarious purposes led first in the ninth century to the reservation of the cup at Mass to the priest and then in the sixteenth century to the practice of placing the Host on communicants' tongues rather than in their hands, as had been the custom for centuries. This datum of liturgical history illustrates a larger point: the precincts of presence needed to be guarded against the faithful who were endlessly resourceful in breaching them. The same Vatican officials who hoped the saints and the Virgin Mary would be effective emissaries of Roman authority feared and mistrusted these figures in their relationships with ordinary people, especially when ordinary people claimed to have direct sensory encounters with them.[29]

Presence forever exceeds the bounds set for it. This is the perennial dilemma of Catholic authority. The power of the Church depends on offering access to supernatural presence while at the same time controlling who gets such access and when. "Popular" devotions are rarely ever utterly independent of ecclesiastical authority. The great Marian cults of the nineteenth and twentieth centuries flourished in large part because Church authorities not only sanctioned but also enthusiastically participated in them. It is impossible to draw a definitive line between "popular" and "elite" practice in Catholicism. Vatican officials sometimes found themselves in the delicate diplomatic position of having to investigate the devotional enthusiasms of colleagues; not infrequently, they were compelled to put their own practices under scrutiny. But the presences in grottoes and woods, in waters and oils, and on altars and dressers in the homes of the devout forever slip beyond the reach of official control. By the same token, because modern Catholic reformers have often viewed popular practices of presence as impediments to the church's coming of age, they very often found themselves isolated from the very people they aimed to liberate.

*   *   *

A caricature it may be, but Catholics = presence, Protestants = absence is what most Catholics at most times until very recently (and many still: see Cardinal O'Connor's sermon, quoted in the Introduction) have said about Protestants, including Lutherans (whatever the subtleties of Lutheran sacramental theology); it is what Protestants have said about Catholics (despite contestation over presence within Catholicism at different times); and it is how both have lived in the world in relation to each other. Presence / absence is the pivot around which other differences, accusations, lies, and hatreds have spun.

Catholics in the United States in the middle years of the twentieth century, for example, maintained that support in the country for birth control exemplified Protestantism's failure to acknowledge the holy in the material. Modern contraception was an expression of Protestantism's corrupt and decadent disembodiment. On the other side, some years ago I did fieldwork among Catholics in rural Nebraska, where towns were once divided between Catholics and Lutherans, the borders between them carefully policed, and meetings between Catholic and Lutheran boys and girls across the boundary strictly forbidden. Catholics who grew up here in the 1940s and 1950s told me that as children they were ashamed of their large families, because they knew that Protestants made fun of this gross display of Catholic fleshiness. Protestants are not material; Catholics are overly, excessively material. Still today, fear of fecund Catholic bodies circulates in the public debate over migrants coming into the United States from the Catholic south.[30]

As it happens, according to a relatively recent innovation within the Guadalupanan tradition, the beloved Mexican holy figure, Nuestra Señora de Guadalupe, who is a living presence on the border and accompanies migrants on their dangerous journeys across the deserts northward, is pregnant. Her hands are serenely folded above the fetus inside her. The caricature, Protestant / absence, Catholic / presence, names a real difference that is felt and acted out, that contributes to popular theologies, and that is consequential for social interactions and religious misunderstandings. To the present day, and to the horror or bemusement of non-Catholics, Catholic statues weep tears of salt and blood, they move, they incline their heads to petitioners—as in the diocese of Sacramento, California, where in November 2005, five months after the diocese was brought near bankruptcy as the result of a $35 million settlement of sexual abuse lawsuits involving thirty-four victims of ten priests, a statue of the Blessed Mother in a Vietnamese Catholic church leaked from her eyes what local people took to be blood.[31]

Presence in this sense—Jesus's flesh chewed on and his blood drunk, bits of saints' bones and clothing kissed and whispered to, visions of the Virgin Mary and the saints, the presence of the holy signaled by sweet scents and bleeding statues, the consecrated Host taken into the streets in great processions in order to bring Jesus out among the people, and so on—has been repellant, strange, dangerous, and horrific to Catholics' neighbors over the centuries. It has been fascinating and at times compelling to them as well. Presence in this sense contravened ordinary human experience. It was inconsistent with new scientific knowledge in various fields of inquiry. It was inconsistent with modern epistemologies. It erased the distance between heaven and earth. Catholics emerged from the Eucharistic debates and confessional wars of the sixteenth century as the people of fleshly, embodied, living, and literal presence, and it was as the people of presence in this sense that Catholics entered the modern era.

* * *

"Religion" as the word is commonly used today took shape at the same time that violent conflict over Christ's words at the Last Supper was tearing Europe apart, and "religion" is fully marked by the circumstances of its origin. Emergent understandings of "religion" in the seventeenth and eighteenth centuries would not only be free of presence; they would offer a safeguard against it.[32]

"Religion" is derived from "Protestantism." This is the dominant view among scholars of religion today, but it is only partially accurate. It is true that one of the sources of contemporary meanings of "religion" was the effort by theologians and philosophers working in Protestant environments from the seventeenth century forward to articulate a universal account of religion free of denominational specificity and the virulent conflict it spawned. But it is historically more accurate—and theoretically and historiographically more generative—to say that "religion" was the creation of the profound rupture between Catholics and the varieties of Protestantism over the question of presence, of the ongoing and intensifying caricatures of each other's theologies and rites of presence, and of their mutual denunciations for practicing what in their respective judgments was not really "religion." Protestants, according to Catholics, address themselves to a god who is not there. Catholics, according to Protestants, address themselves to a god who is grossly material, disgustingly and overly "present." The extended semantic connotations of "Catholic," "Protestant," and "religion" derive from the relations *among* these terms and from their historical inheritances, not from a single trajectory that goes in a direct line from "Protestantism," which is itself not a singular entity in any case, to "religion."

Sacred presence was so fiercely stigmatized because of its conscious and unconscious association with Catholicism. Protestants may have had their own experiences and theologies of presence, but Catholics remained the once and future exemplars of unacceptable practices and experiences of sacred presence and the template for non-European peoples' idioms of presence. Charges of religious cannibalism, idolatry, and gross materiality traveled back and forth across the seas, with traders, soldiers, and missionaries. "Pagans" and "savages" in South America, Asia, and Africa, on the one hand, and Catholic peoples in Europe, on the other, were constructed in explicit relation to each other in the first age of European globalization. When they encountered indigenous special beings in distant lands and the rituals addressed to them, Protestant missionaries, serving as the advance guard of commerce and empire, labeled them "popish," which was synonymous in their lexicon with "savage," "primitive," and "demonic." The use of such language was nearly always the prelude to and legitimation of efforts to uproot and destroy native practices.[33]

The encounters of Catholic missionaries with native peoples, on the other hand, were haunted by the similarities they, too, saw between Catholic and pagan practices. Viewing the latter in terms of the metaphysics of real presences, Catholic missionaries were often better able to glimpse and describe the reality of local gods, although in most cases this did not diminish their determination to destroy these gods and their cults. Catholic missionaries experienced an anxiety of ontological proximity, which they resolved with one of two arguments. The first, introduced by Christian apologist Justin Martyr in the first century of the Common Era, held that Satan in his wiles had seduced native populations into the worship of evil by means of depraved copies of Catholic rituals. "What is most astonishing about Satan's envy and desire to compete with God," Jesuit missionary José de Acosta wrote back to Europe in *Natural and Moral History of the Indies* (published in 1590) about Aztec and Incan religious practices, "is that not only in idolatries and sacrifices but also in certain kinds of ceremonies he has mimicked our sacraments . . . especially the sacrament of communion, the loftiest and most divine of all." Demonic mimesis was one of the earliest modern theories of comparative religion in the globalizing age of the sixteenth and seventeenth centuries. Pagan idols were really real, but they were evil. Satanic mimesis of Catholic sacraments was an affirmation by

inversion of the Catholic supernatural; the victory of Catholic missionaries and armies over these evil pagan gods and their worshippers was
proof of Catholicism's truth.[34]

Others were led to a different conclusion by the similarities they perceived between pagan and Catholic practice. Intellectually formed as
many of them were in the "Aristotelian-Thomist conceptual scheme," a
minority of Catholic missionaries, Bartolomé de Las Casas foremost
among them, drew on philosophical concepts of natural law and natural
reason to argue that worship of the gods was inherent in human nature.
What was satanic mimesis to others was to these thinkers empirical
evidence of an innate, intuitive, and universal religiosity in humankind.
Such theological considerations led Las Casas not to a defense of human
sacrifice but to an understanding of it as being anthropologically akin
to Christ's sacrifice on the cross, to the glory of Christian martyrdom,
and to the celebration of the Eucharist. Generated amid the intellectual ferment of early modernity, rooted in late medieval traditions of
Catholic theology, and made exigent by encounters with others who
were at once recognizable and not, this discourse of the "religious" profoundly altered the idea of religion itself.[35]

The study of comparative religion as an academic discipline is thoroughly implicated in this history and it is deeply marked by its dialec-
tics of familiarity and otherness, natural and demonic. Literal, material
genealogical links connect the Eucharistic conflict of the sixteenth
century, its importation by traders, missionaries, travelers, and soldiers,
to the lands colonized and conquered first by Catholic, then later by
Protestant European, powers, and the development of the academic
study of religion. Scholars of religion in the metropolitan centers of empire in northern Europe and the United States mined the reports of
merchants and missionaries for evidence in developing theories of "religion" as a universal phenomenon in human civilizations.[36]

The idea of the "fetish" encapsulates this genealogy. The biography
of the fetish begins with seventeenth-century Portuguese Catholic
traders, who used the word *fetiços* for ritual objects they encountered
in the non-Islamicized black societies in Benin and the Congo. The Europeans viewed these unfamiliar things—how could they not?—"as

the heathen equivalents of the little sacramental objects common among pious Catholics," historian William Pietz writes. Fetiços were thus endowed from the start with familiar Catholic associations. The "crusading Portuguese," in the common logic of Catholic colonial strategy, sought to substitute authentic (meaning Catholic) presences for their local demonic counterparts by "replacing idols with crucifixes" and fetiços with statues and images of Catholic saints. That Catholics could operate in this way in the mission fields, that they possessed the media and metaphysics to make such efficacious substitutions, was sometimes the envy of their Protestant counterparts. Were savages capable of conversion, Protestant Willem Bosman wrote, glumly and jealously, in *A New and Accurate Description of the Coast of Guinea* (1704), Catholics would be more successful at it than Protestants, because the two, pagans and Catholics, "already agree in several particulars, especially in their ridiculous Ceremonies." Eventually Dutch Calvinist merchants on the Gold and Slave Coasts took up the word "fetiços," which had by that time entered the lexicon of European travelers, and imbued it with the full Protestant horror of the Catholic real presence.[37]

The fetish, conflated with Catholic devotional and sacramental things, became one of the "bad objects" of Protestant empire, objects of purported evil that were used to draw a moral and political distinction between the older Catholic empires, in which the worship of idols / fetishes flourished among local peoples and their European conquerors, and the new, enlightened Protestant empires, in which such practices and the things associated with them were prohibited for the religious and political good of all, especially of the natives. In the poet John Milton's global vision, literary historian W. J. T. Mitchell writes, summarizing a theme from *Paradise Lost* (1667), "Satan is the spiritual leader of the rival Catholic empires who enslave their colonial subjects, and maintain them in a state of brute savagery by encouraging their idolatrous religions." This was the same sort of brute savagery in which the Catholic Church maintained European peasantry, according to Protestant political philosophers and travelers. Political and religious freedom, in this context, from the seventeenth century forward, meant, among other things, liberation from real presences, or superstitions, an argument that resonated well into the twentieth century in the nagging doubt that Catholics were capable of democracy.[38]

Then, in the final stage of the history of the fetish, modern theorists of religion, from David Hume to Tylor, used the notion of the human-made thing-that-lived as the foundation of their general theories of "primitive religion" and of "religion" itself. The "fetish," in its subsequent place in religious theory, bore the full inheritance of sixteenth-century controversies over presence and the Protestant repugnance with Catholic doctrine and practice. Theorists of religion, like travelers and merchants, assumed a correlation between African fetishes and Catholic devotional and sacramental things. Comparisons of "savages" and "primitives" from different regions of the globe were central to the emerging discipline of the study of religion.[39]

In an early text in the emerging academic field of the critical study of religion, *Elements of the Science of Religion,* published in 1897, Dutch evangelical scholar of religion Cornelis Petrus Tiele maintained that all human beings possess a religious impulse, an "original, unconscious, in-nate sense of infinity," which is the same in all times and places—a nontheist universalizing view of "religion" that dates to the seventeenth century. Here Tiele echoes Calvin's *sensus divinitatis.* The subject matter of the study of religion, according to Tiele and other scholars of reli-gion at the time, has to do with the particular forms this impulse is given in specific social, cultural, and political circumstances. Religions de-velop, Tiele said, in an evolutionary progression that ascends over time from the primitive to the advanced. The forms given the religious im-pulse are more or less sublime, more or less ethical, and more or less debased, depending on social conditions, different histories, and varying levels of civilizational attainment. The Hebrew prophets gave the clearest ethical expression of the human religious impulse; the ancient Greeks its most beautiful aesthetic forms. But the religious impulse motivating the great achievements of morality and art of ancient Israel and Greece was the very same as that among "the savage who bedecks his poor idols with gauzy cloth and all kinds of finery" and "the simple minded vo-tary of Rome, who bedizens his Madonna with gilded crowns and showy drapery." Such arguments, associations, and prejudices were commonplace in the study of religion as it developed in the nineteenth and twentieth centuries. Africans and Mediterranean Catholics, distant "primitives," Catholic peasants and factory workers closer to home, the fetish, the Madonna, the idol, the image—here was a taxonomic swirl of identifications all pivoting around the premodern Catholic other.[40]

* * *

Literary critic Roberto Calasso observes that the Greek word for "god," *theós,* has no vocative case. "*Theós* has a predicative function," Calasso writes. "It designates *something that happens.*" Before the advent of modern epistemology, before the arrival of "religion" within the boundaries of Enlightenment reason, ethics, and linguistics, and before the codification of "religion" in national constitutions and diplomatic treaties, the woods, homes, and forests of Europe, its churches, statues, relics, holy oils and waters, and shrines were filled with the presences of spirits, pre-Catholic, Catholic, or a hybrid of the two. These beings were really there. Max Weber famously referred to all this as "enchantment," which he contrasted with modernity's disenchantment. Humans lived alongside and in the company of supernatural presences. They called on these extra-human presences to witness and to intervene in the affairs of life, domestic and social. From these presences, humans sought protection of their bodies and souls, property, kin, animals, towns, and families. Jesus was there in flesh and blood on the altar, in the Host, in the priest's hands, and supernatural beings were everywhere, experienced in all the modalities of the senses. "There was a time," says Calasso, "when the gods were not just a literary cliché, but an event, a sudden apparition." Things happened between humans and their gods. But that was then.[41]

The divide between presence and absence, the literal and the metaphorical, the real and the symbolic, the natural and supernatural, defines the modern temperament. In *The Natural History of Religion* (1757), philosopher David Hume predicted a day soon coming when modern men and women would not be able to even imagine that, once upon a time, humans walked on this planet believing that the gods were really present to them. Hume was thinking specifically of Catholics and Catholic

sacred presences, but he was using Catholics and Catholicism met-
onymically, to stand in for all people who see themselves in relationship to such otherworldly beings. Modernity exists under the sign of
absence. The reimagining of the relationship between God and humans
that commenced in the early sixteenth century introduced an ontological
fault line that would eventually run through all of modernity.[42]

It would run through the nascent field of the academic study of religion, too. Contemporary theorist of religion Jonathan Z. Smith identifies the "fundamental issue that yet divides" scholars of religion as that
"between an understanding of religion based on *presence* and one based
on *representation*." "Representation," as I understand the distinction
Smith is making, refers to the understanding of religious practice and
imagination as being about something other than what they are about
to practitioners. This something else may be human powerlessness, false
consciousness, ignorance, hysteria, or neurosis. It may be a social group's
shared identity of itself. Whatever it is, religion is not about itself. All
of this is further evidence that the fathers of Trent were right about
Zwingli. "Modern religion" is an assemblage of symbols, which are defined by anthropologist Clifford Geertz, in his discussion of "religion,"
as "tangible formulations of notions, abstractions from experience fixed
in perceptible forms, concrete embodiments of ideas, attitudes, judgments, longings or beliefs." The symbol is not an experience of something, but a sign or a representation of it. Signs symbolize, but as critic
George Steiner writes, signs "do not transport presences."[43]

Religious theorists assumed that religions of presence would die out
as the human species evolved to higher forms of consciousness. Modern
Protestantism, as scholars of religion who were themselves well-educated
Protestants or post-Protestants conceived it, was in this sense what all
of human civilization was heading toward. It was the future of humanity
itself. Theorists more ambivalent about their Christian inheritances, such
as the former Quaker Tylor, envisioned a time when reason and science
would fully supplant all religious irrationality. In the meantime, they
conceptualized religion as the response of awed and terrified "primitives"
to the opacities of nature and society, a kind of proto-science in which
gods, demons, and spirits were evoked as causal agents at the limits of

understanding or as "survivals" of a way of being human that was inevitably and necessarily disappearing, albeit at varying rates of speed in different societies.[44]

Catholics were not included in this future. Not only had Catholics not evolved with the rest of Western Christianity; the evidence of the centuries after Trent was that Catholics were actually regressing. Catholics were, if anything, an impediment to the evolution of the species. Modern understandings of religion and religions in this way told a story about time organized around the Catholic / Protestant, presence / absence axes. In his history of the making of modern consciousness, for example, philosopher Charles Taylor refers to supernatural presence in the Catholic sense as "the *old* model of presence." This "old" has played a big role in the interpretation of religion and religions. A then / now construction determines the contours of religious theory, mirroring the movement from a corrupt Catholic *then* to a free and rational modern *now* that organized Western history generally.[45]

Working within this temporality, early British scholars of Asian religions reconstructed them in the image of the confessional divide within Christianity. The South Asian religions that came to be known as Hinduism, with grinning demons and embodied deities present and responsive in manifold forms to humans on feast days, in shrines, smells, sounds, and colors, was Asia's Catholicism. Hinduism had fouled the pure waters of Buddhism, Asia's Protestantism. According to the great modern French scholar of Buddhism Eugène Burnouf (1801–1852), the Buddha, unlike the "the Brahmanical incarnations of Vishnú," did not come "to show the people an eternal and infinite god, descending to earth and preserving, in the mortal condition, the irresistible power of the divinity. He is the son of a king who becomes a monk and who has only the superiority of his virtue and his science to recommend him to the people." Designating Buddha the Luther of the East, the first Western scholars of Buddhism, distinguishing themselves from the Catholic missionaries that preceded them, imagined their work in uncovering the real Buddha of history and text as analogous to that of the sixteenth-century reformers. The power of the "Buddha's" "humanity," according to the modern scholars who invented the "Buddha," "was such that it could overthrow the great weight" of the culture of miracles, sacrifices, and rituals into which the Buddha was born, just as Luther liberated Christianity from the weight of Catholicism. As Donald Lopez Jr. writes, the modern "Buddha," as "discovered" by Europeans, "appealed particularly to the anti-Papist sentiments of Anglican Englishmen and Presbyterian Scots," as well as to Catholic-born anti-Catholic continental scholars. These would free Buddhism from the sordid accumulations of the superstitious past by recovering the original and true Buddhist gospel from the decadent accretions of devotion, ritual, and doctrine. The study of religion itself would make a crucial contribution to winnowing the old from the new.[46]

The phrase "modern religion" has always entailed both descriptive and prescriptive dimensions. It inscribes one way of being religious as "religion" itself. Anthropologists discovered people coming face to face with their gods in environments safely distant from metropolitan centers, while at the same time a powerful professional taboo, which has endured until relatively recently, prohibited studying religions in "civilized" societies. One of the tasks of early anthropologists seems to have been to reassure moderns that such religious phenomena happened only elsewhere, among people living in a time out of time. Psychologists diagnosed experiences of presence as neurotic or psychotic, reinterpreting them as hallucinations, hysteria, projections, and delusions, the productions of unsound or frightened minds. When they had the power to do so, these new scientists of the psyche dispatched to asylums men and women who came face to face with their gods. The absence of the gods became a sign of mental health, whereas their real presence, in the "old" Catholic sense, was a symptom of mental illness.[47]

The absence of the gods has grounded what anthropologist Webb Keane calls "the moral narrative of modernity" and underwritten its cultural capital. There are certain ways of being in the world, certain ways of imagining and inhabiting reality—"reality" that includes the circle of relationships, the scaffoldings of power, and the horizon of what may take place in any given world—that are tolerable, and others that are not. By confining the gods to the inner life of individuals, to the edges of the modern, to the corners of the human mind, and to the past of the species, theorists of religion in the emerging academic disciplines of sociology, anthropology, comparative religion, and political science thus contributed to the constitution and legitimation of the modern state and to the formation of the modern subject as citizen. The absence of the gods from the ordinary affairs of life was a fundamental prerequisite not only for good citizenship in the modern liberal nation-state, but also for social membership and recognition. Practices of presence marked out those who engaged in them as figures of suspicion, persons of uncertain civic loyalties, ill fitted for democracies until such time as they or their children or grandchildren learned how to worship as they were supposed to worship. Language, law, and aesthetics (for example, what people may experience before a work of devotional art safely housed in a museum and how they may experience it) enforce absence, as does a sensorium to which the gods are not available by touch, taste, sound, smell, or sight. The civic domain, along with the realms of finance, labor, and commerce, would be free of the disruptive intrusions of the gods. Where the names of the gods were mentioned—in courts of law, for example—it was to summon the gods to give cold and silent approbation of the authority of the state and its legal system. But the gods did not speak or act on their own behalf or on behalf of their clients in the public sphere. The gods were as remote as stone or ice.[48]

Thus, to be a modern person meant precisely to free oneself from superstitious and infantile subservience to, and dependence upon, supernatural figures, those really present in bread and wine, as well as those in plaster, paint, water, and rock. This maturation is literally what Immanuel Kant meant by "enlightenment." Hume's *Natural History* is as much a handbook to the requisite manners and postures of the enlightened cosmopolitan, to a way of comporting oneself in the world, as it is a critique of religions of presence. Polemicists, theologians, jurists, and philosophers mapped other polarities onto presence / absence, including rationality / irrationality, the impossible / the possible, past / present, female / male, primitive / civilized, and dark skin / white skin. Practices of presence became—and to a great extent they remain—the province of people of color, women, the poor and marginalized, children and childish or childlike adults, the eccentric, the romantic, the insane, and those unhinged by life experiences that overwhelm their reason.[49]

So, not surprisingly, "religion" in its ideal or normative modern forms may be talked about without the gods. The gods were absent from accounts of religion as a "sense of the infinite," as an interior sensibility or apprehension. They appeared as tropes, metaphors, and distortions of language in philological, ethnological, and folkloric scholarship on ancient myth and ritual in various cultures. The gods are there only obliquely and abstractly in conceptions of "religion" defined in terms of human ethical duties vis-à-vis an amorphous, impersonal, and spiritualized "divinity." There are anthropomorphic theories of "religion," certainly, but to say that the gods are a function of cognitive processes contributes little to understanding the intersubjective interactions of gods and humans present to each other and the consequences of such encounters. In any case, the location of the faces of the gods in the clouds is another expression of the normative and disciplining edge of theory: the gods are in the clouds, and that is where they ought to stay. Gods make no appearance in Geertz's influential definition of "religion," nor do they have a role to play in Talal Asad's equally influential critique of Geertz. Against Geertz, Asad asks, "How does power create religion?" He does not write, "How does power create the gods?" which might have raised at least the theoretical question of whether, once created by power, the gods do not turn around and trouble or thwart the agendas of power, as Catholic Church officials are surely able to attest. "Religion" comes already fully contained within its limits. So the gods were obsolete in early modern religious theorizing, already on their way out as living entities involved in the real lives of men, women, and communities, and they remain largely absent from theories and histories of religion today.[50]

* * *

Readers who doubt what I am saying about the enduring authority of absence might pause here to check in with their own assumptions and values. Those readers who do not take the gods to be present in the old sense either in their personal religious practice or in their understanding of "religion" are likely to judge as disempowered, at best, if not pathetic, a modern woman whose husband is unemployed, who promises hard-earned and scarce resources or personal sacrifice to a plaster statue of a saint, as Catholic women have done for centuries, in order to secure that holy figure's aid in finding work for her husband and keeping her family from destitution and shame. If the gods do not really act in space and time, then women in these circumstances are better off going out to look for work. (They often do so, in fact, with the gods accompanying them.) When the saints fail to respond to their petitions, it seems at least a little ridiculous and sad for women to vent their frustration against them by doing some sort of harm to these unresponsive holy beings, such as breaking statues or burning images of them, if such material objects are taken as symbols or representations rather than the gods really present. Is this anger not better directed against the real sources of oppression, where it might have some real-world effect? Such behaviors are the very embodiment of working-class women's terror, alienation, and helplessness, according to accounts of religion in which the gods are not taken really, materially, physically, actually to act in history. How readers approach such questions has to do with whether they understand the gods and other supernatural beings as real or symbolic.

* * *

At the same time, the modern anxieties about and prohibitions against presence generated an enduring and intense longing for it. Ostensibly secular moderns have time and again gone in search of "someone livin' . . . that could look out and see yer," to borrow Tony's pal Emmings's phrase. They most often believed they might glimpse this someone or something Other among those upon whom the various costs of industrial and colonial modernity fell most heavily. These modern searchers have "hunted the elephant" in working-class neighborhoods, they have dragged "themselves through the negro streets at dawn looking for a fix," and they have sought out the presence of the gods among the poor and outcast. They have called the insane, and sometimes their own insanity, holy. South Asia has been a favorite destination among modern seekers, during and after the colonial period; southern Italy has likewise fascinated, for its ruins, its proximity to Africa and Islam, and its "primitive" and pagan religious practices so thinly veiled by Christianity. There have even been intermittent crazes for Catholicism, albeit in an idealized medieval version of it that had little to do with contemporary Catholics. Romantic moderns have wanted the people whose lives did not conform to the normative modern to remain that way, so that they might continue to be enjoyed as exciting alternatives to modernity. This was admittedly an impulse at odds with the civilizing imperative, but there were always more moderns determined to exterminate the "primitive" than to revel in it, and to punish those moderns who did.[51]

Such yearnings for the outcasts of modernity did not fail to have positive outcomes, among them the rise of the study of comparative religions. But even the most seemingly benign cases did little genuine or permanent good. When desire became demand, the living people in whose temples, bodies, and dwellings presence was sought were occluded, disciplined, and denied, their ways of life erased by the voracious consumption of what these others were imputed to have of what the consumers lacked. The endpoint of such quests, in any event, was often enough the museum case, the costume cabinet, or the lovely ruin.[52]

* * *

In December 1955, the American writer Flannery O'Connor, who was Catholic, wrote a letter to her friend "A.," as this cherished correspondent is identified in O'Connor's collected letters. It describes an encounter O'Connor had had some years earlier at a dinner party at the home of formerly Catholic writer Mary McCarthy and her husband. "She departed the Church at the age of 15," O'Connor writes about McCarthy, "and is a Big Intellectual." O'Connor had been brought along to dinner by the poet Robert Lowell and novelist Elizabeth Hardwick, who play a role in this story somewhat like Lester Bradley's in Father Chetwood's tale, before the upper-class Protestant's conversion to Catholicism. In the very early hours of the morning, the subject of the Eucharist came up in conversation at the table. O'Connor got the sense, she says, that "being Catholic," she was "obviously supposed to defend" Catholic Eucharistic theology. McCarthy told the others that as a child, when she was still Catholic, she believed she was receiving "the Holy Ghost" in Communion, "he being the 'most portable' person of the Trinity," but now, as an adult, she views the host as "a symbol," "and . . . a pretty good one" at that, O'Connor reports.[53]

The description of the Host as "a symbol" had been a red flag to Catholics since Zwingli, of course, and so it was to O'Connor now. She describes herself as becoming very agitated: "I then said, in a very shaky voice, 'Well, if it's a symbol, to hell with it.'" "That was all the defense I was capable of," O'Connor concludes, "but I realize now that this is all I ever will be able to say about it, outside of a story, except that it is the center of existence for me." "All the rest of life," she tells A. at the end of this story, "is expendable."

O'Connor's distraught riposte on behalf of the real presence of Jesus in the sacrament of the Eucharist in the old Catholic, nonsymbolic sense of the word "presence" recapitulates within the staging of a dinner party the history I have reviewed in this chapter. The conflict that erupted with such tremendous destructive power in the sixteenth century is not the key to modernity. But neither is it merely one strand among others of a complex genealogy. In all its theological variations, conceptual subtleties, liturgical enactments, and contemptuous caricatures, the fissure of presence / absence has run through the center of Western culture and through all of the modern world wherever the armies, missionaries, and merchants of Protestant and Catholic empires landed, which is to say almost everywhere.

The question of how the human and the divine, the natural and the supernatural, are related was not resolved among Christians in the sixteenth century, or in subsequent centuries either, in practice or in theory. When, in 1942, an African American Catholic periodical in Chicago declared that the "living Stations of the Cross"—recently introduced at one of the city's black Catholic parishes, Corpus Christi, in which black men and women from the surrounding neighborhoods acted out scenes of Christ's Passion before large, mixed-race audiences—marked "a return to Catholic customs practiced in medieval times, *before the influence of Protestantism affected austerity and artificiality in church behavior,*" another installment was made to this history. The African American boys in Chicago's Bronzeville in the same period, Tony's near contemporaries, who defended themselves when they were caught defacing a newly constructed Protestant church with the argument, "this ain't no church[,] not a real one!" made another, as did Cardinal O'Connor when he publicly chastised the South African priest for giving the consecrated Host to people who—he said—took it merely as symbol. Such is the *longue durée* of the presence / absence divide.[54]

The deep intimacy of O'Connor's comment that the real presence is the center of her life and everything else is expendable shows how the question of what Jesus meant when he said at the Last Supper, "take," "eat," "drink," and "do it in memory of me," opens out and is implicated in many other aspects of life. I want to say *all* other aspects of life, because how, where, and when humans encounter their gods; how, where, and when the living interact with the loved and feared dead; how, where, and when the gods enter into the relationships among family members, between the sick and the healthy, and among citizens are all immensely important matters, possibly the most important. Not every day and not in everyone's life, but when these relationships matter, they really matter.

* * *

There is little she can say about the literal fleshly realness of God's presence, O'Connor tells A., "outside of a story." She seems to be suggesting that this is a reality better shown than argued for in polemical exchanges. I share O'Connor's intuition. In the chapters ahead, I tell many stories about human encounters with real presences. But to begin thinking about the life of special beings in relation to other lives, it was necessary to have reviewed first the animus against presence, its roots in the theological controversies in the sixteenth century, and the long legacy of hostility between Catholics and Protestants, and then the diffusion of the animus against presence throughout the globe, its embeddedness in modernity, and its implications for religious theory and historiography. There are historical, philosophical, political, and doctrinal reasons for the scarcity of theoretical language for real presences and for the mistrust of them when they do manage to make an appearance, the haste with which they are translated into other terms. But as Tony says, "I can't say Y'ere not there."

Two

ABUNDANT HISTORY

Y EARS ago, I stopped by chance in the town of Knock, County Mayo, Ireland, to fuel my car. I asked the gas station attendant how it was that Knock boasted such an enormous church with a plaza evidently built for tremendous crowds, as well as its own airport. Do you not know what happened here? he asked me. I did not. Are you Catholic? he asked. I am, I said. Not a very good one then, he said. He condescended to explain to me that on August 21, 1879, the Virgin Mary, along with several other holy figures, appeared beside the church wall to a cluster of villagers that grew to number around fifteen as the evening wore on and the sacred figures lingered in Knock. "Here," the gas station attendant ended his story, "the transcendent broke into time."[1]

* * *

Many times in the 250 years since Hume's confident prediction that the gods really present would soon be forgotten, vast crowds have gathered at the places on earth where the Mother of God had appeared, sometimes to single visionaries, at other times to groups of people (as happened at Knock), most often to small clusters of boys and girls of varying ages. Often, Mary's arrival coincided with times of war, convulsive social change, or crisis in the Church, and sometimes all of these. The age of Marian visionaries has been increasing over time. In the 1980s, the Blessed Mother appeared to older children, adolescents, and adults, most famously in Medjugorje, in the former Yugoslavia, but in other countries as well, including the United States. As word of Mary's presence on earth spread among the families and neighbors of the visionaries, local people, the devout as well as the doubting, came to the place where Mary had been, sometimes when she was still standing, speaking to the visionaries, or else where she had promised to return. These men and women went to observe the relationship between the Blessed Mother and the ones seeing and listening to her and responding.[2]

The first on the scene were cautious and skeptical, even suspicious. They had known the visionaries for years in more ordinary circumstances, after all. How was it that heaven had revealed itself to these unkempt children of poor and troubled families or to these ordinary adults, whose lives in all their mundane, sometimes unsavory details were so well known to everyone? But however tentative and uncertain early witnesses may have been, they nevertheless brought themselves to the places where the Mother of God had made herself visible and audible to humans. Perhaps it was precisely because the Blessed Mother came to people whose stories were so familiar and recognizable, so much like everyone else's stories, that townspeople were drawn to the visionaries and eventually came to trust what the visionaries said they were seeing and hearing. The bodies of the seers, their gestures, the sounds they made, and the movement of their eyes registered the Virgin's presence for those not privileged to see her for themselves. These others might at least witness the refraction of Mary's presence in the seers' bodies, just as the words and gestures of the priest at the altar during the Eucharist made Jesus present again, as he was at the Last Supper, for the congregation to see. The apparitions of the Blessed Mother and the sacrament of the Eucharist were both occasions of a distinctly Catholic mimesis of presence.[3]

Over time these venues, once obscure, now made holy and famous—infamous, to skeptics and rationalists—attracted larger and larger crowds, from farther and farther away, until at last, in the case of many Marian apparitions, pilgrims began coming from around the whole Catholic world. All the media of modern communications, from the telegraph and newspapers to radio, television, and motion pictures, carried news of the apparitional events, and all the media of modern transportation brought pilgrims to and from the sites. In recent years, websites dedicated to Marian apparitions have proliferated. Each apparition attracted a following that took *this* manifestation of the Virgin, this embodiment of her, as its own and felt a special intimacy with *this* Mary. The Blue Army of Our Lady of Fatima, for example, was devoted to spreading the message of impending global disaster and the call for repentance and conversion that the Blessed Mother had delivered to three small children in Portugal in 1917. But Our Lady of Fatima's devout knew and loved Mary's other images, too. The Virgin has many names and faces, but she is a single holy figure. Her faithful hold together the Virgin's singularity with her plurality in their experience of her. Devotion to Mary in the various forms she has taken for her visits constitutes a global web of connections and stories, of devotional objects and images exchanged, and of the circulation of souvenirs, postcards, e-mails, websites, texts, and instant messages.[4]

Marian apparitions substantially increased in number throughout the nineteenth and early twentieth centuries, and Mary's visits became still more numerous in the last decades of the twentieth century following the apparitions in 1981 at Medjugorje. Our Lady of Medjugorje came in troubled times, as the Blessed Mother always does. There was civil war perilously close to the site of Mary's appearance in Croatia, and bitter theological and liturgical divisions within global Catholicism. Our Lady of Medjugorje attracted a vast international following that included many members of the Catholic hierarchy, among them Pope John Paul II. Just as the new railway lines facilitated the growth of Marian devotions in the nineteenth century, inexpensive airline flights and package pilgrimage tours did the same for Medjugorje. The visions there continued for many years, and Medjugorje became the template for other late modern apparitions. The Medjugorje seers, most of them teenagers at the time of the apparition, traveled around the Catholic world as the mouthpieces of the Virgin's summons to repentance and reform in these dangerous and evil times.

The name that Catholics gave to the age of the ostensible absence of supernatural beings really present in the old sense was "the age of Mary."

The phrase seems to have first appeared in *The True Devotion to Mary,* a pious work by a seventeenth-century churchman, Saint Louis-Marie Grignion de Montfort (1673–1716). Monfort's book was lost until the nineteenth century, when its rediscovery contributed to the resurgence of Marian devotionalism at a time when the Catholic reaction against modern materialism, positivism, and rationalism had reached a peak of intensity. But *The True Devotion to Mary* was written at the very dawn of the modern age. In some Western imaginations, the world that followed the splintering of Christendom and the institutionalization of the various understandings of what Jesus meant when he said "take and eat" was, from its inception, thought of as a time of particular intimacy between heaven and earth, embodied in the person of the Blessed Mother. Expectation and anticipation of Mary's visits were essential to modern Catholic consciousness. Catholic children throughout the world in the later nineteenth and twentieth centuries eagerly prayed for Mary to appear to them. They were attentive to unusual lights in local skies or sweet scents in the air, hopeful that such natural anomalies signaled the Blessed Mother's approach. (See the description of the little girl's claim to have seen the Blessed Mother in the sky over a Nebraska farm in the 1950s in Chapter 4.) The intense desire of children to see Mary with their own eyes endowed modern Catholic childhoods with a sense of ontological drama and excitement, as well as of the nearness of the sacred, which endured into adulthood.[5]

* * *

Here the transcendent broke into time. The conjuncture of transcendence and temporality, the particularity of *here* and the no-place or beyond-all-places of *transcendence,* exemplifies the erasure within Marian devotional practice of categories and boundaries otherwise kept distinct. It was *here,* in Lourdes, that Mary appeared to a girl named Bernadette Soubirous in 1858. Bernadette reported that she had seen a young woman ("younger than sin," in French Catholic novelist Georges Bernanos's words), whom she identified as the "lovely lady." She also called her *aquero,* or "that one," in the local dialect. In the sixteenth vision, the lady named herself the "Immaculate Conception." The doctrine of this name, which Pope Pius IX had officially promulgated in the papal bull *Ineffabilis Deus* four years before Bernadette's visions, holds that Mary was born without original sin, the only human being other than Christ himself of whom this was true. Protestants found the doctrine of the Immaculate Conception soteriologically outrageous and deeply offensive because it makes Christ's sacrificial suffering and death unnecessary for this one human being. American prelates had lobbied unsuccessfully in Rome against the official proclamation of the doctrine, fearing anti-Catholic reprisals back home.[6]

Pilgrims to Lourdes then and since, most of them gravely ill or disabled (known at the shrine as *les malades*), bathe in water from the spring that bubbled up miraculously from the spot at Bernadette's feet where the Lady told her to dig during the ninth apparition (see Figure 1). (Today, the site is streamed live twenty-four hours a day on the shrine's website.) It is *this* water, *here,* coming unexpectedly and anomalously from dry earth, that pilgrims want to drink, to pour on their wounds or the bodies of loved ones in pain. But then what to make of the fact that Catholic pilgrims go to human-made reproductions of the Lourdes grotto in parishes far from the site of Mary's appearance on earth, to drink and bathe in (ordinary) waters flowing from plumbing (more or less) hidden in artfully arranged (sometimes artificial) rocks? All around the Catholic world there are such reproductions of the site where the transcendent broke into time in Lourdes. Is Mary really present *there* or *here?* Pilgrims to these mimetic grottoes almost always know that the water at the sites comes from local reservoirs. One such "replica" was built in 1937–1939 on the grounds of Saint Lucy's Church in the northeast Bronx (see Figure 2). "I remind people that the water is public water," Father Robert Norris, pastor of Saint Lucy's in the early 2000s, told a reporter. "There is no unusual source." Yet, despite his insistence, Father Robert complains, "people think" the water "has certain qualities." Pilgrims take this Bronx water as having miraculous powers because in some way these waters *are* the waters of Lourdes, although Our Lady of Lourdes's devout in the Bronx also know these waters come through the pipes of the city's reservoir. In a distinctive and common

FIGURE 1 A holy card of the ninth apparition at Lourdes, "Bonamy, Edit. Pontif. Poitiers; Déposé," undated, ca. 1870–1900. CCI / The Art Archive at Art Resource, NY.

FIGURE 2 A boy filling a container with healing water at the dedication of Our Lady of Lourdes Grotto in 1939, Saint Lucy's Church, Bronx, New York.

sort of devotional double-mindedness, the water is both ordinary and extraordinary; it is identical and not to the water at Lourdes. And it holds the power of the Blessed Mother's presence.[7]

Contradictions, erasures, and absurdities abound in the practices and sites of Marian devotions. The boundary between private and public experience is blurred in the places where the Virgin Mary is encountered, where the transcendent not only breaks into time but gets involved in the nitty-gritty of people's affairs, too. The heat of the assembled bodies becomes most intense directly in front of the miraculous image, within the ambit of its gaze. Here, the picture or statue is sometimes close enough to touch, certainly close enough to see and be seen. Pilgrims speak aloud their deeply held needs, fears, and desires to images of the Virgin, and they do so in the presence of others, who see and hear them, too, just as the Blessed Mother does. Standing before an image of the Virgin Mary, or at a place where she appeared, is an intensely private experience and a thoroughly public one. There is a heightened sense of intimacy among pilgrims at these sites, an awareness of each other's needs and vulnerability and of mutual dependence. The carefully, if subliminally, maintained distances between modern bodies, the spatial surround that buffers each individual's autonomy, are erased, as volunteers and family members offer physical support to pilgrims who cannot walk on their own, feed or wash themselves, or take care of their intimate bodily needs. With strangers helping out, family members awkwardly carry the non-ambulatory the final yards to healing waters or a sacred image or object for them to kiss. Strangers have offered me cups of cold water at shrines on hot days. If I was unfamiliar with a shrine's customs, others there instructed and encouraged me. They provided me with what I needed but had not thought to bring: a taper with which to light candles, for example, a bottle to fill with holy water, or a towel to dry my face on a humid afternoon. Shrines where the gods are present to human beings are also places where people's bodies press close together, with their breath on each other's skin and the smells of their skin in each other's nostrils. The boundaries of single subjectivities dissolve in fluid environments of desire, need, and hope, conscious and unconscious, in the Blessed Mother's presence.[8]

The public nature of sacred shrines extends outward, beyond the face-to-face interactions of pilgrims with each other and with the holy figure. Marian shrines have served as wellsprings of nationalist sentiment. Our Lady of Guadalupe, for example, unquestionably belongs to Mexico and to Mexicans, including Mexican migrants in the diaspora and their children. She is a nationalist avatar, the Mother of Mexico, as well as *la madre querita*. Guadalupe is so fully identified with the nation that to see her is to see Mexico. Mary as Nuestra Señora de Guadalupe does not "stand for" or "represent" Mexico. She is the living embodiment of Mexico. At the same time, national or regional images of the Virgin Mary have been the focus of conflict *within* modern nations, getting caught up in internecine strife. In confrontations between the Church and the secular liberal Mexican state in the mid-nineteenth century and again in the 1920s and 1930s, to continue with this national example, Catholic patriots conscripted *la Virgencita* in their campaigns against their secular liberal counterparts. By the time of independence, "many Mexicans thought of themselves collectively as the children of Guadalupe," and yet, only a little later in the history of modern Mexico, "there was competition between Guadalupe and the constitution of 1857."[9]

During the Second World War, American Catholics believed that saying the rosary readied Catholic soldiers for battle, making them more courageous than their non-Catholic counterparts, fiercer in combat, more accepting of the prospect of death. "You are a Catholic!" a U.S. Army officer reported telling himself on the eve of battle, in clipped martial cadence. "You grab those beads and fall asleep trying to say them. . . . You sleep. You are ready the next day—ready to go. You might even be happy about it." This officer told the people back home that he carried the rosary they had sent him into battle. He referred to it as his "ace in the hole." After the war, Our Lady of Fatima became the avatar of resistance among American Catholics against Communism. She stood with them on the front line of a conflict that Catholics in the United States and around the world understood as both political and ontological. Fatima was Catholicism's—and therefore the West's—greatest weapon in the supernatural Cold War, a confidence that was eventually vindicated, Our Lady of Fatima's devout assert, by the fall of the Berlin Wall and the end of Communism.[10]

But nationalist sentiments and ideological certainties may be eclipsed along with racial and cultural boundaries in the shared expression of common human need before the Virgin Mary and in mutual love for her. Places where the Blessed Mother has appeared or shrines that hold especially beloved and efficacious images of her become sites where immigrants and migrants of different races and from different nations come together. This is the case even, perhaps especially, when everyday interactions among these diverse peoples, outside the gates of the shrine, are troubled. At the Bronx Lourdes, Haitians, African Americans, and Albanians share holy water with the Italian Americans into whose neighborhoods in the Bronx and Brooklyn they have moved, and Mexicans and Guatemalans new to the city chat with longer-resident Puerto Ricans and Cubans, with whom they compete for jobs and housing. Some of the Haitians go the grotto to serve the vodou spirits as well as to say their prayer before Our Lady of Lourdes, who is also the beautiful and powerful Ezili Dantò. Most Sunday afternoons in the summer, a yellow school bus drops off at the shrine African American pilgrims from a Baptist church in another neighborhood. They gather at the foot of the great crucifix that stands out in a space densely populated with life-size, brightly colored images of the Virgin Mary, the saints, and the angels. Marian shrines, even those most closely associated with a particular community or region, create alternative publics of supplicant men and women that reach across seemingly solid divisions of nation, region, race, and ethnicity. The Virgin Mary does not completely erase such boundaries, but she troubles them.[11]

There is always an excess of expression and experience at Marian shrines—too many candles; too many statues and images; too many rosaries; too much desire, anxiety, and need; and too many souvenir stores hawking too many things. At Lourdes, in the days following the initial apparitions, townspeople and visitors began setting out candles at the site, as many as fifty-eight in the small space of the grotto by Easter Sunday of that year. Plaster images of Mary also started to multiply, to the chagrin of local authorities still uncertain in their assessment of what was happening in the town. Over the succeeding weeks, the statues became ever more elaborately decorated. Visitors today may be unprepared for the excesses at Lourdes and other shrines to Mary and the saints: the proliferation of souvenir shops overflowing with great heaps of rosaries and statues of the Blessed Mother and other holy figures; the great piles of wax or tin images of body parts that pilgrims buy to place at the Virgin Mary's feet in petition for healing; the stacks of holy cards, alongside umbrellas, playing cards, toys, and crockery ashtrays imprinted with images of Mary; the vast throngs of people wanting to buy something; or the endless, repetitive droning of Marian hymns and prayer just outside the door or on recordings blasting inside. This has offended church officials and Catholic moderns, too, who tell the devout that such tasteless messiness crowds out the real meaning of the sites. These critics fail to see that excess itself is the meaning.[12]

* * *

What words or categories of historical and cultural interpretation are there for phenomena such as these? Apparitions of the Virgin Mary and the devotional practices that follow them have played an important role in the making of many aspects of the modern world. Marian apparitions established experiential bonds between the intimacies of personal life and the destinies of states. The Blessed Mother was called on to be an ally in the shaping of the centralized papacy in the nineteenth and twentieth centuries. Vatican officials in consort with Catholic dictators mobilized her in their campaigns against liberalizing impulses in Europe and throughout South America, and even the most corrupt, decadent, and violent regimes, those that massacred the poor and tortured and disappeared dissidents, claimed her as patroness. But so also did many liberals and revolutionaries. Devotional entrepreneurs effectively commodified and marketed appearances of the Virgin Mary, embedding them in local, national, and international economies. In the biopolitical struggles that succeeded the political conflict of the Cold War in the United States and other Western nations, the Blessed Mother was made into a warrior against abortion and contraception and a model of obedient and submissive femininity. But because the Virgin Mary confounds expectations, Catholic women have continued to pray to her for what they need and want in their lives as they really are, which exceed the limits of clerical idealizations of their lives.[13]

Historians have established all this by now. There does not seem to be more to add to the existing narratives, only more case studies to be appended to the list. But such accounts of the Blessed Mother's role in the modern world remain resolutely within the interpretive field of modern historiography, within the limits of what may be thought and remembered according to the authorized interpretive categories. The political, sociological, and ideological loom large, along with the technological, scientific, and economic. Marian apparitions, devotions to the Blessed Mother, men's and women's relationships with the Virgin Mary, and pilgrimages to Marian shrines are translated into social facts. The Blessed Mother either contributes to the making of the modern world, however paradoxically or ironically, or else she gets in the way of it. Underwriting all of this is a particular metaphysics, according to which religious practices are more or less distorted refractions of the real circumstances of life. They are representations of social or psychological facts, symbols of something else, but nothing in themselves.

The confident translation of the stories men and women tell of their encounters with the supernatural into language that makes these stories about something else is based on the pervasive assumption in modern scholarship of the "always already mediated nature of cultural relations." The social determines and accounts for all experience. In theories of the world as always already mediated, discourse is prior to and constitutive of experience. Not surprisingly, therefore, the discursive is what needs to be studied when one sets out to describe and study religious experience. Discursive formations of power create religious experiences, emotions, and perceptions. Religions are *social constructions,* in modern intellectual orthodoxy. In turn, religion underwrites the hierarchies of power, reinforces group solidarity, and also, if more rarely, functions as a medium of rebellion and resistance. From this perspective, Bernadette's encounter with *aquero* and other such meetings of the human and the gods really present to them are events fully constituted and anticipated

within the discourses, technologies, and vicissitudes of power in the social worlds of modern France and global Catholicism. The key words
here are "produce," "create," "structure," and "construct." These terms
limn an epistemology in which causal explanations premised on some
version of social construction, whether political, psychological, or demographic, are sufficient. This is modernity's ontological singular.[14]

Such interpretations share the assumption that what is happening
when the transcendent breaks into time is not what appears to be happening to the men and women to whom it is happening, nor is it what
they say has happened to them. What participants say, as a matter of
fact, does "not faithfully represent actual historical occurrences." They
may be the first to go to when studying an event in history, as the archive of the event, but they are the last to go to for an understanding of
it. These encounters with supernatural figures really present simply
cannot exist within modern scholarship as they exist in the experience
of the devout. Going further, it is assumed that there *must be* disconnection, appropriation, and translation as preconditions for historical
understanding. Social structure and discourse are endowed with a reality
that real presences lack or of which they are distorted instantiations.
Scholars in many different fields may be just as intolerant of whatever
is in excess of the social as religious reformers are.[15]

Anthropologist Michael Jackson refers to this process of translating
their reality into *our* reality as the "inequalities of presence." The only
question that remains, then, has to do with social, semantic, and psychological origins. What in the human brain, in the working of social
power, in the depredations of powerless and ignorance, or in the structures of discourse *causes, creates, produces,* or *constructs* experiences of
the supernatural, of the dead, and of the Blessed Mother and the saints?[16]

* * *

That particular religious expressions and experiences arise within specific
social environments, in specific historical contexts, with their distinctive
densities of power is evident. To state the obvious: In the southwestern
Pyrenees, where Bernadette grew up, short, ghostly female entities who

lived in the woods were familiar creatures of local folklore that pre-
dated Christianity. It was not uncommon for young women in Bernadette's time to catch glimpses of these figures in the local woods and
grottoes. In the months leading up to Bernadette's encounter with
aquero, there were other visions in the forests surrounding the Soubirous
home, which contributed to a local atmosphere of supernatural expectation. This was on top of political and religious tensions. Controversy
over the doctrine of the Immaculate Conception was in the air. Bernadette's relationships with the significant women in her life, especially with
her mother and the woman who had been a surrogate mother to her but
then turned abusive and cruel, were fraught with conflict and disappointment, suggesting social psychological motivations for the child's
vision of a kind and attentive female spirit. Catholic authorities in
Lourdes and Rome were determined to assert their authority and control
over Bernadette's visions, and Our Lady of Lourdes was soon absorbed
in the Catholic politics of antimodernism, especially in the competition
between Catholicism and science, the medical and the miraculous.
Bernadette's experience of *aquero* arose within a particular context.[17]

But it does not follow from this that the context accounts for or explains the experience or what becomes of the many lives touched by it
in the (often very long) afterlife of the experience. Such narratives of
the social origins and consequences of experiences of the gods really
present can never be exhaustive for many reasons, beginning with what
those on the scene say, which is that the gods *came to them.* The genre
of Bernadette's vision may not have been uncommon in the area, but
nevertheless, Bernadette and her family and neighbors were surprised
by her vision. Bernadette's *aquero* was experienced as an other. This other
chose, of her own volition, to come to the young woman in the grotto.
Even when persons take a step toward supernatural presences, by praying,
making a pilgrimage, or, in Bernadette's case, by going out into the forest
to collect firewood, there is always the sense that they are responding
to a supernatural presence that has come to them. Human beings meet
real presences in the midst of living their lives, but the purposes and
intentions of the gods who come have yet to be discovered. These matters are not fully known in the encounter, nor are its consequences for

the seers, their relationships, the future shape of their lives, or the world in which they live. More is inevitably opened in culture, individual lives, families and communities, and the church than is foreclosed by such events.

The testimonies visionaries give of their experiences are not exhaustive, either. Both those who see and hear and their interlocutors sense that there are levels and dimensions of what is happening to and around them that are not completely within their grasp. To understand any experience, including an experience of real presence, involves relationality, conversation, doubt, and ambiguity. It entails tracking back and forth between one life and other lives, as Bernadette and her family and neighbors did in their efforts to begin to understand events in the woods outside the village. But they did not succeed in containing the experience, which was probably not, in any case, their goal. "Life might be understood as precisely that which exceeds any account we may try to give of it," and this includes accounts of our life and the life around us that we give to ourselves, as well as to others. No life is so thoroughly embedded in given structures of meaning, discourse, and power as to be fully accounted for by them, just as meaning, discourse, and power are rarely hermetic, coherent, unidirectional, and stable. Narratives of encounters with the saints are simply not isomorphic with experience, just as the holy figure is not completely identified with any one social environment. These stories are incomplete, contingent, and intersubjective. They are shot through with "unknowingness," studded with "opacities." Talk about the Blessed Mother and the saints is contingent upon the unpredictable supernatural figure and the never fully knowable lives of the others with whom stories of what the Blessed Mother has done are shared. Such stories are always in three voices, at least. There is the Virgin Mary, the one speaking, and the one listening. In these exchanges, aspects of one's life previously unknown or unacknowledged may be discovered. The imagination takes hold of the world as the world takes hold of the imagination. This all belongs to the experience itself and to its history. "Human culture, like consciousness itself," Jackson writes, "rests on a shadowy and dissolving floe of blue ice, and this subliminal, habitual, repressed, unexpressed, and silent mass shapes and reshapes, stabilizes and destabilizes the visible surface forms." Bernadette was not an already, once-and-for-all fully formed subjectivity when she entered the grotto where she saw *aquero*. Her experience of the supernatural other did not arise on securely and fully constituted discursive grounds, nor was it completely containable in the stories that first Bernadette and then others told about their experiences of her and of Our Lady of Lourdes.[18]

The Blessed Mother lived in others' lives and they lived in hers. The apparitional figure standing in the grotto was at once known and unknown. She was an appearance. No story about what happened or happens at Lourdes is ever a secure medium of world making or meaning making, subject formation, or power because the narratives of this experience are never free of the interplay of the known and unknown, conscious and unconscious. There is always an excess of intersubjectivity in encounters with the Blessed Mother and the saints, and there is excess in the narratives that precede and follow from them, too. The experience arises on the shadowy and dissolving floe of blue ice.

* * *

The postulate of absence, along with the totalizing claims of discourse, makes it difficult to work from inside the experience of those who have encountered sacred presences outward toward the environment within which these experiences have their destiny, rather than the other way around. It is nearly impossible to let such experiences be as they are to those involved in them without yielding to the imperative to explain them (away). Any account of religious phenomena as social constructions runs the risk of distorting and diminishing these phenomena precisely *as* historical and cultural realities, because such phenomena are not merely this. What becomes of Bernadette at Lourdes if the question of whether the Blessed Mother *really* appeared is cordoned off by means of the famous epistemic bracket? What is made of the millions of others who have since called on Our Lady of Lourdes to heal them or a loved one? In its harshest formulation, which may seem to some as its most realistic and responsible formulation, if the supernatural figure has not *really* appeared, then the visionary is a psychotic; the others are dupes. Looked at carefully and openly, fully aware of the prohibition against presence in modern historiography, such explanations begin to seem inadequate in all ways—politically, existentially, ethically, and socially—because they are empirically inattentive to the actual experience. There is something more going on in the grotto at Lourdes or its replica in the Bronx than can be accounted for by "social construction" or "discourse."

In a commentary on Sir James George Frazer's massive compendium of the history of religions, *The Golden Bough,* philosopher Ludwig Wittgenstein expressed his dissatisfaction with the explanatory ambitions of social science, which he acerbically called "the stupid superstition of our time." The theoretical and historical aim of Frazer's magnum opus, published in twelve volumes between 1890 and 1915, was to fully explain the origins and evolution of religious myth and folklore, beginning with ancient paganism and "primitive" religion and ending with the unmasking of Christianity as merely one religion among many. Frazer's hermeneutical key was the supposedly universal impulse to overcome death's terrible and mystifying finality with visions of an afterlife. By demonstrating continuity between "primitive" and "savage" beliefs and modern Christianity, "especially Roman Catholicism," Frazer, who fancied himself "the undertaker of religion," also wanted to show once and for all how "primitive" and "savage" Christianity itself was. In Wittgenstein's view, however, all Frazer achieves with this massive compendium of religious data is the recasting of the unfamiliar in terms of the familiar, which Frazer does, says Wittgenstein, in order "to make [religious phenomena and practices] plausible to people who think as he does." This represents, to Wittgenstein, a serious and massive failure of the intellectual imagination. "How impossible for him," he says of Frazer, "to understand a different way of life from the English one of his time!" The everyday life of the theorist and historian becomes the ground for judging the experience of others.[19]

There is an unconscious motivation to this imperative to explain, Wittgenstein says, an anxious need to take hold of "the strangeness of what I see in myself and in others." The explanation itself is almost irrelevant. What matters is that whatever the scholar finds intellectually, ethically, or emotionally alien to his or her way of being in the world is safely isolated and secured by sanctions that have the authority of science. *The Golden Bough*, in other words, is a twelve-volume hysterical symptom, to borrow Freud's language here (and overlooking Freud's fondness for Frazer's work), a reaction-formation against the strangeness of the alien other. *The Golden Bough* is not a written work, but (literally and theoretically) an overwritten one.[20]

Modern historiography, French Jesuit historian Michel de Certeau writes, "endlessly presupposes homogenous unities (century, country, class, economic or social strata, etc.) and cannot give way to the vertigo that critical examination of these fragile boundaries might bring about." Scholarship serves to contain ontological "vertigo." In an intellectual culture premised on absence, the experience of presence is the phenomenon that is most disorienting, most inexplicable. This puts the matter of "translation" and "bracketing" into a new light. Constraints on the scholar's imagination become, by means of his or her scholarship, constraints on the imaginations of others, specifically those whose lives the scholar aims to represent and understand. There is a double intellectual tragedy here, for once their reality is constrained by ours, they no longer have the capacity to enlarge our understandings or our imaginations. This is the price of ontological safety.[21]

* * *

Historian and philosopher Frank R. Ankersmit, in a manifesto for a new historiography of experience, calls for the liberation "of the history of historical experience from the heavy and oppressive weight of (the historian's) language and [for] unearth[ing] experience from the thick sedimentary strata of language covering it." In more evocative, explicitly Christian, language, theologian Marilyn McCord Adams makes a similar challenge. She writes, "Saint Paul says, the Spirit groans within us with sighs too deep for words, and we respond with babbling, even unconscious acquaintance." There are experiences and events in history and culture that are in excess of available languages, that even undermine the capacity to speak in the old tongue, but instead require new languages. "Like mother-love," Adams continues, "the Sprit's presence strengthens, empowers us to grow and learn." Subjectivity is not singular. There is only intersubjectivity. Humans are always accompanied, and any account of a single human life must include these others that accompany that life, for better and for worse. Adams concludes, "Our Paraclete and inner teacher, the self-effacing Spirit, is ever the midwife of creative insight, subtly nudging, suggesting, directing our attention until we leap to the discovery of the '$2+2=5$.' Human nature is not created to function independently, but in omnipresent partnership with its Maker." The presence of the other is the precondition of creativity, in a process that unfolds over time, in the ongoing relationships between humans and the accompanying beings, human and extra-human. The end is potentially radical: a leap beyond the insistence of any contingent "reality" on itself as "reality," toward that which is unthinkable in the world as taken for granted. It is a leap toward what Adams represents as the "$2+2=5$."[22]

The alternative to a historiography without gods is one that allows another reality to break into history and theory, not to destroy them but to enlarge them. Inquiry premised on a postulate of presence entails relinquishing the authority and control that adhere to the postulate of absence. An empiricism of the equation $2+2=5$ would be sufficiently capacious to acknowledge the excess, the more that is fully in, but not fully of, the social, without imprisoning it—to borrow Campion's word—in anxious theory and method. There is something awful about the gods really present, and their awful presence requires an empiricism of the visible and invisible real. What is necessary is not writing, certainly not overwriting, but a kind of un-writing, to allow what is denied to break through.

* * *

Before the apparition at Lourdes became the subject of local controversy; before politicians, clergy, and scientists had staked out their positions; before historians recalled that similar events had occurred in the region in earlier times; before the trains started running on improved national railroad tracks; before the souvenir shops opened; before the ceramic plates, shot glasses, and ashtrays were stamped and the medals struck, there was the face-to-face meeting of Bernadette and *aquero*. Before everything else there was the event of the appearance of the human and the divine to each other. All the other things happened, and continue to happen to the present day, because of what happened to Bernadette, then to gradually expanding circles of kin and neighbors, circles that finally came to include millions of Catholics around the world. All this happened, in other words, because of the abundant event of presence, and all this is evidence of the event's abundance.

What identifies an abundant event in history and culture? A density of relationships was at the core of the Lourdes event. The young girl who stood before the apparitional figure brought into that moment her own history of relationships; intricate webs of long-standing relational histories connected the first cohort of spectators at the grotto. They had the experience of seeing their daughter, niece, cousin, and neighbor in intimate communication with a figure they had also been in relationship with over the years. They knew the Blessed Mother under other names from their own lives; she bore the secrets and stories of their relationships to her as well. The Virgin Mary is not so much seen in apparitions as she is recognized by the visionary and by the ones around her (or him). What is really real about the Marian event at Lourdes and the experiences of visitors at its many replicas is the real presence of the supernatural in relationship with humans. The abundant event serves as a focusing lens for the intricacies of relationships among a group of people in a certain place at a certain time.

The relationship between the Virgin Mary and the devout is like other intimacies, but the analogy is not exact. The difference is ontological. The Blessed Mother is a supernatural figure of infinite power, compassion, and love. She is the Mother of God, the mediator between the almost inconceivable Trinity and human beings. She protects humans from divine judgment, which she also threatens them with. Based on past experiences and stories, the devout may surmise how she *may* respond to their petitions, but they cannot predict it. The Blessed Mother also chastises her devout, demands great sacrifices from their lives and bodies, and warns them of dire consequences should they not heed her. Intimacy does not imply safety, comfort, or security. Modern critics of cults of presence such as that at Lourdes are correct in seeing them as contexts of human limitation, powerlessness, and vulnerability. But they are also the contexts of much more, a more that becomes visible through the postulate of presence.

In the presence of this figure, people's imaginations become larger and more efficacious in their actions upon the world. In the unlocked environment of the devotional relationship there develops "a separate sense that reaches through the barriers exercised by the limits of consciousness." Much becomes possible that otherwise was not. Time may become fluid. Past / present / future, as they are, as they are hoped for, and as they are dreaded, may converge. Spatial boundaries, between here and there, oneself and another, may give way. Relationships also come under the power of the unlocked imagination, relationships between heaven and earth, between the living and the dead, among persons as they are and persons as they are desired to be by themselves and others. In the abundant event and all that follows it, a certain kind of intersubjective receptivity and recognition may become possible, on earth and between heaven and earth, an awareness of being seen and known, of seeing and knowing, so focused that in certain circumstances it may seem intrusive and threatening; in others, deeply compassionate and supportive. Objects come alive. "On the theoretical line between the subjective and that which is objectively perceived," psychological theorist D. W. Winnicott writes, a unique creativity becomes possible. Winnicott contrasts this creativity of the interstices with the attitude toward the world that he calls "compliance," by which he means a posture of deferential acceptance of "reality" as it is given in any contingent world as reality itself. This givenness of the "real" dissolves in the abundant event. Anthropologist Paolo Apolito has written powerfully of this dimension of Marian apparitions at Oliveto Citra in Italy. "It was as if," Apolito says, "the obviousness of everyday perception underwent a drastic overhaul and the world appeared composed of new presences in old forms. . . . All was left suspended between ordinary perception and the possibility that all of a sudden something might emerge from the depths of the unspoken, breaking out of the accustomed surface of things, creating an opening that might suck the everyday order into metahistorical reality. Out there, in an instant, infinity could erupt." Out there, in an instant, the transcendent could break into time.[23]

The abundant event is not exhausted at its source. Presence radiates out from the really real event along a network of routes, a kind of capillary of presence, filling water, relics, images, stories, and memories. "Routes" include the far-flung pathways of commerce, production, and consumption that develop out of the abundant event; networks of devotional affiliation (for example, the Blue Army of Our Lady of Fatima); and the travel itineraries that carry the sick and their families to the shrine. Formed and shaped by the abundant event, the routes are media of presence that reach out beyond the place where the transcendent broke into time, in the stories people want to tell about their experiences of presence, in the many images and objects associated with Lourdes that find their way into Catholic homes around the world, and, of course, in the water carried away from the site in little plastic bottles in the shape of Our Lady of Lourdes, capped with a bright blue crown; or sent by post to friends; or taken from the many replicas of Lourdes in less representational containers such as plastic milk cartons or jelly jars; or poured into automobile radiators by devout drivers who want to get a few more years out of their old cars.[24]

*   *   *

Religion is not transcendent, or not in the way the word is commonly meant. The example of "Lourdes water," drawn from the city reservoir and pumped from pipes arranged to replicate the original miraculous source, circulating through the hot engines of automobiles, serves as a fit emblem of what I mean by the non-transcendent nature of religion. The idea of religion's transcendence is a modern one. When the word "transcendence" is used in everyday speech to refer to religion, it has two different functions. It protects "religion" by disentangling it from the compromises and equivocations of social life and political power, preserving religion in this way as a source of judgment and hope in the world as it is given. This is the "religion" that Christian political theorists mean when they speak of prophetic religion, religion as refusal and resistance, as a beautiful and divine madness, exemplified by figures such as Saint Francis of Assisi or Saint Joan of Arc, that disrupts hierarchies of social oppression and injustice, and as the inspiration for envisioning new possibilities for human life. The idea that religion is transcendent, however, also serves to keep the social sphere free of it. If religion is transcendent, then the gods ought not to involve themselves in affairs that are not "religious." If they do so, it is called "superstition."[25]

But the routes of presence go right through the material and political circumstances of everyday life. The gods are regularly summoned into the spaces where humans suffer and where they inflict pain on each other. The implication of this nearness of the gods to humans as they live in the world is that the gods are not innocent, nor are the practices and media of presence associated with them. The gods may align themselves with some against others. They may be called on to sanction or witness acts of violence, even to do violence. And because the gods are not transcendent but immanently present, humans are compelled to ask whether the gods have caused the pain and suffering of men and women, and if so, why. Or why do the gods stand by and do nothing while humans suffer? This may bring the ones suffering to the conclusion that they are responsible for what has happened to them, that pain, disaster, and death are their just deserts. In this way and others, the gods really present may contribute to further entrapping humans in injustice and degradation. Theorists of religion have described such moments, when men and women are confounded by the inattention and otherness, if not the actual evil, of the gods, as occasions when humans struggle for rational comprehension and explanation of the cosmos. But this emphasis on the empty logic of theodicy misses the existential depths of these times, the sense of radical abandonment and betrayal by one (or more) of those who ought to have been present.

So the Blessed Mother makes herself visible at particular times, but this does not mean that at other times she is not there. She is there in the water taken from Lourdes, in the images of Guadalupe tattooed on the bodies of gang members, in the brightly colored images printed on holy cards, and in groups of people saying the rosary together. "Breaking into time" is not quite right. What the gas station attendant may have meant is that while the Blessed Mother was always present to her devout, on those nights in the lee of the great church in Knock, she was there in a special way that affirmed for her devout the reality of her continuing presence in their everyday lives.

* * *

Does such an approach to events in the past require a particular kind of historical sensibility on the part of historians? Ankersmit thinks so. "Historical experience," he writes in a discussion of the historian Johan Huizinga, "is the historian's 'response' to the 'call of the past.'" "There is in the case of historical experience," Ankersmit continues, "a 'communication' between the historian and the past excluding all that is not part of this most private and intimate communication." It is striking in this regard that on the very first page of a recent and superb history of Lourdes, the author alludes briefly to her own experience of physical distress. "My work on Lourdes," she writes, "became part of a personal voyage, an act of sympathy with nineteenth-century pilgrims." The world of the pilgrims is not utterly alien to the historian, or cannot remain so. There is commonality in the shared vulnerability and contingency. In visiting Lourdes, this historian describes how her sense of being an alien at the shrine is slowly eclipsed as she becomes caught up in the work of helping other pilgrims who cannot help themselves. She tells of being "directed to help a mother care for her adult son who was incontinent, paralyzed, blind and deaf." In the end, she was not "converted," she says. (But why is conversion even an issue, important enough or necessary to mention?) "The experience" of being there, however, she says, "completely changed my approach to the topic" and her relationship to the past. Here the historian breaks into time.[26]

Abundant events, which are not exhausted at the source, and which are characterized by the face-to-face experience of presence, may very well also draw historians into an unexpectedly immediate and intimate encounter with the past, whether or not they are "believers." Ankersmit's description of the relationship of the historian to the past uncannily echoes aspects of what takes place at shrines of the Blessed Mother and the saints. The past may act upon us in such a profound way as to erase our intentions of remaining outside of it. This is the vertigo of abundant history. It comes upon historians as a result of their training and disciplining. But it may be that this is what abundant historiography is: approaching events that are not safely cordoned off in the past, that are not purified, but whose routes extend into the present, into the writing of history itself.

Three

HOLY INTIMACIES

T HERE is a change of scale now in this chapter, from the great apparitional events that so captured modern imaginations and generated vast global enterprises to intimate occasions when humans and gods come face to face, in nearly secret or hidden places—certainly places hidden from history—amid the realities of mundane everyday life. This is where people ordinarily find themselves, and it is also where humans and the gods most often find each other. The venues of intimacy between humans and sacred figures in the pages ahead are a hospital room in the United States in the mid-1990s, small circles of women praying the rosary in an industrial city in the last days of the Second World War, and two homes on either side of the border between the United States and Mexico in the late 1950s. One of the stories has to do with a shrine whose origins are shrouded in mystery and legend, as the past of most Catholic shrines are; another with a mostly forgotten apparition of the Virgin Mary, as the majority of the Blessed Mother's appearances are lost to history and memory; and the third with a Mexican American girl's devotion to the Sacred Heart of Jesus that went unnoticed amid the surrounding urgencies of migration, domestic violence, the difficulties of speaking one's experiences in a strange tongue, and the challenge of finding work. To study the intimacies with the holy that arose in these places and times, it is necessary to go below the surface of what is remembered and authorized as history.

I will call such intimate encounters between humans and the holy "abundant events." I mean by this those occasions, often times of crisis, when supernatural figures who may or may not have been known before come to humans and make their presence more immediately known and felt, as well as all that follows from these encounters. Abundant events always take place within densities of intimacies, at whatever scale they occur. Relationships are essential to understanding modern religious history at all levels, including relationships between humans and the gods. For the women in the three stories I tell in the following pages, the relationships they entered into with holy figures that came to them were as momentous and consequential as Bernadette's with *aquero* standing before her. So this is not about moving from global to local, from public to private, or from the register of the social and political to that of the emotions. Nor is it a question of the difference between memory and history. The relationships of humans with the gods really present trouble such insistent distinctions. The experiences and encounters I relate in this chapter are private *and* public, past *and* present, matters of memory *and* history, at once illegible to power *and* inextricable from its structures. The point is that humans and gods meet each other every day, in the thick of life's circumstances, not only in distant grottoes or hillsides. "The miraculous occurs out of the midst of the mundane," a contemporary anthropologist writes in a study of "extraordinary experience" in northern Kenya, and so it is in North America, too.[1]

* * *

The young, heavyset doctor slipped into the small room sideways, squeezing through the nearly closed door, not opening it wide. He was obviously anxious and uncomfortable to find himself there in front of us. Lizzie sat in her street clothes on the examining table in the center of the room, gripping her husband's hand. Just before the doctor arrived, she had joked about wanting a cigarette. Lizzie was a doctoral student in the social sciences at the time, working with me at the university. She and her husband had asked if I would come with them to the hospital to hear the result of blood tests she had taken earlier in the week, after months of feeling sick, debilitated, and exhausted. The room's harsh white lighting seemed overly bright and somehow dirty at the same time. It drained the color from our clothes and our faces. In my memory, the room is lit like an empty bus station late at night.

"I have very bad news for you," the doctor said abruptly. Lizzie began sobbing into her clenched fist. "There are good kinds of leukemia," he went on, "and bad kinds, and you have one of the worst kinds." To my initial confusion, he seemed to be saying something about the city of Philadelphia, until I finally understood that this was the name of the chromosome associated with the kind of leukemia Lizzie had. There was no truly effective treatment for it. The doctor made some further nearly inaudible comments about consultations that Lizzie would need to schedule with oncologists in the days ahead in Indianapolis to see about available procedures and new trials. He said he was sorry again. But he had nothing else to add. He may have asked if we had questions, but we were too stunned and sick at heart to think of anything. Then he walked out of the room and out of the story that until that moment was Lizzie's life but that was already becoming something no longer completely hers. This happened on a freezing, damp January evening twenty years ago in a small hospital in southern Indiana.

Months later, after many arduous sessions of chemotherapy, Lizzie was waiting for a bone marrow transplant. During this trying and exhausting time, she was either impossibly thin or else swollen almost beyond recognition from the medications she was taking. There were periods of disorientation and dementia. Most days she could not move from her bed. She was losing her eyesight. The world's perversity further manifested itself in a sudden infestation of foul-smelling ladybugs in Lizzie's clean and cozy home in the southern Indiana woods. Her doctors in Indianapolis had begun to harvest bone marrow cells from her body in case the transplant was unsuccessful. If it failed, and there was a good chance that it would, we understood there was no further hope for her. It was around this time that billboards appeared alongside rural southern Indiana roads advertising the quality of the services at a local hospital with the confident and cheerful slogan, "We'll make cancer afraid of you!" Cancer was not afraid of Lizzie.

In the middle of all this, a friend of Lizzie's who had just returned from a trip to the Southwest brought back for her a Ziploc bag filled with holy dirt from El Santuario de Chimayo, a Catholic shrine set in the foothills of the Sangre de Cristo Mountains outside Santa Fe, New Mexico. The shrine at Chimayo is the most popular Catholic pilgrimage destination in the United States, "the Lourdes of America," as its enthusiasts call it in the competitive spirit common among Catholic devotions. Thousands visit Chimayo throughout the year; several estimates put the figure at over 100,000 annually. On Good Friday, pilgrims walk long miles through the night along the roads and highways of New Mexico toward the shrine. Many of them are barefoot. Some carry heavy, hand-carved wooden crosses, with the names of family members needing prayer painted on the wood of the cross in thick black strokes. The crosses are left at the shine on Easter Sunday as offerings in petition or thanksgiving.[2]

Pilgrims arriving on Good Friday in 2014 greeted each other and shared incidents from their journeys. As at all shrines, some of those at Chimayo on any given day are tourists, but most are there to seek help or to give thanks for help received for themselves or for a friend or relative. Sometimes tourists become pilgrims, whatever their intention when they set out. On this Good Friday, vendors along the road just outside the shrine were doing a brisk trade in rosaries, sno-cones, tacos, and tortillas, along with images, statues, and T-shirts of Jesus, the Blessed Mother, and the saints. Long lines of pilgrims waited patiently in the warm spring sunshine to enter the sanctuary.

The shrine dates to the early nineteenth century. On Good Friday in the year 1810, according to legend, a man named Don Bernardo Abeyta was out in the hills near Potero performing the customary Holy Week rituals of the penitential fraternity to which he belonged when he saw a bright white light shining up into the sky out of the ground ahead of him. Clawing at the earth with his bare hands, as Bernadette would do some years later at Lourdes—there is a strong chthonic element to early modern and modern Catholic apparitional culture—Don Bernardo discovered a buried crucifix bearing the black Christ of Esquipulas. Devotion to this figure originated in Guatemala in the sixteenth century. By Don Bernardo's time, it was the most popular devotional cult in the Americas, with a string of shrines dedicated to Our Lord of Esquipulas following the trade routes from south to north. The location of Don Bernardo's discovery had a pre-Christian history as well, having been a healing site for the Tewa people, who believed the soil there had curative powers. The black skin of the buried corpus was mottled with age and crusted with dirt.[3]

The parish priest, summoned out to the hills by Don Bernardo, carried the crucifix back to town in solemn procession. But the townspeople awoke the following morning to discover that the crucifix had mysteriously returned to the hole in the ground where it had been found. Not to be deterred, the priest went out and brought the crucifix back to town again, and again, that night, the black Christ returned to the hills. After the third time this happened, the priest finally bowed to the evidence of what was clearly the wish of the crucified Lord of Esquipulas and permitted Don Bernardo's family to build a chapel over the hole from which the black Christ had been exhumed.

The shrine remained in private hands for a century. Then, as its popularity waned in the early 1900s, the Spanish Colonial Arts Society bought El Santuario de Chimayo and donated it to the diocese of Santa Fe. The numbers of visitors grew during World War II, when the families of Mexican American servicemen came to pray for the safety of their sons, fathers, and husbands overseas, and afterward, when they returned to express their gratitude or to grieve. From these postwar years to the present, the shrine at Chimayo has thrived and grown as a tourist attraction and sacred site, adapting in various ways over time in response to the changing society around it, as well as to the liturgical and devotional transformations of the post–Vatican II era in the Church.

The hole in the earth was left open like a portal or a wound. The devout believe that dirt scooped from this hole has healing powers and that as the hole empties during the day, the dirt is miraculously replenished, although they also see the shrine's caretakers regularly refilling

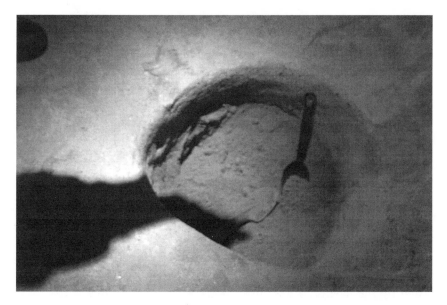

FIGURE 3 The well of holy dirt, El Santuario de Chimayo. © Jessica Rinaldi/
Reuters/Corbis.

the declivity with soil carried in buckets from a mound behind the sanctuary, just as the pilgrims at the Bronx Lourdes see the pipe that pumps
city water down the rocks of the artificial grotto (see Figure 3).[4]

Lizzie was raised Catholic but stopped going to church just after
making her First Communion. Now she decided that she must make a
pilgrimage to Chimayo before the bone marrow transplant. She was
fiercely determined to do this and would hear no objections or concerns.
Her friends, most of whom were not Catholic, attributed Lizzie's single-
minded fixation to her despair or to her intermittent dementia. But
Lizzie's husband, who was also not Catholic, supported her, as did her
parents. Then, a few days before she and her husband were scheduled to
leave for the Southwest, Lizzie's beloved grandmother died. Lizzie wanted
to cancel the trip and instead go to Iowa for her grandmother's wake and
funeral, but her father insisted she proceed with her original plan. So,
with her vision dimming to shadows and in deep grief over the death of
her grandmother, Lizzie boarded an airplane for New Mexico. The whole
way, she held on tightly to the bag of dirt her friend had given her. Lizzie

77

arrived in Santa Fe weak and in pain, but she and her husband went straight to *el posito* (the little well), as the hole in the ground from which Don Bernardo is said to have lifted the black crucifix is called. At the time, the roads to Chimayo were badly marked and poorly paved, making the journey there from Santa Fe especially arduous.[5]

El Santuario de Chimayo is comprised of several nested rooms that open up into each other. The main sanctuary is the biggest space; the next is the "offering room" or the "milagros room"; the smallest houses *el posito*. To reach the well of dirt, pilgrims must first go through a small doorway in the side of the sanctuary, so low-hung that most have to nearly double over to pass into the long rectangular room of offerings. The walls of this room are hung with crutches, canes, eyeglasses, and medical prostheses left behind in witness of the miracles that have taken place, there or as the result of prayers said there. Statues of saints, donated by the devout, are grouped together on a card table at the front of the room. Handwritten messages of petition or thanksgiving, describing the many misfortunes that had brought the writers to Chimayo, are fixed to the walls. People are so anxious to leave these messages, a priest at the shrine told me, that if they have nothing to tack them up with, they set them out lovingly and carefully on the old wooden pews that line the room. There are photographs of people hoping for a miracle: a married couple that wants to have a child but cannot conceive, for example, and a man whose family is praying that he will stop using drugs. There are many photographs of men, women, and children who were miraculously healed or saved from harm, as well as drivers' licenses, military dog tags, and sonogram images of fetuses. A small shrine to the Infant Jesus as Santo Niño de Atocha, protector of small children, sits midway through the room, a shrine within the shrine. Baby shoes are piled up at the tiny feet of El Niño, who is said to walk about at night in aid of sick children. Some devout maintain that this image was found in the hole along with the crucifix, making it another instance of the excess of presence.[6]

At the time of Lizzie's visit, this room of miracles was a great heaping and disordered jumble. It has been cleaned up since. Today, the messages pilgrims write are collected and displayed outside the sanctuary, many in a newly built visitors center. A local shopkeeper I spoke with in 2014 had mixed feelings about such organizational efforts by the clergy. He referred with derision to the new arrangement of written prayers as "a filing system," but he also acknowledged that it was "a [much needed] way of grouping offerings that [both] honors them and cleans the room out." Many hundreds of photographs of people in various stages of life remain in the room, however, as well as in a number of *nichos,* or mini-shrines, built in recent years on the grounds of the shrine. In my experience of many different Catholic shrines around the United States and Europe, such attempts at the purification of devotional excess are rarely if ever successful, and so it is at Chimayo. The *nichos* are crammed with pictures of children and teenagers, graduation and prom photographs, formal marriage portraits, pictures of servicemen and servicewomen in uniform, and photos of sick people in hospital beds, tubes trailing from their noses and arms. Some pictures have text written on them ("I miss you, Dad"). There are also photographs of celebrations, parties, and family gatherings, and many pictures of men and women of all ages holding babies. "People bring pictures," a young woman explained to me, as her grandmother listened to our conversation, "so that they can ask other people to pray for them." Pilgrims tell each other their stories or repeat accounts they have heard about miraculous events at the shrine. A story made the rounds in the late 1990s among visitors to Chimayo that a bright light had shone forth from the chest of a woman who was cured of breast cancer during her visit there, as if the miracle of Don Bernardo's discovery had been literally reproduced in this woman's body. (See Figure 4.)[7]

Many of the photographs and messages tell stories of men and women who have died or been killed in automobile accidents, in street violence, or from illness. The appearance of pictures of the doomed and lost alongside expressions of hope and thanksgiving suggests that the families and friends of the people in the photographs have perhaps accepted these endings as God's will. But even if this is so, it does not mean that all their doubts and questions have been resolved or all their sorrows healed. There is an unfolding and perpetually unfinished quality to the walls of photographs and narratives at Chimayo. This is a function of the sheer

FIGURE 4 A *nicho* at Chimayo, with objects left by pilgrims in gratitude or petition, photographed by the author during Holy Week, 2014.

multiplicity of them, as well as the regular appearance of new ones every day, so many faces looking out from an extraordinary moment in the middle of life and so many stories. The shrine's communal narrative of hope and anguish never ends.

Lizzie and her husband stopped to read some of the messages and to look at the pictures. Then they ducked into the smaller room that houses *el posito*. Bending with her husband's help, Lizzie sank her hands into the cool, dry dirt in the open well. The room was full, but other pilgrims waited respectfully and patiently as Lizzie painstakingly sifted more dirt into the bag her friend had given her. The soil in the hole is sandy and fine. When pilgrims scoop it out, a pale cloud rises up into the air and people in the little room feel the gritty soil crunching between their teeth. Visitors to the shrine invariably report that they feel supported and encouraged by the people around them. A woman with fibromyalgia who made a pilgrimage to Chimayo in 2006, for instance, described weeping at the edge of the well of dirt and slowly becoming aware of "strangers radiant in their hopeful sadness" smiling at her. When Lizzie stood up to leave, the others in the room stepped back to make room for her to pass. They saw how pale and weak she was.[8]

Back home in Indiana, Lizzie began three days of full-body radiation in preparation for the bone marrow transplant. She arrived at the hospital on the appointed day with her husband. She had the little bag of Chimayo dirt in her hands. It was Lizzie's firm intention to take the dirt from *el posito* with her into the bone marrow transplant unit and keep it near her, maybe even on her, during the procedure. The doctors were incredulous at first, then outraged. They told Lizzie there was no way she was bringing a bag of dirt, of all things, into the hospital, of all places. "Well, then," Lizzie said to them, "I'm not coming." An angry standoff developed. Lizzie refused to be separated from the bag of holy dirt. The doctors would not permit the dirt to be taken into the hospital. The bag of dirt put her at grave risk of infection, they told her. Lizzie refused to listen.

*   *   *

The origin stories of many Catholic sacred sites seem remote and strange. They are more like dreams than history, and, like the recollection of dreams, they survive in broken fragments, distortions of familiar things, and strange imagery. Once told, such tales are mostly forgotten, especially in contemporary contexts, or else they are repurposed as quaint lore in souvenir pamphlets and guides for tourists and pilgrims. (I collected many of these at the shrine in Chimayo.) But the story of the light rising from the chest of the woman cured of breast cancer, this alignment of a body in pain with the miracle of the shrine's origins, suggests that the intimacy between heaven and earth that occurs at the shrine begins in the narratives of Don Bernardo's discovery. At Lourdes, Knock, Fatima, Chimayo, and other such venues in the history of modern Catholicism, stories of the transcendent breaking into time are media of presence, too. There are different legends about Chimayo's origins, but all have in common "an association between the crucifix and the healing earth there."[9]

The dirt returns us to the fetish. Lizzie's Ziploc bag is an unthinkable and scandalous confusion of the supernatural and the material, as the real presence of Christ in the Eucharist was to many reformers in the sixteenth century. Recall Zwingli's disgust. Pilgrims rub the dirt onto their bodies or the bodies of the relatives they have accompanied to the shrine. They mix the sandy soil with water or soda pop and drink it down. They lower sick or troubled children into the ground and scoop dirt over them as a blessing and a prayer. They make mud plasters to apply to the parts of their bodies or the bodies of friends and relatives that are in pain; they press the muddy dirt to leg braces and casts. They stand barefoot in the dirt, quietly praying alongside others in the room, who are also suffering. In these ways, in the medium of the dirt animated by the crucifix that had lain in it, the pilgrims come into intimate contact with real presence at Chimayo. The dirt is the physical reality of the gods become close, as close as the skin on the body, as close as the bodies of the pilgrims to one another at the shrine.[10]

* * *

One evening in the summer of 1944, a "Detroit housewife," as she is commonly identified in Catholic periodicals of the time, was overcome with terror for her six brothers in the service. She had already lost one brother in the war. Now she was frantic to come to the aid of the others. But they were so far away from her and in such grave danger; the intensity of her fears was in direct proportion to her awareness of her powerlessness to do anything for them and to the enormity of their vulnerability. In a panic, she began turning the pages of her missal, "looking for something, I did not know what," until at last she came upon a story about an appearance of the Blessed Mother in Naples, Italy (a reference, most likely, to Our Lady of Pompeii). "I INSTANTLY KNEW THAT THIS WAS IT!" The Neapolitan Madonna had promised that she would intercede on behalf of anyone who said a fifty-four-day novena rosary ("3 novenas of petition and intention, and 3 of thanksgiving"). Right away, the Detroit housewife began the novenas, "and as I finished each one, I gave it to OUR BLESSED MOTHER as IF SHE WERE STANDING BEFORE ME." (The letters are capitalized in the original.) Handing over her fears to the Blessed Mother, the woman felt a deep peace and reassurance. "The thought came to me," she said, "that I have nothing to worry about." Her brothers were safe.[11]

"Then came the battle of Iwo Jima." On her way to Mass, the Detroit housewife heard a radio announcement that "the battle was on in all its fury." Shortly afterward, she received a letter from one of her brothers, who told her he "was on a troop ship, and that they were going to settle a little matter with the Japs." After years of virulent racist wartime propaganda against the Japanese that cast them as reptilian monsters, and simply after so many years of war, the Detroit housewife had all the imagery she needed to picture the most horrific fate for her brothers. A neighbor she told about her fears for her brother said quietly, and ominously, "I will pray for him." "At these words," the Detroit housewife reports, in words commonly used to describe Mary's grief at the foot of her son's cross, "I suddenly had a great sorrow pierce me." Sitting down in her kitchen, the thought came to her, "I must save my brother."

So she determined to rededicate herself even more fervently to what the U.S. government had been telling women it was their responsibility to do and to think. She promised Uncle Sam to donate more blood, buy more war bonds, and collect more scrap metal. "Tomorrow I will donate my blood; I'll give a pint, then walk out and walk back and give another pint[.] They'll never know the difference. I am going to buy more bonds. I'll take the money out of the grocery money. I'm going to save every tin can, every piece of paper. I JUST HAVE TO SAVE MY BROTHER." Then, as she was making these anguished and desperate promises, the Detroit housewife heard a voice saying to her, "YOUR BLOOD WILL NOT SAVE YOUR BROTHER. YOUR BONDS WILL NOT SAVE HIM. YOUR TIN CANS AND YOUR PAPER WILL NOT SAVE HIM." The woman knew it was the Blessed Mother speaking to her, not in a dream or hallucination, but really present.

A more subversive message is not imaginable. Women had been hearing, for years by this time, from all the men in public authority on the home front, that it was their duty as wives and mothers, sisters and daughters, to support their men overseas and prove their loyalty to the nation at war by selling bonds, collecting scrap metal, and giving blood. Citizens generally, but women in particular, were encouraged "to think of themselves as personally connected to the battlefront and to imagine the repercussions of their everyday action for the combat soldier." Women's sense of helplessness was shadowed by guilt and recrimination. Catholic clergy delivered this message to the women in their congregations, ardently endorsing the war and calling women to their duty as Catholics and as American citizens. The Catholic theology of the suffering and sacrificial woman—"I will donate my blood"—gave supernatural sanction to the "tradition of maternalist patriotism" in the wider public discourse. The entire apparatus of the American government, with the cooperation of business, industry, labor unions, religious leaders, and Hollywood celebrities, had been mobilized for years to establish an intimate connection between women's home front contributions and the well-being and survival of fighting men. A short time before the Blessed Mother appeared to the housewife in Detroit, popular and iconic singer Kate Smith, speaking on the radio on behalf of a war bond drive, told listeners, "When we buy War Bonds . . . what we're really doing is buying our boys back." Smith closed her pitch by quoting a man who had lost a son to the war. "I'd give anything, all my money, or my health, or my own life," she reports the man as saying, ". . . to buy my boy back from the war."[12]

But now the voice of another woman, with even greater authority than Kate Smith, tells the Detroit housewife, just when her terror is most acute, that participating in the war effort as she had been told to do would not help her brothers. "The VOICE stopped." Mary seems almost cruel in confronting the woman with such dreadful honesty at this precise moment. Or it may have been that the Blessed Mother was expressing what the Detroit housewife already knew but was forbidden by the demands of "war-mindedness" to say, and acknowledging feelings not permitted in a context in which every gesture and emotion on the home front was represented as consequential for the lives of servicemen, the success of the war, and the survival of the nation. "Then before me," the Detroit housewife resumes the narrative of her vision, "appeared Mt. Surabachi [*sic*]." In imagery reminiscent of newsreels she must have seen, she describes the faces of marines, taut, filthy, and terrified. In one hand, she says, they carry their guns; in the other, they pull themselves up the cliff face. "Every figure stood out so distinctly that were I to see those men again I could recognize everyone. Then Mt. Surabachi [*sic*] disappeared."

Catholic women set up shrines in their homes during the war, placing images of the saints and the Blessed Mother alongside photographs of the soldiers in the family for whom protection was being sought, a wartime representation of the communion of saints, not only between heaven and earth, but also between home and the distant battlefields. It may have been that the Detroit housewife had such a shrine in her home and that she was praying in front of it when Mary appeared to her. Such details are missing from the accounts that eventually appeared in the Catholic press, in which the Detroit housewife is glimpsed only fleetingly. It was the Church's practice to treat such instances of human and divine interaction very cautiously and with suspicion, and this was reflected in the reports of this wartime abundant event in the Catholic press.

* * *

One morning some years ago, when I was doing fieldwork in South Phoenix, Arizona, a woman I will call Natalie sought me out to tell me her story. She had heard about my project from a friend of hers. Natalie was an exquisitely poised woman. She was dressed for work on the days we met and she sat very straight during our conversations, her hands folded in her lap. Natalie was born in Mexico in 1948. Her father died when she was still an infant and some time later her mother remarried. When Natalie was three years old, the family moved to a mining town in southern Arizona where her stepfather had found work. During these years when they were living in the United States, Natalie's family "traveled back and forth across the border" all the time, Natalie told me, sometimes as often as every other week, to visit Natalie's maternal grandmother. These visits were a delight to Natalie. "What a joy it was," she said, "when you went over the little hill and I knew my [grandmother's] house was right there."

Her grandmother had a picture of the Sacred Heart of Jesus on the wall above her bed. Every night, Natalie said, her grandmother knelt down before the image to pray. A crown of thorns circled Jesus's exposed heart and a shining cross rose up from its center, as if it were a sword's blade piercing the blood-red organ. Natalie called this simply "a very important picture." There was a tone in her voice when she said this that made me suddenly uneasy about the story she was slowly unfolding around this image. "That's where I learned devotion to Jesus," Natalie went on. "Because I would see her," she said about her grandmother. "I could see her pray." Her grandmother entered what to the young child seemed like a trance as she knelt before the image of the Sacred Heart. "And I would look at her and I would see her. She had such peace and tranquility in her . . . though her life was so hard for her." Her grandmother's husband, Natalie's grandfather, was an alcoholic who physi-

FIGURE 5 Currier and Ives, Sacred Heart of Jesus, 1877–1894, lithograph, from the collection of David Morgan. Note titles in English, French, and Spanish. This image or others like it would have been for sale in Mexico.

cally abused his wife. But by the time of Natalie's childhood visits, he was out of the picture. Before Natalie and her brother went to sleep at night, their grandmother blessed them, making the sign of the cross, "in Spanish," Natalie specified, on their foreheads. Natalie's mother did this at bedtime in their Arizona home. (See Figure 5.)[13]

Natalie broke off here to tell me that when she was a little girl, this grandmother had taught her how to make the sign of the cross. Natalie stood at the side of her grandmother's bed, the older woman sitting behind her. Then her grandmother took the first three fingers of Natalie's right hand and pressed them together, a sign of "the three-in-one" of the Trinity, Natalie explained, and slowly moved the girl's hands through the arc of the blessing, from her forehead, to her heart, to her left shoulder, then her right shoulder. Natalie asked her grandmother who had taught her how to make the sign of the cross. Her grandmother replied that her own grandmother, Natalie's great-grandmother, did, when Natalie's grandmother was Natalie's age.

Returning to her story, Natalie said that she had been held back in school in Arizona because she did not speak English very well. So she was a little older than the other children in the catechism class when it came time to prepare to make her First Communion. The class was taught in English, which was common practice in American parishes on the border. Natalie struggled, but she described herself as an eager and attentive student. She applied herself so assiduously to her lessons that the priest teaching the class often singled her out for special praise. One day he said to the other children, "See"—he pointed to Natalie— "she can't speak English like the rest of you, but she really wants to learn." Natalie's mother did not speak English very well either, but her stepfather did, because he had already spent some time in the United States when he was a younger man. Natalie said that it was in this catechism class that she began to learn to speak English.[14]

The first question in the catechism, from which Natalie learned English, along with the basic doctrines of Catholicism, is, "Who made us?" The answer is, "God made us." "Who is God?" the next question asks. "God is the Supreme Being who made all things." "Why did God make us?" "God made us to show forth His goodness and to share with us His everlasting happiness in heaven." Eventually Natalie would learn, as the answer to the tenth question in the catechism, that "God knows all things, past, present, and future, even our most secret thoughts, words, and actions." God is everywhere. "Does God see us?" "God sees us and watches over us with loving care."

It was now, just when she was about to make her First Communion, that her stepfather began sexually abusing her. From here on in our conversation, Natalie referred to her stepfather as "the ugly gorilla." The ugly gorilla threatened to hurt Natalie's mother and younger brother if she told anyone what he was doing to her. Before making their First Communion, children were required to go to confession. This put Natalie in a terrible bind. Like many children who are sexually abused,

Natalie believed she was somehow at fault. If she did not confess this to the priest, as she thought she must, she would knowingly receive Christ really present in the Host with a mortal sin on her soul, a most grievous offense that would put her at risk of eternal damnation. Anticipating this, the ugly gorilla warned Natalie that if she said anything to the priest, he would find out and punish her. The nine-year-old girl felt forced to choose between the risk of hell and her stepfather's brutality. During this time, the ugly gorilla bragged to Natalie that he had killed a man. He forced her to look at gruesome pictures he had collected of bloody and dismembered bodies. The priest who taught the catechism class also heard the children's confessions. Despite her stepfather's warning, Natalie told him. The priest listened, but in the end, he told Natalie, in her words, "there was nothing even he could do."

So Natalie began to confide in a statue of the Sacred Heart of Jesus that stood inside her parish church. This was the same figure, in a different form, as the one over her grandmother's bed. "It was through the Sacred Heart of Jesus," Natalie said, "when I went to kneel to him that he told me he was with me." Often she would sit in church and "talk to the Sacred Heart of Jesus, this beautiful statue." Natalie used masculine pronouns to describe the image, but most often she simply referred to it as "the Sacred Heart of Jesus." "And he would always console me," she went on, "and tell me that it was okay, that he loved me. I was his child and he loved me and it was okay." Suddenly telescoping in time from childhood forward, as she often did when we talked, Natalie added, "and it's been like that throughout my life." I asked Natalie what drew her to this image of the Sacred Heart of Jesus. "It's his eyes," she said, again using the present tense. "It's his eyes, the way they are fixed, penetrating, such peace and comfort that I get from him. Even when things were going on at home, I would sit and I would pray and I would pray [sic] like I used to see my grandmother pray."

*　*　*

Natalie, Lizzie, and the Detroit housewife were not suffering because they found themselves in circumstances that did not make sense to them. They suffered because the circumstances they found themselves in were all too clear. Their worlds had given way to awful transparency. They saw just what was expected of them and they knew exactly how the people around them would enforce this expectation. Any step they took in the world as it was given to them only drew them more deeply into a reality that was made against them. The mundane world had become claustrophobic, futile, and dangerous.

Shaping Lizzie's fate was the modern history of women's disempowerment in medical settings; the asymmetries of power and knowledge between patients and doctors; the many ways, in language, gesture, the multiplicity of specialists, and the decreasing length of and opportunity for social interactions between patients and physicians, as well as in the shape of hospital architecture and design, that this discrepancy in social capital is performed; the coerciveness and constraint of contemporary medicine, often beyond the intentionality of actors within these environments, as a result of the imperatives of law, finance, insurance, and accreditation; and the geographical isolation of the spaces and times of contemporary medicine from the ordinary places where people live, a distancing that began in the mid-twentieth century and has increased over time. The Detroit housewife was confronted with the full authority of the government and public opinion in wartime, which demanded that she and other "housewives" like her stoically, cheerfully, and loyally contribute to the national war effort. This expectation carried heavy emotional freight and a powerful undertow of accusation. Natalie's suffering arose from the terrible silence that is often imposed on children who are sexually abused; their abandonment, denial, and dismissal by persons around them; the added linguistic isolation in the context of an unequal bilingualism, in which one language provided greater access to public expression and visibility; and the guilt that sexually abused children feel, exacerbated in this case by the ambiguous discourse of sin, the canonical protocols of confession, and the limits of a child's comprehension of Catholic moral teaching.[15]

Lizzie, the Detroit housewife, and Natalie were abandoned, but abandonment does not adequately describe the intersubjective reality of the three women's lives in this moment. They were not so much abandoned as repulsed. They were silenced and denied just when they most needed the people around them to see and to recognize them. These others, from whom recognition was sought but not found, glimpsed broken and disjointed shards of the women's experiences, whatever these others would allow themselves to see. The doctors caring for Lizzie presumably had experience with other cancer patients' abject terror and loneliness. They must also have known from their own lives how difficult it is to put such deep and insistent fears into language. The Detroit housewife's neighbors, certainly her parish priest, would have seen and approved her redoubled fervor at the public tasks she was assigned. The priest in the confessional knew that his best catechetical student, about to make her First Communion, was being raped. Once these traces of the women's real lives surfaced, however, they were ignored or denied. The "world that lies between people," in Hannah Arendt's phrase, was erased. This world is "the thing that arises between people," Arendt says, ". . . in which everything that individuals carry with them innately can become visible and audible." The effacement of intersubjective reality happens between people, too, just as the world's creation and ongoing existence do. To see this thing that arises between people disappear must have made the women's despair and isolation all the more terrifying.[16]

Not to be recognized in one's social world "endangers the identity of human beings." Individuals stand out against their social worlds in times of crisis, which is a kind of intimate exile, an experience of exposure and invisibility at the same time. It is to be isolated within their local surroundings, although the people around them continue to look at them and although their images register on the retinas of these others. Just as the workings of their environments are coming into ever-sharper focus, the one standing out against her social context is becoming less substantial, less present. Lizzie, the Detroit housewife, and Natalie were at this extremity of danger. They were at risk of becoming subjects of what others wanted, expected, needed of them. Many factors converged to constitute this risk, including the socially constructed and discursively authorized roles and identities made against them as young women, which expected them to be a good patient, a patriotic housewife, and a silent victim, respectively. What was wanted of them in these precise circumstances, in other words, was compliance, to use Winnicott's term, the deep and willing conformity to the demands of the other that this, not that, was the way they were supposed to be, a compliance so deep and willing that it came to feel like oneself.[17]

The opposite of compliance is the creative engagement with what is given as reality in such a way that both the self and the world are taken up and set in motion. But Lizzie, the Detroit housewife, and Natalie could get no purchase on their circumstances, no traction. They spoke, but they weren't heard. They were in pain, but their suffering was purposefully denied. They were fully visible, but they were not seen. Their efforts to bring themselves into the world that lies between people were disallowed (by the hospital protocols Lizzie encountered), forbidden (the Detroit housewife's fear for her brothers and her deepening sense of the futility of her efforts to protect them), and denied (Natalie in the confessional). Moreover, the three women's silence and invisibility were necessary to the well-being of the people around them, who were protecting themselves and securing the stability of *their* worlds by not seeing or hearing the women. This turned the women into functionaries for the maintenance of these others' realities. The women were summoned to be for these others, and to cease being for themselves in relation to others.

Then the transcendent broke into time.

*　*　*

Observing the standoff between Lizzie and her physicians, nurses at the hospital devised a compromise that allowed Lizzie to keep the bag of dirt close while at the same time placating the doctors and protecting her health and the well-being of other patients in the bone marrow unit. They put the Ziploc bag of holy dirt inside another plastic bag and sealed it. There were two windows between Lizzie and her visitors (another instance of nested space, as at Chimayo). One looked out from her room into a corridor, then through another window in the corridor on the opposite wall into the area where Lizzie's visitors stood to see her. The nurses taped the bag of holy dirt to the *outside* of the window of Lizzie's room. The bag of dirt was *inside* the hospital, then, separated from Lizzie by a thin pane of glass, visible to her as she lay in bed, and visible also to her visitors as they looked through the parallel window in at her. "It was there with me" is how Lizzie describes this.

I went to visit Lizzie in the hospital just after the bone marrow transplant. She was so thin and pale that she was nearly transparent. But she was definitely there, just as the bag of dirt was. The reality of her presence in the world was substantiated by images of her life outside the hospital that were affixed to corkboards on the walls of her room. There were pictures of friends, of happier times and places, of her animals, and of her home in the woods. There were notes and many images of angels, because it was that time in late twentieth-century American religion when angels seemed to be everywhere. The bag of holy dirt was there, too. But it was ontologically different from these other instantiations of love and connection, to recall an earlier point. The bag of dirt was the presence of the supernatural really real there in the hospital. It may be that the faces of absent friends and the notes in their handwriting acquired reality and presence of their own by virtue of their proximity to the bag of dirt. Most visitors were not allowed to enter Lizzie's room. When friends and family looked at her from outside the corridor that separated her room from the hospital and she looked at them from her bed, the bag of dirt hung in the shared field of vision between the windows, as if it were hovering in the air. The presence of the sacred in the bag of dirt was physically closer to Lizzie in these weeks than anyone besides her husband and the many medical personnel who came and went. Lizzie had managed to contaminate the medically purified space with presence.

* * *

"OUR BLESSED MOTHER APPEARED." The Blessed Mother made herself visible to the Detroit housewife. "Dressed all in black," she reports, Mary "stood as though a thousand swords were piercing HER heart." The Blessed Mother was showing that she knew from her own experience what the Detroit housewife was suffering. "Tears were in

HER eyes, and HER forehead was wrinkled as if from great sorrow." Then Mary spoke to the woman in front of her, "WHAT ARE YOU WAITING FOR? COME AND GET YOUR GROUPS." The Blessed Mother gave the Detroit housewife a vision within the vision. She and the woman entered a small, white house, one of four that the Virgin revealed, and there they saw a circle of gray-haired women "on their knees." "In their faces," the Detroit housewife described them, "was such bitter grief as if each had a son who was about to be hanged, and . . . GOD alone could save him." These women were in as bitter distress as she was. Then, "I saw a bomb coming through the roof, and again it appeared as though only GOD'S hand could stop it. That was the only hope." The Blessed Mother explained to the Detroit housewife that the older women were praying the rosary together. "WHEREVER THESE GROUPS WILL GATHER, I WILL GIVE THEM PROTECTION. I SHALL BLESS THEIR HOMES. I WILL BE IN THEIR MIDST." She gave the visionary precise instructions. "TAKE THEM THE FIRST WEEK; ANOTHER THE NEXT, ETC. ONCE A WEEK, TIME 7:30 P.M., HOUSE BY HOUSE, STREET BY STREET." As the story was reported in the Catholic press, the unnamed housewife protested that she was unworthy for such an assignment. "NO, BLESSED MOTHER, I CAN'T." But Mary had a confidence in her that the woman seemingly lacked in herself at that time, when she was so anxious about her brothers and when she was feeling so impotent. The Detroit house-wife describes the Blessed Mother's reaction to her fearfulness: she looked "straight into my face." "RUN, MY CHILD," Mary said to her, an image of Jesus in the background now, "YOU CAN SAVE YOURS, MINE MUST DIE." She reassured the Detroit housewife, "YOU JUST ASK, I WILL DO THE REST."

Then the Blessed Mother described what the postwar world would look like. She did so in language and images that directly confounded any popular anticipation or official promise that protracted war is fol-lowed by good times for the victors, and she challenged the eternal pro-pensity of the winners to forget the costs of war. The Blessed Mother insisted that war's most intimate wounds be acknowledged and con-fronted. This was the vision of war's aftermath as women would experience it in their homes, in the bodies of their husbands and brothers, fathers and sons. In the Blessed Mother's words: "THIS WAR WILL END SOON. BUT ARE YOU GOING TO FORGET THE DEAD SO SOON? YOU MUST PRAY FOR THE DEAD, FOR THOSE IN HOSPITALS, FOR THOSE WHO ARE BLIND, FOR THOSE WITHOUT LEGS AND ARMS. YOU HAVE MUCH TO PRAY FOR. YOU MUST PRAY FOR SUN, FOR RAIN, FOR CROPS. YOU MUST PRAY FOR THE PARALYZED."

This was the origin of what came to be called the Block Rosary. In the last days of World War II, families in city neighborhoods and parishes met in each other's homes in rotation, one the first week, another the next, as the Blessed Mother had stipulated, to recite the rosary. An image of the Virgin Mary traveled from home to home. The family hosting the week's gathering burned a candle in their front windows to signal the presence of the holy. The candle illumined the service stars that families posted on their windows to indicate the number of their men at war, the numbers lost. A rural counterpart of the Block Rosary developed after the war. The Block Rosary remained popular through the 1950s and 1960s.

*   *   *

Five years after Natalie had made her First Communion, she and her mother were together at home one day when they heard the warning buzzer at the mine sounding in the early morning quiet. Natalie's stepfather had been abusing her for all these years. "When we heard those buzzers real loud," Natalie said, "we knew something had happened in the mine, and so it was either a death or it was someone hurt and the whole town would go over." She and her mother ran out of the house. When they got to the mine, they learned that Natalie's stepfather had been killed in a terrible accident. "He was crushed underneath a mine. He was totally crushed." The year was 1959. Searchers found his body later that day. After they buried him, the family began a nine-day period during which relatives and friends came over to the house to socialize.

*   *   *

The Detroit housewife expressed doubt that she was capable of carrying out the Blessed Mother's wishes. Mary interrupted her to reassure her that she was. After so many years of war and fear, there was good reason for the human woman in this exchange to be hesitant and uncertain. It is not unusual for people in such circumstances to come to this pass, to be gripped by radical self-doubt, when they are "obliged to rethink and reconsider the relationship between what we can and cannot change, comprehend, or endure." Regaining one's balance in the face of this existential dread—existential, but again also thoroughly socially constructed—is an intersubjective process. Humans make a detour to the other en route to coming back—not to their senses, but to relative poise and composure in the face of their inner sense of hopelessness— just as to be repulsed in the detour is to have that interior apprehension confirmed by another. Here the other to which the detour is made is a supernatural figure. In *A Place on Earth,* the novelist Wendell Berry describes something happening to one of his characters "as if in answer to a prayer that he has not even thought of praying." If the prayer is unspoken, who knows what is being prayed for? Who knows what the answer to the unspoken prayer might be?[18]

* * *

The Detroit housewife's story suggests that the supernatural figure that comes in response to prayer may hold knowledge of the inner desires and needs of the person praying or seeing, including knowledge the subject himself or herself lacks but discovers in relationship to the supernatural figure. To put this in other language, the holy figure is the bearer of the "unthought known." The detour to the other opens up possibilities hitherto unimagined or actively denied ("YOU HAVE MUCH TO PRAY FOR"). As with figures in dreams that say or do things the dreamer recognizes as true although she had not previously realized it, so, too, with the supernatural figures encountered in the circumstances of everyday life. Living within webs of relationships with men, women, and children, the supernatural figure holds the unconscious, unspoken, or unacknowledged wishes of humans, what they cannot bear or accept about themselves. They encounter these hidden desires and truths in the intentions, actions, and demands of the supernatural figure that comes. "People speak each other's disowned voices," psychoanalytic theorist Adam Phillips writes, and so do the Sacred Heart of Jesus, the Blessed Mother, and the bag of dirt. They speak the disowned and disallowed voices of the people praying to them. This means, among other things, that prayers may be answered before they are spoken or even thought. It also means that prayer is not unidirectional or univocal, but dialogic.[19]

The Blessed Mother lifted the terrible burden from the Detroit housewife and the other women who took up the Block Rosary of believing they were singularly responsible for the safety and survival of their men overseas, as the voices of public authority had been telling them for years. The import of the Virgin's message was that the *only* thing the women could reasonably do for their men was to pray along with her and other women who have suffered and are suffering like they were from grief, terror, and helplessness. But what to make of the vision's odd detail that the sons of the older women praying were to be *hanged?* Death by hanging is meted out in wartime to traitors and to soldiers who desert. What had these men done to deserve the punishment of the gallows? Whom had these "sons" betrayed or abandoned to deserve such an ignoble fate? This image of men facing the hangman's noose in the housewife's vision may have been the Blessed Mother's acknowledgment and recognition of women's anger at having been betrayed by their men, who left them behind to go off and die in faraway places. In this way, the Virgin Mary troubled the deep alignment of subjectivity and patriotism required by the modern nation at war.

The Detroit housewife's account of her vision ends with the Blessed Mother's summons to institute the practice of the Block Rosary. It ends, in other words, with Mary getting the "housewife" outside of the walls of her home, in which her fear and helplessness had grown to such terrifying proportions—"GO," Mary commands her—and into the company of other women like her. "I . . . put on my coat. I went to the door and said, 'I'll be back in ten minutes,'" the Detroit housewife says. "I went to the door of the house across the street, opened it without knocking, walked in and asked for 'mother.'" When the woman of the house comes to the door, her neighbor tells her, "OUR BLESSED MOTHER was here AND SHE WANTS US TO PRAY THE ROSARY IN GROUPS—all mothers to pray for their sons in the battlefields." The vision ends with one woman going out to find another woman; the Detroit housewife enters this other woman's home as if it were her own, "without knocking." As Phillips says, "When two people speak to each other, they soon become inextricable: words are contagious."[20] Published by the Block Rosary Lay Apostolate, this account of the Detroit housewife's vision ends with a note from the "biographer," a man named Nick Schorn: "I have interviewed the 'neighbor' several times. She substantiates all parts of the story in which she was personally engaged." Later versions will leave out most of the details, including the vision of Mount Suribachi, the visit to the neighbor, and the Detroit housewife's clear if unspoken expectation that Block Rosaries were to be women's practice, which she shared with the Blessed Mother. The postwar history of the devotion begins with Schorn's coda.

Just how unsettling and dangerous the Blessed Mother's message to the Detroit housewife was surfaces clearly in the fate of the Block Rosary after the war and in the Church's treatment of the Detroit housewife. In a severely worded article published in the popular Catholic periodical *Sign Post* in 1951, Passionist father Aloysius McDonough identified concerns that had arisen among Church authorities regarding the new devotion and the presumed visionary. Catholics in the United States are free to make what they want of "the 'Detroit visions,'" Father McDonough begins, although the quotation marks make plain exactly what he thinks of them. He commends the Detroit housewife's decision to "stay in the background—unnamed and except to a very few unknown," although whether this was actually her choice or whether it was imposed on her is not known. Then, as if speaking to her directly from the page, he warns, "The vanity of a religious fakir feeds on notoriety." Is the Detroit housewife a fakir?[21]

The import of the threat is obvious. Were she to step forward and identify herself as the one to whom the Blessed Mother had come, the Detroit housewife would be publicly exposed as a religious fraud and humiliated. Her experience would stand revealed as trickery or delusion, magic or madness. Catholics must "distinguish sharply," Father McDonough goes on, *as a condition of participating in the Block Rosary,* between the woman to whom the Blessed Mother had come to speak, on the one hand, whose status within the Church remains uncertain, and the practice itself, on the other, which "is in perfect harmony with the explicit appearance of Our Lady of Fatima." The priest thus drives a wedge between the Detroit housewife and her vision, between her and the Blessed Mother, and between her and women everywhere the Block Rosary is said. The Detroit housewife's mental stability had become a question, too. Another article in the Catholic press at this time referred to the unnamed women's encounter with the Virgin Mary as "a series of visions or dreams," and not even she "can be sure which" it was. This is the politics of presence.[22]

The Block Rosary is acceptable, Father McDonough continued, because "it is a variation of the Family Rosary Crusade." This is a reference to the hugely popular postwar devotional campaign founded by the Irish-born father Patrick Peyton, CSC. A handsome and photogenic priest with a thick head of silver-white hair, Father Peyton was a master of modern communications media and a relentless self-promoter who embodied the postwar American Catholic ideal of the hypermasculine clergyman. The message of his rosary campaign, delivered in a soft, old-country burr that soothed and thrilled fourth- and fifth-generation war-weary and upwardly mobile Irish Americans, was that the most effective way of repairing the world, thrown into turmoil by the absence of men from their homes, was to restore the patriarchal family. Relations between men and women in working-class Catholic families before the war had in fact been considerably more fluid in response to economic exigencies than Father Peyton's postwar evocation of a domestic great chain of being suggests. Rather, the Rosary Crusade contributed to the innovation of the postwar Catholic middle-class, suburban, nuclear family, a sociological and demographic transformation to which Father Peyton gave the Blessed Mother's approval, mobilizing her for the coincident agendas of Church and nation after the war. Catholic men would perform their restored prominence by leading their wives and children in the nightly rosary. In his admonitions to American

Catholic women, Father McDonough neatly subsumes the Detroit house-wife's Block Rosary under Father Peyton's Family Rosary Crusade, making Father Peyton the public face of the devotion and pushing the unnamed Detroit housewife ever deeper into the shadows of Cold War American Catholicism.[23]

Peyton himself contributed to the disciplining of the Detroit house-wife after the war. She had arranged to meet Peyton during his 1947 rosary campaign in Detroit. This meeting never took place. The hand-some and romantic priest was dashing off to the airport en route to yet another great rosary gathering, as the story was told in the Catholic press, when the woman arrived to meet him as they had scheduled. With no time to talk, Peyton left her in the hands of a local businessman, Nick Schorn, "a tough old bird," as one Catholic reporter called him. This was the man, quoted above, who in a short time, and as the result of this encounter with Peyton, would become the Block Rosary's national executive. "I sized her up rather skeptically as she told her tale," Schorn told a reporter, his name and diction evoking the fictional hard-boiled private investigators of the period. But he decided in the end that she was "sane and sincere." Schorn moved quickly to assert his au-thority over the Block Rosary as he just had done over its founder's sanity. After briefly serving as chairman of "the Block Rosary Lay Apos-tolate Committee of Detroit," he went on to promote himself to the title he had created: "National Director" of the Block Rosary Lay Apostolate. He ran the organization out of the basement of his home in a Detroit suburb. Father McDonough gives Schorn's address in his article, but instructs readers—that is to say, women—interested in organizing a Block Rosary first to seek the permission of their parish priests. The Blessed Mother had neglected to mention this detail.[24]

What really troubled Father McDonough was the idea that the women who gathered to recite the rosary might *talk* with each other before or after praying. His article closes with a string of warnings, de-livered in a staccato burst. No one family (meaning no one woman) is to "monopolize" the devotion! There is to be no expression of "private needs"! Socializing before or after the rosary is strictly forbidden! "No refreshments are to be served"! Visitors are to depart silently from the hosting home at the conclusion of the rosary! No talking in the doorway, no protracted farewells! The devotion is to be enshrouded with a veil of women's silence. When he is finished, Father McDonough again reminds his readers, now duly cautioned to be suspicious and wary of the Detroit housewife, that if they want to sponsor a Block Rosary, they are to write to Schorn for approval.[25]

Father McDonough's precise, even strident effort to constrain women's behavior underscores what the Block Rosary was meant to be: an intimate forum in which women who recognized one another's circumstances and suffering might come together in the Blessed Mother's company and share their worries and doubts with her and with each other. Among women between heaven and earth and on earth, the intimacy that the Blessed Mother promised in the vision-within-the-vision that she gave the Detroit housewife appears to terrify Father McDonough and other Catholic writers after the war. This is what Father McDonough aims to prohibit. The Detroit housewife, her sanity simultaneously certified and undermined by male authorities, is fleetingly identified in one or two articles after the war as "Mrs. Mary E." before disappearing forever. In Schorn's 1952 invitation to families to participate in the Block Rosary, "Why the Block Rosary?" the vision itself is erased; instead, Mrs. E. "decides" to form a Block Rosary, and she is given the "definite admonition" by the (unnamed) "director of the world-wide devotion" not to "go out alone" at night.[26]

The Detroit housewife's abundant event is eclipsed today by the later history of the Block Rosary, when it becomes an artifact of the apocalyptic Marian anti-Communism that took shape around the figure of Our Lady of Fatima and flourished among Catholics in the United States in the 1940s and 1950s. But there is a sleight of historical hand here. The encounter between Mrs. E. and the Blessed Mother took place during the war, not after it. The visionary was anxious not about Soviet power but about her brothers' safety in the Pacific and the futility of the assigned patriotic duties in doing anything for them. The Blessed Mother said nothing about Communism, nor did she manifest herself as Our Lady of Fatima, a connection that was first made by postwar commentators and authorities. The bomb that comes through the ceiling in the vision is not identified as atomic. The Block Rosary was indeed mobilized in the postwar struggle against Communism, but the Cold War interpretation ignores the reasons the Blessed Mother herself gave for her appearance. It also ignores what transpired first between the two women, one human, the other supernatural, who had come face to face with each other in a specific time and place, and then among the groups of women praying together as the result of this encounter.[27]

* * *

"Illness is the night-side of life," Susan Sontag writes on the first page of her study of illness as metaphor. By the time of her journey to Chimayo, Lizzie had moved deeply into this nighttime, and she knew there was still further to go. Her bag of dirt, which had no face, no eyes with which to see and to recognize her pain, appears to mark some outer limit of comprehension and communication that the suffering woman had reached. From one perspective, the dirt is bare materiality.[28]

A contemporary theory of trauma holds that "trauma creates a structural deficit, wound, or 'hole' in the mind where representation ought to be." Trauma's reality, the reality of what happened to cause the rupture or deficit, is "disassociated from all semantic-linguistic-verbal representation." It is representable, according to this theory, solely in the forms of icon, image, drawing, and painting. Chimayo appears to be the literal enactment of this theory of trauma. The shrine bleeds copiously. Bright red blood pours down nearly every saint's statue and image of Jesus there. The statue of Jesus crucified that hangs above the main altar drips blood. Dark blood flows down the front of Jesus's chest from both arms and head, pooling under his breastbone. All around the shrine grounds during Holy Week in 2014, people wore T-shirts depicting Jesus on the cross in bright red ink that looked wet and sticky, with the slogan "A blood donor saved my life" splashed across the back. Pilgrims pinned to their clothing pictures of their loved ones in distress. Everything in Chimayo communicates the realities of pain. Suffering pilgrims and their families enter an environment where they are surrounded by icons, images, and objects of trauma. All of these things are media of objecti-fication, metaphors of pain's terrible agency. They bring the interior re-alities of suffering, which are so resistant to speech, out into the world where all can see them.[29]

This takes us part of the way toward understanding Chimayo. The shrine is indeed a space for that which cannot be represented elsewhere. But this theory of a "hole" in the mind where representations of trauma ought to be falls short as an analogy to the hole in the ground at Chi-mayo because *el posito* is not empty. The little well is a paradoxical hole, a seeming emptiness that is in fact full. The dirt from the portal in the earth at Chimayo is a route of the excess of real presence. The dirt is enlivened for having been the repository of the crucifix of the black Christ of Esquipulas and it bears the enduring touch of this sacred figure. Christ is present in the dirt, at the shrine, and however far away the dirt is carried. The presences animating the dirt include all the figures, human and divine, visible and invisible, sick and well, living and dead, that meet at Chimayo. These others at the shrine have suffered or are still suffering from their experiences, the traumas that brought them to Chimayo. But at the same time, they are also actors in their lives. Like Lizzie, they chose to go to Chimayo. They did everything necessary in terms of preparation, packing, making arrangements, getting transpor-tation, and so on, to get there.

This duality surfaces in the messages on the shrine's walls, which are missives of abjection, detailing disastrous and destructive events, but also acts of self-expression that invite others to take note of them. The message writers ask these others, on heaven and earth, for prayer. They express—to these others—their faith and hope for healing, often in ex-plicit contradiction of medical authorities. They recount the moment of crisis and its extended circumstances. They describe missing persons as if they are asking other pilgrims to be on the lookout for them (and perhaps they are). They disclose their families' intimate and even shameful secrets. In this way the messages on the walls constitute a com-plex and multileveled devotional genre that reports facts, expresses de-sire, acknowledges the presence and role of sacred figures, and asks readers to recognize what has happened and to share the hope for what might happen at the same time that it offers them encouragement, compassion, and solidarity.

One pilgrim to Chimayo recalled that while reading through the messages on the walls she realized she "was praying for strangers, asking for their miracles to occur." She *found herself* praying for these others; she was taken up into their stories without intending to be, as if the texts had called her out in prayer. Looking for a word to describe such occasions when one person's experience becomes another's, when one person's being in the world is so deeply apprehended by another that their lives touch at a very deep level, the anthropologist working in Kenya quoted above reaches for the Catholic concept of transubstantiation. Such interpenetrations of lives, she writes, are "transubstantiations of experience." "We are in contact with the world, we make the world as it is for us through our being in it, and we share world [*sic*]." In such cases, "signs do not present the world in another form, but rather *are* an aspect of our being in the world at another moment, at every moment."[30]

The signs on the walls are not there to be read, in the ordinary sense of reading. Rather, the narratives draw pilgrims into the stories in such a way that, by the act of reading, they are situated in the larger and shared story of human suffering that is always unfolding at the shrine. The images and narratives are media of transubstantiation. The ones reading and looking are asked to recognize the suffering of others as they find their own distress reflected back to them in the medium of these other lives. One family's or one person's pain is interleaved with others. Recognition becomes mutual. Through these exchanges new possibilities are discovered. A pilgrim suffering from a serious illness wrote of her visit to the shrine that she felt a sense of hope there that she had not "in the hospitals and doctors' waiting rooms that had dominated [her] life these past few months." This hope was not an idea or a feeling she had. It was a reality in her body in the presence of others. The dirt is the medium of these presences within presences within presences. The messages created a vibrant connection between visitors to the shrine on any given day and other pilgrims who were not there on that particular day but who had been before on other days. The dirt holds all of this.

The room of *el posito* is very small. To move around in it requires a heightened attentiveness to the movements of others' bodies that are often, like oneself or a loved one, hobbled by pain or sorrow, or who are assisting someone who is so hobbled. People stumble, hesitate, struggle. But at Chimayo, as at other shrines I have visited, there is a kind of spontaneous coordination among pilgrims, a grace of movement that comes from visitors' attunement to one another. This is especially so around *el posito*. The mutual awareness that hovers at the border between consciousness and unconsciousness is an instance of what a contemporary writer on spatiality terms "simultaneous perception." The senses take in, at varying levels of consciousness, the multiplicity and the movements of the surroundings. By virtue of this, individuals are connected to their environment and to others around them, as well as to the place itself. This makes possible a mutuality deeper than words, a matter of the body, moving inward and outward at the same time, and a stronger "sense of humanity's pressing problems and unfinished business." Simultaneous perception speaks of the mutual recognition that is located in bodies in relation to each other and to things within space, a radical intersubjectivity that at the shrine in Chimayo brings together humans and supernatural figures. Presence is realized in the synchronous movement of bodies in relation to each other; in the mutual speaking of stories, one's own and others'; and in shared distress.[31]

* * *

The ex-voto tradition in Italian and Spanish Catholicism, the practice of commissioning local artists to paint scenes of abundant events as media of acknowledgment and gratitude, depicts the miraculous intervention of holy figures in a moment of crisis as the immediate and definitive resolution of that crisis. Storm-tossed sailors are saved from drowning, the sick child is healed, the trapped driver is spared the oncoming train bearing down on his car on the tracks, and in each case the holy figure hovers at the upper edge of the image but fully within the narrative and pictorial frame. In contrast, Natalie's account leaves open the time of the miracle. Her story suggests that the event of the transcendent breaking into time may be an extended process in a temporality contiguous with but not identical to the time of pain and suffering. When the transcendent breaks into time, the result may be a lack of closure rather than the making of meaning, instantaneous healing, or the restoration of comprehension. So it seems to be in Natalie's story. There was a long time between Natalie's first prayer to the Sacred Heart of Jesus and the accident in the mine, and I do not know whether Natalie wanted the earth to bury her stepfather, but she did not conclusively know this either, even after so many years.

The Sacred Heart of Jesus offered Natalie no "cosmic guarantee," Geertz's phrase for what humans seek from religion and what religion ostensibly provides. Rather, the abundant event created the lack of closure. The event of the Sacred Heart's intervention put an end to the abuse, but at the same time it served to introduce a new and seemingly permanent inconclusiveness to Natalie's story and an anxiety that hovered just beneath the surface of her days. Did she want this to happen? Did she will her stepfather's death, did she desire it, did she cause it? The outcome of Natalie's prayers subverts the customary expectation that religion in any simple sense provides comfort, assurance, and meaning. It may be that other domains of culture such as law, consumerism, politics, and education offer a more definite and attainable meaning and purpose that religion not only fails to provide, but actually troubles. Natalie's engagement with the Sacred Heart of Jesus led to a lifetime of questioning and uncertainty. This is what she went out of her way to share with me that morning in South Phoenix. It is not that the Sacred Heart made things worse, but that encounters with real presences disrupt ordinary expectations, neat plotlines, and the usual routines of life. This lack of closure may very well have been the miracle Natalie had been praying for unwittingly.[32]

* * *

"The common world," Arendt writes, "remains 'inhuman' in a very literal sense unless it is constantly talked about by human beings." I take "talked about" here to refer to the ways that lived worlds are made and sustained in webs of relationships and rounds of conversations. Lizzie, the Detroit housewife, and Natalie were denied access to their respective common worlds. They lived in an airless present in which the horizon of the future was closed. They were without reason to hope.[33]

Then the holy figure, who was of their worlds but who also came to them from outside their worlds, broke into the space and time of the crisis. The women were able to disclose themselves to these figures, who, in turn, recognized the women and acknowledged the truth of their experiences. The process of recognition, on earth and between heaven and earth, was not passive. In each case, the women took a step toward the holy, and the holy responded. Nor was it unidirectional. There is always a "double directionality" to recognition, psychoanalytic theorist Jessica Benjamin writes; recognition moves along "two-way streets." Recognizing the holy figure, the women were recognized in turn, and then things changed.[34]

Lizzie remained sick, the Detroit housewife was frightened for her brothers until the war's end, and Natalie's stepfather continued to abuse her for years. But "the space within the world which men need in order to appear at all" had been opened. Genuine action in the world is "completely dependent on the presence of others," Arendt writes. While Arendt probably did not intend this, for the above women these others included the presence of the gods. Once recognized and attended to, Lizzie, the Detroit housewife, and Natalie found it possible to stand as themselves on the grounds they were given to stand on.[35]

It may appear at first that Natalie's story is different because, unlike Lizzie, who was able to have an effect on how she would be in the hospital, and unlike the Detroit housewife, who got to say the rosary to the Blessed Mother, who had come to her, and to do so in the company of other women who recognized each others' lives, Natalie found a way to express her genuine feelings in the company of others, but she continued to be abused until the mine caved in on her stepfather. Caution is in order here, however. Among the reasons why the sexual abuse of children is so deeply destructive of their identities is the fact that the victims often accept responsibility for the abuse. Natalie and I did not talk about this, specifically. But it may be that once she had found the

Sacred Heart near her home and was able to tell him what was happening to her, this burden was lifted, even though the abuse went on. It is certainly the case that Natalie marks the moment she discovered and turned to the Sacred Heart as a tectonic shift in the story of her abuse.

*   *   *

The broken world is lived through and survived, but the brokenness is not forgotten. This suggests that religion is less about the making of meaning than about the creation of scar tissue.

Lizzie still sleeps with the bag of Chimayo dirt under her pillow, more than twenty years after the night of the diagnosis in the southern Indiana hospital. Her eyesight remains poor and she has trouble walking, although she has courageously continued to work toward her academic degree. The dirt has been ground down into even finer powder as a result of Lizzie's handling it all these years. At night, when she prays, with the bag of dirt nearby, Lizzie asks the Blessed Mother "to pray with [her] to God." Lizzie says that she cannot be without the bag of dirt because "it has the whole history" of her illness and survival. The dirt holds her memories. After she told me this, she went on to recount once more in the medium of the dirt all the stages of her experience, from the diagnosis through the bone marrow transplant. "It was in the hospital with me," she said of the bag of dirt, "and it has been with me ever since."

The Sacred Heart of Jesus, Natalie told me, has "been with me ever since" the days of abuse and of her stepfather's death in the mine. Through trials and tribulations, she repeated, "the Sacred Heart of Jesus has always been with me." Today Natalie keeps the picture of the Sacred Heart that once hung on the wall in her grandmother's bedroom in her own bedroom in Phoenix. When her grandmother died, she said, "that's all I wanted from the things she had was that one picture, which was the Sacred Heart of Jesus." Natalie's grandchildren come to see her and they climb into her bed the way she and her brother did at her grandmother's home many years before. Natalie described the room in her home to me. "I have the Sacred Heart, I have the Virgin Mary, I have the crucifix and I have other pictures." Her grandchildren want to sleep in her bed. "I think my bed—they come in and they all just kind of gather in there and they like it. They find peace. And I talk to them about the angels and I try to show them about religion."

How the Detroit housewife lived with her memories is not known.

So the arrival of the holy figure did not offer a pathway out of the world, an escape from reality, as some theories of religion have it, or sub-mission to it, but rather *a pathway back into the world*. The holy figure did not make pain, suffering, and violence endurable; one way or an-other, humans have to figure out how to endure what befalls them, and they do not necessarily need religion for this. Rather, the holy figure made it possible for those in pain and distress to reenter their lives, however those lives were. Lizzie went to the hospital after Chimayo as a woman who was very sick, but who had a life whose reality would not be denied by the protocols of bureaucratic medicine, the anger and authority of her doctors, or the stipulations of science. The Detroit housewife found a way to express unacceptable emotions in wartime and to make it possible for other women to express themselves, too, to each other, in circles of mutual recognition and conversation. Natalie refused to accept the reality and inevitability of the abuse or responsibility for it.

*   *   *

What readers see and think as they encounter the events described in these three stories depends fundamentally on what they hold to be the nature of reality, based on their own experiences, their own lives, and, if they do not live in a world populated by sacred beings, whether they are able to imagine life in such a world. "Our understanding of others," anthropologist Michael Jackson writes, "can *only* proceed from within our experience, and this experience involves our personalities and his-tories as much as our fieldwork," as much as our archival research. There is no methodology that permits escape from this. The reader's subjec-tivity in encountering and interpreting such experiences, whether they are designated religious, sociological, or psychological, is inextricable from research and interpretation. This is an epistemological position, but, as we have seen earlier in this chapter, it has an existential edge. As

Wittgenstein argued, interpretation may become and often is the medium for controlling the incomprehensible, incoherent, silly, shameful, uncomfortable, or dangerous. We are reminded that there ought to be no safety in encountering the experience of others, especially their experience of real presences.[36]

What happens if instead of translating these stories into the alien categories of social and cultural theory, we say that these lives are this way, just as our lives are, or may be, another way, whatever way that is? "Interpretation," Phillips writes in a discussion of "truth" in psychoanalysis, "can be a refusal to listen." The aim is to enlarge our understanding of what happens to the world as a result of these ties between heaven and earth. This entails a struggle between their categories and the categories available to scholars of religion in history and culture in which neither is given primacy. Otherwise it will be said of the study of religion, to borrow from Jean-Paul Sartre's critique of Marxist social and psychological theory, that "it situates but no longer discovers anything."[37]

* * *

Recently I returned to the recording I have of the conversation in which Natalie told me about her abuse. It is nearly impossible to listen to, because of what Natalie is saying and because she speaks so softly. At one point, clearly shaken by what Natalie has been telling me, I ask Natalie whether the Sacred Heart enabled her to *resist* her stepfather. This comes after a very long silence, during which I was trying to compose myself. I am almost pleading with Natalie to tell me she found in the image a source of power. In my voice, one may hear the emphasis in religious scholarship over the past several decades on empowerment, the enduring impulse to situate all religious experience and practice on the axis of power / powerlessness, and an echo, from further away in the modern history of critical theories of religion, of the radical critique of religion as promoting submission, self-alienation, victimhood, and passivity. I wanted to protect Natalie from such criticism, which I knew would come when I told her story in academic settings.

One of the things I have found over the years, however, is that very rarely, if ever, do the people we scholars of religion talk with and write about need our protection, because what we are protecting them from is the judgment and condescension of critical theory. In other words, we are protecting them from ourselves. Natalie was having none of it. "Resist?" she replied, as a question to my query. "No." But because Natalie and the Sacred Heart of Jesus are two different beings, and because the Sacred Heart of Jesus had his own plans and intentions for Natalie that were different from hers, Natalie has been able to say that she is not sure if her prayers to this figure are what brought the mine down on her abuser. This was the Sacred Heart's greatest gift. He freed the child and the woman she became from the long shadow of justice achieved by vengeance and violence. Otherwise, Natalie would have been bound to the ugly gorilla by guilt for the rest of her life.

* * *

The gas station attendant's language was elegant, solemnly cadenced, almost liturgical in its expression. "Here, the transcendent broke into time." Word of the Blessed Mother's appearances to the young Bernadette and of the spring of water that bubbled up from the dry earth under the girl's hands threw first the little town of Lourdes and then the whole Catholic world into a great paroxysm of excitement, which really has not ended from that time to today. When the three priests came out of the smoking ruins of the Immaculate Conception Church in the Bronx on December 23, 1923, walking in procession with the Blessed Sacrament in their covered hands, as described in the Introduction, the people outside fell to their knees on the wet and muddy sidewalk before God really present. These are stories of grandeur and high drama, as befits the encounter of human beings with the sacred. Or so it might seem.

But such stories threaten to occlude the far more common and quotidian nature of abundant events and the grittier and nastier circumstances in which the gods come to human beings. Natalie's bond with the Sacred Heart of Jesus and Lizzie's holy dirt—both unknown to anyone but their closest friends and family—and the Detroit housewife's now forgotten or rewritten wartime vision of the Blessed Mother all arose within the culture of presence. In all of them, the holy figure was experienced as coming to them, as seeking them out, through a friend (in Lizzie's case), in a vision (the Detroit housewife's), or by means of memories of a beloved relative's devotion (for Natalie). The holy figures came within webs of relationships and they belonged to those webs. The seismic movements across the Catholic world following Bernadette's vision underscore the potency of the more hidden encounters described in this chapter. The abundant events described in all cases are on a continuum; they are not radically different, and they each must be understood in relation to the others. This is especially true for Bernadette's vision. The grim and hard facts of the three women's stories are a reminder of what it is that the little, blue-capped bottles of holy water, the postcards, and the ashtrays and other souvenirs surround at Lourdes: namely, the trainloads of men, women, and children in the greatest distress, their bodies aching, sweating, and soiled, arriving all day, day after day, at the shrine in France; the lives they lead in the local environments from which they have journeyed to Lourdes; the enormous pool of healing water, fed by Bernadette's spring, into which they lower their bodies or their bodies are lowered, and from which they drink; and the hopes and terrors they and their caregivers carry with them to Our Lady of Lourdes. There are no gradations of real presence; there are only different circumstances of its experience, different lives, and different consequences.

Four

PRINTED PRESENCE

L YDIA was born in 1921 in a German Catholic farm community in central Nebraska. She recalls, "I knew there were non-Catholics [around us] but we never associated with them. When we walked home from school we were not allowed to walk past the Protestant church." As her mother lay dying after the birth of her tenth child, "her last baby," Lydia says that the priest who came to the house to administer the sacrament of extreme unction cut a small piece off a holy card of the Sacred Heart of Jesus that was "setting on a little table alongside of [my mother's] bed" and put it into the dying woman's mouth. "They gave her the head of the Sacred Heart," Lydia says. "A picture. They cut the head off the Sacred Heart and made [my mother] swallow that!" Earlier in the conversation Lydia recalled the nun who prepared her and her classmates for First Communion telling the children that if they accidentally bit the Host, the blood would run. The thought of Christ's blood running down her chin, Lydia says, "scared me *so bad* when I went to Communion" afterward. The little girl watched her mother's body, wrapped in a sheet, being carried out of the house. "She couldn't just die and leave ten little kids," she remembers thinking to herself.

* * *

A dying woman being fed a piece of printed matter: this already suggests that *print culture* is an odd rubric for anything having to do with

Catholic practices of presence or the excesses of devotionalism. After all, it was the destruction of Catholic images in the sixteenth and seventeenth centuries that helped usher in the age of print in the first place. Before the sixteenth century, written and illustrated texts and sacred presence were fully entwined in Christian culture. Afterward, in the age of the printing press and of vernacular translations of the gospels, devotional print became "Catholic books in a Protestant world."[1]

Again, this is not a matter of an absolute Protestant / Catholic divide, although, again, important differences do follow this fault line. Protestant reformers directed Christian attention away from the crowded sensory world of Catholic sacred space to the pages of the Bible. Here Christians might read the narrative of salvation, if not quite for themselves, nevertheless with the text in their hands, the text as preached and interpreted by ministers more or less learned—the emphasis on pastoral education varied in different times and places and among Protestant denominations. The texts were to be read, moreover, within communities whose membership was determined by informed assent to well-defined doctrines, creeds, and theologies. Even when scripture was read at home, the minister's authoritative interpretation remained the hermeneutical key. This way of approaching printed matter anticipated and contributed to modern secular reading practices. But in neither Protestant nor secular contexts does it involve eating printed images or words or feeding them to the sick and the dying.

This chapter turns to the place of printed images of Jesus, the Blessed Mother, the saints and angels, and the dead in twentieth-century American Catholicism, and to printed words by them, about them, or addressed to them—on holy cards, in missals, in prayer books, in comic book lives of the saints, in reproductions of European masterpieces of religious art, in pamphlets, in fiction, and so on. Catholics in the United States, as elsewhere, used such printed things in many ways and contexts; they read books about the saints and looked at pictures of the Blessed Mother, just as they read and looked at nonreligious texts and images. But devotional print was not simply a vehicle of ideas in this world; it was itself a medium of presence, like Natalie's statue of the Sacred Heart of Jesus, Lourdes water, and Lizzie's bag of dirt. And so "reading" and "looking" do not exhaust what Catholics did with printed presence, what sorts of relationships they entered into with printed things.

The adults responsible for the formation of children in the faith used all sorts of printed matter with children. These varied uses of print by these men and women at this time serve as the case studies in printed presence in this chapter; the specificities of American society in this period make these uses distinct and particular, as much as they are recognizable in the *longue durée* of the history of the Catholic book. Catholics understood religious instruction to be the duty of families, but in practice, for most of the twentieth century, the task fell primarily to teaching sisters. These women, who were better educated than their predecessors (and became more so as the century proceeded), developed and published pedagogies, curricula, and classroom exercises, which all entailed particular techniques of reading and looking. They also generated, collected, and had children prepare a huge array of printed materials. The Bible does not have much of a role in this chapter, although Bible stories do. The aim of this pedagogy of presence, by which I mean the project of religious formation in which printed presence played an essential role, was to cause children to know themselves as being members of the communion of saints, living every day in the company of supernatural figures really present to them.[2]

Printed presence was on the front line of religious and moral antagonism between Catholicism and what Catholics consistently called in these years, right into the 1960s, "pagan civilization." This was their designation for the commercialized entertainments and consumerism of modern American society, which they saw as particularly and perniciously exploitative of the young. Pagan civilization included competing secular printed idioms, such as comic books, trashy movie magazines, and bad novels. Catholic educators believed that modern Americans who were not Catholic did not fully appreciate the power for good and evil contained in the acts of reading and looking and, as a result, they were failing to protect their children and the nation from the dangers of evil print. This sense of being radically at odds with secular print media infamously led some Catholics after World War II to burn great pyres of comic books in parochial school yards. An underlying question of this chapter is what we learn about modern practices and understandings of reading and writing in the world when we look at them from the perspective of what Catholics did with presence in print.

* * *

I recently bought a cache of holy cards on eBay that included several images of the Sacred Heart of Jesus, of the sort placed on Lydia's mother's tongue many years ago. eBay has become the great repository of discarded Catholic media of presence from the pre–Vatican II era. There are thousands of holy cards for sale on the site (along with monstrances, ciboria, chalices, Communion patens, and tabernacles, among other sacra). The cards I have in front of me, like others I have bought, arrived at my door in an overstuffed padded envelope, carefully wrapped in Sunday newspaper supplements, with absolutely no information about the cards' provenance. I contacted the seller to see what he or she might be able to tell me. All she knew, the seller wrote back, was that the cards came from the estate of a woman in Colorado who died in 1972. A member of this woman's family had contested the estate sale, so for forty years the house had been sealed, pending the resolution of the dispute. "This was a true time warp like I have never seen," the seller described the dead woman's long-empty house.[3]

From evidence on the cards themselves, I see they once belonged to someone named Elsie H., who lived in a German-speaking Catholic town in south-central Illinois between 1911 (the first handwritten date on any of the cards) and 1950 (the last), somewhere near Techny, Champaign, Mount Vernon, Belleville, and Centralia. These locations are all specified on cards commemorating special occasions in local churches, such as the twenty-fifth anniversary of a priest's ordination, school graduations, or parish missions. Based on what the seller told me, then, it is likely that the cards are two or three times removed from Elsie H. Unlike other forms of Catholic print from earlier ages, for instance, books of hours or medieval lives of the saints, mass-produced modern holy cards are generally not collected, preserved, and archived. If they are historical documents at all, they are ones that have fallen haphazardly though time's folds until, in this case, winding up on my desk via the Internet. But in their contingency and fragmentation, the cards are like most of the other sorts of documents that historians must rely on to find ordinary men and women in the past. Elsie H. accumulated the cards throughout her life. What kind of records are these, and what do they tell us about Elsie and her world, about Catholicism, and about the place of print in this world?

Simple wood-block-print holy cards existed as early as the mid-fifteenth century. But it was the introduction of lithography at the end of the eighteenth century, along with other developments in industrial printing technologies, that made possible the mass reproduction of holy cards and their wide distribution throughout the Catholic world. The earliest centers for the design and printing of cards were in Europe, in particular in Germany, where the lithographic process was first developed, and in France, especially in the print shops around Saint-Sulpice in Paris. It was not long before holy cards, along with chromolithographs of Jesus, the Blessed Mother, the saints, and the angels, were being printed in the United States as well, for the burgeoning Catholic immigrant communities of the nineteenth century and later for increasingly prosperous third- and fourth-generation American Catholics with sufficient income to purchase such printed matter for themselves and their homes.[4]

Elsie H.'s collection reflects this global circulation of sacred images. She had cards from Germany, Italy, Spain, the United States, Belgium, Hungary, Canada, and France (including one from rue Saint-Sulpice). Specific printing houses are identified on some cards, among them Krause, Gräer and Company (Germany), T. F. Édit. Pontif (Paris), B. Kühlen (Munich), C. and N. Benziger (Einsiedeln, Switzerland), Fritz Schemm Kunstantsalt (Nuremberg), Serz and Co. Edits (also Nuremberg), Jos. Vorfeld (Kevelaer, Germany), R. A. Co. (Italy), and, in the United States, B. Herder (St. Louis) and Edward D. O'Toole (New York). The text on most of the cards printed in Europe is in English, suggesting that they were intended for the large American Catholic market, although American Catholicism is polyglot and international and there are cards in Elsie's collection in Hungarian, German, and

French, as well as Latin. A number of Elsie's cards show missionary saints encircled by indigenous peoples on their knees in what European artists imagined as native dress, with prayers for the missions printed on the back of the cards. How conscious Elsie was of the international dimensions of her collection is impossible to know. At the very least, the cards constituted an ambient surround that made visible Catholicism's presence nearly everywhere on the planet. To hold the cards, to pray with them in one's hands, to collect and save them, and to give them away as gifts was to associate oneself with the universal Church and the communion of saints, as one participated at the same time in the always also local and intimate devotional world of modern Catholicism.[5]

From the nineteenth to the mid-twentieth centuries, the cards shared a common devotional aesthetic. Jesus, the Blessed Mother, the angels, and the saints were depicted in warm colors, lovely blues, sanguinary reds, burnished golds, and Franciscan browns, their halos shimmering and bright wings glowing, all this heightening the drama, emotional intensity, and movement of the imagery. Such cards were everywhere, a great river of color flowing through the everyday lives of Catholics. An essential medium of piety and social life, given as gifts, rewards, and mementos, the cards were especially ubiquitous in the lives of Catholic youngsters. Parents were urged by religion writers to put holy cards "of the type that will have a special appeal to the very young" on the walls around their babies' cribs so the children would go to sleep and wake up in the company of the Blessed Mother and the saints. "A small picture of Saint Stephen on the wall," the father of a boy named Stephen advised other parents in a 1958 issue of a Catholic family magazine, "can become a regular acquaintance now to form the basis for a full-blown friendship later on." He proposed children be encouraged to "kiss the piggies" of the image of "the good saint's bare feet." Point to images of the Virgin Mary on the cards, Catholic mothers were told, while saying to their children, "[This is] God's Mamma," as if it were literally a photograph of the Blessed Mother. Using holy cards in this way, a teaching sister wrote in 1945, parents ensured their children grew up in an environment of the sacred really present to them in a medium that engaged all their senses. Lay out holy cards in front of a small child, another educator recommended as a playtime activity, and ask him or her to point to Jesus, then to the Blessed Mother, and then to the angels and to different saints, as the child's mother names them, making it a game of devotional mnemonics. Holy cards were said to be more useful for distracting fidgety toddlers in church than rosary beads clicking noisily against the wooden pews.[6]

Children loved holy cards. The colorful aesthetics and dramatic imagery were compelling to young imaginations. They wanted them and they were happy when they received them. A Nebraska Catholic woman who grew up in the late 1940s described her feelings as a girl about a holy card of Saint Thérèse of the Little Flower: "You kind of thought that, when you looked at them, how pretty they were. And I think that drew you towards them." Children had their own uses for holy cards. They collected and counted them, traded them for candy, mixed them up with images of Hollywood celebrities cut out of magazines and newspapers, and played games with them. Given holy cards as rewards for good behavior or academic achievement, children cherished them as special tokens of recognition, often keeping them all their lives tucked away in missals or bureau drawers.

Children customized and personalized the cards. In Elsie's collection, for example, is a card of the Immaculate Heart of Mary (an image of the Blessed Mother standing on a crescent moon, her arms open wide, a bright flame rising out of her exposed heart) onto which someone, perhaps Elsie, has sewn a small balsa-wood cross with dark red string. On the back of another card, the following prayer is typed: "Savior of the World, Save Russia! 300 d. [anyone who says this prayer is granted an indulgence of 300 days off time in purgatory] Sweet Heart of Mary, be my salvation. 300 d." Another of Elsie's cards, a four-sided one that opens like a little booklet, is in the shape of a Communion wafer. On the front of the card is a raised image of a golden chalice out of which a white Host rises. Inside, a sword goes laterally through a bright red heart. This prayer is written in beautiful cursive in thick, burnished gold ink: "Jesus, my love, my only love, I seek for no one but Thee. I hold me [*sic*] all Thy own, my God. Do as Thou wilt with me."

*   *   *

Differences over printed matter were internal to Catholicism as well. The papacy took full advantage of modern print technology in its campaigns after the Council of Trent to impose universal norms of order and regularity on the church and to prevent abuses in doctrine, liturgical practice, piety, and the life and education of the clergy. Print was also marshaled against what the hierarchy considered popular superstition. At the same time, print's capacity to spread heresy, to popularize and to serve as media of unauthorized devotions (as in printed lives of unrecognized saints or images of them), and to document and disclose ecclesiastical malfeasance—this is the long memory of print—has made Catholic authorities in Rome and around the world wary of print's many forms. Rome has repeatedly asserted its authority over the written word and printed images in the modern era by means of censorship, licensing, and the actual confiscation of prohibited publications. Books forbidden to the laity were kept caged in Catholic libraries. Pope Paul VI abolished the official list of prohibited books in 1966—it was another pope of the same name, Paul IV (1555–1599), who promulgated the first papal Index of Forbidden Books in 1559—although this by no means ended Rome's condemnation and prohibition of disapproved authors and texts. The archives of Catholic institutions are cautiously guarded. Local bishops have also been careful about print circulating in their dioceses, devotional or otherwise, particularly print associated with forbidden or not yet approved practices. Of course, Catholics did not have a monopoly on censorship in the modern era.[7]

But print was not an effective mechanism of control because print itself was another medium of presence in the hands of ordinary people. Print's capacity for appropriation and excess only increased in the age of mechanical reproduction, when printed presences proliferated in images and cards, souvenirs and prayer books. One example of the limits of Church authority over devotional print is that of Padre (now Santo) Pio of Pietrelcina. The miracle-working Franciscan's cult was promulgated by means of images, hagiographies, and holy cards, in direct contravention of concerted efforts on the part of both local diocesan and Vatican authorities to curtail, censor, or suppress the cult. Many of the holy cards of Padre Pio, which were in circulation already in his lifetime,

SERVO DI DIO
Padre Pio da Pietrelcina
CAPPUCCINO

* Pietrelcina   † S. Giovanni Rotondo
25 maggio 1887   23 settembre 1968

FIGURE 6 Cover of a booklet with prayers for the canonization of Padre Pio, dated 1971, with a miniscule piece of cloth stained by his blood, in the lower corner, from the author's personal collection.

were adorned with a minuscule piece of cloth bloodied by the friar's wounds, affixed behind a little plastic window on the card, transforming the image into a relic (see Figure 6). Such veneration was unusual in the case of a living miracle worker, and the Church strongly disapproved of it. The excessive reproduction of holy cards and other printed things, then, was both a boon and a danger to church authorities.[8]

To introduce the anxieties of Church authorities over devotional print culture is not to distinguish between "official" and "popular" attitudes and practices; in print culture, as in all other areas of Catholic life, this boundary is rarely, if ever, stable. The tumultuous and conflicted story of Padre Pio ends with his canonization during the pontificate of John Paul II, after all, who had a warm, personal devotion to the Southern

Italian holy man, and who himself is now canonized, as Saint Karol Wojtyla, and whose image appears on holy cards today. Catholic print idioms arose and existed within the culture of real presences, and Catholics throughout the modern era treated printed things as media of presence, even as the antithesis between the two—print / presence—was increasingly characteristic of modern approaches to print.

* * *

The majority of Elsie's cards are rectangular, but several take other geometric forms. Some are in the shape of a particular feature of cathedral architecture—a nave, for instance, or a lancet window. These cards, long and narrow, tapering to an arch at the top, look like miniature shrines, and Elsie may have used them this way. Some cards are cut out in the shape of the body of the holy figure depicted, from halo to feet, to form a silhouette.

One card in Elsie's collection, for example, is a cutout figure of the child Jesus holding a cross, adorned with a crown of thorns. The holy child and the cross are affixed to a textured, lacelike screen, the top of which is in the shape of a Host that rises above the rectangular plane of the card. "The Cross is thy salvation" is printed along the bottom edge of the card. Some of these silhouette cards have a strip of stiff paper affixed to the back, making it possible to stand them up like little paper statues. A number of cards are printed with prayers, calibrated to particular indulgences, to be directed to the figure on the front. One of these, titled, "A Communion Prayer," bears the poem, "O Holy Virgin Mother / Prepare my heart to hold / Your Son Divine, as you prepared / The stable dark and cold. / Cleanse it from every sin-stain, / Soften it with a prayer, / Then light it with the warmth of love / And place your baby there." A silhouette card of the Blessed Mother, her head bowed slightly to the viewer's right, reads, "She is the unspotted mirror of God's majesty, and the image of His goodness."

On many of Elsie's holy cards, techniques of trompe l'oeil create the impression that the figures depicted are stepping out of the cards toward the viewer. On others, the heart of Jesus or Mary, pierced with swords, crowned with thorns, and dripping blood, appears to pulse above or in front of the cards. This impression of presence was further amplified in the twentieth century with the process of lenticular printing, which made possible 3-D images that shifted when the card was moved—the saint's eyes opened / closed; Jesus on the Cross / Jesus on Easter morning—giving the images the quality of apparitions. The cards strain toward an immediacy and intimacy in their depictions of Jesus, the Blessed Mother, and the saints, so that people came to think of them as almost photographs of the saints, to imagine that the saints really looked like this. It is as if such cards were reaching toward presence, in excess of the limits of print itself, making visible what was true of all holy cards, and of all devotional print.

*   *   *

Before cataloging the various forms of mid-twentieth-century print culture available to young Catholics, there is the question of who these youngsters were and what the adults who gave them holy cards, taught them penmanship, or created new classroom exercises in religion for them thought about younger generations of Catholics between the 1930s and the 1950s. Not all Catholic children went to parochial elementary school, but many did, especially later in the century, when Catholic classrooms became overcrowded. Catholic children not in parochial school attended religion classes on weekends in their parishes, in vacation schools, or in released time periods in the middle of the week. The numbers going to Catholic high schools were smaller because there were fewer of these schools. This latter circumstance contributed to the growing panic among religious educators from the 1930s on that the church was losing its older children and teenagers to the seductions of popular culture.[9]

In a paper published in the *Journal of Religious Instruction* in June 1933, Father George Vogt, a frequent commentator in these years on religious education, employed the starkly militant terms common among Catholic religion teachers to describe the contemporary circumstances in which these teachers found themselves. "The fight is against a complete culture," he wrote, "a complete civilization—a pagan civilization." Once upon a time, according to Father Vogt, "society and the home were Christian" (meaning Catholic), so all of society and culture cooperated in the formation of young people. But today, "we find a widespread and influential culture allied against Catholic principles and Catholic life." The "only complete and adequate defense is to oppose our own culture to that of paganism." Amid "the surging allurements of the senses," influential educator Reverend Florence Sullivan, SJ, warned in an address to Catholic educators in 1930, Catholics must develop new and compelling ways of presenting the living faith to children and adolescents or else perish. Youngsters had become the new front in the long engagement between Catholics and modernity in the United States.[10]

The apprehension evident in Fathers Vogt's and Sullivan's calls to educational arms was not caused by the economic crisis of the 1930s, and it did not abate at its end. The lingering aftereffects of the anti-Catholicism of the 1920s probably contributed to it, as subsequent anti-Catholic outbursts may have as well. But the anxiety arose within American Catholicism too, not in response to threats from the outside. It was the tone of midcentury Catholic pedagogy. Intensifying during the Second World War, when, as we have seen, the Detroit housewife was caught in the midst of wider fears among Catholic leaders about the war's erosion of family hierarchies, the fear that something was going wrong among Catholic children and teenagers reached fever pitch during the Cold War. Catholic educators repeatedly sounded the alarm that the worst aspects of pagan, materialist modernity were penetrating into Catholicism. This runs as a dark thread through religious formation, as clearly evident at the end of the 1950s, the age of the juvenile delinquent, as it was in the early 1930s, the era of the boy gangs.[11]

To respond to the difficulties and risks of religiously forming Catholic children in a secular culture, up-to-date Catholic religion teachers set out to raise the standards of religious education. Although they regularly expressed ambivalence about modern educational philosophy, on the grounds that its resolute naturalism left no place for the supernatural, the new methods and media that teaching sisters introduced for children's religious formation were fully in line with contemporary understandings of the child and with current educational theory. The vowed women religious responsible for teaching the faith led dedicated and disciplined lives and had very high expectations of the children in their care. They understood youngsters to develop particular intellectual, moral, and emotional capacities at various ages, just as secular educational theorists said. But they worked within an environment that made no special allowances for children in terms of moral formation, doctrinal instruction, or devotional and sacramental practice. Catholics prided themselves on this. They believed it was indicative of the metaphysical and moral truth of Catholicism, in comparison with their modern American "non-Catholic"—meaning Protestant—counterparts. These other Americans were adrift in "shifting sureties," in the words of a Catholic family magazine in 1959, and had little of real substance to give their children, only empty symbols and moral relativism, a view that goes all the way back to the sixteenth century, as we know.[12]

A model religion curriculum prepared in 1930–1932 for the Archdiocese of Chicago under the joint direction of Father Daniel F. Cunningham, the city's diocesan superintendent of schools, and the Graduate School of Education at Marquette University provides a sounding of what Catholic religion teachers were beginning to think children needed to know in order to be fully formed in the faith. In first grade, children are introduced to "love of the Christ Child," which "is more important at this age than any knowledge of doctrine," according to the authors of the curriculum. Following Pope Pius X's decree on early Communion (1905), it became the responsibility of first-grade religion teachers to prepare children to receive the Sacrament. First Communion preparation continued in grade two, when "a better understanding of, and a more significant spiritual life" was to be inculcated in children. Religious art was key here. Second graders were to be taught to recognize scenes from the life of Christ in various paintings by Guido Reni, Bartolomé Esteban Murillo, and Heinrich Hofmann, among others. They were also to have learned to recite from memory at least eight "formal prayers," including the Act of Contrition, and to be competent at performing "religious practices," such as "bowing at the name of Jesus" and "tipping [one's] hat or bowing as one passes church." In third grade, children encounter "The Public Life of Christ." In the fourth, the main subject is "Old Testament history." Grade five is when children learn about the popes and saints of Church History. A large part of the fifth-grade religion curriculum was to be dedicated to "great saints of the Middle Ages" and "the Revolution," as the Reformation is called, thereby conflating events of the sixteenth century with the fiercely anti-Catholic political turmoil of the eighteenth. Fifth graders also studied the Council of Trent. Among the recommended vocabulary words for this grade were "apostasy," "Jesuits," "heretics," "infallibility," "schism," "atrocities," and "reign of terror." "Protestant" appears nowhere in the lesson plan. Also in grade five, children learn about the vessels of the holy liturgy, "the consecrated paton [*sic*] and chalice, the blessed ciborium, lunette, and monstrance, and the thurible or censer, the sanctus bell, the processional cross." Grade six was dedicated to memorizing the different parts of the Mass, which in the list provided by the authors of the curriculum number forty-two, from "prayers at the foot of the altar" to "Ite Missa Est." It is in grade six, then, that children learned the words of institution. "Christian doctrine" is taken up in grades seven and eight. Students are expected by now to follow the Latin Mass in their missals. The words they must know include "transubstantiation," "purgatory," "invisible," "sacramental," and "communion of saints." They ought to have memorized the prayer for the dead, "Eternal rest give to them, O Lord, and let perpetual light shine upon them."[13]

Both the richness and the contradictions and tensions of twentieth-century Catholic religious formation of children and adolescents in the United States are evident in this ambitious program. Religion instructors are encouraged to address the full sensorium of childhood—sound, movement, color, smell, and taste—as befits a religious imaginary in which the supernatural is fully present to the senses. But they are also enjoined to drill children in the highly technical terminology of Catholic doctrine in all its scholastic opacity. This required of children enough linguistic facility to be regularly quizzed on doctrine, if not actually to understand it. There was much to be memorized: formal prayers; ritual gestures; the names of the vessels and utensils of the Eucharist; the responses, in English and Latin, to the priest's prayers at the altar during Mass ("P[riest]. Introíbo ad altáre Dei." "S[erver]. Ad Deum qui laetí-ficat juventútem meam"); the criteria distinguishing mortal and venial sins; technical theological terminology; the meanings of the colors of the priest's vestments in the different seasons of the liturgical year; the questions and answers in the catechism (word for word in preparation to recite them in class, ideally without stumbling or error); the different kinds of grace; the lives of the saints, and so on. Finally, the model curriculum proposes an affective pedagogy with the aim of awakening a lively and passionate faith; yet it stresses "formal prayers" for all grades. Formal prayers included "ejaculations," which were short exclamations ostensibly uttered spontaneously. "Mother of Love, of Sorrow, and of Mercy, pray for us," is an ejaculation, as are "O sweetest Heart of Jesus, I implore that I may ever love Thee more and more," and "Blessed be the Holy and Immaculate Conception of the Blessed Virgin Mary." These are all from the fifth-grade curriculum. Ejaculations were scripted, too, in other words; spontaneity itself was to be disciplined.

Already by the late 1930s, teaching sisters were beginning to chafe under the inconsistent, often conflicting aims and requirements of Catholic religious formation. Sister Mary Consilia of the Dominican House of Studies in Washington, DC, expressed this dissatisfaction in very strong language in a 1938 paper: "We all want suitable courses of study in Religion," she writes, and "we agitate for courses that will produce practical results." Yet most "often a teacher finds herself in a position where she spends every religion period doing what? Driving, driving, answers, answers, answers." Diocesan religion requirements, motivated by the professionalizing and standardizing imperatives evident elsewhere in American education, demanded "this or that number of answers to be learned verbatim per year and that, measured out into weeks and then into days, means as many as four or five questions per day piled onto the memory load." The only possible way of meeting such quantified targets was by resorting "to the line of least resistance," namely, "memorization."[14]

What gives Sister Consilia's complaint its urgency is her conviction that the likely result of all this misguided and overzealous memorization, testing, and quantification was the failure to prepare young Catholics adequately for the spiritual and moral challenges of modern life. "Breathing the unwholesome atmosphere around them," Sister Consilia says, young Catholics are "gradually setting their standards to conform with those about them." Her evidence for this assertion was young people's indifference and insouciance before the real presence at Mass, which she had observed herself, she says, on many occasions. Catholic children and teenagers are behaving toward Jesus in the tabernacle, says Sister Consilia, as if he were not there, and in this sense, Catholic adolescents were becoming just like the Protestant boys that tormented Tony in the story with which this book opens. Catholic religious instruction, with its dogged emphasis on rote memorization, was failing young people and by extension the church and the nation.[15]

Father Vogt's response to the overlapping dilemmas of the contradictions of Catholic religious education and the vulnerabilities of young Catholics in a society that was ever more sophisticated at stimulating and appropriating these youngsters' desires and fantasies was clear and straightforward. "We must seek to influence the child," he writes in the paper cited earlier, "in every department of life, in his thought, his imagination, his play, his leisure, and in his prayer." Children's religious formation was to be based not solely, or even primarily, on their intellects, but especially on the stimulation of their emotions, desires, and imaginations. By means of vivid imaginations properly excited and bodies rightly disciplined, youngsters would enter the company of supernatural figures really present to them in the sacraments and in their everyday lives; by means of their emotions properly directed, they would desire to do so. "The main objective of the religion teacher," Sister M. Evangela, SSND, addressed her colleagues in an article in the *Journal of Religious Instruction* in January 1945, ". . . is to capture the child's will for Christ and His cause." The way to do this is *"through desire."* The great danger of the modern world was disordered desire, so children's thirst for holiness "must be strong enough and steady enough to vanquish rival desires. . . . It is therefore necessary to discover the road which leads to desire." The aim was to be able to say of all their students what Sister Mary Marguerite, CSJ, a widely published educator and devotional writer, said of one of her students, Mary, in 1941, that she "lives in a world of angels and saints." "I wanted the children I had under my care," Sister Mary Marguerite elaborates, looking back over her many years in the classroom, "to begin to live in company with God, the angels and saints, and to really want heaven and to want to do something to attain it."[16]

But there was a grave problem with this strategy. Religion teachers were afraid that they would so excite children's imaginations, already overstimulated by secular popular culture, with the reality of the supernatural, of presence in their everyday lives—angels, the souls in purgatory, hell, the miracles of the saints, apparitions of the Blessed Mother, healings—that children would countenance ontological impossibilities, metaphysical horrors, and forbidden things. In a 1930 public lecture widely circulated among Catholic educators, Father Sullivan comments that the religious instructors of his time tended to view a child's imagination as "a pest or an enemy." The pestilential and the inimical were the inevitable shadow side of Catholicism's high evaluation of children's imaginations. What was so richly creative was also potentially destructive. A teaching sister, writing in a professional journal in 1946, saw danger ahead in what she called the "thirsty imagination of children."[17]

Here, then, were the dilemmas and contradictions of mid-twentieth-century Catholic religious formation: How were teachers to ensure that children knew themselves to be living in the company of the communion of saints, of supernatural figures as present as or even more present to them than their mothers and fathers, aunts and uncles, given the emphasis in Catholic school requirements on the precise memorization of doctrines, rules, and rubrics, all of which religion teachers also wanted their students to know? How were they to give children a deep grounding in the tradition, as the model curriculum sought, but with the vivid and embodied understanding that the tradition was living? The desires and imaginations of young Catholics needed to be stimulated and enlivened, but without making youngsters even more vulnerable to the seductions of pagan modernity. The pages of Catholic professional and devotional journals through the middle years of the century were preoccupied with these challenges, dangers, and risks, as were the meetings of Catholic educators. Overarching all of this was the fear, which Sister Consilia, for one, spoke clearly, that by growing up in a pagan civilization, Catholic children would lose the embodied experience of the real presence. This was the environment through which printed media of presence circulated.

*   *   *

Many of Elsie H.'s cards are signed in pen or pencil, I assume by the people who gave them to her. Most of these signatories are nuns, although several priests also gave cards to Elsie, as did a number of friends. In each case, the handwriting is clearly distinct from Elsie's, which I can tell because she has written her name on the cards, too. Elsie was careful to record the names of the persons who gave her cards, and sometimes the occasion of the gift. One card reads simply, "Received from Jack P." (The full name is given on the card.) Two cards commemorate the visit of the apostolic delegate to the United States in 1941; the date is written in Elsie's hand. Several nuns gave Elsie more than one card, perhaps because they taught her in different grades, or because they knew her through different life stages. One sister in particular seems to have been especially fond of the girl. She gave Elsie many cards over the years.

There are messages on some of the cards. A card of devotions to Mary for the Marian month of May, given to Elsie by Sister M. Stella, assures the girl that she is remembered in the sister's prayers. Another is a "remembrance of your birthday, November 4, 1913," signed "Reverend P." On the back of another image, of the child Jesus looking down on a little cross and crown of thorns nestled in the straw of his crib in the Bethlehem manger, this is written in pencil: "In remembrance of a sincere friend who shall always remember you in his prayers and communions," signed "Hugo E. S., Nov. 3, 1914." Below the image on the front are the words "To save us, Jesus bore his Cross and thorns." Did Hugo mean to signal some resonance between Jesus's loving sacrifice and his gift of prayers and communions to Elsie? It is a sad card, with its association of Bethlehem and Golgotha, and a palpable melancholy hovers by association over Hugo's signature. But the card is also charged with desire, sacred and profane. Another card is printed with a poem, "The Ladder of Love," which reads in part, "Some days are dark and dreary / Others are sunny and sweet, / But what are all but a ladder of love / Leading to God's dear feet." A trellis of roses borders the poem. On the back is the date, "August 1941," and this message: "I may fail visibly to show how I sincerely feel—but my prayer will never change nor will my thoughts of you." It is signed, "S.M.G. [or O]." Two languages, one printed, the other handwritten, are interleaved on this card and others: the affective language of modern Catholic devotionalism is borrowed to articulate feelings between persons, specifically between vowed religious and younger people, that might otherwise not be expressible. Catholics spoke in many different registers, at home and in public, but the devotional language of intimacy is what they used when they gave each other holy cards. They held on tightly to these cards in prayer, memory, and desire, over many years.

* * *

Here is the promised catalog of mid-twentieth-century Catholic print culture for children. It is long, but still incomplete. (1) Prayer books, cards, and pamphlets for all ages, some of them for specific occasions, such as novenas, First Communion, parish missions, devotions, and holy days; (2) illustrated books of Bible stories; (3) coloring books and picture books with strong metaphysical, devotional, and moral content that invited children to color images of the Blessed Mother, Jesus, the saints, and angels in colors the children would have known from holy cards and stained glass windows as being the correct ones to use for various figures; (3a) coloring books of the Eucharist, which helped children learn with their hands the sequence of colors in the liturgical year, the priest's movements on the altar, and the rubrics of the Mass; (3b) coloring books illustrating various moral dilemmas, such as *Angel and Imp at Home Paint Book,* by Jesuit father Daniel A. Lord, founder of the Queen's Work press, a prolific publishing enterprise that throughout the twentieth century issued many different kinds of printed materials for children and adolescents (including, for example, *Tony*); (4) lives of the saints for children and youngsters at various ages, in the form of coloring books, illustrated stories, and full-length novelized hagiographies, in which the saints' lives were retold as adventure stories of the sort other American children read, with the difference that the Catholic ones were true; (4a) comic book lives of ancient, medieval, and early modern saints, introduced as Catholic alternatives to the booming comics craze but as chilling and gory as the secular comics Catholic educators so excoriated (more on this later in the chapter); (4b) comic book accounts of young saints, many of them nearly contemporary, such as the Italian martyr Saint Maria Goretti, an eleven-year-old Italian girl who was murdered in 1902 as she resisted a farmhand who was trying to rape her, or Jane Bernadette McClory, a farm girl from Trowbridge, Illinois, not far from where Elsie H. lived, who promoted devotion to the Sacred Heart of Jesus; (5) popular magazines for younger and older children, among them the *Junior Catholic Messenger, Our Little Messenger, Young Catholic Messenger,* and *Treasure Chest of Fun and Fact,* all published by the Dayton, Ohio, company, George A. Pflaum, and distributed in large bundles by subscription to parochial schools around the country; the contents of these magazines included tales of heroic adventurer priests who explored the North American continent before the Protestants arrived; cowboy yarns with no particular Catholic subtext; sports tips; animal stories; breathless accounts of exciting new technological and scientific achievements, and, during the Second World War (in cooperation with the Commission on American Citizenship, founded at the Catholic University of America in 1939), tales of patriotism and the Catholic contribution to American history—all set in close proximity to illustrated lives of the saints and other Catholic content so that, if only by association, cowboys, athletes, inventors, and scientists all somehow seemed Catholic, too; (5a) fiction written in demotic language for children and adolescents, often with lively and popular young priests and nuns as main characters; in a storyline common to this genre, especially in the 1920s and 1930s, gangs of misguided boys or girls in urban settings are transformed into or revealed to have been angels with dirty faces, although some of them die violently and all of them suffer horribly along the way; later on, the gang will be replaced by cliques of misbehaving middle-class teenagers with too much time and money on their hands, who buy too many things and yearn to be popular by the pagan world's standards, which almost always leads to death and destruction; (6) holy cards by the millions; (7) missals, in English or Latin, with descriptions accompanied by little drawings in red of what the priest was doing on the altar during Mass; (7a) picture books about the Mass for younger children; (8) scapulars, which are small paper images of holy figures affixed to two pieces of felt on a string and worn around the neck, with one image in front and the other in back; (9) cards distributed at wakes and funeral homes, generally with a picture of Jesus, the Blessed Mother, or one of the saints on the front and a small image of the deceased on the back; these were not specifically intended for children, but children collected them nonetheless; (10) the *Baltimore Catechism,* first issued at the behest of the bishops who met at the Third Plenary Council in Baltimore in 1884, then revised in 1941, and reprinted many times (some editions with illustrations); it was the major pedagogical device for teaching children and adolescents the terminology of Catholic doctrine; (10a) other catechisms, in the languages of various immigrant communities, used in part as a way of preserving mother tongues among American-born and raised children (although English was in most places the required language of catechetical instruction, as in Natalie's case); (11) workbooks for elementary school teachers for how to illustrate lessons in doctrine and morals with stick figures drawn on the board; (12) scrapbooks of European art, assembled by teaching sisters and students, depicting scenes from the lives of Christ, the Blessed Mother, and the saints, to train children to recognize these figures on sight; (13) small pamphlet-sized "vacation guides," offering advice for how to spend the summers in a Catholic way, particularly outside Catholic contexts and beyond the supervision of nuns and priests; (14) colorful certificates offered by the Pontifical Association of the Holy Childhood (a society in support of Catholic missions, founded in the nineteenth century) as part of a fund-raising effort, to commemorate American children's "adoption" and naming of "pagan babies" in far-flung Catholic missions; (15) flash cards of the words of prayers or responses to the

FIGURE 7 First Holy Communion remembrance, 1934, Church of Saint Mary Magdalen, on East 17th Street, New York, since destroyed. Author's private collection.

Mass, in English or Latin; (16) guides to making a good confession, to help children examine their consciences by providing them with a list of sins explained in such a way that children were made to understand it was within their capacity to break *all* of the commandments, including the commandment against murder, for instance (which they would do by harming an animal or "killing" someone's reputation by spreading gossip about them); (17) large, colorful certificates made to look like elaborate diplomas that commemorated a child's First Communion (more common before the Second World War) (see Figure 7); (18) religiously themed cutout books, for example of the stable in Bethlehem, of priests to be moved around cutout altars, of vestments to dress the priests with, of the saints, and, in one of Father Lord's publications, of the Roman Colosseum, with little cutout Christians, gladiators, and wild animals to allow children to enact scenes of martyrdom for themselves; (19) purity guides for teenagers; (19a) manuals and periodicals, which begin to appear in noticeable numbers early in the century, for teaching up-to-date, middle-class manners and expectations to teenagers; (20) Catholic high school yearbooks; (21) dramas (hundreds of them), usually written by vowed women religious, most often about an incident in a saint's life or a moral crisis confronted by a modern boy or girl, to be used as scripts for producing class plays, allowing children to act the parts of saints and martyrs.[18]

*　*　*

There was also a robust practice of *unprinted* but nonetheless textual (with words and images) presence for children, created by children themselves, under supervision. To explain what I mean by this, I have to begin with handwriting. Catholic teaching sisters spent an enormous amount of time and effort during the school day instructing children to write correctly, legibly, and *perfectly in cursive,* as these women understood the perfection of script. The aim of this insistence on proper handwriting was a clean, even beautiful page; it was also meant to teach self-control, concentration, and precision. Perfect penmanship was particularly stressed in religion classes, where the discipline of the hand was practiced as an especially effective way of disciplining children's imaginations and bodies. The perfection of handwriting was an end unto itself—so precisely accomplished that it was possible years later to guess, from the cast of an adult's cursive, by which order of nuns he or she had been taught—but it was also a devotional practice. The obedience, aesthetics, and perfection expected in penmanship had metaphysical significance.

"Speaking of penmanship in connection with religion seems a small matter," Sister Mary Leo, supervisor of the Pittsburgh Sisters of Mercy, explains in a 1943 article in the *Journal of Religious Instruction,* "yet there is no subject in the curriculum that affords a better chance to teach and inculcate in the minds of little ones respect for the persons and things about which they write." When children scribble "the Holy Name of Jesus" in pencil, Sister Leo says, the writing itself is a prayer. "Ask the children sometimes when they have written Blessed Sacrament, Holy Communion, Mass, what they were thinking about while they were writing these words," Sister Leo proposes. Some will say "nothing"; others will say they were rushing to finish the assignment. But these are not acceptable responses when what is being written is God's name, or the Blessed Mother's, or that of a saint. Children ought to have the Blessed Sacrament in their minds as they write the words "Blessed Sacrament," the Blessed Mother when they write "Blessed Mother," and so on. The result of this practice is prophylactic in the pagan civilization in which these children live. "If children are taught to respect the Holy Name in writing it, the danger of profaning it later on in life is lessened." Moreover, "thinking in religion," Sister Leo concludes, "will help [children] think in other things."[19]

The devotional work of the hand, in the many forms it takes, is rooted in the awakened and disciplined desire for the really realness of the sacred. Sister Leo, thinking within the Catholic devotional economy and articulating assumptions about the relationship between the hand, the heart, and the mind that were common among mid-twentieth-century Catholic educators, says that the writer's interiority becomes visible in the quality of his or her penmanship. Handwriting *makes visible,* in ink and graphite on paper, supernatural realities in the mind and heart, and, in turn, it reinforces these realities by embodying them in the hand. This understanding of the relationship between writing and reality goes back to the fourth century. Practiced as Sister Leo urges, with attentiveness to the supernatural figures or phenomena being written about or drawn, penmanship is another medium of real presence. The Blessed Sacrament in the mind becomes the Blessed Sacrament visible and present on the page in the world.[20]

Practices of handwritten and hand-drawn devotional print arose within this milieu of presence in script. A teaching sister in 1931 planned a Mass to be followed by a party in honor of the Immaculate Conception. She asked her pupils to write out invitations to their favorite saints; then the children put these messages in a mailbox for their guardian angels to deliver. Another sister instructed her first graders to make gift tags, signed, "With love, from God," which they affixed to objects in their classroom. Children regularly prepared "spiritual bouquets," pages of handwritten prayers—the *entire* Our Father and Hail Mary, and Glory Be to the Father, many times—given as gifts on special occasions to parents, teachers, and parish clergy. Making a spiritual bouquet was usually a group project; writing together became a way of praying together. The time and sacrifice the preparation of spiritual bouquets entailed, the ache in children's hands, their bodies tensed over the paper straining to write the prayers out perfectly, were integral to the gift. Sisters also encouraged children and teenagers to write messages to their patron saints or guardian angels, a practice one teaching sister described in 1947 as "the *soul* talking freely, without reserve, to one who could understand and help." In preparation for confession, children traced the outline of their hands on a piece of paper and marked each finger with one of the sins they had committed that week. Then, in the confessional, their hands became mnemonics of their moral lives.[21]

* * *

On the back of a card that shows the Infant Jesus resting at the place where the horizontal and vertical beams of the cross meet, Elsie has written, "S. E. Elsie H.," in her familiar childhood script. Is she testing what her name would look like if she became a nun? According to the practice of the time, Elsie would not have been allowed to keep her given name, so "S. E. Elsie H." may be a child's fantasy of becoming a nun while remaining herself. Did Elsie use the card as a medium of imaginative possibility? Was writing out her signature a way of playing with her destiny? On the front of the card is this prayer, taken from Thomas à Kempis's *The Imitation of Christ:* "Grant me thy grace, most merciful Jesus, that it may be with me / And labour with me and continue with me unto the end."

* * *

Through practices of printed and unprinted presence, teaching sisters sought to develop among children a supernaturally realist imaginary. They taught youngsters to cultivate the devotional art of visualization, through which, using images or stories of incidents from the New Testament—in particular those in which the Blessed Mother plays a role—or the lives of the saints, children and adolescents would insert themselves into the scenes and feel in their bodies what they imagined the figures shown were feeling. Youngsters were expected to be able to visualize different moments of Jesus's agony so vividly and precisely, for example, that they saw themselves walking beside him on the crowded and dusty streets of ancient Jerusalem, the ferrous smell of his blood in their nostrils. The practice of devotional visualization was neither fully interior nor fully exterior to the self. The distance between what was seen—on the holy cards children held and looked at while they were praying, in illustrated stories about the Blessed Mother and the saints—and the one looking became fluid. The texts and images were spaces in between, which children were invited to traverse by visualization. In the 1950s, these devotional techniques were put to powerful political purpose among American Catholics when children used them to put themselves in the scenes of Catholic martyrs being persecuted and killed in Communist nations, adding a supernatural immediacy to Cold War rhetoric.[22]

Children's (internal) visualizations of the sacred took place within the (external) surround of printed images and stories, in their homes, churches, and parochial schools. The result was that a child's guardian angel looked like the ones in pictures, as did the faces of the Blessed Mother and the saints. Recognition fostered an understanding of Bible stories and the lives of the saints that was empathic and intimate. "Let's suppose you are one of those children who were with Jesus that day when He was tired and the Apostles wanted you to go away," Sister Marilyn, OSF, from New Alsace, Indiana, asks her younger students, as she describes in a 1957 article. "You remember, that was the last time you talked to Jesus on paper. [This is a reference to an earlier written meditation exercise in the class.] Now you've been a good friend to Jesus ever since. Pretend that you have come to see and speak with Him whenever you could. Now this one day when you are coming home from school, you hear a lot of talking and laughing as you pass the courthouse. You look into the yard and there you see soldiers laughing and making fun of your friend, Jesus. You see one soldier spit on His cheek. Another says, 'He calls Himself a king, so He has to have a crown.' He pushes a crown of big thorns on Jesus' head. Now the soldiers run back into the courthouse to get a raggedy old cloak to throw over Jesus. While they are gone, you can speak to Jesus. Now write what you would like to say to Him."

When the children are finished writing, Sister Marilyn says, she collects the pages, but does not read them out loud or show them to anyone. Children will eventually learn to do this visualization exercise on their own as a regular practice, and perhaps even "some poorly instructed" parents, Sister Marilyn adds hopefully, might be "drawn into a closer union with our Lord" by seeing their children at prayerful writing. As other "suggested activities," Sister Marilyn proposes that children draw themselves into a picture of a guardian angel that teachers distribute; write letters to Jesus during Advent, telling him what they plan on giving him for his birthday; make valentines for Jesus in February; collect images of the Sorrowful Mysteries in a book during Lent to aid them in their visualization prayer practice; and, in May, construct an altar of cardboard and cloth for the Blessed Mother.[23]

* * *

The thin pages of old Catholic missals are interleaved with holy cards, printed prayers, old shopping lists, notes from friends, and other printed and written miscellany. Catholics kept their missals throughout their lives; the books were among the things left by the dead and inherited afterward by children and grandchildren, nieces and nephews, whether they wanted them or not. In a little cardboard box, I keep my two grandmothers' missals. One of them is in Italian and Latin; the other was a First Communion gift to my Sicilian grandmother, dating to the very early twentieth century. My old *Saint Joseph Daily Missal* is stored with them. On its translucent pages, little drawings in red depict the priest's movements on the altar, which were otherwise hidden because in 1959, when the missal was published, celebrants kept their backs turned to the congregation. The words of the Consecration, in Latin and English, are in bold black ink, underlined with thick crimson bars. As they turn the pages of their deceased parents' missals, surviving children may encounter evidence of what they cherished about their loved ones, along with evidence of what they had hated and aspects of these lives of which they had no idea.[24]

Looking at an image of the Sacred Heart, a woman is distressed to find herself thinking about her emotionally and religiously oppressive father, who was devoted to this representation of Jesus and compelled his children to be so as well. An older man holds a holy card of Saint Jude and recalls his alcoholic father, who had introduced him as a boy to this holy figure. He says, "In his own little ways [my father] would show us, you know, his faith." Another woman contrasts her recollections of her overbearing and cold father with the famous image of Jesus welcoming children to sit at his feet. The movement of printed presence from hand to hand, life to life, does more than disclose the bonds among people; it creates them, intervenes in them, and reshapes them. Presence is real, but because presence exists in networks of relationships, to be in relationship with presence is not always safe, and it is sometimes intrusive, unnerving, and even dangerous.[25]

* * *

Anxious notes sound throughout the century in articles written by priests and nuns about the consequences of the pedagogy of presence. The goal is to form "normal" boys and girls in the faith, a School Sister of Notre Dame warned in 1934. "We do not want any of our children to cultivate a habit of saying edifying things, or to look forward to a lingering death and an early grave; nor do we want them to be turned aside from the desire of holiness because of such unattractive associations." A decade later, a Midwestern teaching sister told her colleagues that it was their responsibility to sift out the implausible from the lives of the saints they gave children and to avail themselves of critical historical resources that allow such discernment. Only by taking such care with printed material will those responsible for the religious formation of the next generation "be saved from the danger of misleading young minds in regards to fictitious stories of the saints," Sister concludes, and misrepresenting "romantic content" for the truth.[26]

But this was yet another conundrum of printed presence: How were teachers to make children understand that they lived in the immediate company of supernatural figures, that they belonged to the communion of saints and were destined for heaven, as the catechism said, without introducing distortions into their desires and imaginations as a result of their overzealousness? The ubiquity of printed presence, its everyday quality, ought not to obscure the intensity with which children who were well disciplined in the practices of presence encountered it. Some children fainted on hearing or seeing—or visualizing—overly graphic accounts of martyrdom. The story of Iroquois warriors gnawing off Saint Isaac Jogues's fingers at the bone, for example, a favorite among American Catholic writers for children, caused some children to pass out, sometimes before the first knuckle. "It is very painful to have your nails torn out," one children's author informs young readers in book on Isaac Jogues. "They crunched Blackrobe's forefingers till I [the narrator], lying the space of three canoes away, heard the bones crack." "And when I looked at him again," the child who is telling the story says, "his two nice hands were not nice any longer . . . they were as wild red rose buds."[27]

Why describe the gore in such detail? Why not omit the crunched bones and grisly stumps and instead tell what modern educational theorists would have called age-appropriate stories of the virtues of saints that conclude with morals and models of good behavior for children to emulate? Isaac Jogues, after all, is a paragon of grit, loyalty, and courage. Is this not message enough? Patricia, a teaching sister born in 1942, told me that as a child, she believed that the way to become the saint she fiercely desired to be was to die a horrible death as a martyr for the faith. We were talking in a nearly empty convent in a small town in central

Nebraska on a beautiful day in early summer 2001. She put it more graphically: The surest way to become a saint, Sister Patricia elaborated, was to be "bathed in blood." She said this in the context of remembering reading as a girl the life of Saint Maria Goretti. The Italian girl was stabbed "twelve or thirteen [times], something like that," Sister Patricia said. "With a butcher knife," one of her roommates, a sister in the same order, chipped in, recalling images that had endured in her imagination for more than fifty years. (See Figures 8–13.)[28]

The reason Catholic children's writers almost never omitted the gore, even in stories for younger children, was that the gore was essential to the culture of printed presence. The figures on Elsie's cards were not merely good; they were holy. They lived in infinite excess of the good. This was their "bathed in blood" quality, in Sister Patricia's words. Teaching sisters and children's writers were mindful not to recast the lives of the saints as embodied virtues. Writing about the life of Saint Aloysius Gonzaga in a 1943 picture book called *Miniature Stories of the Saints,* Father Lord tells the very young readers for whom the book was intended that Saint Aloysius did not simply take care of the sick, which would have been the good and virtuous thing to do; he brought sick people into his own bed, while he slept on the floor beside them. This was the excess of holiness beyond morality. Hearing this, the more devout Catholic children were all but compelled to ask if they were capable of such heroism.[29]

"What a divine intimacy is possible for a child of God!" Sister M. Brendan of Marywood College in Pennsylvania exclaimed in a paper written for a professional conference in 1938. Introduce the children in your care, she urged religion teachers, to "the Little Secret" of "aspiratory prayer," in which every breath taken is a prayerful recollection of God's "Presence." "Nothing at all matters except that each of us becomes a saint," another teaching sister told children in 1953. But how do "normal" children breathe prayers and how do they become saints? Surrounded by images and stories of Jesus, the Blessed Mother, the angels, and the saints; taught to insert themselves as culpable and compassionate contemporaries into Jesus's Passion and Mary's sorrows; and regularly reminded of the insufficiency of mere goodness against the standard of

FIGURES 8–13 The graphic book depicting the life of Saint Maria Goretti, "The Blood-Stained Lily," by Mary Fabyan Windeatt, from *Treasure Chest of Fun and Fact* 6, no. 5 (November 9, 1950), with drawings by illustrator Mart Bailey, whose credits included many secular comics of just the sort that Catholic teaching sisters fulminated against in this period, among them "The Face" (1940). Courtesy of the American Catholic History Research Center and University Archives (AGUA), the Catholic University of America, Washington, DC.

I CAN SEE THEM NOW: ANGELO, MARIA, MARIANO, ALEXANDER, ERSILIA, AND LITTLE TERESA.

IT MUST HAVE BEEN HARD TO KEEP THE HOME TOGETHER.

YES, BUT THE CHILDREN WERE A WONDERFUL HELP.

COULD YOU TELL US ABOUT THOSE EARLY DAYS?

AND ESPECIALLY ABOUT MARIA?

OF COURSE.

IN 1899 THE GORETTIS WERE SHARECROPPERS NEAR NETTUNO, ITALY. WHILE THE OTHER CHILDREN HELPED IN THE FIELDS, 9-YEAR-OLD MARIA ACTED AS HOUSEKEEPER.

DINNER'S READY, MOTHER.

WE'LL BE RIGHT IN, MARIA.

I'M STARVED!

SO AM I!

QUIET, CHILDREN, WHILE WE SAY GRACE.

MARIA HAD BEEN STABBED 14 TIMES. WHEN HER MOTHER AND THE NEIGHBORS ARRIVED—

MARIA! WHAT HAPPENED?

ALEXANDER TRIED TO MAKE ME SIN... B-BUT I WOULDN'T....

MY BOY DID THIS?

HOLY MOTHER OF GOD!

LOOK! MOTHER'S FAINTED!

SOMEBODY GET A DOCTOR!

THE 11-YEAR-OLD MARTYR FOR PURITY LIVED ONLY 24 HOURS. AS SHE LAY DYING IN THE HOSPITAL...

MARIA, DO YOU FORGIVE ALEXANDER FOR WHAT HE DID?

Y-YES, WITH ALL MY HEART. I WANT HIM TO BE WITH ME IN HEAVEN.

SENTENCED TO PRISON FOR 30 YEARS, ALEXANDER ONLY SNEERED WHEN TOLD OF MARIA'S WORDS. THEN ONE NIGHT—

MARIA! IS IT REALLY YOU? ARE YOU IN HEAVEN?

YES, AND I'VE BEEN PRAYING FOR YOU, ALEXANDER. HERE—TAKE THESE AS A LITTLE GIFT FROM ME.

TOUCHED BY GRACE, ALEXANDER DID REPENT AND WAS RELEASED FROM PRISON IN 1924. HE THEN ENTERED A CAPUCHIN MONASTERY AS A LAY HELPER AND IS STILL THERE TODAY PRAYING AND DOING PENANCE.

PLEASE KEEP PRAYING FOR ME, MARIA.

WHAT A WONDERFUL STORY, MRS. GORETTI!

EVERY BOY AND GIRL IN AMERICA OUGHT TO HEAR IT.

MAYBE YOU'LL TELL THEM WHEN YOU GO BACK HOME? TELL THEM WHAT A TERRIBLE THING SIN IS AND THAT THEY SHOULD BE READY TO DIE RATHER THAN OFFEND OUR LORD.

sanctity, Catholic children were at risk of religious obsessiveness. The unfortunate youngsters who succumbed—and almost every Catholic of my acquaintance either knows a story about a child who suffered from scrupulosity, as this condition is known in Catholic terminology, or was a scrupulous child themselves—anxiously monitored their actions, toted up the most trivial missteps as sins to confess, and repetitively performed devotional activities and moral duties in dread of failure, which usually became the certainty of it. This was the excess of devotionalism embodied in children.[30]

* * *

I noticed one night when I was going through Elsie H.'s cards that she had signed her name twice on a number of them. One signature is in the strong hand of a younger person, signed perhaps at the moment she first received the cards; the other is in the shaky hand of an elderly person. This practice, which I have never heard of or seen in any other context, must have some basis in Elsie's emotions and imagination, in the way she lived in the world. Was she reflecting on the changing shape of her life over time, as expressed in the adjacent signatures, past and present, separated by a lifetime spent in the company of the saints? Was this a way of keeping sacred presence close to her, an older person's version of the holy cards pasted up around children's cribs, so that on each disappearing day, she went to sleep and awoke within sight of these familiar presences? Was she putting herself at the end of her life among the saints, and also within the presence of her dead, the men and women with whom she had spent her childhood, and who gave Elsie many of the cards she had saved and cherished for so long?[31]

* * *

One of the essential differences in how peoples of presence in the old, Catholic sense have lived and continue to live in the modern world in contrast with others is in their approach to works of culture in literature, film, photography, and painting. Among peoples of presence, I include Catholics, although not all Catholics, and not only Catholics, but also people of other religions in which supernatural beings are present to humans in the way that has been associated with Catholics since the late sixteenth century and that Catholics themselves took as their distinctiveness in modernity. The dominant secular view is that images are about nothing beyond themselves; an image is not alive. Yet many modern people have viewed, and continue to view, the practices of reading, looking, and writing as interactions with media of presence. The supernaturally realist imagination, which Catholic religion instructors worked so diligently to form in children, belongs to the history of the modern imagination.

To see this is to trouble any absolute distinctions among modernity, premodernity, and postmodernity, or between the religious optics of the West and those of the rest, with the rest cast as people who approach the productions of culture in a way that is unrecognizable to moderns. The stakes here are very high. Catholic schoolteachers recognized printed presence as dangerous. To treat print as alive with presence may be powerfully disruptive, in particular circumstances, to the self and the social world. What may to some merely be a text or image, not identical to what is represented, may to others be that very figure, present right there in front of them. Failure to understand this can lead to serious grief and worse in hospitals, government offices, law courts, and other modern places that have ostensibly been scoured clean of presence in the old sense.

For all the efforts to exclude them from modern religion and culture by denial, humiliation, force, or theory, presences in print have proved to be resilient. Presence has never been completely or finally exiled from print. It continually reasserts itself despite ongoing efforts to expel it. So the precise question may be how it is that people and polities come to stop experiencing the intimacy of presence in print. How do people learn not to bring print up to their lips, kiss it, sleep with it, or hold it? If we take the practices I have described in this book as another way of living in the world, not an atavism or an aberration, and perhaps even the human norm, then modernity may be better characterized not by absence in print but by the struggle against presence. It demands hard work and rigorous attentiveness to bind the presences in print with disciplinary and exclusionary nomenclature, and still, in one way or another, presence in print exceeds such efforts at binding. Among peoples of presence in the old sense, the works of the imagination are real; they have real consequences in the world. Seeing and reading are practices that expose the self and the community to being acted upon and transformed, for better and for worse, so care must be taken in what is looked at and read. In the mid-twentieth century, Catholics were resisting the flattening of print to a single register and the tendency to understand its viewing as a unidirectional activity. They felt there was something living and moving in the work itself, something there that looked back.

* * *

In a *Treasure Chest* comic book about Saint Joseph of Cupertino, who first appears in this book in Chapter 1 as he soared away from the Eucharistic debates of the late sixteenth and early seventeenth centuries, the saint is shown flying over crowded church pews. Later in the story, a modern-day priest, who is also a pilot, tells a group of boys gathered adoringly around him that "seventy levitations have been proven" for Saint Joseph, more than for any other saint. This is why the Church made Joseph the patron saint of pilots. In another comic book, Don John Bosco is rushing out with the consecrated Host to a dying person's bedside when assassins who are lying in wait to kill him set upon him. Suddenly, a gray dog mysteriously appears and saves him. "But where did you come from?" the future Saint John Bosco asks the dog. "This question was never answered," the story goes on, "although 'Grey' [as the dog came to be called] continued to appear for many years, especially when Father Bosco's life was in danger." But "he [Grey] would never eat . . . [ellipsis in original]." This was a sign of the dog's supernatural origins, as it was of the sanctity of stigmatics and visionaries. All of this really happened, the comic book declared, and all of this was still happening in our own times.[32]

* * *

In the years after the Second World War, Catholic boys and girls in parishes and school yards around the United States set fire to great piles of comic books. The children held hands and prayed while the comic books burned, giving the events the quality of ritual or devotion. At one such bonfire, widely covered in the national press, on Friday, December 10, 1948, a "cold and gray" day, at Saint Patrick's parochial school in Binghamton, New York, the flames rose more than thirty feet into the air from a great mound of 2,000 comic books, as a teaching sister led the children in the battle song of Catholic Action, which went, in part, "We're fighting for Christ the Lord / Heads lifted high, Catholic Action our cry / And the Cross our only sword." (See Figure 14.)[33]

Why were Catholics in the United States burning comic books? One interpretation holds that the comic book controversy brought to a boil tensions within the generation of adolescents that arrived on the scene between the late 1930s and the 1950s, in particular between teenagers who identified with the new youth culture and those who adhered to the norms and expectations of their teachers, parents, and religious leaders. The comic book, which made its appearance in 1935, very much belonged to the new generation, and young people saw it this way. It was their art form, drawn by adolescents for adolescents, and a medium of rebellion. But this was not so for Catholic youngsters, the argument goes. Growing up in a hierarchical religious culture deeply hostile to popular media, expected to obey the Church's rule without question, and isolated in parochial schools such as Saint Patrick's, Catholic youth found themselves at odds with the emerging adolescent peer culture. The fires burned, moreover, at a time of renewed anxiety among Americans that Catholics were out of step with American democracy. Given such assumptions about American Catholicism in this period, not much more has been said about Catholic comic book pyres.[34]

But Catholics in the United States were not uniformly antagonistic to all aspects of American popular culture. Catholic leaders and educators were ambivalent about the American entertainment industry. They feared the insinuation of pagan values into Catholic youth culture, as we have seen, but they also realized the need to approach youngsters in ways they would recognize and appreciate. Catholic educators belonged to

FIGURE 14 Students of Saint Patrick's parochial school, Binghamton, New York, burning comic books, December 10, 1948. "Manners and Morals: Americana," *Time Magazine,* Dec. 20, 1948, vol. 52, no. 25. From the collection of David Hadju, with permission.

professional associations that kept them well informed about new trends in youth culture and adolescent psychology. Catholic commentators did not speak with a single voice, in any case, not even on the subject of comic books. Catholics had become leading figures in all aspects of mass entertainment in the twentieth century, in sports, on the radio, on Broadway, in the movies, and in nightclubs. As a largely urban population, Catholics were among the major consumers of popular media; they had the most at stake in thinking about its effects. This included comic books. As one outraged "Missionary Sister" wrote in 1944, Catholic homes were "practically swamped" with comic books, a contemporary observation that at least ought to raise questions about the mindless-youth-in-a-hierarchical-religious-culture argument.[35]

Still, there is the historical and theoretical problem of what to make of the flames. Book burning is shocking at any time, but it was especially so in the late 1940s. The fires in Binghamton and elsewhere have struck at least one contemporary historian as "disturbingly reminiscent of Nazi book-burnings." This association of Catholics with Nazis is outrageous, of course, and deeply offensive for many reasons, beginning with the numbers of American Catholic young men and women who served in the armed forces in the war and the many who died. Still, the flames capture our attention. Public bonfires in which hated and feared objects are consumed in flames are frightening. But every such event is distinct and book burnings, however much they may look alike, are not always and everywhere the same, just as practices of reading and seeing are not. American Catholics were not burning words when they burnt comic books; they were burning words and images *together,* a genre Catholics had known and been pondering since the early Middle Ages, at least. Pictures were as frightening as, if not more so than, words. Catholic educators were afraid of what might happen to Catholic children whose imaginations were exposed to images of violence and evil, mutilated and dismembered bodies (in particular women's bodies), and the rotten and corrupted flesh of ghouls, and then what might happen to American life as the result of these images.[36]

* * *

The sisters and priests who organized the comic book autos-da-fé knew whereof they spoke, of course. They spent their lives, as we have seen, forming and stimulating children's imaginations in relation to images of violence and evil, mutilated and dismembered bodies (in particular women's bodies), and the sweet and uncorrupted flesh of the saints' bodies, exhumed from their graves. What secular comic book was as terrible and graphic as that of the life of Maria Goretti? The same sisters who protested ghoulish and gory comic books prepared children for making their first Holy Communion by telling them over and over again that if they bit down on the consecrated Host the priest put in their mouths, the Host would spurt blood, a lesson Lydia, with whom I opened this chapter, remembered more than fifty years later. Picture lines of children returning to their places in the pews after receiving Communion, blood dripping from their mouths. What comic book could depict supernatural horror as well?

Catholics understood childhood and adolescence as the times when the imagination was most alive and active, the "most plastic," as one teaching sister wrote in her condemnation of comic books, and so when society was most vulnerable to children and adolescents. Although modern Catholics generally did not share the romantic evaluation of children as innocent and ethereal—healthy children, that is; sick and dying children were another matter—Catholic writers maintained that children's imaginations were open to supernatural realities in an especially intimate and immediate way. Modern Catholic educators cultivated this faculty in their work of endowing children with an embodied experience of living between heaven and earth. But the life of the church was vulnerable to the imaginations of children and adolescents because, if not carefully attended to, disciplined, and oriented to the real, they were easily seduced by the compelling surround of modern images, fantasies, and desires. This was especially so as they got older, precisely when their engagement with the supernatural began to wane, as teaching sisters often noted.[37]

*   *   *

As a result of their religious formation, Catholic children possessed a kind of internal comic book of the supernatural in which they were characters, too. Before Medjugorje, when Mary seemed to come only to children, one of the most exciting supernatural realities available to Catholic youngsters was a direct encounter with the Blessed Mother on earth, as at Lourdes, Fatima, and elsewhere. A woman born in 1948 in a Catholic farming community in Nebraska told me this story about what happened to her one night when she was eight years old: "We were playing outside and it was dark and the farm light, the big yard light, was on, and I looked over toward the barn and I was sure that the Blessed Virgin was up there. And I went running to the house, and I told everybody, 'You've got to go outside because the Blessed Virgin is on top of the barn.' And I can remember them turning on more and more lights to show me that it was the smoke stack on top of the barn, but I was sure it was the Blessed Virgin . . . for about fifteen minutes I thought I was Bernadette. I was just so sure it was." In the year this woman was born, an Italian American boy in the Bronx named Joseph Vitolo saw the Blessed Virgin over a gate in his grandparents' backyard. So prepared were adults to countenance the supernatural claims of children that thousands of Catholics made their way up to the Bronx, to the Grand Concourse, a largely middle-class Jewish neighborhood, to watch Joseph kneel in ecstasy before an empty space in which he saw the Blessed Mother standing. Catholic children looked at the supernatural and the supernatural looked back.[38]

* * *

Catholics were troubled by the moral and political dangers of comics, but what made these worries strong enough to lead to the flaming pyres of comic books was metaphysical and supernatural. Religion instructors were especially concerned about the graphic, lurid, and ghoulish comics, in which the dead rose, monks in cowls appeared as agents of evil, and a hideous darkness teeming with just barely visible demons bore down on human life. The reason they were most concerned about such comics had to do with how Catholics understood the power of images over the body and imagination and the reality of presence in print. Catholics recoiled from what one sister in 1943 called the "grotesquely pictorial and weirdly impossible" in comics. They were fearful of what might happen to children and adolescents when these practiced visualizers entered the titillating and bizarre realms of comics.[39]

Comic books were terrifying because the supernatural was real, because the supernatural really did break into the natural, and because some of the most prominent vehicles of this permeability of the natural and supernatural, and also of paganism and Catholicism, were the souls, bodies, and imaginations of children and adolescents. Comics seemed to Catholics a perverse inversion of their sacred universe. Even more: such tales of ghosts and demons were horrible because they held more than a sliver of truth, as ghost stories did, too. The most popular comics operated according to an unacknowledged metaphysics that Catholics recognized. There were echoes in the mid-twentieth-century comic book controversy of the encounters of Catholic missionaries and chroniclers with the rites and divinities of indigenous peoples in the New World. These alien visual and imaginative realms were taken to be real but perverse, a corrupt and demonic mimicry of the faith, especially dangerous because of their proximity to Catholic sacraments. A similar mimesis was evident in the most terrifying supernatural comics, like *Tales from the Crypt* and EC Comics, which drew for their chills on the dark tropes of the Anglo-American Gothic: demons in monks' garb presiding over grotesque rituals at which a human body, usually a bound female body, was sacrificed on a stone altar. The deepest roots of the romantic Gothic in Europe and the United States were sunk in the modern horror of the Catholic supernatural and fascination with it. As Jesuit scholar Robert Southard said in a public lecture in 1945—just three years before little Joseph Vitolo saw the Virgin Mary in the Bronx, not far from where Southard was speaking—comic book superheroes represented "a kind of duplicate of the Christian ideal [but] with pagan overtones." José de Acosta could not have put it better. Interpretations of Catholic concerns about popular media as moralistic miss the real point. It was never just about comic books. The Catholic criticism of comic books was so fierce because the mimesis was so close. The fires burned in the mirror. The evil of particular comic books was palpable and real.[40]

* * *

In 1954 the great postwar scare forced the harassed comic book industry to introduce the Comics Magazine Association of America, which promulgated a strict Comics Code. This banned, among other things, the use of the word "horror" in titles, "excessive bloodshed," "scenes dealing with, or instruments associated with, the walking dead, torture, vampires and vampirism, ghouls, cannibal and werewolfism [*sic*]." "All lurid, unsavory and gruesome illustrations shall be eliminated," the code directed, and "females shall be drawn realistically without exaggeration of any physical qualities." (One wonders if this stricture leaves room for images of Our Lady of Lourdes, a question that turns on how the word "realistic" is understood, which is a big question.) Cleaner, more wholesome fare, such as *Archie* comics, represented the industry's bid for respectability and continued sales.[41]

Such disciplinary endeavors produce what they aim to prohibit, of course, and by the late 1950s and early 1960s a new generation of comic book artists was furiously contesting the recently formulated limits of the genre. One of the most visually revolutionary and influential of this cohort was Robert Crumb, who was born in 1943, at the start of the comic book scare (which Crumb says he knew nothing about). Crumb's mother was Catholic. Robert and his brother attended Catholic elementary school with his Jewish father's enthusiastic approval; an ex–U.S. Marine, the senior Crumb admired the moral and physical discipline of Catholic schools and considered the nuns saintly and brave. "I was fanatically Catholic," Robert Crumb told an interviewer, "praying all the time. My brother was even more fanatical; he used to walk around with pebbles in his shoes," a self-mortifying practice Robert attributes to his brother's devotion to Saint Francis of Assisi. Crumb remembers fiercely arguing the truth of Catholicism against "super-Protestants" in high school. According to a short biography on Crumb's website, the artist remained "a faithful Catholic until he was sixteen." So a story that begins with Catholic boys and girls burning comic books ends with a Catholic boy rescuing the genre from the artistic mediocrity into which censorship had pushed it.[42]

Crumb's work, which appeared in the underground comics of the 1960s—a genre he helped to create—is voluptuous and sensuous, often disturbingly so, possessed of an eroticism that is shot through with angst and guilt. Crumb attributes this to the influence of his Catholic childhood. The nuns, Crumb says, so thoroughly "formed" his "view of the universe" that Catholicism remains "one of the underlying currents in all the work I do." Crumb means this in a mostly negative sense. "I had such heavy Catholic brainwashing when I was a kid," he told a French journalist in 1999, "and I've been dealing with it ever since." Catholic schools were presided over by "twisted and sadistic women," he says, who enforced a regime of sexual repression, and "when people are forced to deny their natural urges they get weird, twisted and mean." This is the psychological and religious root, by Crumb's own account, of the por-

nographic fantasies, violence against women, and the horrific and titillating images of aggressive and destructive females in his work. "I guess
it's all just left over hang-ups from Catholic school," he mused in a 1980
interview, "where the nuns were these big giant scary women who liked
to pick on little boys so I developed this obsession to 'conquer' these
big scary women and I'm still like that . . . [ellipsis in original]. I never
grew up." "I never will" abandon Catholicism, Crumb remembers himself declaring as a boy to a nun who had just accused his class of future
betrayals, as nuns often did by way of stimulating the morale and commitment of their troops. "Not me!" The evidence suggests that Crumb
kept his promise, and that he never really left Catholicism behind.[43]

But Crumb also hints at a deeper Catholic source of his work than
uncomplicated rejection. "Remember the movie *The Exorcist,* that came
out in 1973?" he asked the French journalist interviewing him. "I was
completely terrified by that movie. I felt really stupid but it got to me
in such a deep way that I realized that I'm not past all that Catholic
crap at all. Even though I think it's stupid, it's still there." What makes
The Exorcist, written by Catholic, Jesuit-educated William Peter Blatty,
so terrifying for Catholics brought up in the middle years of the century
is their—*our:* I have never been able to bring myself to see the film—
deeply embodied sense of the really realness of the supernatural, good
and evil. In this sense and in this context, *The Exorcist* was a documentary, "based on a true story," as Catholic gossip at the time maintained,
rather than a work of fiction, although of course Catholics also knew
it was fiction. Many Catholics of Crumb's age would have been familiar
with the famous and truly chilling story of the exorcism of a young
woman, Emma Schmidt, in a convent in Earling, Iowa, in 1928, widely
reported in the national press. I first heard about it from the sisters in
Nebraska, quoted above, who were connected by one or two degrees of
separation to the convent in Iowa where Schmidt was taken for the
rites.[44]

"In my midteens," Crumb told the *Paris Review* in 2010, "I went
through a brief stage of religious fanaticism but it was very much about
saying prayers and stuff like that, reciting rosaries and spending a lot of
time on that kind of Catholic ritual." By "that kind of Catholic ritual,"

Crumb means the devotional practices of presence. While Crumb names the lingering influence of Catholicism on him variously as guilt, the sadistic nuns, repression, or "mysticism," I think a sensibility of heightened supernatural realism is also at play. The bodies in Crumb's comics are overly present, abundantly embodied. Boldly drawn and so deeply etched and shadowed as to seem three-dimensional, these images are resonant with those on the holy cards Crumb would have seen as a child. His female figures have such outrageously enormous breasts, arms, and buttocks as to seem apparitional; often, the perspective taken on them is from below, as if from a child's point of view. The eyes of his male figures bulge and pop; their Adam's apples wobble as if with a life of their own. It is as if these men were in a kind of ecstasy of terror or desire, or both. Always surrounding men's and women's heads is a churning halo of drops of sweat spun out from their anxious and concupiscent bodies. Crumb's art is so intensely realistic as to become more than realistic, an abundant or hyperrealism, an excess of realism, like the excessive aesthetics of Catholic devotionalism.[45]

*　*　*

By the 1960s Crumb was no longer a practicing Catholic, and the church in which he had grown up was changing. But Crumb and his contemporaries Robert Mapplethorpe, Andy Warhol, and Andres Serrano, all of them raised Catholic, were formed in a world in which images and words were media of sacred presence. They brought a sensibility of Catholic supernatural realism to their work. The irony, of course, was that this made them among the most radical and subversive modern artists.[46]

The occasion for Crumb's interview in the *Paris Review,* from which I have quoted above, was the publication of his illustrated *Book of Genesis,* in which he puts to use his aesthetics of abundant embodied presences in depictions of the holy. The interviewer asks him where he got the idea of what God looks like for the volume. Crumb replies that the figure appeared to him in a dream. God was "very severe but at the same time sort of anguished looking" and "he was warning me about something . . . ," Crumb says, "warning me about this destructive force that was getting stronger, and since He loved Earth or this reality or whatever you want to call it, He was enlisting me to be one of the people to protect this reality from this destructive force." This was exactly the sort of apocalyptic message the Virgin Mary brought to seers in the modern era, of course, and for the same purpose of enlisting their aid. When "trying to figure out how to draw God," Crumb goes on to say, "I remembered that image, which I could only look at for a split second. It was painful to look at his face. It was so severe and so anguished." Bernadette, the children at Fatima, and the Detroit housewife could not have said this more eloquently about their encounters with God's mother.[47]

It was this God so visualized, with whom he was in relationship—a relationship that went back to his Catholic childhood—whose really realness Crumb tries to express in his illustrations for the Book of Genesis. In Crumb's work, the excesses of supernatural presence in modern devotional Catholicism moved to the more creative and daring edges of both American and American Catholic cultures. Here, it contributed to the transformation of late twentieth-century art.

Five

THE DEAD IN THE
COMPANY OF THE LIVING

THE woman sits on the edge of her son's empty bed, saying the rosary in front of a lithograph of the tortured, bloody, and crucified body of another woman's son. It is a month since her youngest son died from a cancer of the blood. The Virgin Mary had foreseen her son's Passion when he was a boy in Nazareth. The woman sitting in her dead child's room has known since his birth that the boy's life would be short—only months long, the physicians told her in the hospital that day. But he survived for five years. His mother recounts this fact with almost delirious joy when she talks about her son's brief life. In the days following the boy's death, the woman felt forsaken and abandoned by God. Why did God permit this innocent child to suffer and die? The years before the boy's death, which is to say all the years of his life, were filled with constant pain. He was often in the hospital for tests and transfusions. The boy's parents, cherishing the times when he was home, veered between hope and despair as every small period of relief was followed by still more dreadful pain and hopelessness. Looking up from her rosary, the woman notices that a small circle has appeared in the corner of the image of Jesus. In subsequent days, the circle grows and changes shape. A decade later this woman and her husband graciously welcome me and a group of friends into their home one evening to tell us her son's story and to allow us to look for ourselves at the miraculous image of Jesus on the Cross.

* * *

This chapter examines relationships between the living and the dying and the dead among Catholics in the United States in the twentieth century; the various ways that Catholics, living and dead, thought and talked about these relationships; and what they did to maintain them, over time, amid broader changes in death and dying in the United States, as well as within Catholicism itself. The dead are not silent or absent in this history. The porousness of the boundary between the living and the dead in Catholicism meant that Catholics' intimacy with the dead was everywhere apparent in devotional art, funerary customs, cemetery practices, and the Catholic habitus itself. Ordinary Catholics knew intimately the presence of death and of the dead. The souls in purgatory, with whom Catholics were in regular communion, were mobilized to frighten children into appropriate behavior toward their parents and ancestors and to create in them a profound sense of personal responsibility, empathy, and love toward the dead, who remained in need of their attention and affection. It served as another sign of Catholic difference in modernity and of the archaism of the Catholic imaginary. The people of real presence were also the people of the living dead.[1]

Catholics for their part emphasized this difference between themselves and Protestants, "Protestants" again being the synonym for "moderns" in Catholic parlance (and vice versa, "modern" meaning "Protestant"). "Other religions may be pleasant enough to live in," a writer muses in a Catholic devotional magazine in 1954, "but the Catholic faith is by far the best to die in." "In my 33 years as a priest," widely syndicated author Father Leo J. Trese exclaimed in 1960, "I have never—I repeat *never*—seen a Catholic in fear of death when the moment of death actually came." Catholics took this confident familiarity with death as another instance of their supernatural realism. They chided men and women of other faiths for allegedly refusing to look death in the face, in all its hard and grim specificity. So deep and pervasive is the denial of death in contemporary America, a priest complained in 1954, that it is evident even among U.S. soldiers in Korea. "We must knuckle down to the fact of death," he scolds, the "we" here being all his contemporaries, Catholic and non-Catholic, civilian and military. In this self-discipline, Catholicism has the edge. "One of the great hypocrisies of our age," another author asserted, using the confrontational tone Catholics assumed when comparing themselves to Protestant moderns, "is the attempt to disguise and camouflage death." The Catholic attitude, in contrast, is "more stern and realistic." Catholics "savor the dank smell of mortality." The border between Catholics and Protestants smelled of incense and candle wax, miraculous roses, and the stench of death.[2]

This was the modern American Catholic politics of death. In a century of mass death, the quality of their dying separated Catholics in the United States from their fellow citizens. One reason why Catholics carried rosaries around with them in their pockets was so that in the event of an accident they would be taken to a Catholic hospital and a priest would be called for the last rites, ensuring a Catholic death. By dying well, moreover, Catholics offered the United States, always at risk of spiritual enervation, access to the really realness of death, because in the redistributive economy of Catholic cosmology, Catholics died for others, just as Jesus did and just as children do, as we will see. Catholic courage and confidence in facing death were a contribution to the moral and political strength of the United States and a warning to Communists at home and abroad. The Catholic way of death paradoxically distanced Catholics from other Americans and at the same time made dying and dead Catholics essential for the survival of the American nation. The politics of death endured into the afterlife. It was forbidden to bury Protestants in Catholic cemeteries, except in situations where not doing so would be the cause of greater evil *to Catholics*. It was also a question whether it was permissible to bury non-Catholics next to their Catholic spouses in Catholic cemeteries.[3]

The deaths of non-Catholics underscored the good fortune of Catholics. Non-Catholics were doomed to hell unless they converted; otherwise, for them, death was the transition to an eternity of suffering. Catholics vividly imagined and graphically depicted the suffering of the afterlife, especially in the religious formation of children. Non-Catholics at the edge of eternal damnation presented a "fertile missionary field," however, and there was spiritual capital to be made of them. Paul Blanshard, a prominent liberal author, assistant editor of the *Nation* magazine, and a major voice of mid-twentieth-century anti-Catholicism in the United States, feared that nuns working as nurses in Catholic hospitals were baptizing the non-Catholic dying or dead, including miscarried fetuses. "If she is zealous," Blanshard describes the alleged ambition of Catholic nurses, "she may add many souls to the Church." The Apostolate to Assist Dying Non-Catholics, founded in 1930 in Cincinnati by Monsignor Raphael Markham, circulated "Prayer Cards for Dying Non-Catholics," printed with Catholic prayers but otherwise "with no appearance of Catholicity about it," for distribution to the non-Catholic dying. The claim of nondenominationalism here is evidence, perhaps, of uneasiness with such an obviously confessional enterprise in the "tri-faith America" of 1944, which was also the time when Blanshard was arguing that Catholicism was antithetical to American freedom. By 1955, the Apostolate to Assist Dying Non-Catholics was able to claim that 500,000 prayer cards had been distributed "and used."[4]

The displayed body of the crucified Christ in all its bloody brokenness was at the center of the Catholic cult of death. This image was ubiquitous in modern Catholicism. Catholics used many different devotional techniques, as we have seen, to bring themselves into intimate proximity to the violence and suffering of Christ's Passion and his mother's grief. The sign of the cross that Tony and other Catholics once upon a time made so insistently, sometimes provocatively, in public was another such practice, and a potent expression of Catholic difference. On my desk as I write is a particular kind of crucifix that was common in Catholic homes for most of the twentieth century. Inside the hollow wooden cross to which the detachable crucifix is affixed is everything a priest needed when he came to a house or hospital to anoint the body of the dying in the sacrament of extreme unction: two candles, a clean cloth, and a bottle for holy water. (These items were included in the purchase of the crucifix.) When the cross-shaped base is placed flat on the table, the detached crucifix fits upright into a slot at its top. There are declivities in the horizontal arm of the cross for candles. Set up like this, the crucifix forms a small altar. The extreme unction crucifix was a popular wedding present. "This sacrament [of extreme unction] effectively and specifically puts the soul at the gate of death," according to one of the many articles on the subject that appeared over the years in Catholic family magazines, "in a perfect condition to confidently and safely enter into eternity."[5]

*   *   *

When the boy was three years old, his parents brought him to a seer and healer, a much-revered figure in the international supernatural underground of Catholicism that developed in the 1970s and 1980s. Some post-Conciliar miraculous phenomena, such as the apparitions at Medjugorje, were officially tolerated, but the great majority of seers, visionaries, and apparitions were local and unsanctioned, or not yet (if ever to be) sanctioned. All this was the bane of diocesan authorities and parish priests; to enter this environment of metaphysical excitement was to step outside the boundaries of orthodox and respectable Catholicism. Many Catholics in this era, including many priests and nuns, moved back and forth across the line between the acceptable and the forbidden. The seer to whom the dying child was brought was physically disabled as a result of a childhood accident. At public meetings, he spoke of his confidence that before dying, he would be privileged to witness the great miracle prophesized by a contemporary European Marian female visionary with whom he was in regular contact. In that apocalyptic moment, he was to be healed of his ailment. There was an aura of supernatural imminence about this seer. Other seers received messages from the Blessed Mother regarding him or were sent by her to him, notifying him of her intentions for him specifically. This excitement can be sensed in written reports of meetings where he was the main attraction. The healer touched the little boy's body with blessed objects.[6]

One morning, shortly after this episode, the boy came out of his bedroom and told his parents that a beautiful man with long hair had visited him during the night. He eventually identified the man, who came only this once, as Jesus. In the following weeks, the boy seemed to become physically stronger, and his parents allowed themselves to be hopeful. They took him back to the seer, who touched the boy again with sacred things, among them, this time, a medal that had been kissed by the Virgin Mary during an apparition. The boy's mother reports that in these days her son was becoming closer and closer to God. As word of the boy's story spread, the network of Catholics on the miraculous edges of the faith began to pray for him. Not long before his death, then, the little boy had entered the company of men and women whom the Virgin Mary regularly visited to deliver messages of impending chastisement and comfort, who lived in an everyday atmosphere of expectation that at any moment the transcendent would break into time, and who were a source of embarrassment and scandal to other Catholics. It was as if whatever separated this world from the next was getting stretched thinner and thinner.

*   *   *

A dying child was the object of intense devotional fascination for modern Catholics in the United States and elsewhere. This was not unique to Catholics. Dying and dead children were cherished characters in nineteenth-century American and British fiction and Protestant piety. But Catholics incorporated children into the devotional tradition of the victim soul, those innocents to whom God gives the gift of suffering in their bodies as a grace for others. It was the pain of children and adolescents, dying so young, that lifted them to holiness in their last distress and linked their fate ontologically with others on earth and in heaven. It also endowed them with supernatural efficacy. Blessings pour out from the bodies of sick children on the edge of death, as Jack Kerouac reported of his dying brother, Gerard, this edge that is also the threshold of the afterlife.[7]

After her son's vision of Jesus, and as his pain intensified, requiring frequent hospital stays, more tests, needles, and transfusions, the boy's mother came to understand that her son's suffering was saving souls, on earth and in purgatory. Her account of the boy's last days in the hospital is graphic. This woman spares no detail in describing the child's failing body. She and her son were seeing what becomes of human embodiment at this point of extremity, and she writes courageously about it. But it is all framed in the theology of the victim soul, transposing the grim and ancient language of martyrdom and sacrifice incongruously to the setting of the modern hospital.

The woman's prose exemplifies the poetics of modern Catholic dying in the twentieth century. Catholic writers insisted that there be no "velvety euphemisms" in descriptions of death and dying, of the sort they said was common among Protestant moderns. "Our Faith makes death so wonderful with the divine assurances of Christ," an author explains in 1939 in *Ave Maria,* "that we do not need the pale similitudes of halting unbelief to obscure it." Rather, "the words 'death,' 'coffin,' 'shroud,' 'grave,' are beautiful . . . because they border on heaven." Catholic spiritual certainty produced a distinctive semiotics of death and dying. This is where the little boy was, then, in his last days: in a modern hospital, hooked up to intravenous lines, and at the border crossing between here and heaven. He had already become a bridge between the living and the dead.[8]

* * *

"The most important moment of our lives is the moment of our death," Father Trese wrote in *Ave Maria* in 1961. "In that moment we are fixed forever in the mold in which death finds us." Death found the little boy with blood cancer shining with transcendent beauty and coming ever closer to God, his mother says, his great suffering a blessing for others. "Upon that single split second of our passing," Trese continues, "hangs our eternal union with God or our eternal separation from Him." At the instant of death, the human stands exposed "with merciless clarity" in the piercing and sudden illumination of "the searching light of God's infinite justice," all the good, all the bad, and all the extenuating circumstances revealed. There was a smile on the boy's face, his mother reports. "For the first time," says Trese, "we shall see ourselves, totally, as we really are." "Even before the sheet has been drawn over our now still face, we shall have stood under God's revealing light." He closes with the somber caution, *"It will happen to you . . .* and we are rushing toward it so fast."[9]

"The hour of our death," in the language of the Hail Mary, was heavily marked in the Catholic imaginary as an occasion of great, perhaps the greatest, danger and grace. In the hour of death there is "the final holocaust of self-will," according to the devotional writer cited earlier who spoke of Catholicism as the best religion for the dying. To accept this sacrifice of oneself willingly "is the supreme act of resignation beneath the hand of God." The writer of another devotional article in 1961 warns that the hour of death will reveal whether the newly dead is "worthy of love or hatred in the eyes of God." It will also make clear to everyone in the dead person's circle of acquaintance just how successfully the deceased had loved others on earth. The selfish die "intolerably alone." Everything that transpires in the hour of death "is the supreme payment due on our debt of sin." In an exquisite, instantaneous moment of simultaneity between heaven and earth, bereaved survivors, looking down on the body of the newly dead, will know the fate of their loved one, who is at that very moment standing before the judgment seat of God. The little boy's smile, as his mother witnessed and reported it, was a sign for all to see of what was happening to him at that very instant.[10]

While many priests were surely compassionate toward the bereaved, there were limits beyond which sympathy and solicitude could not take them. A note in the *American Ecclesiastical Review* in 1954, for example, cautioned clerical readers that in the case of an unbaptized infant, while priests might say a prayer over the infant's body, burial beside the baptized in Catholic cemeteries was forbidden, as was any statement that "the child has been admitted to eternal life even though it [*sic*] did not receive baptism." To ignore these canonical limits risked giving scandal to other Catholics. The fates of the unbaptized and the unconverted on the other side of this life was known, in any case, even if not with complete certainty (a caveat not always specified). For those who die as infants without baptism, there was "some place similar to Limbo," according to the *Baltimore Catechism,* "where they will be free of suffering, though deprived of the happiness of heaven." For the unconverted there would be no happiness of heaven at all; for them there would only be suffering.[11]

But the conditions of the modern world made it increasingly difficult to identify the moment of death and judgment precisely. Medical science and technology, together with the broader social circumstances of dying—which was more and more taking place away from home, in institutions, in hospitals, and at war—rendered the chronology of mortality ambiguous and fluid. This created a problem for the administration of the sacrament of extreme unction. Canon law forbade the anointing of the body more than three hours after death. But how to identify with any confidence the interval between apparent and actual death was a question priests were repeatedly compelled to ask each other and canon lawyers over the century, often in the most challenging circumstances.[12]

For Catholics coming of age amid the social and technological heterogeneities of modernity, then, death in lived experience was the occasion for doubts and uncertainties, theological, soteriological, biomedical, and moral, rather than a time of "merciless clarity," as clerical authors continued to limn it. Not all Catholics in the United States were able to consign their non-Catholic neighbors to eternal damnation, for example, especially when these non-Catholics were relatives, neighbors, and friends, a situation that was increasingly common as the century proceeded and Catholics moved out of the old urban immigrant enclaves into the suburbs, served alongside non-Catholics in war, and began attending non-Catholic colleges and universities. The frequency of clerical queries in pastoral journals about what to do in ambiguous situations at the life / death border is evidence of some American priests' discomfort with the inherited rules pertaining to dying and death. I often heard from Catholics who grew up in the era when the fate of non-Catholics after death was ostensibly certain that their parents and other adult relatives brushed aside this doctrine when they were asked about it, saying simply that all good people went to heaven. Sympathetic priests faced with the grief of mourners in situations of apparent canonical rigidity had recourse to the logic of Catholic casuistry, the practice of discerning acceptable flexibility within the limits of canon law. *All* positive regulations, the editor of the *Ecclesiastical Review* noted as early as 1930, in response to a query about the rule governing the burial of a non-Catholic husband in a Catholic family cemetery plot, "admi[t] of exceptions, for fear of greater evils," leaving it up to individual priests to strike this balance.[13]

Because the border between life and death was not fixed in the Catholic imaginary, death created anxieties and concerns about appropriate relationships between the living and the dead. What did the dead need? What did the living owe the dead? These questions were framed within the context of the prevailing mode of American Catholic public life, rural and urban, in which face-to-face relationships was the preferred mode of social interaction, in the streets, in workplaces, and in politics. This culture of reciprocity, of favors done and favors owed, included the dead. "There are favors that can be done for the dead person," a priest reminded readers in a 1957 pastoral article. He proposed that the living undertake "a program of help that continues through the months and years that follow" a loved one's death, up until the time comes when "it has been certified that the prize of heaven has been given." Then, in due course, the dead would be able to intercede before God's throne in heaven on behalf of the living who had so faithfully taken care of them after death. The "only way our relatives were going to get out of Purgatory," children were repeatedly told, was if children remembered them in their prayers. Getting into heaven from purgatory was like getting a job in the Chicago political machine; it depended on whom you knew. "First you pray for relatives," a woman born in central Nebraska in 1951 remembered the rule from her childhood, "and then for friends and . . . neighbors and then just everybody." "You prayed them out," she added. Prayers for the souls in purgatory were so thoroughly children's responsibility that the two, children and purgatory, came to be intimately associated with each other. There are children in purgatory, popular children's writer Father Gerald T. Brennan told readers of his *Angel Food: Little Talks to Little Folks* (1939), who "are waiting and crying out for you to help them," perhaps just one prayer, *your* prayer, away from Heaven.[14]

"Memory, affection, and reason will not die at death." The dead continue to feel, need, and want the sorts of things living humans do. This is one of the ways the dead remain recognizable to humans. Praying for the souls in purgatory, who were nearly always described as lonely and feeling abandoned, was a way to keep them company. "He is still a member of our family," a recently bereaved parent writes about an infant son that has just died, in a 1964 article in the *Liguorian*. "We should remember his birthday, include him in our activities." The dead baby's siblings "thronged around his body, petted and kissed his face. We took colored pictures of the family grouped around the casket." Writing in the *Catholic School Journal* in the same year, Dominican sister M. Rose Patricia encouraged religion teachers to present the Mass celebrated on the first anniversary of a person's death as a party and to involve the children in their classes in planning for it. "The day people die," the sister wanted children to know, "is their birthday in heaven." She continues, "The one we love in heaven will be anxious to have many others enjoying [his or her] birthday party." Living children will send out invitations to the souls in purgatory in advance of the party, in the form of prayers for them. A few days before the event, "we should think of the day and realize that the person [in heaven] will be getting ready for a birthday party," just as the living children are doing on earth.[15]

* * *

The recitation of the rosary at wakes had long been a source of comfort and reassurance for bereaved Catholics and of benefit to the dead. But at the time of the little boy's death in the early 1980s, the practice had come to be viewed by many progressive American Catholics as out of step with the theological and liturgical reorientations of the Second Vatican Council. This altered attitude toward the rosary at the wake was a sign of broader changes in official teaching about death and dying in the period. "This problem of the rosary and the Christian wake," as a Catholic University of America professor called it in 1965, had become divisive and polarizing, especially when parish priests refused to lead the rosary themselves, as many had begun to do. Saying the rosary at wakes might confuse and alienate non-Catholic family members and mourners, moreover. While the practice was never condemned officially, the rosary at the wake had begun to be subtly, and sometimes not so subtly, discouraged.[16]

In 1964, Pittsburgh bishop John Wright, informing priests in his diocese of his approval for two new services proposed for wakes by the Diocesan Liturgical Commission in place of the rosary, addressed the problem that rosaries at wakes had become for many Catholics. "Some people have suggested that such 'liturgical prayers' [as proposed by the commission] be used at wakes as a substitute for the recitation of the rosary," the bishop notes. But "I am not enthusiastic about the proposed substitution," he goes on, "even though I welcome the liturgical prayer service, on its own merits, for use at our wakes." He promises Catholics in his diocese who are anxious about the fate of the rosary that he "will never say the word that would downgrade" the rosary, "however many or however excellent may be the devotions which supplement it." Wright closes the pastoral letter with the wish that a rosary be said at the side of his coffin during his "eventual wake." And "if by chance," he writes, anticipating a future without rosaries, "no one who comes to my modest wake has with him the beads with which to lead the rosary," then let "an appropriate person" search his pockets. "Underneath my liturgical vestments he will find, unless I have been robbed, the cherished beads with which we priests and faithful people seek to add humble private prayers to those supremely hallowed mementos [of the Last Supper] in the Mass that we give those we love [in Communion] at the altar of God." The link Wright draws between the rosary and the consecrated bread and wine distributed at Communion ought not to be surprising. Both are practices of presence. At the time of Wright's pastoral letter, one of these practices had fallen into the disrepute within the church that many outside the church had for so long held as the other.[17]

The boy's family asked the seer to lead the rosary at the wake. Among the many people in attendance were those who had heard about the boy from the very extensive media of communication among contemporary Marian visionaries and their devout. As family and friends threaded the beads through their fingers and repeated the memorized prayers in the communal drone that soothed and comforted them but irritated and embarrassed opponents of the practice, electric candles on either side of the boy's open coffin began to flicker, then blinked on and off, on and off, through the remainder of the rosary. It was as if her son were saying the rosary along with them, the boy's mother says. The flickering of the light stopped when the rosary ended. The boy was making his continued presence known, as well as showing his approval of the practice of saying the rosary at wakes.

*　*　*

The graphic poetics and aesthetics of the Catholic way of death contributed to the repulsion many American Catholics expressed at the beautification of corpses, as this art was practiced by morticians in the ever-expanding funeral industry, as well as to their disgust with the ostentation of American cemeteries. "Don't let the undertakers doll me up," distinguished educator Sister M. Madeleva, CSC, approvingly quoted her mother Lucy's deathbed wish in 1955. Catholics chastised what they saw as the modern impulse to "disguise and camouflage death." Better the stench of the rotting corpse than the flowers intended to hide it. Catholic writers relentlessly condemned the "conspiracy against death" in the United States, which was everywhere, they said (except for the comics and Hollywood movies, which were filled with violent and bloody death, but only for the purposes of titillation). Pagans who refuse to accept the soul's immortality "fashion an immortality of their own imagination and ingenuity," a writer in the *Liguorian* accused in 1957. But this is an illusory immortality. "They beautify the dead bodies of their loved ones as if they were not dead at all." Modern Americans use euphemisms such as "slumber room" to refer to where the dead are laid out.[18]

"The art of glamorizing a corpse," as one Catholic writer character-ized contemporary embalming practices in 1957, trivialized and degraded the vessel that in life had held God's presence within it. The "preten-sions and artifices" in the treatment of corpses, the "circus" that mod-erns made out of death, distracted from the fact that the body lying on a deathbed or in a coffin had been in life a receptacle for God's body really present in communion and, perhaps only recently, in the sacra-ment of extreme unction. Like a monstrance, the corpse had held the living body of God. The Catholic body became after death another frag-ment of the real presence, like the assiduously gathered crumbs of the consecrated Host. The body, free from sin and receiving God at the Communion rail, was the body now being embalmed and displayed. Tabernacle and corpse were homologous. Just as the mystery and maj-esty of God's presence on earth were inversely displayed in humble bread and wine, so the truth of the resurrection of the dead emerged most clearly and transparently when the reality of death was not denied by being made pretty.[19]

Despite this steady stress on difference and superiority in their way of dying, however, Catholic death practices in the United States gener-ally followed developments in the wider society. Middle-class American Catholics died and their bodies were handled like the bodies of other dead Americans. Funeral homes first appeared in the United States in the 1880s, following the rise in the popularity of embalming after the Civil War, although the "vast majority" of Americans resisted moving the wake from the home. The introduction of funeral parlors coincided with the immigration of Catholics from southern and Eastern Europe to the United States. In nascent Catholic urban neighborhoods, the funeral director or mortician rose to be a figure of local prominence, more so than would have been the case in the old countries. Priests occasionally complained about funeral directors usurping pastoral authority at the time of death. By the mid-twentieth century, "funeral directors," as they had come to call themselves (rather than the nineteenth-century "undertaker"), "orchestrated the death rites for most deceased Americans." This was true for American Catholics as well, and mostly they accepted this. "To those who can remember the abuses associated with a so-called Catholic wake at home," Father John E. Leonard, writing in the *Priest* for his fellow clergy, declared unequivocally in 1960, "the funeral home is the best thing that has happened to grieving survivors."[20]

The reasons Father Leonard gives for his enthusiastic approval of the modern funeral home index the changing world of middle-class American Catholics. Funeral directors, he says, will see to it that everyone is out by ten or eleven o'clock at night. This meant that the custom of socializing in the vicinity of the coffin until the early morning, common at wakes in the home, would disappear. The "absence of refreshments," a development especially highly regarded by Father Leonard, will focus the attention of the mourners ("sincere and otherwise") on why they are at a wake in the first place: to pray for the dead, not to gossip with the living. "When the priest arrives to say the Rosary," Father Leonard says, "everyone joins in," because, he adds pointedly, "there is nothing else to do," nothing to eat, nothing to drink. In the spirit of Father McDonough's admonitions to women thinking about organizing a Block Rosary, Father Leonard singles out for particular disapproval the conversations among "nosey neighbors" and "hangers-on" at old-fashioned wakes. Stripped of all this gossiping, visiting, eating, and simply being together in the presence of the dead, Father Leonard concludes, paganism will be "completely outlawed" from the Catholic wake at last. Cordoning off the dead body and the rites associated with it from life's normal activities secured a more solidly defined boundary between the living and the dead, sacred and profane, modern pagan and modern Catholic—and also between Catholics who were not acceptably modern and those who were.[21]

But for all of Father Leonard's enthusiasm, this was not an untroubled transition. After the war, a lament arose among the children and grandchildren of the immigrants for the passing of the old wake. Kate Dooley, a frequent contributor to *Ave Maria,* condemned funeral parlors in 1957 as "cold and impersonal." "The events of family life should take place in the family home," Dooley says, "and I do not like the implication that a person is no longer wanted there, just because he happened to die." "Across the spotless expanse of Arabian rug," another writer described the contemporary funeral home in 1960, "lies the deceased, scientifically embalmed," resplendent in "the suit-and-tie décor of American cadavers." Everything is "functional" and overorganized. The practice of sending flowers in place of being present oneself is dismissed as the rudeness of a materialist age. Other writers complained that children, boisterously ubiquitous at home wakes, playing around the coffin, are kept away from contemporary Catholic funerals, "as if contagious diseases were connected with them" (it is not clear here if "them" refers to children or to the dead). It was common at the old wakes for children to be lifted up over the coffin to view, often to kiss, the face of the dead. Now, there is "very little weeping" in funeral parlors. People know to control themselves. "Regimented remorse" has replaced real sorrow.[22]

Once the wake had been thus rendered fully rational and respectable, the sense of community, which had been reinforced by the old wakes, drained away, Catholic critics said. The contemporary Catholic wake "is not a place to come for companionship," but "for furtive prayer and uncomfortable sorrow" that reflects "the hurried pace of a sophisticated America and the demise of regional unity." "When I go to wakes today," Rose Grieco, the writer who complained about the sequestration of children in funeral parlors, concluded, "I sense a strangeness in our behavior." Although Italian Americans "know that in times of sorrow, people need other people," "we [Italian Americans] . . . have become assimilated." The loss was not one of ethnic particularity, however, or not primarily, nor was it the passing of local culture. The bustling crowds at wakes seemed now to these second- and third-generation ethnic Catholics, looking back to their childhoods, to have been the "tangible demonstration" on earth of "the communion of saints." It was this intimacy between heaven and earth that seemed to be waning.[23]

* * *

The circle in the corner of the image of Christ grew over the following days and slowly took on the features of the dead boy's face. The woman kept this to herself at first; then she confided it to her husband. He feared for his wife's mental stability, until he saw the image himself. Their other children saw it, too. In the days following the boy's death, his mother had pleaded with God to grant her another sight of her son. It seemed now that heaven had answered her prayer. Telling no one outside the family about what they were coming to recognize as a great miracle, husband and wife struggled to discern more clearly what was transpiring in their home. They were familiar with such supernatural phenomena from the stories told in the circles they had become part of as their son was dying. But such a thing had never happened to *them*. What *was* God's intention? Was this even God's work? One night, the woman rubbed the image with holy water to see if she could make it disappear. Her child's face remained visible in the frame. Then other faces and figures began to appear alongside him: the Blessed Mother and the Holy Spirit, as well as holy people and images that had become popular in the wake of the changes to Catholic devotional culture that followed the Second Vatican Council, among them Padre Pio and the sepia-tinted face of the Christ of the Shroud of Turin, the long piece of cloth said to be Jesus's burial shroud, scored by blood and light with an impression of his face.

Of particular concern to the boy's parents was whether God intended this miracle to be shared for the faith, peace, and consolation of others beyond the immediate family. The woman had a plan for finding the answer to this question. She proposed to God that she would invite one of her friends to view the image without saying anything about the miracle. If this woman did not see the boy, his family would take it as a sign that the miracle was to be kept private. If, on the other hand, the visitor did see the boy's face, they would know that the miracle was for everyone. The woman came and saw the boy's face in the image. Overcome by a feeling of deep peacefulness, as this visitor later reported to the boy's mother, she began to weep. As she did, the Blessed Mother and the Shroud of Turin also appeared to her within the frame of the devotional picture, alongside the boy.

* * *

Catholics do not die alone, Catholics said. They are not abandoned in death. Many Catholics believed that when the moment of death arrived, a loved one would come from the other side to carry the dying across; a number of the middle-aged Catholics with whom I spoke told me they had heard stories about this from friends or relatives. The *Junior Catholic Messenger* counseled children to be prepared to say the Act of Contrition with a dying person if a priest was not available. The anticipation of company, human and supernatural, in the final hour and beyond, distinguished the Catholic way of death from that of pagan modernity, Catholics said. "When the time comes for one of us to die, we [Catholics]," in contrast to "modern man," "gather the family for the prayers for the dying" while waiting for the priest to come, a writer in 1955 described in an article titled "Death in Your Home" that appeared in the devotional magazine *Voice of Saint Jude.* "When death comes close," another author reassured her readers, "so also does God, providing by the wonder of His Own presence, and through the mercy and goodness of friends, the strength, the stamina, we need to see us through." Jesus will be there, too. "Approach death we must," a Franciscan friar counseled in 1955, "why not in the friendship of Jesus," who will "sweeten the anxiety of our last hour." Death itself was personalized as "Brother Death," in the spirit of Saint Francis, and the quality of one's death was said to depend on the "relations" of the dying with this sibling. Catholic death notices recorded publicly that the deceased passed away in the company of a priest and family members with the phrase, "He [or she] died with the consolations of Holy Mother the Church, and was a member of such and such a [parish] society."[24]

But it is one of the conditions of modern life that men and women often die alone; this was true of Catholics, too. Like other Americans in the twentieth century, Catholics died in nursing homes without family members there to pray for them; in hospital beds in the middle of the night; or on distant battlefields, as the Detroit housewife feared would be the case for her brothers. Given the Catholic ethos of accompanied death, this was an unbearable prospect. Just how unbearable the thought of a lonely death was to Catholics is illustrated by the story of the founding of a new devotional society in 1958–1959 in Pittsburgh. One day a woman named Margaret O'Konski happened to stay on in church after attending the last mass of the morning. By utter chance, she found herself the sole person in attendance at the funeral of an elderly woman who, as O'Konski later learned, was named Anna. O'Konski was deeply troubled by the absence of mourners for Anna, who had died "at the county home." "I couldn't sleep remembering that little casket in that nearly empty church." O'Konski recalled. She determined to found an apostolate for "providing friends for those who die friendless."[25]

O'Konski arranged with the men of the diocesan Saint Vincent de Paul Society, who were already pledged to serve as pallbearers at the funerals of "unclaimed [Catholic] bodies," to notify her in such cases. Then she began to enlist sponsors to adopt and enroll the unclaimed and lonely dead in a perpetual Mass society. Among the first sponsors to join her were a group of "Bell telephone girls" who together adopted "12 souls." A ten-year-old altar boy offered his Mass each morning for the departed soul of a Jewish convert his family had adopted. ("Just think, that family will probably be the only one who remembers that soul by name," Mrs. O'Konski mused.) These initial efforts eventually took institutional form as the Spiritual Society for the Unclaimed Dead. Society members attended funeral masses, they accompanied the dead to the cemetery, and they recited the rosary afterward for the peaceful repose of the departed. Each year on November 2, the Catholic Feast of All Souls, members of the Spiritual Society for the Unclaimed Dead brought flowers to the graves of all the dead they had adopted.[26]

That women should take on this role of accompanying the unaccompanied dead is consistent with the role of the Blessed Mother in the Catholic way of death, as well as a function of middle-class Catholic women's newfound time in their postwar suburban communities. Of all the figures, mundane and supermundane, to come to the side of the dying, the Blessed Mother was the being Catholics most confidently expected and the one they most profoundly desired to see there. In the prayer Catholics repeated so often every day that it became the rhythm of their breathing, the Blessed Mother was entreated to "pray for us sinners, now and at the hour of our death." "Our Lady is not a stranger to death," Father Titus Cranny, SA, reassured readers of *Our Lady's Digest* in 1957. "She is [death's] special patroness." Father Cranny describes an incident that took place "in a large city a few years ago" (perhaps the same metropolis that is the site of so many twentieth-century Catholic tales). A group of "dirty-faced street urchins" urgently lead a priest into the basement of a squalid tenement. The priest finds a woman there, dying on a "rusty bed." She is "wrapped in man's overcoat," groaning "in intense pain." But when he attempts to comfort the woman, she raises herself up and spits at him. So the priest sits down on an upturned crate, "amid the welter of soiled laundry, empty beer bottles and cigarette stubs," and begins to recite the rosary aloud. The woman slowly turns toward the sound of his voice. "Her bloodshot eyes" are filled with tears. Calm and peaceful at the rosary's end, she confesses to the priest her "evil" life. After he gives her the sacrament of Holy Communion, she passes away. The Blessed Mother has been faithful to her, just as the prayer says she will be. "Souls in their last agony have many needs," another priest writes in 1956 in an article titled "A Devotion for Life's Most Important Hour," but "none of these compare to the possession of Mary's presence." Accompanying this article is a story about an old woman who is gripped on her deathbed in the poorhouse by the apprehension that "all her good deeds of eighty-one years seemed useless for eternity," whereas her sins "were [as] vivid and as real as [the] living horrors about her bed" in the crumbling room. In deepest despair, the narrative continues, the woman holds up her rosary and exclaims to the Virgin Mary, "Pull, Lady Mother, pull!"[27]

The details and language of these stories—"dirty-faced street urchins," heroic priests, fallen women, "Lady Mother," bodies in pain, and souls in despair—and their infinite repetition in Catholic oral and written culture suggest that we are in the presence here of a distinctive popular genre, the Marian death scene. Such thrilling tales of Mary's appearance at the side of the dying, letting no squalor or darkness deter her—indeed, the more rank the squalor and the deeper the darkness, the more Mary's transcendent beauty and grace shine forth—are not new in Catholic history, but they endured into modernity and existed alongside other expressions of Marian piety. This was the promise of the

Hail Mary. The stories of the Blessed Mother's presence in times of death are another instance of the inverting logic of real presence: the more awful and degraded the context, the more glorious the real presence of the holy. The century's wars provided an especially compelling venue for the Blessed Mother's presence at the hour of death. The "call for rosaries" from the front was said to be "a constant 'repeat order' " during the Second World War. This clamor for rosaries became so overwhelming and urgent that the Holy See approved the practice of making rosaries out of knotted string that was already common among Catholic soldiers and sailors. Catholic airmen who belonged to a society called Our Lady's Knights promised to recite at least a decade of the rosary every day. Catholic soldiers went into battle with rosaries around their necks. According to Catholic writers, so present was Mary at the front, and so evident was the reliance of Catholic soldiers and sailors upon her, that even non-Catholics clutched rosaries and miraculous medals on the eve of battle, hoping either for Mary's protection or for her companionship in death.[28]

*   *   *

After her friend saw the boy's face in the image of the crucified Christ, the boy's mother decided it was time to tell her parish priest what was going on. She had great trust in him. The priest came to the house and stood silently in front of the image for a long while. At last, he went over and rubbed vigorously on the surface of the image. Then he turned and asked the boy's parents, who were standing behind him all this time anxiously wondering what he was thinking, for a photograph of their son. He held the photograph up to the image, comparing them. After this, he asked to see another image of the crucified Christ in order to ascertain, he explained to the couple, whether the phenomenon they, and presumably now he, too, were observing was the result of light reflecting off the image's glossy surface. It was not. When all this was done, the priest told the boy's parents that their son's face in the image was a gift from God in recognition of the family's terrible suffering and grief. Now the boy's mother saw her dead son every day.

*　　*　　*

The period from after World War II into the 1960s was an asynchro-
nous time for Catholics in the United States. The children and grandchildren of southern and Eastern European immigrants and Mexican
migrants were out of joint with themselves and with their environments,
in often uneasy movement between ways of being in the world. Some
had entered the professional classes, although the majority of American
Catholic men were blue-collar workers, which introduced the hidden
and intimate injuries of class into Catholic homes and neighborhoods.
Catholic white-collar workers, male and female, remained connected,
more or less closely, with friends and relatives in the working class, who
may have stayed on in the old neighborhood while others had moved
away. The wives of blue-collar Catholic men had stepped out a little
ahead of their husbands, into the new and increasing number of positions available to women in the postwar service economy. This difference
in workplace, which was also a difference in prestige and opportunity,
exacerbated tensions left over from economic depression and war. There
were constant comings and goings between the older neighborhoods of
first and second settlement and the more prosperous areas of the cities
and the suburbs into which younger Catholics were moving, where it
was common to build the parochial school before the church. When
the church was finally built, moreover, it had little of the weight and
presence of the massive structures that had brooded over the old neighborhoods. Young Catholic couples had Jewish and Protestant neighbors. As mentioned previously, one of the arguments against saying the
rosary at wakes in these years was that the repetitive and nearly incomprehensible murmur of prayers would be unfamiliar to non-Catholics
in attendance and make them uncomfortable. Such an objection would
have been unthinkable twenty years earlier. There were few attempts to
revive the old custom of waking the dead at home, and, in any case,
there were no opportunities to do so. Yet a feeling of loss lingered.[29]

A cranky 1966 article written by an inner-city parish priest for his
fellow clergy on "funeral problems," with the subtitle "towards greater
efficiency," captures some of the conflict in these times among Catholics

about how to mourn and bury the dead. Too many people who have moved away from the city core, Father Harry S. Smith, CSSR, begins, want to be buried from the old neighborhood or to have their parents or grandparents buried from there. Such nostalgia creates a logistical nightmare for priests who must spend hours in city traffic going between the old neighborhoods and the newer ones. Catholics' insistence on burying their dead with rituals from earlier times, when people were living together in densely populated urban neighborhoods, was onerous now in the new circumstances. With visiting the funeral parlor on the night before the funeral, getting back to the funeral parlor early the next morning for the blessing of the corpse before the closing of the coffin, accompanying the dead and the bereaved from the funeral parlor to the church for the mass, and finally making the trip to the cemetery—which was in most cases at considerable distance from the old neighborhood— and performing the desired rituals there, the better part of a day is wasted, Father Smith says, more "if the funeral parlor is located on the other side of the city—and many are—[because] this means driving there and back at night, often through thick traffic and often in bad weather."[30]

In 1965, the priests in the hundred-year-old parish where Father Smith worked conducted 165 funerals. Of these, Father Smith complains, too many were for people who had no connection whatsoever to the parish. Rather, it was done for the convenience of the funeral directors that the families had hired. It is especially galling to Father Smith that the families of the dead expect him to drop everything, even "an important meeting . . . a convert to instruct, hospital rounds to make, or perhaps a diocesan activity to attend," for their convenience and the benefit of their dead. Eliminating the rosary at the wake has helped, he notes, but this is not enough. The new "Prayer Service for a Christian Wake" is just as time consuming and bothersome. The dead and their families seemed to be ensuring that Father Smith spent as much as possible of the twilight of his clerical career in his automobile.[31]

"What can be done to 'update' the funeral ceremonies and yet maintain dignity and decorum plus the proper execution of the liturgy?"

Father Smith has ideas for how to achieve greater efficiency in the rituals surrounding death. First, no more visits by the priest to the funeral parlor, whether for a rosary or a liturgical prayer. Let one of the "emerging laymen" take over, he says snidely, revealing himself to be one of the many American parish priests who were wary, at best, about the laity newly empowered by the Second Vatican Council. No blessing the corpse the next morning. No trip to the cemetery, either. Certainly no passing by the last place where the deceased lived, let alone leisurely tours of the old neighborhood, as many families wanted. It would be best, Father Smith concludes, to hold everything *inside* the church. He concedes that funeral directors, limousine drivers, and cemetery workers will object to his plan, but they do so, the priest avers, for reasons of economic self-interest. Father Smith closes with some glum remarks about what an "indelicate thing" it is to ask family members for his fee for all this at the end of the funeral, so that too often he is not even properly recompensed for all those miles logged and hours spent— wasted—with the dead and their families.[32]

*   *   *

This might appear to be the resentment of one parish priest, left behind in the old church and rectory to contend with all the headaches of costly maintenance, dwindling congregations, shrinking classrooms, and unfamiliar neighbors. But a similar spirit of efficiency and streamlining is evident in the writings of Catholic cemetery professionals in the decades immediately following World War II as well, in their plans for the architecture, landscaping, and administration of Catholic cemeteries. Redesign of older cemeteries or the creation of new ones in this era aimed to replace "the usual multiplicity of monuments" of the old urban ethnic cemeteries with "one central memorial feature." This is the view of a long 1959 article that comprehensively reviews trends in Catholic cemeteries, published in the professional journal *Catholic Property Administration*. The proposed central focus might be a canonically erected chapel or shrine, both to be designed by professional architects. Panels of scripture references, "explanatory material on certain saints," and "great religious truth[s]" around its interior will add a "catechetical purpose" to the new Catholic cemetery, the authors affirm.[33]

Such organization was necessary, Catholic cemetery professionals believed, in order to eliminate the devotional and memorial excesses and chaos of the older cemeteries. They meant by this the mausoleums and privately erected chapels of locally prominent merchants, celebrities, bankers, and criminals. But they also meant the photographs of the dead in oval frames sealed onto marble or faux-marble headstones; the plethora of objects left at gravesites, such as rosaries, statues and images of the saints, and baby shoes; and the massive images of Jesus, the Blessed Mother, and the saints, in poured concrete or carved stone, bent over the bodies of the dead in postures of grief and mourning. The preference among the new Catholic cemetery professionals was for "lawn-level markers." Pleasingly invisible from even a short distance away, these headstones left the carefully tended vista of the cemetery grounds open to the horizon. They also made maintenance easier and less expensive, eliminating overtime wages for unionized gravediggers (an expression of the ambivalence among Catholic elites, including many prelates, for organized labor, especially organized labor within the church). Services for mourners were now to be held at the central location, away from where the dead would be interred, with a view to keeping the grasses kempt and priests and funeral directors out of inclement weather.

These changes would give administrators "better control over the quality of memorialization." Marketing research on reactions to innovative arrangements of cemetery grounds indicated a positive response overall, a cemetery administrator noted with satisfaction in 1961. But by the end of the decade, Catholic educators worried that their students no longer cared about or even knew or understood the contemporary Catholic view of death and the afterlife.[34]

* * *

The boy's mother, confident now that God wanted the miracle to be shared with others, invited friends and neighbors into her home to see the images within the image. Visitors saw their own dead in the frame, alongside the boy, and in the company of holy figures. Sometimes Christ appeared in the image with his arms outstretched protectively over the boy. As at Chimayo, the lives and stories of many people and families became interleaved, their faces comingled, and the miracle became a communal one.

But then some visitors saw in the image *living* relatives of theirs. They immediately became frightened that this meant these family members were fated to die in the near future. The boy's parents did not know what to tell them, how to help them make sense of this unexpected development. There were terrible incidents, the woman told me, as people became very agitated at what appeared now to be prophecies of death. Gradually, as she and her husband thought about the new turn in the miraculous event in their home, they came to the conclusion that God was directing visitors' attention to specific persons in their lives, whether they were alive or dead, so that they might offer them special care and prayers. The appearance of the living in the frame was not a premonition of imminent mortality. Thank God, my friend's mother, who was looking forward to seeing her relatives, living or dead, in the image, exclaimed when the woman explained this to us the evening of our visit. It was a dismal, wet night in June. My friend and I, along with his girlfriend, mother, sister, and brother-in-law—who had just been fired from his job and was in a very edgy mood this evening—all jammed into my friend's car, an old beige Chevrolet Impala. Most of us were second- or third-generation Italian American Catholics. The visit had been arranged months in advance.

The woman and her husband once again struggled to make sense of what God was doing in showing living people alongside the dead in the frame. They listened carefully to what visitors told them about what they were seeing in the image. Some came expecting to get a glimpse of a particular deceased loved one, often a child, but instead saw someone else. Why had God shown them this face and not the face they were hoping to see? This question became especially exigent in cases where the face revealed in the image was the last face a visitor ever wanted to see again, an estranged relative, for example, in whose company it was painful to be, someone who had hurt them or who had been hurt by them. When this happened, the boy's parents wondered if it was God's intention that there be reconciliation between the estranged parties or forgiveness of one for the other. As the numbers of visitors increased, the man and woman were called on more and more to offer counsel and solace and to interpret visions and signs. In conversations with each other and with troubled or elated visitors, they tried to work out God's intentions. They became lay theologians of the miraculous dead, probing the uncertain details of a miracle for understanding.

The woman told my friend over the phone when he was making plans for our visit that we ought to bring along a pound of coffee and a coffee cake. The kind of coffee cake, she specified, with pecans and swirled white icing. It took us more than three hours to make what ought to have been an hour-long trip. The last part of the journey was spent circling a poorly illuminated working-class neighborhood with immaculately tended lawns, almost all of them decorated with images of saints or the Blessed Mother. The couple lived in an aluminum-sided duplex. A brightly lit bay window filled with plants extended out over the front lawn. The boy's mother met us at the door and welcomed us warmly into her home. The coffee and cake she handed over to her husband, standing behind her. He said almost nothing the whole evening, but very amiably shared his cigarettes with us and talked about local sports teams and the television shows he was watching during our visit. It all felt very familiar to me, like a visit to the homes of my aunts and uncles. The woman told us we would have a snack later, after we had spent time with the image.

Among the visitors to the boy's home and to the image of the crucified Christ were Catholics deeply alienated from the church because of "the changes," as they called the various reforms in worship, theology, and devotional life instituted during and after the Second Vatican Council. These angry and disaffected Catholics wondered why the boy's parents, who were otherwise Catholics like them, continued to go to Mass at their local parish church. To worship and adore God, the woman responded, and for the well-being of their souls. The consecrated Host was precious medicine for ailing spirits, she said, and she had no intention of separating herself from it. The couple, by their own account, remained faithful and orthodox practicing Catholics while maintaining their affiliation with the dispersed circles of the heterodox and disaffected. These latter, as I have said, were those most attuned to the supernatural, the miraculous, and visions, such as the appearance of the boy's face in the image of the crucified Christ. When people complained to her that they got nothing out of the new Mass, the woman advised them to receive the sacraments more often. She emphasized the importance of being obedient to the Church. Priests and nuns visited her home to look into the image, where they saw things, too. The boy's parents often said how grateful they were for the support of all of these visitors and for the counsel and spiritual direction of their parish priests.

* * *

"In general, we can say that the new funeral rite is an improvement on the old," a liturgist wrote confidently in the *Priest* in 1970, "in the sense that it does not add to the fear and gloom of the occasion and it permits the bystanders to realize that their grief is normal and even desirable." Using this same phrase, "fear and gloom," another writer around the same time explained that everything fearful and gloomy had been removed from the new funeral rites. This included the dress of mourners: "Traditional black gives way to joyous white." White had become the color of Catholic mourning. The vestments of the priest celebrating the funeral Mass were white, as was the pall covering the casket in the center aisle. The "whiteness" of the Paschal candle that replaced the decrepit, unbleached waxy yellow candles parishes used to put around the coffin "hints at glory," another priest explained in 1970. (He does not say what the old candles had hinted at.) The flames rising up from the Paschal candle "suggest life," not eternal damnation, and "its pillaring stature conveys a sense of strength." Texts stressing judgment were "either amended or eliminated" in experimental funeral liturgies in parishes around the country in 1966. The *Libera me, Domine* "has been suppressed."[35]

Some clerical writers urged caution in introducing such changes into the rites of the dead. They told their fellow priests to be careful not to bruise the sensibilities of mourners at this most vulnerable and fragile time by depriving them of the comforts of familiar devotions. One priest advised holding educational sessions in the parish to explain the new funeral rites. But in the press of ordinary parish life, which bore down even harder now as increasing numbers of men began leaving the priesthood and as fewer were entering the seminaries, alterations in how Catholics mourned, prayed for, buried, and memorialized their dead were instituted with little preparation of the laity. It must have seemed to grieving Catholics that the world around them had gone suddenly from black to white, from sorrow to a joy they did not feel, from mourning to celebration overnight, just when their grief was at its deepest.[36]

The fervor with which the new funeral Mass in particular was introduced by its defenders reflected, among other things, their relief at being able to free contemporary Catholics from what generations of religion teachers and parish priests had made of death and dying earlier in the century. Apprehension at the overuse of death in Catholic culture was already evident in American Catholicism before the council, and it became pervasive after it. Religion teachers fretted that the too-frequent evocation of death, dying, and eternal reward or punishment either to terrify children into obedience or to thrill them with the mysteries of the faith would drive youngsters away from the church as they got older. In "pre-kerygmatic days," as a young priest called the time before 1968, when he was writing, the church, meaning parents and the men and women responsible for the religious formation of children, failed to educate the younger generation "in the good news of Christ." He called for a moratorium on "death sermons" like the one he had recently heard, in which a pastor encouraged his congregation to pray that a nonbeliever well known in the parish be stricken with cancer to lead him to the true faith.[37]

Catholicism had the most profound consolations to offer humans who were suffering and dying and the deepest comfort to those who mourned. "One cannot explain to others, or even to oneself," Gary Wills writes about Ash Wednesday rites, "how burnt stuff rubbed on the forehead could be balm for the mind. The squeak of ash . . . marked the body down for death, yet made this promise of the grave somehow comforting." But this balm was often quite harsh in its application. Death's awesome powers were blatantly appropriated for the ends of authority, control, and power. Here is a description of the fate of a teenager who suffers a graphically described death in a state of mortal sin, written in 1959 for adolescent readers: "Faster than a thought, or the glance of an eye, Joseph Corby was in hell. . . . He heard the unearthly shrieks, shrieks that can only be uttered by the souls of the damned. He smelled the stench of burning and of sin. . . . At once Joseph Corby was immersed in a sea of fire. . . . Bathed in this terrible flame, Joe screamed with pain. . . . An hour passed and he shrieked wildly as if to go out of his mind, and still the pain did not let up. Two hours passed, three hours, four hours . . . [ellipsis in original] months, years, lifetimes, eternities." The author of this vision of hell, Curtis B. Schmidt, SJ, goes on like this awhile longer, before he leaves young Joe Corby to his fate and his readers to their choices. How will *they* die?[38]

Younger Catholics in the United States who came of age during and after the Second World War appear to have become more aware of this abuse of death, resentful of it, and resistant to it. They were more prosperous, better educated, and healthier, and their workplaces were safer. As it was for all Americans, death among Catholics was becoming less common an event in everyday circumstances. The introduction of penicillin during the war enabled American medical practitioners, once constrained to diagnosis and palliation, to heal. "Emphasis upon the resurrection of the Lord Jesus," the priest quoted above on the subject of the Paschal candle reflected, "is a mark of the current age in theology" and of the new liturgies.[39]

This priest goes on to recommend that before the "more public" and "obviously more 'paschal'" funeral Mass in church, a priest from the parish should go to the home of the recently deceased and, in purple vestments, say Mass only for the immediate family. This will allow them to do their "grief work" in private. "Home" here means where the postwar Catholic nuclear family lives, not "home" as in the setting for wakes that promiscuously mixed public and private, family and neighbors, the dead and the living, and children and adults. Writing for each other in this new age of death and dying, priests emphasized the *private* nature of death and mourning. Do everything *inside* the church, Father Leonard had urged. Extravagant displays of grief common earlier in the century at ethnic funerals and burials—moaning, "wailing with green faces of death," kissing and stroking the face of the dead, climbing onto the catafalque, rending garments, tearing skin—were out of place, obscene, in the new ethos of joy and resurrection. Now, psalms "expressive of grief" are recited and passages from Christian scripture read. "Catechesis" is imperative, the priest concludes, "if the rites are to teach the Christian interpretation of death." Catholics were well into the culture of modern professionalism and rationality.[40]

* * *

My wife and I had just had a child, and I found the woman's evocation of the death of her little boy devastating. Her story affected us all this way. The group of us moved closer together on the couch in the living room, except for my friend's brother-in-law. He wandered around the house, pausing occasionally to look at the flickering images on the television. Everyone was smoking furiously; we could barely see each other through the thick gray haze. "I'm not going to make it, God," the boy's mother told us she had prayed after her son's funeral, "this is too much for me to bear." When she described the appearance of the boy's face in the image of the crucified Christ, my friend's mother exclaimed, "It was like a miracle! Like a miracle." "That's right," the woman agreed. "But at first I didn't believe this, and I didn't tell anyone." "She didn't tell me," her husband confirmed.

The woman had learned how to grieve with strangers. It happens, she told us, that she sits up for most of the night on her son's bed with her arms around a distraught parent who has just seen or not seen his or her child amid the others in the image. Although they have done nothing to put out word of the shrine, people have come from all over the world to mourn their dead in the little child's bedroom. "Some people heard about us in India, and came all the way here just to visit."

"Now, do you want to go upstairs to see the picture?" she asked us.

We filed up a narrow carpeted stairway behind the woman to the second floor of the house. The boy's room was very small. There was a bed in it and a bureau along one wall. The image of the crucified Christ faced us as we entered the room. "This is my pride and joy," the woman said. She pointed to a multileveled shrine altar she had built on a surface just below the image. A plaster bust of Jesus, in the image of the *ecce homo,* crowned with thorns and bleeding, stood alongside ceramic figurines of American popular culture icons and statues of saints, among them Francis, Thérèse (the Little Flower), Anthony, and the nineteenth-century Italian saint Vincent Pallotti. All were crowded together on a tiered structure. I had the impression of a pyramid of faces looking at us, beneath the image of Christ crucified, who was also looking down at us with what seemed like sympathy that night.

"This is my shrine," the woman said, a gesture of her arm taking in the images and statues, the bed and the bureau, and at the same time welcoming us into this very intimate space in her world. "I've been building it over the years. Isn't it beautiful? I've got a lot of people here." She meant by this a lot of special beings and her son, although she did not specify this. She might also have meant all the people who had come into this room since she and her husband opened it up to visitors. The room was crowded, in other words, with many presences, visible and not, present and past.

"I'm going to leave you alone to look at the picture," she said. "Remember, don't be afraid! You don't see ghosts here. That's not what we Catholics believe. You see your dead people, and God wants you to know that they're in his care now. You don't have to worry." She took hold of my arm and repositioned me in the small room in order to show the others what to do, how to stand. "Look. If you move around, and look at the picture from different angles, you'll see different things." She pushed my head down gently until I was looking up at the image from a slight stoop. "Like this. You look like this, from underneath, and you may see something different. Now say a prayer that God shows you what you need to see." Then she left the room.

The six of us began to climb over one another, almost like children playing Johnny-on-the-pony in the playground. The room was so small that we needed to support each other as we squeezed past and leaned over one another to look up at the image of the crucified Christ from various angles. "Anybody getting anything yet?" my friend asked, as if we were waiting for a television or radio signal from another world to clear.

*   *   *

Catholics knew that the dead had needs that it was within the power of the living to meet. They expected the dead to be present in the affairs of everyday life. It is no wonder that Catholics objected to the American celebration of Halloween: children's costumes of ghouls and spirits made a mischievous carnival out of the real relations between the living and the dead, and in doing so were playing with some dangerous things. October 31 is the eve of the Feast of All Saints, which falls on the first day of November; the Feast of All Souls follows on the second day of the month. November is the month of the dead in Catholicism. (Some nuns compromised with their students' enthusiasm for Halloween by letting them dress up as saints and martyrs.) No one who encountered the boy's image in the frame seems to have been shocked, horrified, scandalized, or frightened by it—not the parish priest, the children in the family, the family's neighbors, or visitors to their home, including us that night. There was a certain familiarity with the supernatural and with the presence of the dead.

Not once did we did think we were in a haunted house. With the exception of my friend's girlfriend, who was Jewish, all of us had grown up Catholic, in the culture of presence. We had all been to shrines before. Had we thought in a moment of silliness or unease that we were embarked on an occult adventure, the coffee cake and coffee would surely have brought us back down to earth and to our senses. Nor was this a trip to the church's periphery, to which so many supernatural phenomena had been relegated in these years. The boy's mother had made it clear to all her visitors, including us, that she was a faithful and obedient Catholic.

The dead are not easily dismissed, it appears. Not from the company of the living, and not from a religious world that for so long attended to them, both the proximate dead—the dead one knew when they were alive—and the ambient dead—the vast and populous fields of death that surround the individually known dead. The souls in purgatory were both proximate and ambient dead. Nor are the dead easily dismissed from history. The common Catholic practice of praying to free souls from purgatory was a form of ancestor cult, an instance of the many relationships that linked the past and the present in modern Catholicism. The new death rituals instituted following the council officially erected a boundary between private grief and public joy. The newer customs for waking the dead and the rearrangement of Catholic cemeteries clearly aimed to separate the living and the dead for the convenience of the living. But the boy's face in the image, and the many visitors who came to see him and catch a glimpse of their own dead alongside him, tells us that the dead do not go away.[41]

These were the same years as the miracle of Audrey Santo (1983–2007). Little Audrey, as her devout call her, nearly drowned in her family's backyard swimming pool in Worcester, Massachusetts, when she was four years old. Rushed to the hospital, Audrey lapsed into a coma, the result, her family claims, of overmedication. Physicians recommended she be institutionalized, but four months after the accident, her family brought her home. Although Audrey remained unable to move or speak for the rest of her life, her family resisted the word "coma" for their daughter's condition, believing that she was alert and responsive. In 1988 her family took her on an arduous pilgrimage to Medjugorje, where one day she seemed to be nodding her head during an apparition of the Blessed Mother, as if acknowledging what Mary was saying directly to her.[42]

Devotion to Audrey flourished in the Catholic supernatural underground. Her home became a popular shrine and pilgrimage site. So great, indeed, was the press of people who came to see her and to witness the miracles that took place around her that her family eventually replaced one of the walls of their home with glass siding. Pilgrims were able to look in at the girl lying in bed. Audrey's three-sided room was situated on an urban lot just at the edge of life and death. It quickly became a venue of spectacles of presence. The only solid food the young woman consumed were consecrated Hosts; her devout parents believed that this heavenly nourishment sustained her (although they also saw the feeding tube connected to her body). Blood flowed freely at the shrine, from consecrated Hosts and from images and statues around the girl. Her family and her devout believed Audrey to be a victim soul, suffering on behalf of others. On Good Friday in 1996, the priest there to say Mass opened the door of the tabernacle on the small altar in Audrey's room and blood came pouring out of it in a great river. There is now a foundation, approved by the local ordinary, for Audrey's canonization.

* * *

Images began to take shape inside the picture. These are reflections of the light, I told myself, hoping not to see any of my own dead in the frame, and certainly, I pleaded silently, none of my living loved ones. This is light reflecting off the glossy surface of the lithographic reproduction of the image of the crucified Christ. "Do you see the tall, thin nun over there, standing against the right side of the picture?" my friend asked me. Unbelievably, I did. (I am able to recall the image as I write this.)

Now we all began seeing things. My friend's mother saw her father, whom she had been talking about wanting to see all during the ride to the shrine. My friend's girlfriend saw a man in a tuxedo. She thought it might be her father when he was young. In the image, the elegant man in the tuxedo appeared to be dancing with someone. For reasons she did not explain, my friend's girlfriend found this image upsetting; in a quiet and unhappy voice, she said, "I don't like this." None of us could see him, however. "There's Padre Pio," my friend's sister said. Her husband, in full clown mode now, was doubled over and looking up at the image from below, through his legs. In a loud voice, he said, "Hey, look, from this angle I can see Casey Kasem [who was alive at the time]. Maybe I can get next week's top forty." Later on he saw Fred Astaire.

After about an hour of this—or so it says in my field notes; I cannot believe that we were in there that long, when I look back on the evening—the boy's mother returned and asked if we were ready yet for coffee and cake. First, though, she wanted to show us that what we were seeing was authentic. "Look at this." She held up an identical image of the crucified Christ next to the one on the wall. "Do you see anything in this? Bring that light over here and shine it on this one." She indicated the copy in her hand. "Can you see anything?" The image was empty.

*　*　*

Every aspect of that evening in the little boy's room—our physical closeness throughout, first in my friend's automobile, then on the sofa in the couple's home, and finally in the boy's room; the currents of conflicting and ambivalent moods, needs, disappointments, and expectations that were moving through us and that we were entering; the fluidity of the images in the frame and their intricate entanglements with the circles of significant others, real and imaginary, actual and desired, that each of us brought into the little boy's bedroom that night; the excess of devotional materiality in the room that had the effect of multiplying the faces that we were looking at and that were looking back at us; the couple's emotional warmth and mostly silent supportive presence and accompaniment; the smell of coffee in the kitchen later in the evening and the sound of the television throughout—contributed to my experience then and informs how I have thought about it since.

There is no question, for example, that our physical hyper-closeness to each other in the boy's room, the fact that we were literally climbing over one another the whole time we were in the tight space, and the constant commentary among us, from the somber to the ribald, contributed to what we experienced together. We had become a single organism of mutually activated and influencing sensations. The root of whatever theories may be developed about this shrine and others described in this book is the sheer physicality of such sites and of what takes place there. How does physical intimacy among strangers create shared visions? If it is possible to answer this question in terms of cognitive psychology,

the workings of the human mind, group psychosis, or mutual hyp-
nosis, do any of these begin to account for the emotional density of the
event, the interleaving of memories, desires, hopes, and anxieties that
were carried on the senses that night and in all the years after the little
boy's death?

Throughout this chapter, I have established some of the features of
the social environment within which the heightened visibility of the
dead in late twentieth-century American Catholicism arose. These included the multiple ways of understanding and relating to the dead, in
prayer, ritual, iconography, and so on, that were inherited in Catholic
traditions of devotion, narrative, and visual arts. It also included the persistence into the twentieth century of certain Catholic ways of construing
relations between the living and the dead, along with the profound
social, liturgical, architectural, and theological reorientations of Catholic approaches to death and dying that have the effect of pushing the
dead away. Implicit in these historical contextualizations and descriptions is interpretation. We might want to say the Italian American
working-class woman's vision of her dead son's face in the image of the
crucified Christ was a reaction against the rapid modernization of Catholic death practices and rituals. Or perhaps it was an efflorescence of
the supernatural Catholic underground of the post-Conciliar decades,
born of disappointment with the changes in devotional aesthetics and
practice following the Second Vatican Council. It is impossible to write
these sentences without immediately becoming aware of the flatness and
inadequacy of such explanations.

Such historically apposite interpretations are centered exclusively on
the living, as if the living were the only ones that mattered in this history.
But the dead had their own ideas. The humans in the story, beginning
with the boy's mother, had to struggle to figure out the intentions of
the dead. What did *they* need? This entailed much conversation, intro-
spection, experience, and consultation, all of it over time. These conversations always included the dead. Interpretations grounded in the
empirical evidence of the shrine of the dead boy's face would need to
begin with the fact that the dead took the living by surprise. The dead
forced events. So it seems right from this perspective to include among

the questions that lead to interpretation why the dead chose to make themselves visible in late twentieth-century American Catholicism, what they came to say to the living, what they wanted, why they took a stand at this time, and then in turn what this teaches about life at the juncture of a religious tradition, on the one hand, and changing social circumstances and customs, on the other. The dead, that is, in relationship with the living. The living and dead acted in each other's company and in the presence of the figure of the crucified Christ in the image. It was by means of these intersubjective triads, with all their internal dynamics and possibilities, that the living, the dead, and the crucified Christ together entered the history of late twentieth- and early twenty-first-century American Catholicism.

Looking through the frame in the little boy's room or outward from the glass wall in Audrey's, it is possible to see the dead everywhere in this period of American Catholicism, official and unofficial, most recently in the cults of the dead Popes John XXIII and John Paul II. Migrants from Mexico and Central America brought mortuary devotions with them to the United States, infusing such practices as the Day of the Dead with new potency and visibility in the 1980s and 1990s and capturing the imaginations of Catholics of other cultural inheritances. In the cemetery where my mother is buried in the Bronx, family members tape greeting cards to gravestones on holidays, with warm messages of love and remembrance written inside in the careful script of Catholics. At Christmas, they arrange toys around the stones of long-dead children and on Easter Sunday they set out colored eggs and baskets of chocolate candy that dissolve in the spring sun and rain. Although the little boy's parents did not do anything to publicize the miracle in their home other than face-to-face communications, still thousands came to see the image.

The story of the boy's face in the image of the crucified Christ is another moment in the history of real presences in Catholicism in the United States. It is also an occasion when the intentions of the dead might be glimpsed. The Catholic dead refuse to be permanently separated from the living, as intended by the new Catholic ethos of death and dying, to be relegated to private spaces outside the public view, or to have their needs unrecognized and unacknowledged. The boy wanted to be there in his family's home. The dead of other families who appeared in the frame beside him were eager to console or challenge the living, remind them of their duties, and call them to task for neglecting them. And if what eventually happened to his bedroom is indicative of the boy's intentions, then we can say he wanted his room to be a corridor between the living and the dead, for his family's home to be filled with visitors, and to be upstairs while his parents and their guests were having coffee and cake below.

* * *

"So, what did you see?" the woman asked when we were sitting around the table in their finished basement. Images of the couple's other children hung on the walls around us. The boy's mother was a sensitive and gifted reader of her visitors' moods, especially of any distress they might be feeling. She knew immediately which member of the party needed her assistance. When my friend's girlfriend was finally persuaded to describe the dancing man in the tuxedo, which she did in between loud sobs, the woman leaned over and hugged her. She made soothing and comforting sounds and whispered something in her ear that none of the rest of us heard. Together, we ate the coffee cake ring we'd brought and drank the strong black coffee that the silent husband had brewed for us in an old aluminum percolator pot while we were up in his son's room. "Help yourself," he kept saying, passing his pack of Marlboros around the table. "Go ahead, take one."

The woman embraced each of us at the door and invited us all to come back again. We said we would, but the next time that was free, she said, was in eighteen months.

There were that many visitors to the little room in those days.

Six

THE HAPPINESS
OF HEAVEN

THE playground of my Catholic school in the north Bronx in the early 1960s was a vicious place. It seems silly to say this in light of the much greater horrors of the world, then and since, but the playground was real and immediate to me, and it was dangerous ground. Two children in particular, male cousins from the forbidding neighborhood behind the church, whirled through the playground like demons, before and after school each day, punching and howling, and tearing at other children's clothes and faces.

I watched a circle of boys urinate on a classmate after school one afternoon, a much-tormented boy, whom they had pushed to the asphalt at their feet in the playground. Where were the nuns, who at other times seemed to be everywhere? The boy writhed and screamed under the hot flow, and then pulled himself up, dripping and foul, to make his way home alone through the gridded shadows under the tracks of the elevated train on White Plains Road.

* * *

In the revised 1941 edition of the *Baltimore Catechism,* the compendium of Catholic doctrine in the form of questions and answers that parochial school children in the United States, including those tormenting and being tormented in the Bronx, were made to memorize word for word in the middle years of the twentieth century, the word "heaven" appears for the first time in the fourth question, "What must we do to gain the happiness of heaven?"[1]

* * *

With the other good boys, I mostly accepted the playground's savagery as a normal part of everyday life. But sometimes it became too much for me. Then, if I could get away without being seen—it would have drawn the feral cousins shrieking down on me—I slipped into church through the side door that opened onto the playground. I was an altar boy and so I knew my way around the back hallways and hidden corridors of the church. I crossed the sacristy, where the vestments, chalice, and wine for Mass were stored, crept behind the main altar, past the choir stalls where the friars chanted the morning office, to a side chapel dedicated to Saint Anthony of Padua. The chapel glowed from within with a deep red luminescence, the light from the racks of flickering votive candles burning before the saint. The old women of the neighborhood, and sometimes their husbands and sons, lit the candles, and old women, dressed in black and murmuring over thick prayer books and beads, were mostly the only people I ever saw in the chapel in the middle of the day, when other adults were at work. The place smelled sweetly of incense, candle wax, and the old women's soap.

* * *

The answer is, "To gain the happiness of heaven we must know, love, and serve God in this world."

* * *

The blood pounded in my ears in the chapel's immense silence until I calmed down and my eyes adjusted to the smoky gloom, and then the playground's grip eased on my heart at last. A statue of Saint Anthony, in brown Franciscan robes with the baby Jesus in his arms, stood in the front of the chapel. Behind them was a fresco, darkened and glazed by years of candle smoke and heat, that showed two long lines of men and women making their way toward the open and glowing gates of heaven in the distance up ahead of them. If you stood up close to the wall at either side of the fresco, you would step into the line yourself. The drone of the women's prayers went on and on.

* * *

Question 186 of this edition of the catechism, near the very end of the book, asks, "Who are rewarded in heaven?" The answer is, "Those are rewarded in heaven who die in the state of grace and have been purified in purgatory, if necessary, from all venial sin and debt of temporal punishment; they see God face to face and share forever in His glory and happiness."

* * *

A tall king in a great vermillion cape with ermine piping and a golden crown walked alongside a man in dirty miner's gear. A soldier in a khaki uniform and high-laced brown boots, with a flat World War I helmet tucked under his arm (a detail that completely captured my boyhood imagination), was illuminated by the light pouring out of heaven. Children skipped along holding hands. There were costumes from different periods of history and different parts of the world, and I vaguely remember a slender woman in a slinky, clinging dress. (Is this possible? The mural was covered over in thick coats of glossy yellow paint sometime after the Second Vatican Council, so it is impossible now to check this halting memory. Maybe she was a Roman martyr—perhaps Saint Perpetua or Saint Felicity—or maybe she is a figment of my early adolescent fantasy, or maybe she was all of this.) A fellow in a sharp gray suit and fedora strode along confidently on the road to heaven. I thought he looked like Bud Abbott of the old Hollywood comedy duo Abbott and Costello.

*   *   *

The work that heaven does in culture seems as clear as the work that death does, if for the opposite reasons. Heaven grounds the realness of the otherwise contingent worlds that we humans make for ourselves in the face of the nothingness, chaos, and oblivion that are facts of creaturely existence and the results of the actions and plans of men and women. Our short lives acquire not only purpose but also grandeur and drama when they are set against the horizon of sacred history, the story that goes from the origins of the world to its end. Heaven absorbs the handful of our years into its infinity. The time of societies is likewise short, and, in the shadow of transience, all creations of human communities, their laws, hierarchies, and institutions, are weak and vulnerable. But with heaven's sanction these fragile entities—the rightness of a nation's choices, what is permitted sexually and what is not, the guarantee of truth in a court of law, and a ruler's authority—take on solidity and meaning. The idea of heaven masks the human origins of meanings. The anticipation of heaven's reward gives weight and inevitability to moral decisions—Why shouldn't I do this? Why should I do that?—that they otherwise lack. "Heaven is my witness," people say when they want to be trusted. Those who deny the sacred order are cast out as evil. They are seen as making a pact with the forces of disorder and destruction. Against them the most monstrous things have been done, in heaven's name. The sweet by-and-by, when all be united, there will be no more pain, and all will see the face of God, has been called on not only to compensate for endless suffering and injustice on earth, but to sanctify them. Those who assent to the sacred order are rewarded in heaven. Heaven is the dullest and most obvious of religious imaginings.[2]

*   *   *

In a special, illustrated edition of the *Baltimore Catechism* published in the United States in 1944, there is a set of "study exercises" after the first seven catechetical questions that includes the following: "5. The happiness of heaven continues f_____. 6. To gain the happiness of heaven we must s_____ God. 7. To gain the happiness of heaven we must k___ God. 8. To gain the happiness of heaven we must l_____ God." Further on there is a game. *"Put a ring around the names of the boys and girls who serve God by doing what they know will please Him."* Among the choices for children to think about are: "3. Michael is lazy and always late for Sunday Mass. . . . 5. John does not play in the busy street. 6. William is good to the poor. . . . 9. Gertrude cheats when playing games." In this way, heaven is brought close to everyday activities on earth and becomes less dull; or perhaps, brought close to everyday activities, heaven becomes even duller.³

*   *   *

During fieldwork in rural Nebraska in 2001, I asked a group of men in their forties and fifties how they had understood heaven as children. All were graduates of Catholic elementary school and in most cases Catholic high school as well. "I thought that it would be like a time machine, basically," one of the men said, "where you could get there and you could go back and see what the old West was like, or back in your own time, or you could go way ahead and check everything out. All of this stuff you wanted to see and investigate, that you wanted to know what it was like . . . just see all the things that you, you know, wondered about." Another man in the group added, "I had the idea also that all of those things would be revealed, all the questions I had. And I—I think I got that from some of my teachers, but also my mom, because I had questions and asked her, [and she answered] 'Well, that's one of the mysteries that you will never know until we die.'"

"I loved reading history," another man in the conversation added, "and I loved reading the lives of the saints, and so I was looking forward to meeting some of the men I had read about, like meeting Abraham Lincoln and George Washington and meeting Saint Patrick and seeing the angels." Heaven was a place, the men agreed, where people would be reunited with their dead friends and relatives, even those they had never met, the grandparents or siblings who had died before these men were born. "I remember when I was really young," one of the men said, "I lost a friend and my parents explained to me that someday" he would see his friend in heaven. "Nothing but the good times," he went on. "We'd be riding Shetland [ponies] together."

* * *

Before my mother had begun dying of colon cancer, before we even knew she was sick, my father retired from his work as a machinist and began volunteering at a Catholic cancer hospice in the north Bronx named after the hill on which Jesus was crucified. His task there was to bring the dying residents whatever small treats they wanted during the day: chocolates, milkshakes, cigarettes, and newspapers. In the time they were in the hospice, which could be a couple of days or several weeks, many of them got to know my father well. They liked him. He chatted in Italian with the people from the old neighborhood. "You never know who's going to show up there!" my father exclaimed to me once. One man who had been a chef explained to my father how to cook a real *marinara* sauce. "No onions!" The old man was insistent that my father understood this and accepted it. "*Never* onions in a marinara sauce!" People wanted my father to meet their children and grandchildren when they came to visit. They told him about the lives they had lived, very short lives for some, twenty or thirty years, or less in some cases. My father complimented the women on how good they looked. Many people waited for the days he was on duty there before they let go and died. My father figures that in the years he spent at the hospice, he met several hundred people who died, some of them holding his hand. He anticipates they will all be there to greet him in heaven when his time comes. When my mother became sick, my father left the hospice to take care of her.

* * *

The man who imagined riding Shetland ponies in heaven with his friends had a sister named Margaret Mary who died in her early twenties of leukemia, when he was just eleven years old. "My sister went directly to heaven," he told me. "I mean, I couldn't see she ever did anything wrong." Margaret Mary was the oldest of eighteen children, much loved by her siblings and parents, who simply could not accept the fact of their daughter's and sister's death. They denied the reality and severity of her illness until the very end. Soon after Margaret Mary's death, her mother began telling the other children that one day the Church was going to recognize their oldest sister as a saint. She stored Margaret Mary's things in the attic to have them ready for use as relics after her daughter's canonization. "So I felt she went to heaven," Margaret Mary's youngest brother continued, "and I felt if she's in heaven that I can talk to her and that I can ask her for help."

* * *

"Do me the kindness to come here everyday for a fortnight," the apparitional figure at Lourdes asked the young Bernadette, who was kneeling before her, and then she said, "On my part, I promise to make you happy, not in this world, but the next." I take this translation of Bernadette's Lady in White from a "playlet" for Catholic children by Sister Mary of Grace, CDP, published in the *Catholic School Journal* in December 1934.[4]

* * *

The stoma in my mother's side was raw and open; "meaty" is how my father described it, "like an organ." "Aren't you happy," my mother asked him in the hospital when she came out of anesthesia, "that I don't have the tumor anymore?" My father did not have the heart at that moment to tell her that the tumor was inoperable and that the doctor had had to do an emergency colostomy. When the doctor finally did tell her, my mother shrugged her shoulders and said, "Well, what are you going to do?" Every day my father cut a little patch of cloth to fit over the opening, dressed the stoma, and attached a new bag to his wife's side. He assured her there was no smell; she fretted about this constantly. "You lose all dignity," my mother told him once while he was cleaning her, but my father says it never bothered him to do this. Every night she took out her teeth and gave them to my father to clean. "Your mother was spunky right to the end," my father says. She chased him out of the bathroom so he wouldn't see her taking her teeth out.

* * *

"I remember very vividly the Q and A from the *Baltimore Catechism*," a woman named Marlene told me. She had grown up in the 1960s in a Colorado town "where we had a lot of army bases," she said. "'Is there salvation outside the church?'" Answer: "'No, there's no salvation outside the church.' And I thought, 'Okay, that takes care of my mom.'" Her mother was Protestant. Marlene married a Catholic man and raised her children in the church. When her oldest daughter, a talented and popular athlete, died suddenly and unexpectedly in her early twenties from an undiagnosed heart condition, Marlene said, "Our faith was definitely the rock of our lives." Some years ago, she and her husband chose to live in an intentional community in Phoenix, with other Catholic families gathered around a Catholic parish, with a pastor sympathetic to them.

Recalling the time after their daughter died, Marlene's husband said, "We endure. It's something we endure and . . . as we go through life together . . . indeed there is this wonderful mystery of us all being, all eventually being [called] to great sacrifice and our own life is not our own. Ultimately, everything we think we have, and have been given, is going to be given back again." In the autumn, when she was a child in Colorado, Marlene helped her father rake the leaves in the backyard, "and we were burning them . . . and I remember watching the flame, that fire, and thinking of hell." Marlene had been baptized Catholic, like her father, and, as Catholic authorities required before permitting a marriage between a Catholic and a non-Catholic, she was being raised Catholic. Looking into the flames, Marlene thought "especially about my mom," who was going to hell because she was not Catholic. Marlene no longer believes this, but she says it took her many years not to imagine her mother in eternal flames, a fate her mother would have avoided if only Marlene had been able to convert her to Catholicism, which she was not.

*　*　*

My mother stopped eating in her last month of life. My father sat next to her bed, begging her to take a spoonful of ice cream or applesauce. I tell him he was very brave during that time, and he answers me, "How was I brave? She was the one who was brave." Then she lost the strength to make it the short distance from her hospital bed in the living room to the bathroom. One night she fell under the bathroom sink. No longer as strong as he was when he worked in the factory, my father knelt beside her, unable to lift his wife from the floor. "Help me," he said to her. "Help me lift you." The two of them struggled until she was upright and he could maneuver her into the old beach chair my father used to push my mother around the apartment's linoleum floors. She did not want to sit in a wheelchair.

*　*　*

"And he who was sitting on the throne said, 'Behold, I make all things new!' And he said, 'Write, for these words are trustworthy and true'" (Rev. 21:5). Catholic theologian Romano Guardini, reflecting on Saint John's vision of heaven, understands it as the awakening to "the full maturity of love." All creation is included in this love. "The huge heart of the God-man, which once lived in terrible solitude, 'abandoned' by all, even by the Father, will triumphantly enfold all things that will exist in it, manifesting its radiance everywhere. Everything will become luminous."[5]

*　*　*

"We used to sit there at night and talk," my father told me one afternoon, two years after my mother's death, when he and I were alone together in their apartment. My parent's marriage was tumultuous, although I am probably the least capable of judging it because I experienced it all as a child. Their arguments were terrifying to me. They fought often, bitterly, for reasons they could name and for others that were buried deep in their histories, in their parents' and grandparents' lives, and in the hidden injuries of class in the United States. Sometimes neighbors called the police. These huge men with guns and ballpoint pens and notepads in hard leather pouches creaking on their wide hips sat in the kitchen with my parents, drinking coffee in the sudden and shocking calm that had descended following their arrival. But at the end of my mother's life, my parents found themselves at peace. This did not have to do with the certain promise of heaven. My mother asked my father one day, "Do you think it's all true? Is there anything to it?" Is what true? I asked him. "Heaven," he said. "Is there really a life after death?" Did she doubt this? "You have to wonder," my father said. "I don't know. Who really knows?"

* * *

"And I heard a loud voice from the throne saying, 'Behold, the dwelling of God with men, and he will dwell with them. And they will be his people, and God himself will be with them as their God. And God will wipe every tear from their eyes. And death shall be no more; neither shall there be mourning, nor crying, nor pain any more, for the former things have passed away" (Rev. 21:3–4).

* * *

I wonder about my mother's doubt, trying to align it with the history of Catholicism in this period and to think of how it speaks to religious history and theory. Was this evidence of the dissolution of Catholic certainty in the late modern world, after the changes in Catholic theology and ritual following the Second Vatican Council? While the men and women who traveled through the supernatural underground of the post-

Conciliar church began to see visions in these years, there seemed to be no visions for my mother in her last days. Was this a function of her times?

My mother fits a certain common profile of change in American Catholic history. She was born on New York's Lower East Side, lived most of her life in the Italian north Bronx, but she died in a more prosperous working-class suburb populated by others who had left the old neighborhood, as she had done, in the 1980s and 1990s. "Left" is not quite right. My mother had been displaced from two old neighborhoods, first from Lower Manhattan by the construction of Stuyvesant Town, and then from the Bronx when drugs and violence had finally completely taken over their neighborhood. "They would offer me crack on the sidewalk," my father remembers of this Bronx neighborhood. "They stood in front of the old Jewish school and asked me if I wanted crack." She worked as a secretary for the Jesuits at Fordham University, where in the 1960s she got caught up in the excitement of the church's liturgical and social transformations. My mother used to say that half the nuns and priests at Fordham who left religious life to marry each other had met in our living room over macaroni and red wine. She became a Eucharistic minister for the Fordham University church. Anthropologist Ellen Badone, who has studied the attitudes of contemporary Catholics in Brittany toward the afterlife, found that since Vatican II, heaven has faded in its vividness and urgency. One man told Badone, "Now there aren't any more fires in hell. They've installed central heating! The road to heaven used to be rocky and difficult. Now it has been paved and they're going to take us there by car."[6]

Others in the contemporary world do not have such doubts as my mother's. I mean those who call down the wrath of their gods on people they condemn and who know with absolute conviction that heaven is for them and for those who think like them. "Heaven" in the mouths of these men and women comes closer to the word's dullest and most predictable meanings, the horizon of certainty that lifts human prejudice, meanness, and power to the authority of the sacred. My mother was never very political, so her notions of the afterlife lacked the borrowed assurance of political rage and social hate. Still, there may be a religious historical context for my parents' late-night conversations about what might come after death.

But I've also wondered, thinking about the two of them holding hands in the room that had become my mother's hospice and would soon be the room in which she died, whether there is something in the constitution of human life, consciousness, and culture that draws humans to doubt something the more real it is to them. What is not doubted is never known as really real. Who cares about such anodyne realities enough to doubt them? So those who do not doubt, who will not allow themselves to doubt, must look elsewhere for the means to make their worlds real for themselves and others, to destruction, violence, and enmity. But the closer humans move to what is real to them, the more their doubts and uncertainty rise.

Then a time comes when they find themselves asking others to come near, to help them not to resolve but to hold the doubt and uncertainty together with them. "Holding" is used here in Winnicott's sense, the essential support given, without which humans are brought to "a sensation of infinite falling." Holding is a form of "loving," Winnicott says, a way of living together with attentiveness. It creates the possibility for the one so held to engage the tumultuous world, not with absolute confidence, but at all; "to experience anxiety associated with disintegration," but not to be disintegrated by it. But to be held in extreme circumstances is dangerous, especially when the ones holding include powerful supernatural beings; there is profound risk involved. If "we cannot exist without addressing the other and without being addressed by the other," then these times of such profound vulnerability and exposure also threaten both humans and holy figures with nonexistence, with disappearance. However one understands the circumstances in which the Detroit housewife, Lizzie, Natalie, and the others in this book found themselves, it must not be thought that such times were easy, that the way forward was always certain.[7]

These men and women, living and dead, human and supernatural, called upon in urgent times, have appeared throughout this book, among them Bernadette's neighbors, *aquero*, Lizzie's husband, the women gathered around the Detroit housewife, other pilgrims at Chimayo, the Sacred Heart of Jesus, and the quiet husband of the woman who saw her son's face in the image of the crucified Christ. Scholars are also asked to stand in the place of these men and women, as Natalie asked me to do when she came to tell me the story of the mine that fell on her step-father, which may or may not have been the work of the Sacred Heart of Jesus, or as Lizzie did when she asked me to accompany her to the hospital the night of her diagnosis. In this sense, scholarship entails risk, for the person whose world has been entered by the scholar, but for the scholar, too, whose own certainties ought to be on the line in the encounter. It it because of this risk, however, if it is taken, that scholarship also creates possibilities for engagement and relationship.

On the evidence of the questions my mother asked my father late at night, heaven is not, or not always or necessarily, the banal guarantor of human pretension or authority, or the ground of cosmological meaning. Rather, it is the limit of knowing and an invitation to conversation, recognition, and accompaniment at the extremity of life. The great hole that death opens in the world distracts from this simpler fact. But it ought to be clear by now how infrequently real presences are encountered by humans in their solitude; and when they are, it seems that the presences themselves draw the people to whom they come out into company, for better and for worse.

* * *

What is heaven then? Guardini continued. "Interior and exterior will be no more, only the presence of the reality that is love. Love is the permanent state of creation. Identity of interior and exterior: that is heaven."

* * *

People who needed something from Saint Anthony lit the candles that burned in front of the statue. I lit candles there, too, when I was a boy. We wanted some sorrow to pass, or to ask the saint to help with a terror we could no longer bear on our own or with a family crisis that would not end. The banks of candles burning before the saint held the neighborhood's inner history, just as Lydia's twice-signed cards in some inchoate way held hers, and as the photographs on the walls of Chimayo, the children's shoes left at the image of Santo Niño, and the heaps of rosaries held the history of the people who came there. The burning candles made prayers and needs visible in flame. Outside the chapel's windows, the brakes on city buses hissed, the elevated train made the flashing and screeching turn from Webster Avenue to White Plains Avenue, and children in the playground yelled and screamed at each other. In the smoking light of the votive candles, the mural of heaven shimmered and darkened. Revelation ends, Guardini points out, "in the simple intimacy of the name once given God on earth, 'I, Jesus . . . am the root and offspring of David, the bright morning star." The boy on the playground grew up to become, among many other things, an astrologer.

Seven

✳

EVENTS OF

ABUNDANT EVIL

A LL heaven pays attention to the Eucharist," Monica told me. We were talking about her struggle over the years with the incapacitating terror she experienced on those occasions when she was able to bring herself to Mass. "I think the Holy Eucharist more than anywhere else is the meeting of heaven and earth." The entire company of angels is present at Mass, Monica said, with the Blessed Mother and all the saints. Monica is in her early fifties today. After many years of working in nonprofits, she has recently begun devoting more time to counseling survivors of clerical sexual abuse, for whom she has coauthored a manual of spiritual healing. Monica was sexually abused over a period of many years, beginning when she was a small girl, by a ring of pedophile priests living together in the rectory of her home parish in northern New England. "All those who have passed," Monica adds, are at the Eucharist, too, the beloved dead. But for many years Monica stayed away from Mass because she could not bring herself to enter a church. All of heaven and earth, living and dead, persons mundane and supermundane, may come together at the Eucharist, but not Monica, and not other survivors of clerical sexual abuse, not always, or not consistently, often not openly, and not without tremendous effort.

Just as there is a factor of the *more* to religious consciousness and experience, so there is a more to the suffering of men and women who were sexually abused as children or adolescents by priests, a metaphysical excess of psychic and physical pain. For them, the abundant event was an event of abundant evil. The supernatural power and authority of the priest derive from his special role in making God really present on the altar during Mass. Apostolically descended from Christ and the apostles, the priest is a literal and material connection to Jesus the High Priest at the Last Supper, a link in a fully embodied sacerdotal genealogy. By the grace of his ordination, the priest is the *alter Christus,* the other Christ, "configured to Christ ontologically," in the words of former pope Benedict XVI. At the moment of consecration, a popular 1957 children's guide to the Mass explained, "the Priest changes the bread into the Body of Jesus, then he raises the Host for all to adore. . . . The Priest changes the wine into the Precious Blood of Jesus, then he raises it for all to adore." Without "the Priest," there is no Eucharist. Not even the angels may say Mass. Martin Luther and other sixteenth- and seventeenth-century reformers rejected this doctrine of the priesthood as an intolerable arrogation of authority that was properly God's alone and an interposition between humans and the divine. But it is fundamental to the Catholic imaginary and to the material reality of the real presence. It is also what makes the abuse of youngsters by priests and its consequences over time for their lives distinctly Catholic in nature, compared to the abuse of children by sports coaches, for example, or high school teachers, as horrendously evil as these cases are, too. "There is no one" among the victims of clerical sexual abuse, Monica told me, "who was not abused in a Catholic way." No survivor with whom I spoke ever accused God of abusing him or her. But being abused by a priest was to be abused at one degree of separation from God.[1]

* * *

The Eucharist is a thoroughly social event. The modern American parish was the epicenter of local Catholic life and the Eucharist was its major sacramental occasion. Every hour of every day, in the neighborhood, suburb, or small town, the transcendent broke into time in the midst of the gathered Catholic faithful. The mystical body of Christ, and then, later in the century, in the language of Vatican II, the people of God, comprised neighbors, relatives, friends, teachers, enemies, schoolmates, and playground bullies, among others. The miracle of bread and wine become body and blood through the actions of the priest happened everywhere around the world, as Catholic children's periodicals regularly illustrated, from the deepest depths of the ocean to the very top of the highest mountain. It happened under brutal Communist regimes, where heroic priests put their lives at risk to bring Christ really present to the people. The Eucharist was an event at once utterly ordinary and unimaginably extraordinary, local and universal, temporal and eternal.[2]

Weekly attendance was required at the Eucharist under the pain of mortal sin, but the vast majority of American Catholics went to Mass much more often. The adults responsible for children's religious formation, in particular vowed women religious, were passionately committed to the task of endowing children and adolescents with the truth of the real presence, as we have seen. This gave Catholic religious formation an intensely erotic aspect. I mean by this nothing necessarily untoward, but rather a deep psychological and devotional intimacy between adults, who wanted to awaken in their young charges desire for God really present, and children, who desired to please these adults by feeling in their bodies what was expected of them. This devotional eroticism was there in Elsie's collection of holy cards (see Figure 15). Children were afraid of disappointing priests and nuns because they feared them, but also because they loved them. Desire was the aim of this pedagogy and its method. Real presence was the medium of the implication of adults and children in each other's lives and the focusing lens of this desire. It was the violation of the bodies of children and adolescents in this sacred world—bodies that had been or were being deeply formed to the reality of real presence—by privileged agents of the holy that constituted the particular pain and dilemma of the Eucharist among survivors of clerical sexual abuse.[3]

The abuse crisis in modern Catholicism was not caused by the intimacies of this environment, but it arose within them, and predator priests exploited and distorted the pedagogy of presence for their own ends. Children did what priests compelled them to do sexually because

O Sacred Heart of Jesus
inflame my heart with
the love of Thee!

9129 Ⓦ   MADE IN ITALY

FIGURE 15 An announcement in the form of a holy card of a parish retreat to be held in St. Francis, Wisconsin, February 1922. The card, which was printed in Italy, reads, "O Sacred Heart of Jesus, inflame my heart with the love of Thee!" Author's collection.

they were physically overmastered and frightened. They did so also because they were raised to obey priests *unconditionally*. In language common among survivors, one man described his abuser as "a little god." Youngsters knew they must keep their abuse secret. Few of the adults in the parish, very often including their parents, acknowledged that a priest was capable of such evil. Monica says that her mother, who steadfastly denied evidence and discounted rumors of abuse, "actually chose the priest over me," when she rebuffed Monica's attempt to tell her what was happening. Another survivor recalled that his father, who was unaware that a parish priest he admired was regularly masturbating his son, drove the boy to the rectory in the afternoons, delivering him, as this survivor sees it today, to his abuser. Parents allowed priests visiting their homes to tuck their children into bed, despite the adults' suspicions or discomfort and regardless of the stories making the rounds in the parish about these priests. If an abused child's parents recognized what was happening, moreover, and tried to act, they were often met with denial and resistance. If they persisted, they encountered recrimination and retribution, from other priests, teaching sisters, chancery officials, and their neighbors. Some members of a suburban Chicago parish in 2013 sought to "exorcize"—literally, not symbolically or metaphorically—two women who had prayed, during the time set aside at Mass for public petitions, for two girls abused in the parish by a visiting priest. The sexual abuse of children and adolescents was deeply situated within the relational networks that constituted the parish, which were disclosed and sanctified at the Eucharist. The sexual abuse of children betrayed and sundered these bonds, turning them toxic and evil.

The holy proved to be the best hiding place for evil. Predator priests prowled behind the veil of the tabernacle in full view of the congregation. Children and adolescents were abused in the sacristy, where priests and altar boys robed before Mass. They were abused during Mass. One predator priest forced a child to fellate him at the altar. Another priest, a highly regarded, widely read liturgist and theologian in the 1970s and 1980s, assured one of his victims that taking the priest's ejaculate into his mouth was "another way of receiving Holy Communion." Their privileged intimacy with God really present endowed predator priests with a sense of entitlement over the bodies and souls of children and adolescents and contributed to their impunity. Predator priests prayed with children as they were abusing them; they ordered or entreated their victims to pray for them afterward; they promised to pray *for* their victims, as if the children were at fault for what had been done to them. In these ways, predator priests brought God fully into their acts of sexual violence as witness and ally. Victims became confused about God's intentions, especially when an abusive priest told his victims that his sexual violation of them is what God wanted for them.[4]

The horrific proximity of evil to holiness, most publicly on display when a predator priest took God's body in his hands and lifted it up to the congregation that included his victims, provoked in some of the abused the most visceral anger and an unsublimated desire for super- natural retribution, at the time of their abuse or later in their lives. Monica remembered being at a Mass said by one of her abusers and thinking at the elevation of the Host, "You can't keep holding that Eu- charist [up over your head] without losing." She imagined the Host (now the body of Christ) getting heavier and heavier until it had taken on the weight of an immense stone, which the priest was no longer able to hold aloft. Then it fell and crushed him to death. "One day," Monica believed, this priest "would turn a corner in that evil rectory and God was going to—KAPOW!" Today, Monica recognizes these as a help- less child's fantasies. "But that rectory was imbued with the evil of these guys," so she sat at Mass, imagining God taking revenge on all of them, for her. This immense anger was one of the many sequelae of the abuse and one of its most corrosive.

* * *

At different times in their lives, survivors of clerical sexual abuse find it impossible to go to Mass and impossible not to go to Mass. None of the survivors I came to know stopped attending Mass after they were abused. They were youngsters, after all, and neither their families nor the nuns and priests in the parish would have allowed them to absent themselves from this serious obligation. Nor would it have occurred to the youngsters themselves, good Catholics as most of them were, re- spectful of the clergy, and devout and faithful in practice, as predator priests knew them to be. Sexually abused youngsters also went to Mass because they did not want to live in a state of mortal sin, adding more guilt to lives already overburdened by it. But even into adulthood, when they were contending with broken marriages, substance abuse, and psy- chological turmoil, the survivors I know continued going to Mass. They say they did so because their families and friends expected this and because they wanted to give a good example to their children. They also did it because they were struggling to appear normal on the outside, when on the inside they felt utterly abnormal. "I didn't belong in church," recalled Mary Rose, a survivor in her mid-seventies when I first met her, of the time when, as a young wife and mother, she was actively involved in her parish, "and people knew I didn't belong. It's like they knew but didn't know."

These were the long years of "the absence of words," when survivors kept their abuse secret from their spouses and friends. Their abusers had threatened or pleaded with the youngsters to remain silent. This was a secret between them and God, their abusers said. Victims feared it was a mortal sin to say something bad about a priest; they would go to hell if they spread "lies" about a priest. They were ashamed for what had happened and they felt guilty about it, as children who are sexually abused often do, as if they were responsible. Isolated in these ways, they experienced themselves at a remove from the people around them at Mass. After the liturgical reforms of the Second Vatican Council made space for the laity in the celebration of the Mass, survivors became readers, deacons, and Eucharistic ministers. They served on parish councils. They taught their own children how to make the sign of the cross and how to pray, and they prayed with them. But always they remained disassociated from this self who was participating in parish activities, going to Mass, and taking God's body and blood in their hands at Communion.[5]

The Eucharist was not safe for survivors, moreover. If a sacred place is where "men and gods are held to be transparent to each other," as religious theorist Jonathan Z. Smith has proposed, survivors experienced this transparency as a raw and scorching invasiveness. Being abused was like having the skin ripped off her body, Monica says, and at Mass, her "nerves were on fire." Sitting in church as a girl, she imagined all the statues of the saints around her having had their skin ripped off, too. They appeared to her as skeletons. Monica says she was terrified that the people around her in church "could see my sin." A trusted priest abused Cesar, a young man from El Salvador, shortly after he arrived in the United States after a harrowing journey across the southern border. Cesar said that afterward, when he was at Mass, "I [felt] that everyone knew about my situation." It was as if what happened in secret were now projected on a screen inside Cesar's transparent body, visible to everyone. As a result, survivors of clerical sexual abuse felt, in Monica's words, "at the mercy" of the people around them everywhere, but especially in church, at Mass.[6]

They were at the mercy of God, too. While some survivors remember their childhood God as a loving one, more often, Catholics raised before the 1970s say that as young children they were taught an angry and punishing God, who saw and judged all things. Survivors questioned why this omniscient and omnipresent God, from whom no secrets were hidden, was absent when they were being abused. Mary Rose pleaded with this God for an end to the sexual violence inflicted on her by one of God's ordained representatives on earth. The abuse continued for three years and, "by the time it was over," Mary Rose recalls, "I learned that praying didn't help because God didn't hear me." Was this because God wanted her to be abused? "God sent you to me as a gift," Phyllis's abuser told her. She was fourteen when this priest gave her a cup of drugged eggnog at a Christmas party. She woke up later that night naked in his car, with the priest on top of her, sobbing with remorse. A psychological counselor who works in a Church-sponsored program says she has to tell survivors over and over that "God didn't allow this to happen" and that "God was crying with you after it happened." But survivors have trouble accepting such reassurance. As Cesar says, "God is perfect. He knows why he permits things to happen. He has a purpose." But did God's purposes include what the priest did to Cesar?

"I don't know what I feel in God's company," Bernard told me toward the end of one of our conversations. Bernard is a retired engineer, sixty-five years old. A popular priest seduced Bernard into an intense sexual relationship that lasted until the boy became too old for the priest's tastes. Like Monica, who is a close friend of his, Bernard is a leader in a diocesan program for survivors. He knows most of the survivors of clerical sexual abuse in the region of the country where he lives today. In his experience, Bernard says, survivors of clerical sexual abuse generally do not know what to feel about God. "The emotional tie with that priest went sour," he says. "Why wouldn't that spread to God and everyone else?" It becomes hard to trust God again. "You just don't trust the people around you, you don't trust yourself, and you don't trust God." Because the Blessed Mother is less powerful than God, several survivors told me that she cannot be held accountable for what happened, and so they feel closer to her. Among Catholics, as we have seen, the Blessed Mother is petitioned and feared because she is so powerful; but among survivors of clerical sexual abuse, she is recognized as having stood by ineffectively in mute witness of divine complicity in the sexual violence of priests against them. For much of her life, Monica says, she loved Our Lady of Lourdes and faithfully said the rosary, but she was "hurt with God." The judging God of mid-twentieth-century Catholic childhoods might come crashing into a boy or girl's life at any moment, in the form of a fatal or disfiguring accident, the sudden onset of pain, or some other dreadful occurrence. There is ample textual evidence in Catholic children's literature to support such memories of the harsh and retributive character of God.

*   *   *

Some months before she died, Mary Rose arrived at one of the monthly Monday-night meetings of a Chicago-area group of survivors in a highly agitated state. These men and women, all of them over sixty-five years old now, have known each other since the early 1990s, when they belonged to the Chicago-based organization for survivors called "the Linkup" (Survivors of Clergy Abuse Linkup). Mary Rose was visibly ill at ease for an hour or so before she finally spoke up. In the weeks since the last meeting, she said, one of her grandchildren had become perilously ill, and Mary Rose *found herself* calling on God, she told us, with great emphasis, in this dire situation. She was horrified by what she saw as her unthinking and spontaneous recourse to prayer. "How could I stoop so low," she cried out aloud in the room, "to ask that God who abandoned me over fifty years ago for help?" The words and gestures of the prayers had come unbidden to her mind and body, without her intention or assent. The others in the room knew from their own experience that the nuns would have done their work well in forming Mary

Rose in the faith. Her relationship with God really present had been pressed deep into her bones and sinews, as it had been in theirs. With awkward motions, Mary Rose pounded the coffee table in front of her in tearful frustration. It was as if there was another Mary Rose, the creation of Catholic religious formation, who dragged the anguished grandmother Mary Rose to her knees in prayer. Over the succeeding weeks, Mary Rose sent the group a torrent of tortured emails, berating herself for having humiliated herself before the God who had been absent for most of her life. At the same time, she asked us to pray to this same God for her granddaughter.[7]

* * *

For survivors to go to Mass risks an excessive and transgressive intimacy with the congregation in the pews around them and with the God who is outside of them and also in their bodies after Communion. Monica's image of skeletons is apposite. For her and for other survivors, the sacred place became a place of terror. They experienced *themselves* as transparent in that place, while others, on heaven and earth, remained opaque, their bones and organs covered and protected by their skin. Because they had kept their abuse secret, their transparency in the sacred place intensified their vulnerability and left them with the sensation that they were simultaneously utterly visible and completely invisible. "God remained stonelike and silent," Monica says. Yet God was really present, too. As Bernard told me, it was not safe to be in God's company. The transcendent breaks into time; the holy is present in matter; Jesus is really present in the consecrated bread and wine; and, for survivors of clerical sexual abuse, the real presence of the sacred in the Eucharist was not awesome but terrifying.

One Sunday, shortly after divorcing her abusive and alcoholic husband, Marie was at Mass when suddenly "everything went black." A priest visiting her family had raped Marie in the churchyard of their rural parish; later that same day, he also raped one of her sisters and a female cousin. All were little girls at the time. Marie had been going to Mass her whole life, but in the days preceding the black Eucharist she had been increasingly fearful that God was angry with her for leaving her violent husband. The "black screen" fell again the following Sunday. Both times, Marie says, "I was so frightened [that] I just sat there and cried and cried and then I walked out." Marie's childhood God had been especially cruel. "God's going to get you," her mother had taunted her, over and over. As a child, Marie imagined God writing down all the bad things she did, "but never any of the good things." When her husband beat her or when their financial circumstances became desperate because of his alcoholism, Marie wanted to turn to God for help, but "I felt I was not worthy of God's attention." Now this God who had been tallying up her sins since childhood appeared to be taking vengeance upon her at last. After the black screen fell the second time, Marie stayed away from church for years. She tried to have her marriage annulled, but the priest overseeing the process said there were "insufficient grounds" for doing so. Marie broke down when she told me this story. "What are [sufficient] grounds?" she asked the priest. "For [my husband] to kill me?"

Marie's black screen marks the limit of experience and vulnerability that she had reached at the Eucharist, in God's real presence. It was the border of the tolerable. She could not go beyond it at this time in her life. Psychologists Jody Messler Davies and Mary Gail Frawley, who work extensively with victims of sexual abuse, say that these men and women are hyperalert to any aspect of their environments that may trigger the disassociated experience of the self as radically other that is one of the enduring consequences of childhood sexual abuse. The boundaries of survivors' subjectivities are fragile, Davies and Frawley write, and there is "always the hypervigilance that controls access to the interior." As a result, survivors of sexual abuse have trouble "playing," a word Davies and Frawley use in the Winnicottian sense as the "intermediate area of *experiencing*" (in Winnicott's words) that exists in between "the inner reality of the individual and the shared reality of the world that is external to individuals." Moving between the "subjective and that which is objectively perceived" is a source of human creativity, Winnicott says, but it is also "liable to become frightening." There is a precariousness to play. New ways of experiencing and moving the body may be tried in play. The boundaries of self and other are explored, transgressed, and reestablished. There is the prospect of absorptive solitude in play without fear of impingement. Unfamiliar sensations and novel possibilities for life and relationship arise. "On the basis of playing," Winnicott says, "is built the whole of man's existential existence."[8]

The encounter of humans with supermundane beings really present, at shrines, in visions and apparitions, in the sacraments, and in devotional practice creates such an intermediate area. Nearly everyone who has made an appearance in the preceding pages of this book—Lizzie, Natalie, the Detroit housewife, Elsie H., the dead boy's mother and the visitors that made their way to her home, my mother at the end of her life and my father caring for her—was at play in his or her world in this sense. But for survivors of clerical sexual abuse, play stopped at the black screen, even if it had been possible before. Marie's experience appears to be the opposite of the abundant event. The descent of the black screen locks the environment that the abundant event unlocks. Sacred space— the space between themselves and God, the space that is at once inside, outside, and at the border—becomes for survivors not a place of creation but a place of truncation.

As was the case with Lizzie, the Detroit housewife, and Natalie, survivors were seen but not recognized. However, in the case of survivors, the lack of recognition they experienced was *in church, before God*. They carried the abuse in their bodies and in their memories, where they also carried their experience of God, the Virgin Mary, the angels, and the saints. But they told no one about the abuse, not even their spouses. They spoke of everything but this. They led double lives at home and in their parishes and had trouble recognizing themselves, especially in church, among the people in the pews around them and before the eyes of the sacred. It was as if, in the experience of survivors of clerical sexual abuse, a crack widened along the floor of the nave and made its way through survivors' bodies and psyches, then up through the center of the altar, beneath the holy ground on which the priest stood with the Host elevated above his head. It was hard enough for survivors not to fall into the widening abyss. But the abyss was always there. Any gesture by the priest on the altar, any image or devotional object, a candle's flame or the sound of a bell, the scent of wax and incense, even a movement caught out of the corner of their eyes, might erase the distance between now and then, here and there, and render the trauma present again. So a time came when each survivor I spoke with found it increasingly painful and intolerable to go to church.

There were many reasons for this breach, among them anger at God or other Catholics, or a direct encounter with what seemed to survivors as the church's hypocrisy for judging them sinful while it promoted and protected predatory priests, or their own invincible shame, or disgust with priests generally. Monica stopped going to Mass when she moved in with her boyfriend after college. "How can that church tell me not to sleep with this man, [a way of living] which is normal," she recalls asking herself back then, "when all those abnormal priests [have] already slept with me?" (Monica observed here in our conversation that phrases like "sleeping with" remained her language for the abuse, in what she now sees as her naïveté.) Several survivors I have spoken with described being at Mass one day and suddenly thinking, "What am I doing here?" Some survivors tried going to other churches, but they found that their alienation and anger extended to these faiths as well.

What I have learned, however, in my conversations with survivors is that even after they had decided to stop going to Mass, they remained deeply attached to the Eucharist on some level of their being. Survivors were well aware of the hold of their fully embodied childhood faith on them, as Mary Rose's story indicates. But they also spoke of a deep sense of loss *as adults* when they stopped going to Mass. "If I can't believe that God is really present on the altar in the consecrated host," Bernard argued with himself at the times when his alienation from and anger toward the diocesan hierarchy were at their most intense, "then I have nothing." Some survivors seemed taken aback by their enduring attachment to the Eucharist. A seventy-three-year-old survivor in a Southern city, Jim told me that as a child he was frightened to serve Mass when his abuser celebrated, because he knew that on these mornings the priest was likely to corner him in the sacristy "and fondle me." Then Jim would be forced to watch when this priest "would give mother and daddy Communion with the same hands." Still, Jim told me, "I *loved* the Eucharist."

For the past twenty years or so, Jim has not gone to Mass, except for family weddings and funerals, but he insisted, "I *still* love the Eucharist." Phyllis described her return to Mass after being away for several years as a hunger in her body. "I felt a need for the Eucharist," she told me, "so I just went back."

This all looks like the compulsion of victims of sexual abuse to remain fixated on the site of their abuse and to put themselves in proximity to their abusers. All the survivors I have come to know have been in psychotherapy at one time or another in their lives; they are well aware of this interpretation of their behavior and they recognize in it something of their attachment to the Eucharist. They do not discount it altogether. But they finally find such accounts unconvincing or incomplete. There is nothing simple or unambiguous about survivors' attachment to the Mass, and Phyllis's stark statement, "I just went back," masks the intensity and duration of survivors' struggles with the Eucharist. They approached the Eucharist with ambivalence and anger, but also with desire and need. The Eucharist had always been there, they knew, wherever they were in their lives, and the Eucharist would always be there if they wanted it, as they knew. Throughout her younger life, Monica said, when she was furious with the church, she "didn't question the Eucharist." I heard this from many survivors: what held them close to the church or drew them back, sometimes despite their conscious intentions or desires, was this attachment to the real presence in the sacrament of the Eucharist.

*　*　*

This connection was evident in a comment made to me by Anna, a child psychologist today, who told me she wants nothing more to do with the church. "I don't have much spirituality," she said. "I can't make myself believe in what I see as the smoke and mirrors of Catholicism." A priest who was a friend of her father's abused Anna when she was a young teenager. Anna and I happened to be talking just after Pope Benedict XVI announced his resignation, when the world's media appeared to be riveted by the drama unfolding in the Vatican. But in Anna's view, Benedict's departure was "not going to make much difference in the long run," because the Church, she said, is too effective at keeping people "close," meaning too effective at forming Catholics who would be compliant and silent. Some survivors refer to Catholics who are oblivious to the reality and implications of the clergy sex abuse crisis as "the sheeple of God."

In the early 1990s, Anna made the difficult decision to come forward with the story of her abuse to officials in the diocese where it had taken place, as many survivors were doing at the time. Anna's diocese responded with an organized campaign of legal and psychological harassment. "They went after every record in my life," she said, including medical records. Under oath, she told the diocese's lawyers that she had never had a survivor of clerical sexual abuse as a client in her therapeutic practice, which unintentionally opened "a door for them to go through." She said the lawyers threatened to subpoena "client files of everyone I had ever worked with." Fearful that the diocese would publicly disclose her story, Anna eventually dropped any reference in the lawsuit to the potential effects of the abuse on her professional career, because "I didn't know how people would react, knowing I had a sex abuse history." I asked Anna what she had hoped for in coming forward. "To get the church to pay attention and not to move guys around and to take some sense of responsibility." Yet when she talks about turning away from the Eucharist, Anna's language becomes more tentative. "I don't know if there's a God," she told me on one occasion. She has stopped going to Mass, but she says this "is like watching the Technicolor go out of something." The world "fades all to gray."

Without mentioning her by name, I asked Frank, a priest who was abused by priests first as an altar boy and then again as a seminarian, what spiritual advice he might give to Anna. The essential thing, Frank said, is "understanding that God had nothing to do with this," meaning nothing to do with the abuse. "You can't have a relationship with God," Frank continued, "and not be vulnerable." But while survivors would benefit from a restored relationship with God, they are the people least able to accept God's help. This is because they are so terrified of entering into relationship with God again. "All relationships have their vulnerabilities," Frank said, perhaps especially the relationship between the God of early and mid-twentieth-century American Catholicism and survivors who had encountered this God as children. Survivors do not want to feel exposed and at risk, Frank says. This is the excess of the pain of clerical sexual abuse, its factor of the more; borrowing Sister Patricia's phrase from Chapter 4, it is the "bathed in blood" quality of clerical sexual abuse. In Frank's words, "It robs you of your relationship with God." To be able to affirm that "God had nothing to do with this" was to take a step toward opening the possibility of a relationship with God again.

* * *

What does "God had nothing to do with this" mean? This is the classic affirmation of Christian theodicy: God endows humans with free will, but God is not responsible for the evil they do with it. But Frank framed this not as a theological proposition, or cosmological reassurance, or the "therefore" to a rational argument about the infinite goodness of God and the logical impossibility of this good God doing bad things. Rather, Frank framed "God had nothing to do with this" relationally and pragmatically. The statement is meant to redirect survivors toward questions of intersubjectivity, of the self in relation to others, including God. The violence of the abuse affects all relationships, as Frank well knows, so he seems to intend "God had nothing to do with this" as a move outward, toward a restored capacity for intimacy, with God and others. What does "God had nothing to do with this" mean in this broad, intersubjective sense?

On one reading, it says that the abuse was not God's plan for a particular survivor. To have been sexually abused by a ring of evil priests was *not* Monica's destiny; being abused by a priest is *not* what Phyllis was created for, whatever her abuser told her. Nor was the abuse Monica's or Phyllis's responsibility. Survivors were working through these issues in therapy, as I have said. But because the men and women who came to know themselves as "survivors" were abused in sacred spaces by men who were "like a God" to them, extricating themselves from the gnawing sense of guilt and culpability that the abuse engendered was a matter as much between heaven and earth as it was between people on earth. Rejecting any notion that they were born with an evil destiny freed survivors from the dreadful sense of exposure they experienced most exigently in church, but elsewhere in their lives as well. It restored the skin to their skeletons.

On another reading, "God had nothing to do with it" means that the event of the abuse was without meaning. Almost all of the survivors I have spoken to say that the abuse made them stronger people or endowed them with a greater capacity for love. This seems to imply purpose. But viewing such claims through the lens of Frank's comment, which is how I think survivors would want them viewed, disconnects them from any notion of divine causality or intention. Saying or hoping that good came out of evil, Frank tells the survivors he counsels, does not imply that God therefore sent the abuse as a challenge or opportunity. If anything besides pain and suffering comes out of the abuse, it is what survivors do with what was done to them. On the other side of guilt and fate, both of which offer meaning and control of sorts, survivors come face to face with the inevitable fact of their vulnerability in a world not governed by God or fate. This heightens their sense of intersubjective danger, Frank says, and makes them fearful of intimacy, but from this comes the possibility of freedom in their relationships, with God and others.

To be able to say, "God had nothing to do with this," finally, is also to recognize that God did nothing. Frank's suffering frames his theology. When he discovered that priests had abused thousands of other children and adolescents besides him, in the United States and elsewhere in the Catholic world, "that's when I had trouble with God." How did God let this happen? Then, when he refused his bishop's admonitions to silence, Frank was ostracized in his own diocese. This added to his anger. "Where are you in all this?" Frank recalls asking God. "That's the spiritual struggle," he explained to me, this question of where God is in the contemporary campaign against child abuse in Catholicism, which seems to ebb and flow with the unpredictability of public attention and the interest of the news media. God watches, seemingly unmoved and disengaged, as bishops protect the retirement pensions of pedophiles, while Frank has lost his home, parish, and regular income. He is prohibited from functioning as a priest, while priests accused but not convicted of sexual abuse remain at the altar. But Frank continues to bring himself into God's presence in prayer.

Frank told me a story about a Catholic woman he met in the hospital when he was a parish priest. She needed a heart transplant and she was praying that God would send her a heart. She fearfully confessed to Frank, "I don't want God to be mad at me," so she was being careful to pray in such a way as not to give God offense. But Frank said to her, "You're sitting here waiting for a heart! What more can God do to you?" He encouraged her to be transparent to God in prayer, which meant, as Frank put it, "praying angry." "Read the Psalms!" Frank says. "How angry are they? They're some of the angriest prayers we have." The Psalms are also, Frank added, some of the most beautiful and loving prayers. The Psalms display the full range of emotions that characterize the human relationship with God, in all its moods and troubles. "The spiritual journey," Frank says, "is all about people who have problems with God." This is another way of saying that religion as it is lived is all about people who have problems with God.

* * *

For years, prelates and diocesan administrators moved predator priests surreptitiously from one diocese to another, keeping their crimes secret and putting more and more children in harm's way. Law enforcement agents, district attorneys, and journalists, many of them Catholic, colluded in protecting local parishes and dioceses from scandal. Cowed by the ontological stature of the priest, anxious not to give scandal to the church, victims kept their abuse secret. They did not even have a language, many survivors said of these years before they spoke out, to name what had been done to them. How do you speak publicly about the unthinkable, unsayable thing the *alter Christus* did to you in private? But the victims of clerical sexual abuse lived in times of tremendous change within Catholicism in the United States and around the world.[9]

Two historical developments in particular were profoundly consequential for adults who had been abused as children by priests. The first was the transformations in Catholic theology, worship, and ecclesiology, slowly implemented in the 1970s and 1980s, following the Second Vatican Council. The second was the public disclosures in the national media of clerical sexual abuse in the United States, beginning with Father Gilbert Gauthe in Louisiana in 1983, then emerging with renewed intensity a decade later with Father James R. Porter in Massachusetts in 1992. These revelations made clear the extent of the crisis in Catholicism and spurred the creation of a national movement of survivors of clerical sexual abuse. The two shifts, in lived Catholicism and in the status of survivors, coincided.[10]

"I think that was the turning point," Bernard said about the years after the council, "when the pedestal that the priest was on began to crumble." "The priest is just another schlub among the schlubs," is how Frank puts the revelation that followed public disclosures of clerical sexual abuse. Theologically, Bernard says, the Church awoke to the fact "that there are people out there in the pews!" In the council's ecclesiology, the church was "the people of God," a "community," in Bernard's rendition of it, not a hierarchical structure with laity at the bottom and the ordained clergy at the top. The specific language Bernard used to characterize the transformations of the Church by Vatican II—secrecy / disclosure, hiddenness / transparency—is especially resonant among survivors. That these words describe both the imperatives of conciliar reform and the existential dilemma of survivors in the years without speech underscores Bernard's idea that the implementation of the council's agenda was the turning point in his and other survivors' personal lives. With the mandated changes to the Eucharist, the priest's actions on the altar were no longer "hidden or secret"—still quoting Bernard—and "the theology of the mass had become more visible and transparent." An inadvertent, if not unforeseen, consequence of this reorientation of the liturgy was the decline in the status of the priest, who in the view of the laity and the priests themselves went from being "like a god" to a figure closer to the human than the divine, if not fully humanized, even though enough of the aura of their special ordained vocation clung to priests to facilitate decades more of abusing children and adolescents.[11]

Transitioning from Latin as the church's sacred language to local vernaculars; rearranging church interiors, including repositioning the altar to face congregants and the elimination of the Communion rail that separated the altar from the pews; taking the Host in the hand rather than having it placed by the priest on the outstretched tongue; and offering the cup of consecrated wine to the laity for the first time since the early Middle Ages—the purpose of these transformations in the manner of celebrating the Eucharist was to achieve "the full and active participation by all the people" in the Mass. Even with all these changes, however, the full renewal of the liturgy remained incomplete. "Further substantial or radical adaptations" were on the horizon, the widely syndicated liturgical writer Father Joseph Champlin promised in 1977 "as the particular needs of the people demand them." The horizon of worship had been opened, seemingly to infinity.[12]

The renewal of the Eucharist, which theologian and historian Massimo Faggioli designates as the central transformative action of the council, either initiated a season of searching and experimentation in prayer and worship throughout the seventies and eighties that generated new ways of being in relationship to God, the Blessed Mother, and the saints, or it reinvigorated older ones. The vision of the dead boy in the image of the crucified Christ was one instance of such post-Conciliar religious creativity within the Catholic traditions, as was the multiplication of visionaries and healers on the margins of Catholic orthodoxy in this period. A more loving and compassionate God replaced the retributive and judgmental God of pre-Conciliar Catholicism. "Love was the yardstick you measured everything against," Anna recalled of this changed theological environment, which she encountered in Catholic high school and college. "If it wasn't loving, it wasn't God." The whole idea of the time, Phyllis told me, "was to develop a personal relationship with God."[13]

It is not necessary to draw the before / after distinction in any absolute sense to see that however partial the implementation of the council's agenda was in different dioceses and parishes in the United

States, reflecting the frequent tension between the local and the universal in Catholicism, and however much particular bishops and priests endorsed or impeded renewal, a profound reorientation had occurred in the Church's everyday theology, psychology, and practice. There was a real shift in the tectonics of power between clergy and laity within the church and between church and society. "A sense of religious self-confidence," historian James O'Toole writes of these years, "opened the possibility that lay people might not follow the church's lead if such a course made no sense to them." This included lay parish leaders, who refused to remain silent about the behavior of predator priests, and Catholic journalists, law enforcement agents, and district attorneys who would not violate the ethics of their professions to protect and shield these priests. Instead, these new Catholic professionals clearly judged the actions of predator priests as criminal; they investigated them, made the crimes public, and prosecuted them.[14]

*   *   *

One morning shortly after the story of Father Porter broke in the national media, Frank, who was a parish priest at the time, found himself with a free hour after a woman called to cancel her scheduled appointment with him. He decided to watch some daytime television, which, he emphasized when he told me this story, he almost never did. Channel surfing around the networks on the big-screen television upstairs in the rectory's lounge, Frank came upon a Geraldo Rivera special on victims of clerical sexual abuse. That was it. Frank says he was stunned to realize in that instant that this is what *he* was, a victim of clerical sexual abuse, and that he was not the only one, as he had long thought he was. "If I didn't find out that others had been abused," Frank told me, "I might have just been content," by which he meant that he would have gone on numbly with his inwardly deeply troubled, externally competent life, thinking there was something irreparably wrong with him as a human being. Contact information for SNAP (Survivors Network of those Abused by Priests) scrolled along the bottom of the screen. Frank called the number shown and was invited to an upcoming SNAP event.

It was on his way there, Frank says, that "it occurred to me that here I was a priest about to walk into a room of people who were abused by priests." He pushed on to the meeting. The rest, as Frank says, is history, meaning the convergence of his personal, secret history with the increasingly public history of the survivors coming together in organizations such as SNAP and Linkup.[15]

I have heard nearly identical stories from many survivors. Bernard was riding in the car with his wife when they chanced upon an NPR report on clergy abuse in Chicago. He pulled over to the side of the road and began sobbing. "The light bulb went on," he says. Bernard had been married twenty-two years but he had never said anything to his wife about the abuse. Around the same time, Phyllis's sister asked her one night in a telephone conversation why she had married her first husband despite the fact that no one in the family thought he was a good man. Phyllis replied that she was drawn to him because he looked like Father Martin (the priest who abused her). Having gone this far, Phyllis went ahead and told her sister the whole story of the abuse. Her sister had just heard a news report about SNAP, and she mentioned it to Phyllis, who had never heard of the organization before. Phyllis says her first response was, "Hooray, there's a whole group of people like me."

For Frank, Phyllis, and many others, becoming a survivor was a process of recognition. They recognized themselves in the stories others were telling, just as others recognized themselves in theirs. This path was not completely individual, nor was it fully charted by the survivor movement, neither internal nor public. Survivors had been struggling, more or less consciously, more or less successfully, with the consequences of the abuse, trying as they did so to understand the shape their lives were taking. But as they tell this story, they could not have finished this process without discovering each other. Frank recalls of that first meeting, "We were all devastated hearing each other's stories." Mutual recognition is at the heart of the survivors' movement. "You're just not alone anymore," Frank remembers thinking, "you're not crazy." It was uncanny that weekend, Frank said, how people's stories resonated with one another. "We would just about complete each other's sentences even though we had just met." Frank joined Linkup. He found that organization's emphasis on pastoral care and spiritual recovery more compatible than SNAP's approach, which emphasizes lawsuits, public pressure on the Church, and organized protest, although, like all survivors I have spoken with, wherever they fall on the spectrum of relationship with the institutional Church, from bitter rejection to full participation, Frank acknowledges the importance of both approaches. He eventually became a trusted figure at the annual Linkup meetings, a spiritual adviser to other victims of clerical sexual abuse into the 1990s, when many more survivors were coming forward with their stories.

For survivors such as Frank, Phyllis, and Monica, the discovery of themselves as victims of clerical sexual abuse and ecclesiastical malfeasance was at the same time the exacerbation of their questions about God's culpability. But it also opened the way for them to find God for themselves. Being in the company of others speaking their stories afforded survivors the recognition they needed to bridge their silent and isolated interiorities with their public and visible personae. In turn, this unfolding process of integration made it possible and even imperative for them to search out a God adequate to the persons they were discovering themselves to be and the persons they were becoming. This was not the God of their childhood inheritance. Survivors' searches for a different God would take place in the changed religious environment of post-Conciliar American Catholicism and the growing movement of survivors of clerical sexual abuse.

* * *

"What more can God do to you?" Frank had asked the woman in the hospital waiting for a heart transplant. To have seen God at God's worst is to be liberated from the old relationship with an omnipotent and omniscient God. "The state of omniscience," Jessica Benjamin writes in her study of sadomasochism, "gives birth to domination." Omnipotence dissolves the boundaries between the one who is omnipotent and omniscient and the other parties to the relationship, who are neither. The tension between the self and others as distinct beings breaks down. But by having God's number, and at the same time detaching themselves from the idea that God had anything to do with their abuse, survivors discovered a capacity within themselves in relation to others to restore the necessary tension, enough that they might be capable of standing once more in the real presence without the black screen falling.[16]

Survivors became free not only to express their doubts, their sense of betrayal, and their anger with God, but also to consider the articulations of their feelings as prayers spoken to God. There is a hard edge to Frank's theodicy. Survivors, he says, ought to meet God without illusions about God. Or perhaps it is better to suggest that they see God for who God is. This does not drive them away from God, or it need not, in Frank's theology. Rather, it permits them to address God fearlessly, to open their lives in all their turmoil to God, who must take them as they are. This is another instance of the shifting tectonics of power in the immediate post-Conciliar Catholic world. In relationships that are not trapped in the domination / submission dynamic, "both subjects become partners," Benjamin writes, "in a process that fosters both recognition and difference." They are "co-creator[s] of interactive patterns."[17]

* * *

Because all of the survivors I know were either the children of alcoholics or used drugs and alcohol themselves to dull the feelings of shame, guilt, and inadequacy they were left with by the abuse, they all participated at one time or another in twelve-step programs, such as Al-Anon and Alcoholics Anonymous. Some survivors have been going to meetings off and on for decades. Here, they encountered the Higher Power, or "God-as-I-understand-him," as Norman, a survivor I often got together with after his Saturday-morning AA meetings, described the God substitute or placeholder that Alcoholics Anonymous asks members to affirm. The Higher Power can be anything, Norman said, "even that doorknob over there." This radically protean entity mystified me. Anything? A doorknob? The idea, Norman replied, was "to turn our lives over" to an entity outside themselves, to be able to say, "Here, I can't control my drinking, so I give it over to you. Take away the urge to drink." Give it over to the doorknob, Norman added. The Higher Power was a god without qualities, "more a source of energy and light," Phyllis said. "Recovery programs depersonalize God," according to Monica, when we were discussing her involvement with AA and Al-Anon. She meant this as a positive comment.[18]

But who was the Higher Power *specifically* to these Catholic men and women who were abused within the idioms of the tradition in which they had first encountered God really present? Survivors' responses to my questions about the Higher Power were consistently framed in the negative. "Not a person," Bob, another survivor, described the Higher Power when I asked him, as if this alone were the most important identifier of the entity. "Not the Catholic God," Phyllis said immediately, when I asked her this question. As Phyllis's prompt response suggests, the Higher Power served survivors of clerical sexual abuse as a rejection of, and alternative to, the invasive and judgmental God of their childhoods, and derived its efficacy precisely from this difference. The Higher Power, said Frank, also a longtime member of Alcoholics Anonymous, "is the God you didn't know before." The Higher Power is not the Catholic God; the Higher Power has no features; the Higher Power is unknown and unfamiliar. The Higher Power is an unencumbered entity.

This deity without attributes, without hands, eyes, and ears, could not impinge on them, not threaten their boundaries and their fragile selves. The "depersonalization" of God in Alcoholics Anonymous in the form of the Higher Power, Monica said, made the Higher Power "accessible" to her and other survivors. The period when she was most active in the organization, Monica told me, was at the time in her life when "God wasn't human because all humans could hurt me." In these painful days, the Higher Power came "without all the images laden with pain" that the Catholic God had accumulated. Survivors distinguish among the various modalities of God they have known over the years: the mean God, the loving and forgiving God, the violent father God, and the God who weeps and suffers with them. The Higher Power is one of these gods. The history of their changing relationships with the various faces of God indexes their changing social circumstances as well as the conditions of their being at any time and place. *This* was my God then, they say, but *this* is my God now. The sequence in which these gods come over time varies among survivors, and it is rarely a unidirectional progression from a god of retribution to a god of compassion (as nineteenth- and twentieth-century theorists of religious evolution maintained was the case for civilizations as well as persons in their developmental models). Survivors resist the notion of progress because they have watched themselves fall into darkness again and again. The Higher Power as these survivors of clerical sexual abuse described it is an absence that opened in the place of a presence that was too threatening and dangerous, too much to bear.

But eventually, the bond between victims of clerical sexual abuse and this spiritual entity whose primary significance was its being "not the Catholic God" became unsatisfying. As Monica put it, she wanted "a personal connection." "The Eucharist is tough to shake," Frank says, "being so close to God, because you're actually receiving the body and blood." With the Higher Power, and with the gods of the other faiths they tried along the way, there was no one to wrestle with, to accuse, to be angry with, and to find a way to love and be loved by again; no one who would recognize them, no one with whom they might be in relationship, which is a comment not about these other gods, clearly, but about these survivors in relation to them. Precisely because the Higher Power was not the God of whom it needed to be said, "God had nothing to do with it," survivors seemed to have been drawn back to the Catholic God.

To recall an observation of Jessica Benjamin's I cited in relation to Lizzie and the Detroit housewife: in their changing relationship with God in the years after the Second Vatican Council and then later in the company of other survivors, Natalie, Bernard, Monica, Phyllis, and others had found the "two-way street" or "double directionality" of recognition and intersubjectivity. Double directionality occurs only in "a relationship in which each person experiences the other 'like a subject,' another mind who can be 'felt with,' yet has a distinct and separate center of feeling and perception." In such a position, Benjamin continues, "the subject attains a sense of history and of responsibility for destructiveness as well as an acceptance of loss and an appreciation of the independent existence of the other." The two together create out of their mutual engagement and recognition what Benjamin calls the space of the third. This was the space these survivors began inhabiting with the God they found in their years of searching. Being in this space with God contributed to their emergence from isolation, anger, and disassociation. For some, it made it possible to return to the church on their own terms. It helped others be done with the church at last. But for most of the survivors with whom I spoke, it enabled them to move in and out of church on their own terms.[19]

* * *

In her early adulthood, Monica said, everything about being in church frightened her. She felt herself at the mercy of the people in the pews around her, for reasons we have already seen. "Everything was about safety," Monica went on. But she wanted to be near the real presence, so Monica entered upon a long period of covert Mass attendance. In the city where she was living in these years, there was one church in which she felt especially safe because its great columns offered her protection and secrecy. She hid behind the columns. "You can really go and hide at Saint X's," she recalled, "and still be at mass."

During this time, Monica went for Holy Thursday services at a university Catholic center near her office. Following Mass on this day, the Blessed Sacrament is exposed through the night at a side altar. Monica made a great occasion of Holy Thursday. All week long, she plotted how she was going to get into church and close to the Blessed Sacrament without being seen, and then how she was going to get out again. On the day itself, she had her hair and nails done; every year she bought a new outfit. It was so exciting, Monica said, to anticipate being in the company of the Blessed Sacrament again. At the end of the evening service, when the priest brought the golden monstrance with the consecrated Host at its center out from the main altar to the side chapel, where it would reside through the night until the next morning, Monica followed at the back of the procession. Then, "I'd sit there all night long."

This was not Monica's only secret meeting with God. Sometimes she visited suburban churches and hid in her car in the parking lot, watching, and sometimes resenting, people going to Mass seemingly easily and without fear. She kept a close eye on the church's front doors. When a certain quality of rich and resonant silence fell over the parking lot— Monica identified it as a palpable shifting in the currents of the air that she was able to feel in her body—she knew it was the time of the Consecration inside the church. Then "in just those few moments," the outside walls of the church "didn't exist anymore" and "I would be close to God on the altar."

By the early 1980s, Monica had begun going regularly to Mass again. When she was a child being abused "in that rectory [that was] imbued with the evil of [those] guys," the other parish in her hometown was in the care of Franciscan friars. This was a safe place for the little girl—Monica describes the Franciscans as "very loving"—and now, as an adult, she was drawn to an inner-city Franciscan church near her work. She felt particularly safe with a priest she had gotten to know and she was careful to check the posted weekly schedule to make sure to attend his masses. "Once I knew that I could go to that church and be safe," Monica says, "I would go every day." At first she sat in the back, in the last row of pews, but gradually, over time, she moved forward in church, closer to the altar, finally settling on a regular place in the middle. But she was not completely comfortable. Then she had an experience that changed this.

On one of her visits to the Franciscan church in the city, she noticed people going somewhere down a flight of stairs. Monica felt compelled to follow them to see what was below. "I had to go into the basement," she explained, "to make sure it was safe." In the lower church, she came upon a statue of the Franciscan friar, Saint Anthony, holding the Infant Jesus in his arms, as this much-revered and beloved holy figure is usually depicted (see Figure 16). For obvious reasons, the sight of "a priest holding a baby," in Monica's words, was deeply disturbing to her, and she wanted to run away, out of the church, back into the streets, and never return. But some power, she says, held her in place. She stayed, breathed deeply, and calmed down. Monica began to visit Saint Anthony every day. "It was almost like drinking a little poison," she told me. She was building up immunity to her pain and fear by bringing herself into relationship over days and weeks with this sacred figure.

FIGURE 16 From Elsie H.'s collection, Saint Anthony and the Child Jesus, printed on card stock, with a small, bendable prop in the back to set the image upright. The saint's halo is broken. Penciled on the back is the date "1936."

Finally, one day, she was able to be in Saint Anthony's company for a longer period of time than ever before and with much less distress. The Holy Spirit, as Monica came to understand, was holding and supporting her through this. Monica refers to her visits to the saint in the basement of the church as her "little pilgrimage." Now, when she goes to visit Saint Anthony, she is sometimes overcome by "joyful weeping." The image has become, in Monica's words, "a healing talisman."

Monica understands this episode in her life in two registers. Psychologically, she was desensitizing herself to an image that evoked horrific memories of her encounter with evil. Religiously, she was on pilgrimage, not back to the Eucharist, because she had been attending Mass regularly by this time, but toward less fear in church, less shame, toward becoming a more visible presence there. In the first instance, she was taking the initiative to work through her terrors; in the second, Saint Anthony and the Holy Spirit were shaping events. In the one register, Monica was acting; in the other, Monica was being acted upon. Monica was both the subject of her life and subject to it.

* * *

It may be that awareness and acceptance of this double reality—subject of / subject to—are what being with the holy really present offers survivors. The intersubjective encounter with the sacred other(s) is always, as we have seen throughout this book, an engagement with oneself and one's world in all the modalities of being. Something happened to Monica as a result of this movement between ways of being in the world, because afterward she was able to be less secretive and less hidden before God. The oscillation between ways of being in the world, ways of experiencing herself in the world and in relation to herself, constituted for Monica an opening outward. It proved to be a new way of living with the reality and the memory of the most awful time of her life and everything that followed afterward. Monica became more present to the God present to her, and in this way to herself and to the other people in her world as well.

There are several reasons why phrases such as "coming back" or "returning to" are inadequate as descriptions of survivors' experience of the sacred over time. For one thing, as I have noted, many of them remained in some relation to the real presence all their lives, however tormented, fractured, angry, or intermittent this was. They remained in a sense poised over their relationship with the holy, which is why it seems sometimes that it takes relatively little to restore even the most brutally abused survivor to the Mass and relatively little to drive them bitterly and far away again. Going "back" to the Eucharist is both nearly impossible for survivors, because of the full horror of their experience, and at the same time always imminent, because of the power of their attachment to the Eucharist. "Back" also implies a finality that is not and for most survivors will never be again. Monica is freer in church now, but she is not completely free. This version of freedom was closed to her and other survivors by the actions of predator priests (as it was to Natalie by her stepfather, to Lizzie by her cancer, to the grieving mother by her son's death at such a young age, and so on).

For this reason, survivors despise the word "healing," which they call "the H-word." In their experience, others impose "healing" on them as an imperative to silence. "Healing" effaces the full pain of their experience and posits an end to this pain that survivors do not recognize from their lives. "Healing" also sets a limit to the growth and change available to them, as it curtails their anger. But I also think survivors' resistance to "healing" points to a deeper truth about the meeting of the human and the divine really present, and about the ambiguity of this encounter in human experience. The child or adolescent sexually abused by a priest is acted upon. This is one of the grimmest experiences of human passivity and powerlessness, and it contributes fundamentally to the shape of survivors' lives. But before Saint Anthony on the lower level of the same church where she was finally able to stand forth a little more openly, Monica began to experience the interplay of acting and being acted upon and to acknowledge and accept this dynamic. The modalities of human being are not separate; the challenge is to live with them both. In this process of discovery, survivors take a step toward the sacred, as Monica did in the parking lot, among other places, but the sacred must also take a step toward the survivors. Survivors make themselves present to God, the Blessed Mother, the saints, and the angels, who make themselves present to them. Agency and intentionality are not, as we have seen throughout this book, all on the side of the human or all on the side of the divine. Let me illustrate what I mean here by looking again at Marie's story.

One Sunday, a long time after her experience of the black screen at Mass, a neighbor invited Marie to accompany her to the Eucharist. The revelations of clergy sexual abuse had begun to break by this time. Marie was apprehensive about being back in church, but, as Frank said, the Eucharist is tough to shake, and so she went to Mass with her friend. Marie took her friend's invitation as the first step of the holy toward her. Then, during Mass, the pastor of the church stood up and, "with tears in his eyes," Marie recalled, "apologized to all the victims of sexual abuse [by priests]." This was the second step of the holy toward her. The next day, Marie drove back to the parish alone to tell this priest, "You touched my heart . . . you really brought me back to the Catholic Church." Many survivors have told me this, that there was some movement toward them—something a church official said, a response on the telephone when they called the diocese, another Catholic's reaction to their story—which they always interpreted in supernatural terms as signs of divine recognition, acknowledgment, and welcome. It was the step God and other heavenly figures took toward the restoration of their relationship.

Catholicism contributed to the creation of victims of sexual abuse out of the bodies of children and adolescents—that is to say, it created this crisis out of its own future and within the tradition itself—and then it compounded the horror by refusing to listen to or believe them, or to take steps to protect them and other children. The situation began to change following the public revelations of the abuse, the determination of survivors to hold the Church accountable, and the vast sums of money lost by the Church in court cases. There are procedures in place today for the protection of children and adolescents (although these rules are sometimes violated still). Monica, who is among the most devoutly

Catholic of the survivors I know, deeply learned in the tradition, believes that the evil done by predator priests will haunt the church until this generation dies away. In the meantime, survivors will make something of what has been made of them.

Although they are careful always to emphasize that they do not in any fashion mean to say that being abused was a good thing, a number of survivors have told me that because what happened to them as children or teenagers severed their bonds with the gods they thought they had known, they felt free to become more conscious and intentional about finding a relationship with a God that would be good for them. In this sense, and only in this sense, the abuse served a larger purpose in their lives. "You can love better for the hell you went through," Monica tells other survivors. Bernard says that when he looks at the "reality" he was given as the result of the abuse, which, over the years, has included severe alcoholism and a deep and abiding anxiety, along with the fragile peace and strength he has found in recent years, he wonders "if it was a curse or blessing" to have been abused.

* * *

"Is prayer easy?" Frank asked me rhetorically when we were talking about the difficulties of prayer, or of being in relationship to the God really present. Prayer is *not* easy, he went on, or "not all the time. But should it be? No, I don't think so." There is "suffering, death, and resurrection" in the spiritual life, Frank continued, and this dynamic of dying and coming alive is repeated many times in a person's life, daily in some survivors' lives. "This is the constant thing," Frank believes. "I would like to live in the resurrection, but it's not my experience that that's how it is." So, "when you engage God, it's the complete package," suffering, death, and resurrection. "It's hard and messy."

The gods that survivors find and the gods that find them do not always make life better or worse. Survivors move in and out of relationship with the Eucharist and with the God who becomes really present in the Mass, as well as with the angels, saints, and Virgin Mary. "God came to me in the cruelty," Monica told me, "in my suffering." She added, "We find blessings in the thorns." Monica's comment is given added resonance by her daily practice of praying before a crucifix fashioned for her by a friend out of barbed wire, twisted and coated black. Here, Monica says, she confronts the abyss and chooses between light and dark. If she is able to. When she is not, she retreats into her room and waits for time to pass. "When I look at that crucifix," Monica says about her daily prayer practice, "I see the resurrected wounds." Survivors contend with God and in the contending new possibilities for being arise, for better and worse. No rites mark this quotidian movement, and it is rarely free of pain or risk. As Monica says, "I am that now, a resurrected wound."

EPILOGUE

A Metric of Presence

THE internecine debate among Christian theologians in the sixteenth century about the nature of the divine body in the Host
hardened over time into the stark dichotomy between presence and absence, which then became the metric for mapping the religious worlds
of the planet. The origin of the map's coordinates, the zero point
from which all the other elements are computed or constrained, was
Catholics = presence (in the old sense), Protestants = absence. Unsubtle or
even incorrect as this formula may be as theology or ecclesiology, the
metric nonetheless was used wherever Europeans and Americans in their
global adventures found the gods really present. It was deployed closer to
home as well, to determine legally, for example, which religions or religious practices were intolerable in a democracy or modernizing nation
and which were legally permissible. Ambitious or desperate figures of
other cultures and classes, caught in the global vise of modernization
and industrialization, saw the utility of the presence / absence dichotomy
and adopted some version of it for their own ends and ambitions.

Scholars of religion made an essential contribution to this work of
mapping modern religion, translating the abundance of practices associated with peoples' relationships with special suprahuman beings
really present (in the Catholic sense of presence) into a singular and normative "religion" from which these beings were absent. The nomenclature

of presence / absence gradually expanded to include other terms, and other hierarchies attached themselves to it. In time, as modernity evolved, the gods were severed from the media of their representation, which became signs and symbols, not embodied presences. As a result, there are people everywhere in the contemporary world who live beyond the range of modern epistemology and historiography, and there are religious practices and imaginaries for which there is no name, other than in the language of diminishment and obsolescence. But this religion has refused to go away. The officials who make the rules to constrain and contain the gods nonetheless catch sight of them, though maybe only as hauntings. There are benefits to this illegibility. To be legible means to be vulnerable to the schemes and demands of various officialdoms, local or foreign, and to all the laws and technologies that have been developed to control the gods and the practices associated with them, from zoning regulations to developmental scales of religious evolution to constitutional safeguards. But whether everyone sees them or not, the gods are there.

This book I is a work of history as theory and theory as history. As such it is grounded first of all in my commitment as a historian to empirical research. I started with what Catholics in particular circumstances said about their encounters with supernatural presences and what followed from them. Then I worked outward from this empirical base toward theoretical issues. The case studies all have to do with Catholics. But because of the roles that Catholicism, the Catholic doctrine of the real presence, and the Catholic imaginary played in the shaping of modern consciousness, the case studies also offer unique critical purchase on the study of religion and history. Catholicism became the paradigmatic religion of real presence; as such it was the template through which Europeans approached and understood other religions, from the late sixteenth century forward—in other words from the age of Zwingli, Trent, and Calvin on. Another way of putting this is that in addition to being historical actors in their own right, Catholics have also been good to think with (to borrow Claude Lévi-Strauss's famous observation about the usefulness of animals in anthropological theorizing).

But it is not a question of merely plugging the gods and Catholics back in; the gods have always been there, after all, if only as ciphers, and so have Catholics. Rather, what is called for is a fundamental rethinking of the study of history, beginning with how "history" is constituted in the first place, in both its content and its method, and of the study of "religion," again beginning with its most basic coordinates. The gods never departed lived experience. They insistently reached through the bars of language, law, and theory erected around them. I am proposing that we let the gods out of their assigned places and that we approach history and religion through a matrix of presence. Once the gods return and once their presence is acknowledged, functionalism yields to a messier, less predictable, and perhaps less recognizable past, one that is not bound to a single account of human life or to a single, short period of time or to a single ontology. From the perspective of a metric of presence, it may be that—contra Hume—one day historians and scholars of religion will find it impossible to believe there ever lived on this planet counterparts of theirs who thought it was possible to study history or religion without the gods as interlocutors and provocateurs, as agents of both the given and the impossible, as malignant spirits, as harbingers of excess, as the ones who hold the memories that individual humans and entire societies forget, as bringers of succor and of pain.

To be in relationship with special beings really present is as old as the species and as new as every human's infancy. This is how most of the world is religious today, from India to China; across and between the cities and rural areas of Asia; the market stalls, highways, and factories of Thailand and Taiwan; among Muslims in Europe, Indonesia, North Africa, and the Middle East; in taxis driven by immigrants in Copenhagen, Paris, and New York; in basement vodou shrines in Brooklyn; among the haredim in Jerusalem; and in the resurgence of devotion to old and new saints across the former Soviet lands.

On a blistering day in mid-August 2011, traveling in the former Soviet republic of Georgia under the aegis of a program on "Anthropological Approaches to Religion and Secularism," I watched men and women press their faces into the loose soil of the grave of a recently buried monk at an Orthodox monastery. The dead monk's body was believed to have healing powers. People put bits of the topsoil from his grave into their mouths; they poured corn and olive oil onto the grave in petition or thanksgiving. What struck me most about the festivities, which coincided with renewed hostilities between the Russian and Georgian governments, was the party spirit among the people there. Everyone was dressed up in the sort of outfits more commonly worn in nightclubs. As the oil dripped down off their faces into the soil, pilgrims shrieked in delight, like people do when they get to the waterfall on amusement park waterslides, and in something more than delight, too. Vendors were hawking T-shirts, little plastic icons, and holy cards. People picnicked, flirted, passed around drink and food, and played on the monastery's grass with children and babies.[1]

I know that these men and women, pilgrims and tourists, brought all kinds of stories and needs into the space of the shrine, and I also appreciate the range of emotions that may have been circulating that hot afternoon through the intergenerational family groups gathered together on blankets or folding chairs. I did not talk with any of the pilgrims, so this level of the day's spirit was not available to me. But what I saw were people having a good time being out in public in each other's company and in the company of the dead and buried monk, who was right there with them after all, rather than being consigned to the underground existence that would have been his fate in the Soviet era.

The future that Hume envisioned for the human race has not happened yet. The gods were not turned back at the borders of the modern. The unseeing of the gods was an achievement; the challenge is to see them again. If the presence of the gods in the old Catholic sense is an absolute limit that contemporary scholars of religion and history refuse to cross, then they will miss the empirical reality of religion in contemporary affairs and they will fail to understand much of human life.

NOTES

BIBLIOGRAPHY

ACKNOWLEDGMENTS

INDEX

NOTES

I draw on three separate periods of fieldwork in this volume. (1) The visit to the shrine described in Chapter 5 took place in 1988; for the account that appears in this book, I worked from the field notes I took at the time. (2) Between 1997 and 2001 I did fieldwork at sites around the country, including Nebraska, Louisiana, and Arizona, for a project on Catholic childhoods in the past and in contemporary memory. I recorded many of these conversations (as I did with Natalie), most of which took place over a period of weeks in people's homes, and I also took notes, during and after the conversations. This research was funded by the Lilly Endowment and Indiana University. Participants were fairly evenly divided between men and women; most were around forty-five years old or older, including some very elderly people whom I met in nursing homes; everyone knew I was doing research for a book, in which I would quote our conversations, using pseudonyms and altering some of the specifics of their stories to guard their identities. (3) Beginning in fall 2012, I began talking with adult survivors of clerical sexual abuse, in the greater Chicago area and at several locations around the country. I met survivors in a number of ways: sometimes diocesan victim assistance coordinators circulated my name among participants in their programs, who then told survivor friends of theirs about the project; word that I was doing this research traveled also through the survivor movement. Survivors always made the initial contact with me. In Chicago I attended monthly meetings of former members of the Linkup (Survivors of Clergy Abuse Linkup). My method has been to talk with survivors, individually and in groups, and to take notes during and after our conversations. This research, which is ongoing, was funded in the beginning by the Social Science Research Council.

INTRODUCTION

1. All references to the cardinal's sermon are from Mary Ann Poust, "It Was 'Wrong,'" *Catholic New York,* April 9, 1998, http://cny.org/stories/It-Was -Wrong,2636?content_source=&category_id=&search_filter=&event_mode= &event_ts_from=&list_type=&order_by=&order_sort=&content_class= &sub_type=stories&town_id=%20But%20of%20course%20it%20happens%20 every%20day%20without%20any%20onotoriety. The Southern African Catholic Bishops' Conference also publicly reprimanded the priest, whose name was Mahlomi Makobane. My mother's letter appears, under the heading "He without Sin?" which was presumably added by an editor, in the *New York Daily News,* Sunday, April 12, 1998, 12.

2. Historian and scholar of religion Ann Taves, an old friend, gave me the benefit of the precision of her thought and language in the formulation of this paragraph, for which I am grateful. The final version is my responsibility.

3. Christian Wiman, *My Bright Abyss: Meditation of a Modern Believer* (New York: Farrar, Straus and Giroux, 2013), 61.

4. Judith Butler, *Giving an Account of Oneself* (New York: Fordham University Press, 2005), 33.

5. "Priests Save Host from Church Fire," *New York Times,* December 23, 1923, 15. Domenick DiPasquale, whom I have known since our first day of kindergarten together at the Immaculate Conception grammar school, brought this article to my attention. Fordham Hospital was closed in 1976.

1. THE OBSOLESCENCE OF THE GODS

1. Thomas B. Chetwood, SJ, *Tony* (St. Louis: Queen's Work, 1933), 5, 9–11.

2. Ibid., 12–13.

3. Ibid., 17, 19.

4. Ibid., 19, 23–24, 27. Without a moment's hesitation, Tony repeats after Tappy, "I'm a Nigger, I'm a Sheeny . . ." But he is adamant in refusing to say, "I am a Protestant," literally, physically unable to speak these words (22).

5. The information on Chetwood in this paragraph is drawn from "George-town Names Law Regent," *Bulletin of the Catholic Laymen's Association of Georgia* (November 10, 1928), 11; Christian Pangilinan, "A Laboratory for Legal Educa-tion: The Graduate Program at Georgetown Law" (Washington, DC: George-town University Law Center Office of Graduate Programs, 2012), 16–20 (there

is a picture of Chetwood on 16); and *The Official Catholic Directory* (New York: P. J. Kenedy and Sons, 1921), 704. Stephen Schloesser, SJ, helped me piece together this account of Father Chetwood's career.

6. The phrase "confidence and boosterism" is from Jay P. Dolan, *The American Catholic Experience: A History from Colonial Times to the Present* (Garden City, NY: Doubleday, 1985), 350; on Catholicism in the United States in the age of Father Chetwood and the delinquent Tony, see Dolan, *American Catholic Experience,* 349–417; Charles R. Morris, *American Catholic: The Saints and Sinners Who Built America's Most Powerful Church* (New York: Times Books / Random House, 1997), 141–195; James M. O'Toole, *The Faithful: A History of Catholics in America* (Cambridge, MA: Belknap Press of Harvard University Press, 2008), 145–198; and James J. Hennesey, SJ, *American Catholics: A History of the Roman Catholic Community in the United States* (New York: Oxford University Press, 1981), 234–279. The title of Father Hennesey's chapter on the 1920s is "Catholicism Unbound." On the Society of Jesus in the United States in this period, see Raymond A. Schroth, SJ, *The American Jesuits: A History* (New York: New York University Press, 2007), 115–130. The Twenty-Eighth International Eucharistic Congress is discussed in Morris, *American Catholic,* 135–138; Dolan, *American Catholic Experience,* 349–350; and Margaret M. McGuinness, "Let's Go to the Altar: American Catholics and the Eucharist, 1926–1976," in *Habits of Devotion: Catholic Religious Practice in Twentieth-Century America,* ed. James M. O'Toole (Ithaca, NY: Cornell University Press, 2004), 187–188. McGuinness cites the published proceedings of the congress regarding the meeting's aims, which were to "manifest publicly Catholic love, fealty, and devotion to Jesus Christ in the Sacrament of the Blessed Eucharist; to promote and inspire a greater love for Jesus Christ in the Sacrament of the Altar, and to endeavor to make reparation for the outrages which have been committed against His Divine Presence in the Tabernacle" (187). These works all discuss American Catholic education in the period, but see in particular, Timothy Walch, *Parish School: American Catholic Parochial Education from Colonial Times to the Present* (New York: Crossroad Publishing, 1996), 100–168; and Philip Gleason, *Contending with Modernity: Catholic Higher Education in the Twentieth Century* (New York: Oxford University Press, 1995), 62–206.

7. On efforts to restrict Catholic parochial education see Walch, *Parish School,* 152–168; also Hennesey, *American Catholics,* 246–248. Morris argues that the increasingly "secular" nature of American society after 1900 led to the weakening of anti-Catholicism, especially after the end of the great immigration from

eastern and southern Europe, and that anti-Catholicism lingered only in "rural areas where there were few Catholics" (Morris, *American Catholic*, 133). But Protestants and Protestantism, liberal or conservative, rural or urban, were not the sole bearers of anti-Catholic sentiment in the United States, nor was ethnicity the primary ground of difference. Modernity and secularism were themselves utterly Protestant in character and secular moderns were as much the bearers of anti-Catholicism in the United States as Protestants and Protestantism. It was out of this ostensibly secular, but deeply Protestant modern American liberalism that the secular intellectual Paul Blanshard attacked Catholicism after World War II as being alien to modern American democracy.

8. Chetwood, *Tony,* 26–27, 29. Emmings's assignment to the West Indies is an inside joke. *The Official Catholic Directory* (1921) lists Father Chetwood as a missionary in Jamaica. It is also an instance of the Catholic practice of inserting oneself into devotional narratives, a subject to be explored further in Chapter 4.

9. Thomas B. Chetwood, SJ, *Handbook of Newman* (New York: Schwartz, Kirwin and Fauss, 1927), 68.

10. The phrase "rites of violence" is from the essay with this title in Natalie Zemon Davis, *Society and Culture in Early Modern France: Eight Essays* (1965; repr., Stanford, CA: Stanford University Press, 1975), 152–187.

11. On the Affair of the Placards, see Lee Palmer Wandel, *The Eucharist in the Reformation: Incarnation and Liturgy* (Cambridge, UK: Cambridge University Press, 2006), 176–177. Professor Wandel's scholarship was a guide and inspiration to me in writing this chapter. For the story of the girl dipped into her parents' blood, whose name was Agnes Le Mercier, see Mack P. Holt, *The French Wars of Religion, 1562–1629* (Cambridge, UK: Cambridge University Press, 1995), 86. See also Barbara B. Diefendorf, *Beneath the Cross: Catholics and Huguenots in Sixteenth-Century Paris* (New York: Oxford University Press, 1991), 103, and, on the massacre more generally, 93–106; and Arlette Jouanna, *The Saint Bartholomew's Day Massacre: The Mysteries of a Crime of State,* trans. Joseph Bergin (Manchester: Manchester University Press, 2013). "All of the observers," Jouanna writes, "noted the sinister change in the color of the river, which went red with blood" (137). Jouanna points out that not all Catholics yielded to the savagery; some risked their lives to save their Protestant neighbors.

12. I take the story of the butchering of Campion's body from Evelyn Waugh's historically faithful and elegantly written biography, *Edmund Campion: A Life* (1935; repr., San Francisco: Ignatius Press, 2005), 200. One of those asperged with Campion's viscera was Cambridge wit and poet Henry Walpole, who was so

NOTES TO PAGES 18–20

moved by the spotting of his coat with the dying martyr's blood that he became a priest and thirteen years after Campion's death was himself martyred on the gallows at York. On Campion I also consulted Richard Simpson, *Edmund Campion: A Biography* (London: John Hodges, 1896), and Thomas M. McCoog, *"And Touching Our Society": Fashioning Jesuit Identity in Elizabethan England* (Toronto: Pontifical Institute of Medieval Studies, 2013), which is especially helpful on Campion's trial and death, as well as on what was made of his death in Catholic polemics.

13. The comment on the search for "ever closer definition" is from G. R. Potter, *Zwingli* (Cambridge, UK: Cambridge University Press, 1976), 290. On the body in this period, see David Hillman and Carla Mazzio, eds., *The Body in Parts: Fantasies of Corporeality in Early Modern Europe* (New York: Routledge, 1997), and Jonathan Sawday, *The Body Emblazoned: Dissection and the Human Body in Renaissance Culture* (London: Routledge, 1995). Changing and divergent conceptions of the body played an important role in the evolving Eucharistic debates; see Lee Palmer Wandel, "The Body of Christ at Marburg, 1529," an unpublished paper, which Professor Wandel generously shared with me as I was preparing this chapter. Here and throughout this first chapter I have also relied on Caroline Walker Bynum, *Christian Materiality: An Essay on Religion in Late Medieval Europe* (New York: Zone Books, 2011).

14. Martin Luther, "That These Words of Christ, 'This Is My Body,' etc., Still Stand Firm against the Fanatics" (1527) in *Luther's Works: American Edition,* vol. 37, ed. Robert H. Fischer and Helmut T. Lehmann (Minneapolis: Fortress Press, 1961), 3–150, esp. 33; cited in Ronald F. Thiemann, "Sacramental Realism: Martin Luther at the Dawn of Modernity," in *Lutherrenaissance: Past and Present,* ed. Christine Helmer and Bo Kristian Holm, Forschungen zur Kirchen- und Dogmengeschichte 106 (Göttingen, Germany: Vandenhoeck and Ruprecht, 2015), 156–173, esp. 168. Also referenced in this paragraph are Wandel, *The Eucharist in the Reformation,* 72; and Potter, *Zwingli,* 287–315. On Zwingli's 1525 *Action or Practice of the Supper, Remembrance, as It Was Instituted in Zurich on Easter,* see Wandel, *The Eucharist in the Reformation,* 73–74. Reinhold Theisen points out that there were more radical views of the Mass than Zwingli's, all seeking to approximate as literally as possible the simplicity of the Last Supper, as these reformers saw it. In Reinhold Theisen, *Mass Liturgy and the Council of Trent* (Collegeville, MN: St. John's University Press, 1965), 10–16.

15. "Heretics homed in on the horror" of cannibalism throughout early and medieval Christian history, Miri Rubin writes, in *Corpus Christi: The Eucharist*

in Late Medieval Culture (Cambridge, UK: Cambridge University Press, 1991), 359–360, quotation on 360. Christians and pagans in antiquity traded accusations of cannibalism. See Caroline Walker Bynum, *The Resurrection of the Body in Western Christianity, 200–1336* (New York: Columbia University Press, 1995), 33, 41–42n38, 55, 112n190, and 219. For a discussion of associations between cannibalism and the Catholic Eucharist in a contemporary context, see Heike Behrend, *Resurrecting Cannibals: The Catholic Church, Witch-Hunts, and the Production of Pagans in Western Uganda* (Suffolk, UK: James Currey, 2011). "Anna," a survivor of clerical sexual abuse who reappears in Chapter 7, told me that having been sexually abused by a priest as a teenager forced her to "open [her] eyes to a lot of physical things," eventually leading her to see the Eucharist as a cannibalistic feast.

16. On the Fourth Lateran Council and the question of the real presence, see Jaroslav Pelikan, *The Christian Tradition: A History of the Development of Doctrine*, vol. 3, *The Growth of Medieval Theology (600–1300)* (Chicago: University of Chicago Press, 1978), 202–204. The last sentences on the role of Catholic sacramental theology in provoking violence against Jews from the later Middle Ages forward quote Bynum, *Christian Materiality*, 170. On this subject see also Claudine Fabre-Vassas, *The Singular Beast: Jews, Christians, and the Pig*, trans. Carol Volk (New York: Columbia University Press, 1997); Miri Rubin, *Gentile Tales: The Narrative Assault on Late Medieval Jews* (New Haven, CT: Yale University Press, 1999). This paragraph also relies on Rubin, *Corpus Christi;* Wandel, *The Eucharist and the Reformation*, esp. 14–45; and Joseph A. Jungmann, SJ, *The Mass of the Roman Rite*, vol. 1, *Its Origins and Development*, trans. Francis A. Brunner, CSSR (New York: Benziger Brothers, 1951), 103–127.

17. The classic study of early Christian sainthood is Peter Brown, *The Cult of the Saints: Its Rise and Function in Latin Christianity* (Chicago: University of Chicago Press, 1981). I also consulted Brown's *The Rise of Western Christendom: Triumph and Diversity, A.D. 200–1000*, 10th anniversary rev. ed. (West Sussex, UK: Wiley-Blackwell, 2013; first published 1996), 93–165, the phrase "a world without empire" is on 93; Charles Freeman, *Holy Bones, Holy Dust: How Relics Shaped the History of Medieval Europe* (New Haven, CT: Yale University Press, 2011); and Robert Bartlett, *The Making of Europe: Conquest, Colonization, and Cultural Change, 950–1350* (Princeton, NJ: Princeton University Press, 1993). On martyrdom, see Joyce E. Salisbury, *The Blood of Martyrs: Unintended Consequences of Ancient Violence* (New York: Routledge, 2004); W. H. C. Frend, *Martyrdom and Persecution in the Early Church: A Study of a Conflict from the*

Maccabees to Donatus (Oxford: Basil Blackwell, 1965); Candida R. Moss, *Ancient Christian Martyrdom: Diverse Practices, Theologies, and Traditions* (New Haven, CT: Yale University Press, 2012); and Virginia Burrus, *Saving Shame: Martyrs, Saints, and Other Abject Subjects* (Philadelphia: University of Pennsylvania Press, 2008).

18. Gary Macy, *Treasures from the Storeroom: Medieval Religion and the Eucharist* (Collegeville, MN: Liturgical Press, 1999). The citation from Saint Martin's tomb in Tours is from Brown, *The Rise of Western Christendom,* 109–110. Theisen states Luther's position thus: "The Mass is of divine origin, but the added ceremonies are of human invention," in *Mass Liturgy and the Council of Trent,* 4.

19. Wandel, *The Eucharist in the Reformation,* 217.

20. Potter, *Zwingli,* 293; Wandel, *The Eucharist in the Reformation,* 207.

21. On holy men and women being lifted up from the ground and moving from place to place, see the chapter on "Levitation" in Herbert Thurston, SJ, *The Physical Phenomena of Mysticism,* ed. J. H. Crehan, SJ (London: Burns Oates, 1952), 1–31, esp. the list of "levitated Saints" on 31.

22. Waugh, *Edmund Campion,* 176–177. There are several versions of this disputation; Waugh's is consistent with Alexander Nowell and William Day, *The True Report of the Disputation, or Rather Private Conference Had in the Tower of London, with Ed. Campion, Jesuit, the Last of August 1581* (London: Christopher Barker, 1583), https://drive.google.com/file/d/0B9Gzqjp_hcXIOGtTLTJ4dk5 YcXM/view; and John Field, *Three Last Dayes Conferences Had in the Tower with Edmund Campion Iesuite at 18:23 and 27 of September 1581,* the Second Dayes Conference, Morning Session (London, 1583).

23. On the visions of Mormonism's founder, see Richard Lyman Bushman, *Joseph Smith: Rough Stone Rolling* (New York: Alfred A. Knopf, 2005), 144–160, 196–197; on the practices of presence among twentieth-century American Pentecostals, including the television healing ministry, see David Edwin Harrell Jr., *All Things Are Possible: The Healing and Charismatic Revivals in Modern America* (Bloomington, IN: Indiana University Press, 1975); Oral Roberts, *Expect a Miracle: My Life and Ministry* (Nashville: Thomas Nelson, 1995); David Edwin Harrell Jr., *Oral Roberts: An American Life* (San Francisco: HarperCollins, 1987). Popular devotion to Sallman's Jesus is discussed in David Morgan, ed., *Icons of Protestantism: The Art of Warner Sallman* (New Haven, CT: Yale University Press, 1996).

24. The classic study of religious enthusiasm is Ronald A. Knox, *Enthusiasm: A Chapter in the History of Religion, with Special Reference to the XVII and XVIII*

Centuries (New York: Oxford University Press, 1950). The eruptions of religious enthusiasm in the British North American colonies before the American Revolution and again in the newly formed United States in the early nineteenth century offer a case study in the social and political anxieties that religious enthusiasm has provoked. See Ann Taves, *Fits, Trances, and Visions: Experiencing Religion and Explaining Experience from Wesley to James* (Princeton, NJ: Princeton University Press, 1999); Nathan O. Hatch, *The Democratization of American Christianity* (New Haven, CT: Yale University Press, 1989); Jon Butler, *Awash in a Sea of Faith: Christianizing the American People* (Cambridge, MA: Harvard University Press, 1990); Whitney R. Cross, *The Burned-Over District: The Social and Intellectual History of Enthusiastic Religion in Western New York, 1800–1850* (1950; repr., Ithaca, NY: Cornell University Press, 1981). Edward Burnett Tylor's observation about "the Anglican" is from *Religion in Primitive Culture*, vol. 2 (1871; repr., Gloucester, MA: Peter Smith, 1970), 536. That Tylor was a "staunch anti-Catholic," Robert Ackerman writes, contributed fundamentally to the shaping of his cognitive theory of religion. See *The Myth and Ritual School: J. G. Frazer and the Cambridge Ritualists* (New York: Garland Publishing, 1991), 36. Although it is not a major topic of the book, George W. Stocking Jr., *Victorian Anthropology* (New York: Free Press, 1987), offers some hint of the place of anti-Catholicism in the making of British anthropology, esp. 54–55, 81, 87, 113, 189. A humorous but also probing look at the bad blood between contemporary High and Low Church Anglicans is the novel by Michael Arditti, *Easter* (London: Arcadia Books, 2000).

25. This paragraph and the next cover four centuries, three continents, and many historical actors, who in various eras of global history and many different local contexts, from roughly early modernity to the late twentieth century, sought to bring the Catholic Church more or less into harmony with what they saw as the most progressive and positive aspects of the politics, science, arts, and thought of their respective times for the good of both. These modernizers were refusing "to quarantine the sacred" from the world, in a phrase from Stephen Schloesser, SJ, *Jazz Age Catholicism: Mystic Modernity in Postwar Paris, 1919–1933* (Toronto: University of Toronto Press, 2005), 3. I cite here general English-language histories or translations I have found helpful so that readers who are interested may also consult them: John O'Malley, SJ, *Trent and All That: Renaming Catholicism in the Early Modern Era* (Cambridge, MA: Harvard University Press, 2000); R. Po-Chia Hsia, *The World of Catholic Renewal, 1540–1770* (Cambridge, UK: Cambridge University Press, 1998); Raymond F. Bulman

and Frederick J. Parrella, eds., *From Trent to Vatican II: Historical and Theological Investigations* (New York: Oxford University Press, 2006); Louis Châtellier, *The Europe of the Devout: The Catholic Reformation and the Formation of a New Society,* trans. Jean Birrell (Cambridge, UK: Cambridge University Press, 1989); Michel Vovelle, *The Revolution against the Church: From Reason to the Supreme Being,* trans. Alan José (Columbus: Ohio State University Press, 1991); E. E. Y. Hales, *Pio Nono: A Study in European Politics and Religion in the Nineteenth Century* (London: Eyre and Spottiswoode, 1954); Louis Châtellier, *The Religion of the Poor: Rural Missions in Europe and the Formation of Modern Catholicism, c. 1500–1800,* trans. Brian Pearce (Cambridge, UK: Cambridge University Press, 1997; Robert Bireley, *The Refashioning of Catholicism, 1450–1700: Reassessment of the Counter Reformation* (Washington, DC: Catholic University of America Press, 1999); Hugh A. MacDougall, *The Acton-Newman Relations: The Dilemma of Christian Liberalism* (New York: Fordham University Press, 1962); Owen Chadwick, *The Secularization of the European Mind in the Nineteenth Century* (Cambridge, UK: Cambridge University Press, 1977); Karl M. Schmitt, ed., *The Roman Catholic Church in Modern Latin America* (New York: Alfred A. Knopf, 1972); John Frederick Schwaller, *The History of the Church in Latin America: From Conquest to Revolution and Beyond* (New York: New York University Press, 2011); Dom Cuthbert Butler, *The Vatican Council, 1869–1870: Based on Bishop Ulathorne's Letters* (Westminster, MD: The Newman Press, 1962); Marvin R. O'Connell, *The Counter-Reformation, 1559–1610* (New York: Harper Torchbooks, 1974); Jean Delumeau, *Catholicism between Luther and Voltaire: A New View of the Counter-Reformation,* trans. Jeremy Moiser (London: Burns and Oates, 1977); C. A. Bayly, *The Birth of the Modern World, 1780–1914: Global Connections and Comparisons* (Malden, MA: Blackwell, 2004); Edward Wright-Rios, *Revolutions in Mexican Catholicism: Reform and Revelation in Oaxaca, 1887–1934* (Durham, NC: Duke University Press, 2009); Daniel H. Levine, *Popular Voices in Latin American Catholicism* (PrincetonNJ: Princeton University Press, 1992); Robert A. Ventresca, *Soldier of Christ: The Life of Pope Pius XII* (New Haven, CT: Yale University Press, 2013).

26. "Medieval credulity" is from Hans Küng, *Memoirs,* vol. 1, *My Struggle for Freedom,* trans. John Bowden (Grand Rapids, MI: William B. Eerdmans Publishing, 2003), 268. Hearing about Pope John XXIII's visit, on the eve of the opening of the Second Vatican Council, to a popular devotional site—the Holy Family's Nazareth home, which according to medieval legend was carried by angels to the town of Loreto in Italy—Küng was moved to the gloomy

question, "Is such medieval credulity perhaps to be the spirit of the new Council?" "Second line" as a designation for the new generation of liberation theologians is from Juan Luis Segundo, "The Shift within Latin American Theology," *Journal of Theology for Southern Africa* 52 (1985): 17–29. I first came across this reference in Jennifer Scheper Hughes, *Biography of a Mexican Crucifix: Lived Religion and Local Faith from the Conquest to the Present* (New York: Oxford University Press, 2010), 154. Scheper Hughes carefully traces the tensions between liberation theologians and ordinary Catholics, in particular over devotional practices, that haunted even the second line.

27. For a moving instance of this shame, see the letter quoted in the introduction to the third edition of my book *The Madonna of 115th Street: Faith and Community in Italian Harlem, 1880–1950* (1985; repr., New Haven, CT: Yale University Press, 2010), xvii–xviii. I have explored the fate of devotions to the saints in the later twentieth century in "'The Infant of Prague's Nightie': The Devotional Origins of Contemporary Catholic Memory," *U.S. Catholic Historian* 21, no. 2 (Spring 2003): 1–18. For a bitterly recriminatory commentary on how Vatican II–era reformers turned Catholicism into "Protestantism," by an influential American Catholic conservative, see James Hitchcock, *The Decline and Fall of Radical Catholicism* (New York: Herder and Herder, 1971), 13–34 passim. Hitchcock accuses Catholic liberals of rejecting the "Real Presence," instead seeing the Eucharist as nothing "beyond a human invention expressing human needs" (19). On Catholic traditionalists and separatists, see Michael Cuneo, *The Smoke of Satan: Conservative and Traditionalist Dissent in Contemporary American Catholicism* (Baltimore: Johns Hopkins University Press, 1999); a more balanced review may be found in Mary Jo Weaver and R. Scott Appleby, eds., *Being Right: Conservative Catholics in America* (Bloomington: Indiana University Press, 1995).

28. For a useful discussion of the shift toward greater Church control over the miraculous following the Council of Trent, in particular on the use of the language of science to contest allegedly supernatural phenomena, see Fernando Vidal, "Miracles, Science, and Testimony in Post-Tridentine Saint-Making," *Science in Context* 20, vol. 3 (2007): 481–508. Vidal credits Prospero Lambertini, the future Pope Benedict XIV, with introducing the careful use of countervailing evidence of natural causes into the canonization process in the years when Lambertini was "promoter of the faith" and "devil's advocate." Lambertini's aim, Vidal writes, was "to replace the visionary 'excesses' of Counter-Reformation piety and seventeenth-century mysticism with moderate and non-superstitious

forms of devotion" (483). As an example of Lambertini's caution, Vidal cites his judgment in the case of Joseph of Cupertino: because the friar's flights "did not happen *exclusively* on religious occasions," Vidal summarizes Lambertini's position, "they did not *necessarily* have a supernatural cause" (491). But there was sufficient religious evidence and popular support that, later, as pope, Lambertini canonized Joseph in 1753. In the devotional imagination, from the eighteenth through the twentieth century, the flights themselves were taken as signs of sanctity. For a powerful study of the convergence of right-wing politics with practices of presence, see Sergio Luzzatto, *Padre Pio: Miracles and Politics in a Secular Age,* trans. Frederika Randall (New York: Picador, 2010); on Vatican alliances with fascism, see also Frank J. Coppa, *Controversial Concordats: The Vatican's Relations with Napoleon, Mussolini, and Hitler* (Washington, DC: Catholic University of America Press, 1999).

29. Hubert Wolf, *The Nuns of Sant'Ambrogio: The True Story of a Convent in Scandal,* trans. Ruth Martin (New York: Alfred A. Knopf, 2015), 103. Wolf describes the post-Tridentine Holy Roman and Universal Inquisition as having to "protect the hierarchy" from popular claims of supernatural phenomena, which puts a decidedly different spin on the work of this fearsome institution. On extra-liturgical uses of the elements of the Eucharist, see Nathan Mitchell, OSB, *Cult and Controversy: The Worship of the Eucharist Outside Mass* (New York: Pueblo Publishing, 1982).

30. American Catholics produced an extensive popular literature against birth control in the first half of the twentieth century. In writing this paragraph, I referred to the following: Daniel A. Lord, SJ, *Speaking of Birth Control* (St. Louis: Queen's Work, 1930), reprinted twenty-three times by 1947; Ignatius Cox, SJ, *Birth Control Is Wrong!* (New York: America Press, 1930), which proclaims that the Catholic Church is against birth control "because she is sure of herself and of her stand as God-appointed custodian of human morals"; Daniel A. Lord, SJ, *What Birth Control Is Doing to the United States* (St. Louis: Queen's Work, 1936); Daniel A. Lord, SJ, *What of Lawful Birth Control?* (St. Louis: Queen's Work, 1935); Ignatius Cox, SJ, *Birth Control, Birth Controllers and Perversion of Logic* (New York: Paulist Press, 1936); Clement S. Mihanovich, *Whither Birth Control? The Death of a Nation* (St. Louis: Queen's Work, 1947); Ed Mack Miller, *And Baby Makes Seven: A Father Looks at Birth Control* (St. Louis: Queen's Work, 1954). For a history of birth control in American Catholicism, see Leslie Woodcock Tentler, *Catholics and Contraception: An American History* (Ithaca, NY: Cornell University Press, 2004).

31. On the bleeding statue of the Virgin Mary, see "Believers Flock to Virgin Mary Statue 'Crying' Red Tears," *USA Today,* November 27, 2005, http://usatoday30.usatoday.com/news/religion/2005-11-27-marystatue_x.htm; the connection between Mary's blood-red tears and the sexual abuse crisis was made in *The Economist:* see "Tears in Sacramento," January 5, 2006, www.economist.com/node/5364759, which is also the source for the specific details of the settlement cited in the paragraph. That Guadalupe is with child appears to be a modern idea, although it is based on the much older tradition that the belt worn by the Virgin is an Aztec childbearing aid. Contemporary devout say that Guadalupe is pregnant with the future, which converges in the tradition's *longue durée* with earlier apocalyptic and incarnational Guadalupanan beliefs. In any case, Guadalupe's pregnancy has become an accepted and important feature in contemporary devotion. See, for example, Dan Lynch, "The Amazing Truth of Our Lady of Guadalupe," *Catholic Education,* December 2002, www.catholiceducation.org/en/culture/catholic-contributions/the-amazing-truth-of-our-lady-of-guadalupe.html; "The Story of Our Lady Guadalupe," *Michigan Catholic,* November 27, 2013, http://themichigancatholic.com/2013/11/the-story-of-our-lady-of-guadalupe/; and Donald Wuerl, "Our Lady of Guadalupe, the Star of the New Evangelization," *Cardinal's Blog,* December 12, 2013, http://cardinalsblog.adw.org/2013/12/our-lady-of-guadalupe-the-star-of-the-new-evangelization/. The pregnant Guadalupe inspired "millions of Aztecs" to become Catholic, Cardinal Wuerl writes, and for this reason she is the "Star of the New Evangelization," helping contemporary Catholics make Jesus "present" to others. Guadalupe is also taken today as a patroness of the antiabortion movement. More generally on the history of devotion to Guadalupe, see Timothy Matovina, *Guadalupe and Her Faithful: Latino Catholics in San Antonio, from Colonial Origins to the Present* (Baltimore: Johns Hopkins University Press, 2005), and D. A. Brading, *Mexican Phoenix, Our Lady of Guadalupe: Image and Tradition across Five Centuries* (Cambridge, UK: Cambridge University Press, 2001). Tim Matovina helped me puzzle out the matter of Guadalupe's pregnancy as it changed over time.

32. A new literature on the history of the making of "religion" as a discrete object of modern critical inquiry has developed in recent years, as the discipline of religious studies has turned a historical eye on its genealogies. See, for example, Ivan Strenski, *Thinking about Religion: An Historical Introduction to Theories of Religion* (Oxford: Blackwell Publishing, 2006); also Mark C. Taylor, ed., *Critical Terms for Religious Studies* (Chicago: University of Chicago Press,

1998); J. Samuel Preus, *Explaining Religion: Criticism and Theory from Bodin to Freud* (New Haven, CT: Yale University Press, 1987); Guy G. Stroumsa, *A New Science: The Discovery of Religion in the Age of Reason* (Cambridge, MA: Harvard University Press, 2010). The classic work on the topic is Eric J. Sharpe, *Comparative Religion: A History* (1975; repr., La Salle, IL: Open Court, 1986).

33. See, for example, Anthony Pagden, *European Encounters with the New World: From Renaissance to Romanticism* (New Haven, CT: Yale University Press, 1993), 42–46 passim; Jorge Cañizares-Esguerra, *Puritan Conquistadores: Iberianizing the Atlantic, 1550–1700* (Stanford, CA: Stanford University Press, 2006); Sharpe, *Comparative Religion,* 1–26. This anti-Catholic impulse in Protestant missionaries' perceptions of indigenous peoples around the world persisted into the modern era, as did Catholic missionaries' anti-Protestant bias. On later periods, see David Chidester, *Savage Systems: Colonialism and Comparative Religion in Southern Africa* (Charlottesville: University Press of Virginia, 1996); also, David Chidester, *Empire of Religion: Imperialism and Comparative Religion* (Chicago: University of Chicago Press, 2014).

34. José de Acosta, *Natural and Moral History of the Indies,* ed. Jane E. Mangan, trans. Frances López-Morillas (1590; repr., Durham, NC: Duke University Press, 2002), 300, and, more generally, 282–327.

35. "Aristotelian-Thomist conceptual scheme" is from Anthony Pagden, *The Fall of Natural Man: The American Indian and the Origins of Comparative Ethnology* (Cambridge, UK: Cambridge University Press, 1982), 122, see also 119–145; I draw here as well on Tzvetan Todorov, *The Conquest of America: The Question of the Other* (New York: Harper and Row, 1984), 188–190; a different perspective is offered in Daniel Castro, *Another Face of Empire: Bartolomé de Las Casas, Indigenous Rights, and Ecclesiastical Imperialism* (Durham, NC: Duke University Press, 2007). Also helpful in thinking through this paragraph was Stephen Greenblatt, *Marvelous Possessions: The Wonder of the New World* (Chicago: University of Chicago Press, 1991).

36. On Sir James George Frazer and his era, Robert Fraser writes, "There existed . . . in those *fin-de-siècle* times a strong tendency among Protestant-educated ethnologists of an agnostic persuasion to embrace the Catholic interpretation [of totem feasts], since it enabled them to write off the Mass as magical and hence subtly to undermine it. The object was not so much to demythologize the Mass, as, precisely, to mythologize it and hence write it off as spurious." Frazer was delighted in particular with Baldwin Spencer's work at the very end of the nineteenth century among the Arunta, especially by what he read as

Spencer's identification of the Arunta *intichiuma* ceremonies with the (Roman) Catholic Mass, which Frazer took as evidence in support of his views of magic and ritual in *The Golden Bough*. The Mass, an excited Frazer wrote to a friend with reference to Spencer's research, is "sorcery and mumbo-jumbo." In Robert Fraser, *The Making of* The Golden Bough: *The Origins and Growth of an Argument* (New York: St. Martin's Press, 1990), 83–84, also 112–113.

37. William Pietz, "The Problem of the Fetish, II: The Origin of the Fetish," *RES: Anthropology and Aesthetics* 13 (Spring 1987): 23–45, quotation on 37; Willem Bosman is quoted on 39. On the fetish and the making of the modern study of religion, see especially Sylvester A. Johnson, *African American Religions, 1500–2000: Colonialism, Democracy, and Freedom* (Cambridge, UK: Cambridge University Press, 2015), esp. 13–156. Sylvester Johnson is a good friend and colleague and I have learned a great deal from him about the history of the fetish.

38. W. J. T. Mitchell, *What Do Pictures Want? The Lives and Loves of Images* (Chicago: University of Chicago Press, 2005), 166; "bad objects" of empire is on 165.

39. "As a fundamental principle of both individual mentality and social organization," Pietz writes, "fetish worship was the paradigmatic illustration of what was *not* enlightenment." In William Pietz, "The Problem of the Fetish, IIIa: Bosman's Guinea and the Enlightenment Theory of Fetishism," *RES: Anthropology and Aesthetics* 16 (Autumn 1988): 105–122, quotation on 106. See also Birgit Meyer, "Mediation and the Genesis of Presence: Towards a Material Approach to Religion," lecture from October 19, 2012, University of Utrecht, www2.hum.uu .nl/onderzoek/lezingenreeks/pdf/Meyer_Birgit_oratie.pdf.

40. C. P. Tiele, *Elements of the Science of Religion,* pt. 1, *Morphological;* pt. 2, *Ontological* (Edinburgh: William Blackwood and Sons, 1897). The phrase about the "original . . . sense of infinity" is from pt. 2, 233; the comment on the "simple minded votary of Rome" is from pt. 2, 89.

41. Roberto Calasso, *Literature and the Gods,* trans. Tim Parks (New York: Knopf, distributed by Random House, 2001), 5, 4, emphasis in the original; also see Stephen Wilson, *The Magical Universe: Everyday Ritual and Magic in Pre-Modern Europe* (London: Hambleton and London, 2000).

42. David Hume, *The Natural History of Religion* (1757; repr., Stanford, CA: Stanford University Press, 1956), 56. "Such are the doctrines of our brethren the Catholics," as Hume sardonically concludes.

43. Jonathan Z. Smith, "A Twice-Told Tale: The History of the History of Religion's History," in *Relating Religion: Essays in the Study of Religion* (Chicago:

University of Chicago Press, 2004), 363; Clifford Geertz, "Religion as a Cultural System," in *The Interpretation of Cultures* (New York: Basic Books, 1973), 91; George Steiner, *Real Presences* (Chicago: University of Chicago Press, 1989), 121.

44. On ambivalent theorists, see Timothy Larsen, *The Slain God: Anthropologists and the Christian Faith* (Oxford: Oxford University Press, 2014).

45. Charles Taylor, *A Secular Age* (Cambridge, MA: Belknap Press of Harvard University Press, 2007), 448, my emphasis.

46. On the "analogy between the Buddha and Luther," see Philip C. Almond, *The British Discovery of Buddhism* (Cambridge, UK: Cambridge University Press, 1988), 73–76, 123–126; for the impress of Protestant / Catholic polemics on European scholarship on South Asian religions, see Ronald B. Inden, *Imagining India* (Bloomington: Indiana University Press, 1990), 85–130; on anti-Catholic bias in nineteenth-century British scholarship on Confucianism, see Norman J. Giradot, *The Victorian Translation of China: James Legge's Oriental Pilgrimage* (Berkeley: University of California Press, 2002), 79, 88–89, 93, 222–223, 313; in the study of Taoism, see Russell Kirkland, *Taoism: The Enduring Tradition* (New York: Routledge, 2004), 67–68. The use of the history of Protestant / Catholic polemics to interpret, "reform," and rank indigenous religions in Africa and Asia is not to be understood solely as the imposition of an alien inheritance upon non-Europeans. Often enough, local elites were able to appropriate the semantics of Protestant / Catholic difference for their own political and social ends. See, for example, the agendas associated with "Protestant Buddhism" in modern Sri Lanka, discussed in Richard King, *Orientalism and Religion: Postcolonial Theory, India, and the "Mystic East"* (New York: Routledge, 1999), 151–152. Catholicism in the minds of eighteenth- and nineteenth-century European scholars of Asian religions was not the major interest of the historians I have cited, so in these cases and others I am calling attention to what lies hidden in plain sight. Contemporary scholars of religion are also heirs to a history that begins in the sixteenth century, after all, with all its inheritances of anti-Catholicism. More needs to be done on the subject of Catholic / Protestant polemics in the making of Asian religions, but from a perspective that is more attentive to evidence of it. Exemplary in this regard is the work of Donald S. Lopez Jr., who is acutely aware of the impact of the rejection of Catholic metaphysics and practices in the making of Asian religions. Cited in the text is his recent work, *From Stone to Flesh: A Short History of the Buddha* (Chicago: University of Chicago Press, 2013), 209, 169. "For Buddhists," Lopez writes, "the statue is the Buddha, just

as much as the Host of the Eucharist is the body of Christ" (51). It was around the denial of this reality that modern "Buddhism" was constructed.

47. A great case study of the historical trajectory I am describing here is Leigh Eric Schmidt, *Hearing Things: Religion, Illusion, and the American Enlightenment* (Cambridge, MA: Harvard University Press, 2000). Schmidt writes of the late eighteenth and early nineteenth centuries in England, France, and the United States, "hallucinatory diagnoses crept into ever wider realms of Christian experience and practice. . . . To combat this raging source of insanity, reasonable medical men imagined a Christianity of quiet and calm—no bodily ecstasies, no revival meetings, no terror, no mortifications of the flesh, no gulping of Eucharistic wine, no outcries, no demonic agency, no hallucinatory provocations" (192). And, one might add, no gods really present, which is the phenomenon at the root of all these symptoms. See also Michel Foucault, *Religion and Culture,* ed. Jeremy R. Carrette (New York: Routledge, 1999), esp. chapter 1, "Religious Deviations and Medical Knowledge," 50–56. "We can therefore say," Foucault writes, "that there was a 'medicalization' of . . . parareligious experience" in the sixteenth century. By "parareligious experience," Foucault seems to mean human engagements with special beings. Foucault was raised Catholic (55). I also consulted Roy Porter, *Mind-Forg'd Manacles: A History of Madness from the Restoration to the Regency* (Cambridge, MA: Harvard University Press, 1987); Andrew Scull, Charlotte MacKenzie, and Nicholas Hervey, *Masters of Bedlam: The Transformation of the Mad-Doctoring Trade* (Princeton, NJ: Princeton University Press, 1996); and Michel Foucault, *Madness and Civilization: A History of Insanity in the Age of Reason,* trans. Richard Howard (New York: Vintage Books, 1965).

48. Webb Keane, *Christian Moderns: Freedom and Fetish in the Mission Encounter* (Berkeley: University of California Press, 2007), 12.

49. Kant's 1784 "What Is Enlightenment?" may be found, among many other places, in Isaac Kramnick, ed., *The Portable Enlightenment Reader* (London: Penguin Books, 1995), 1–7; also useful for this paragraph was Curtis J. Evans, *The Burden of Black Religion* (New York: Oxford University Press, 2008), chap. 4, esp. 167–168.

50. Talal Asad, *Genealogies of Religion: Discipline and Reasons of Power in Christianity and Islam* (Baltimore: Johns Hopkins University Press, 1993), 45.

51. Marianna Torgovnick, *Gone Primitive: Savage Intellects, Modern Lives* (Chicago: University of Chicago Press, 1990); Marianna Torgovnick, *Primitive Passions: Men, Women, and the Quest for Ecstasy* (Chicago: University of Chi-

cago Press, 1996); Peter Van der Veer, *Imperial Encounters: Religion and Modernity in India and Britain* (Princeton, NJ: Princeton University Press, 2001); Elazar Barkan and Ronald Busch, eds., *Prehistories of the Future: The Primitivist Project and the Culture of Modernism* (Stanford, CA: Stanford University Press, 1995); Celia Brickman, *Aboriginal Populations in the Mind: Race and Primitivity in Psychoanalysis* (New York: Columbia University Press, 2003). "Hunting the elephant" was late nineteenth-century slang for the journeys of upper-class persons into the slum quarters of industrial cities in search of the excitement of real life. See Irving Lewis Allen, *The City in Slang: New York Life and Popular Speech* (New York: Oxford University Press, 1993), 230–231. In American history such searches often led white people into black neighborhoods; see, for example, Nathan Irvin Huggins, *Harlem Renaissance* (New York: Oxford University Press, 1971). The line about "negro streets at dawn" is from Allen Ginsberg, "Howl," in *Howl and Other Poems* (1956; repr., San Francisco: City Lights, 1980), 9. For an elegant fictional treatment of the longing of Western moderns for the "India" of their desiring, see Pankaj Mishra, *The Romantics: A Novel* (New York: Random House, 2000). For examples of the intermittent allure of Catholicism to restless moderns, see Ellis Hanson, *Decadence and Catholicism* (Cambridge, MA: Harvard University Press, 1997); Jenny Franchot, *Roads to Rome: The Antebellum Protestant Encounter with Catholicism* (Berkeley: University of California Press, 1994); and especially the two magisterial volumes by William L. Vance, *America's Rome,* vol. 1, *Classical Rome;* vol. 2, *Catholic and Contemporary Rome* (New Haven, CT: Yale University Press, 1989). For an intensely personal account of the compulsion of Catholicism to non-Catholic Americans, see Richard Gilman, *Faith, Sex, Mystery: A Memoir* (New York: Simon and Schuster, 1986). As I was finishing this book, I read Jean Findlay's powerful account of the conversion of Marcel Proust's translator, C. K. Scott Moncrieff, to Catholicism on the front during World War I, in *Chasing Lost Time: The Life of C. K. Scott Moncrieff, Soldier, Spy, and Translator* (New York: Farrar, Strauss, and Giroux, 2014). This is a very different sort of modern story.

52. See, for example, George W. Stocking Jr., ed., *Objects and Others: Essays on Museums and Material Culture,* vol. 3 of *History of Anthropology* (Madison: University of Wisconsin Press, 1985); Donald S. Lopez Jr., ed., *Curators of the Buddha: The Study of Buddhism under Colonialism* (Chicago: University of Chicago Press, 1995); John P. Burris, *Exhibiting Religion: Colonialism and Spectacle at International Exhibitions, 1851–1893* (Charlottesville: University Press of Virginia, 2001).

53. Flannery O'Connor, *The Habit of Being: Letters of Flannery O'Connor,* ed. Sally Fitzgerald (New York: Farrar, Straus, Giroux, 1979), 124–125.

54. "Negroes Enact the Way of the Cross," *New World* (March 13, 1942), 9, my emphasis; the story about the Catholic boys vandalizing a Protestant church that "ain't no church" is from the chapter "Reverend A. P. Jackson: Tower of Strength" in Timuel D. Black Jr., *Bridges of Memory: Chicago's Second Generation of Black Migration* (Evanston, IL: Northwestern University Press, 2007), 50. These local Chicago instances of Catholics' enduring metaphysical disdain for the Protestant sacred were brought to my attention by a former student, Matthew Cressler, now on the faculty of the College of Charleston.

2. ABUNDANT HISTORY

1. On the apparitions at Knock (in addition to the secondary sources on Marian apparitions cited below), see especially Eugene Hynes, *Knock: The Virgin's Apparition in Nineteenth-Century Ireland* (Cork, Ireland: Cork University Press, 2008); also Michael Walsh, *The Apparition at Knock: A Survey of Facts and Evidence* (Naas, Ireland: Leinster Leader, 1955); James Gibbons, M. Orsini, Henry Formby, John Francis Hogan, and John Gilmary Shea, *Fathers, Martyrs and Queen of the Holy Rosary* (New York: Thomas Kelly, 1880), pt. 2, "The Apparition at Knock," 1–47; M. Orsini, *The Queen of Angels, or, Life of the Blessed Virgin, with a Universal History of the Catholic Church* (New York: Gay Brothers and Co., 1881), 3–13. On Irish Catholicism, see Brendan Bradshaw and Dàire Keogh, eds., *Christianity in Ireland: Revisiting the Story* (Dublin: Columba Press, 2002); Lawrence J. Taylor, *Occasions of Faith: An Anthropology of Irish Catholics* (Philadelphia: University of Pennsylvania Press, 1995). A valuable perspective on Knock is also offered by Edith L. Turner, "Our Lady of Knock: Reflections of a Believing Anthropologist," *New Hibernia Review* 15 (Summer 2011): 121–125.

2. The best general history of modern Marian apparitions is Sandra L. Zimdars-Swartz, *Encountering Mary: From La Salette to Medjugorje* (Princeton, NJ: Princeton University Press, 1991); for a political history of the subject, with an emphasis on Mary's enlistment in antimodern modernism, see Nicholas Perry and Loreto Echeverría, *Under the Heel of Mary* (New York: Routledge, 1988); the devotional literature on Medjugorje is enormous, but see, for example, Mary Craig, *Spark from Heaven: The Mystery of the Madonna of Medjugorje* (Notre Dame, IN: Ave Maria Press, 1988), and Janice T. Connell, *The Visions of the Chil-*

dren: The Apparitions of the Blessed Mother at Medjugorje (1992; repr., New York: St. Martin's Griffin, 2007).

3. "In the Mass," Wandel writes about Tridentine theology, "the priest linked the moment of the Seder corporeally to the contemporary community of the faithful, with his own body overarching the temporal distance between Christ and the living community of the faithful." Through "the movement of [the priest's] hands, his arms, and in the clothes which he had so carefully dressed his person," the priest—universally, locally, and eternally—made explicit the "connection of the Incarnation" to the Eucharist. In Lee Palmer Wandel, *The Eucharist in the Reformation: Incarnation and Liturgy* (Cambridge, UK: Cambridge University Press, 2006), 239, 241.

4. For the Virgin Mary online, see Paolo Apolito, *The Internet and the Madonna: Religious Visionary Experience on the Web,* trans. Antony Shugaar (Chicago: University of Chicago Press, 2005); on Our Lady of Fatima, see Zimdars-Swartz, *Encountering Mary,* 190–219; Thomas A. Kselman and Steven Avella, "Marian Piety and the Cold War in the United States," *Catholic Historical Review* 72, no. 3 (July 1986): 403–424; Una M. Cadegan, "The Queen of Peace in the Shadow of War: Fatima and U.S. Catholic Anti-Communism," *U.S. Catholic Historian* 22, no. 4 (Fall 2004): 1–15; Jeffrey S. Bennett, *When the Sun Danced: Myth, Miracles, and Modernity in Early Twentieth-Century Portugal* (Charlottesville: University of Virginia Press, 2012).

5. On Saint Louis-Marie Grignion de Montfort, see Zimdars-Swartz, *Encountering Mary,* 251–252, 255–256.

6. "Younger than sin" is from Georges Bernanos, *The Diary of a Country Priest,* trans. Pamela Morris (1937; repr., New York: Fount, 1977), 166; on Saint Bernadette and the apparition at Lourdes, see Ruth Harris, *Lourdes: Body and Spirit in the Secular Age* (New York: Viking, 1999); on resistance to the doctrine of the Immaculate Conception in the United States, among Catholic liberals as well as Protestants, see James J. Hennesey, SJ, *American Catholics: A History of the Roman Catholic Community in the United States* (New York: Oxford University Press, 1981), 167; James J. Hennesey, SJ, *The First Council of the Vatican: The American Experience* (New York: Herder and Herder, 1963); William L. Vance, *America's Rome,* vol. 2, *Catholic and Contemporary Rome* (New Haven, CT: Yale University Press, 1989), 15–16, 33–39; David J. O'Brien, *Isaac Hecker: An American Catholic* (New York: Paulist Press, 1992); Patrick W. Carey, *Orestes A. Brownson: American Religious Weathervane* (Grand Rapids, MI: William B. Eerdmans Publishing, 2004), 287–335; Thomas T. McAvoy,

CSC, *The Americanist Heresy in Roman Catholicism, 1895–1900* (Notre Dame, IN: University of Notre Dame Press, 1963).

7. Father Norris is quoted in Andrea Elliott, "Believers Bring Their Aches to Bathe in the City's Water," *New York Times,* October 3, 2004, www.nytimes .com/2004/10/03/nyregion/03journal.html?_r=0; see also Matt Sedensky, "Neighborhood Report: Bronxdale; Solace, Pilgrims, and Maybe a Cure, at a Grotto in the Bronx," *New York Times,* October 28, 2001, www.nytimes.com /2001/10/28/nyregion/neighborhood-report-bronxdale-solace-pilgrims-maybe -cure-grotto-bronx.html. The *Times* regularly covers the "Lourdes of America," as local people call the Bronx shrine, and there are other articles on the topic over the years. The live stream from the shrine in Lourdes may be found at http://en.lourdes-france.org/tv-lourdes/.

8. The buffered individual is a reference to Charles Taylor, *A Secular Age* (Cambridge, MA: Belknap Press of Harvard University Press, 2007), 37–42. Taylor contrasts this with the "porous" self of the "earlier enchanted world" (37–38).

9. Claudio Lomnitz, *Death and the Idea of Mexico* (New York: Zone Books, 2005), 41, 43.

10. Dorothy Fremont Grant, *War Is My Parish* (Milwaukee: Bruce Publishing, 1944), 27. The officer begins his letter home, "You know the Catholic soldier has it all over the non-Catholic lad." In this spirit, see also Gail Shroyer, "Rosary Under Mortar Fire," *Catholic Digest* 15 (October 1951): 30–35. On Fatima and the Cold War, see Cadegan, "The Queen of Peace in the Shadow of War"; Sergio Luzzatto, *Padre Pio: Miracles and Politics in a Secular Age,* trans. Frederika Randall (New York: Picador, 2010), 264–267; on Pope John Paul II (Saint Karol Wojtyla) and Fatima, see George Weigel, *Witness to Hope: The Biography of Pope John Paul II* (New York: Cliff Street Books, 1999), 440; from another perspective, John Cornwell, *The Pope in Winter: The Dark Face of John Paul II's Papacy* (New York: Viking, 2004), 86–89, 171–177; Sister Mary Ann Walsh, RSM, *From Pope John Paul II to Benedict XVI: An Inside Look at the End of an Era, the Beginning of a New One, and the Future of the Church* (Lanham, MD: Sheed and Ward / Rowman and Littlefield, 2005), 135. It was a common and popular trope in the American Catholic press in the early years of the Cold War that the rosary was the Catholic Church's "atom bomb." See Sister M. Pierre, "Our Atom Bomb, the Rosary," *Catholic School Journal* 48 (May 1948): 165–166, cited in Cadegan, "The Queen of Peace in the Shadow of War," 9. See also Sister M. Amatora, OSF, "Mary's Weapon—The R-Bomb," *Catholic Educator* 21 (October 1950): 99–101; Rev. Thomas U. Mullaney, OP, "The Rosary, Our Secret Weapon," *Ave Maria* 88

(October 4, 1958): 5–7, 23; Josephine Quirk, "The Rosary . . . A Weapon against Communism," *Extension* 46 (October 1951): 30–31. Quirk notes that in her visits to hospitals in Berlin immediately after World War II, many "non-Catholics" asked her to send them rosaries from the United States when she returned home.

11. On Our Lady of Lourdes as Ezili Dantò, see Karen McCarthy Brown, *Mama Lola: A Vodou Priestess in Brooklyn* (Berkeley: University of California Press, 1991), 228. This paragraph is based on the many visits I have made to the Bronx Lourdes over the years, but also see Elliott, "Believers Bring Their Aches to Bathe in the City's Water," on the shrine's ethnic diversity. Dorothy Fremont Grant reports that Jewish soldiers, too, valued the rosary. "I always carry the Blessed Mother with me," she quotes a Jewish airman saying, in *War Is My Parish*, 22.

12. Harris, *Lourdes*, 84–91. Harris notes the "intimacy" in the decorations of the statues donated, their customization in the palette of local aesthetics (87).

13. In addition to the works already cited on Marian devotions and modernity, see also Suzanne K. Kaufman, *Consuming Visions: Mass Culture and the Lourdes Shrine* (Ithaca, NY: Cornell University Press, 2005); Paolo Apolito, *Apparitions of the Madonna at Oliveto Citra: Local Visions and Cosmic Drama*, trans. William A. Christian Jr. (University Park: Pennsylvania State University Press, 1998); William A. Christian Jr., *Visionaries: The Spanish Republic and the Reign of Christ* (Berkeley: University of California Press, 1996); Michael P. Carroll, *Madonnas That Maim: Popular Catholicism in Italy since the Fifteenth Century* (Baltimore: Johns Hopkins University Press, 1992); Michael P. Carroll, *The Cult of the Virgin Mary: Psychological Origins* (Princeton, NJ: Princeton University Press, 1986); David Blackbourn, *Marpingen: Apparitions of the Virgin Mary in Bismarckian Germany* (New York: Alfred A. Knopf, 1994). To say "historians have established all this by now" is to acknowledge my profound debt to these scholars, alongside whom I see myself working in this chapter.

14. On the understanding of "experience" in modern social theory, see Martin Jay, *Songs of Experience: Modern American and European Variations on a Universal Theme* (Berkeley: University of California Press, 2005). The phrase quoted in the text is on p. 3. See also Hans Joas, *Do We Need Religion? On the Experience of Self-Transcendence*, trans. Alex Skinner (Boulder, CO: Paradigm Publishers, 2008).

15. The phrase in the text is from Robert H. Sharf, "Experience," in *Critical Terms for Religious Studies*, ed. Mark C. Taylor (Chicago: University of Chicago Press, 1998), 109. Sharf is talking about alien abductions, but he has in view experience in general, and religious experience specifically.

16. Michael Jackson, *The Wherewithal of Life: Ethics, Migration, and the Question of Well-Being* (Berkeley: University of California Press, 2013), 5.

17. See Zimdars-Swartz, *Encountering Mary,* 43–57; Harris, *Lourdes,* 23–54; Carroll, *The Cult of the Virgin Mary,* 115–218.

18. Life as that which is in excess of any account that may be given of it is from Judith Butler, *Giving an Account of Oneself* (New York: Fordham University Press, 2005), 43, "knowingness" and "opacity" on 20–21; the metaphor of the blue ice floe is from Michael Jackson, *Minima Ethnographica: Intersubjectivity and the Anthropological Project* (Chicago: University of Chicago Press, 1998), 16.

19. Ludwig Wittgenstein, *Remarks on Frazer's* Golden Bough, trans. A. C. Miles, rev. and ed. Rush Rhees (1979; repr., Atlantic Highlands, NJ: Humanities Press International, 1991), 1e [this is the numbering of the English translation facing the original German text], 5e. Wittgenstein writes, "Frazer cannot imagine a priest who is not basically an English parson of our times with all his stupidity and feebleness." Brian J. Coman, "Frazer, Wittgenstein, and the Savage Mind," *Quadrant* 48 (June 2004): 14–19, helped me understand Frazer differently, in particular to see the shadow that falls in the later volumes of *The Golden Bough.* I also consulted Anthony Ossa-Richardson, "From Servius to Frazer: The Golden Bough and Its Transformations," *International Journal of the Classical Tradition* 15, no. 3 (September 2008): 339–368; Mary Beard, "Frazer, Leach, and Virgil: The Popularity (and Unpopularity) of *The Golden Bough,*" *Comparative Studies in Society and History* 34, no. 2 (April 1992): 203–224; Robert Fraser, *The Making of* The Golden Bough: *The Origins and Growth of an Argument* (New York: St. Martin's Press, 1990); Robert Ackerman, *The Myth and Ritual School: J. G. Frazer and the Cambridge Ritualists* (New York: Garland Publishing, 1991); and Jonathan Z. Smith, "When the Bough Breaks," in *Map Is Not Territory: Studies in the History of Religions* (Leiden, Netherlands: E. J. Brill, 1978), 208–239. On Frazer as the "undertaker of religion," see Ivan Strenski, *Thinking about Religion: An Historical Introduction to Theories of Religion* (Oxford: Blackwell Publishing, 2006), 139–140.

20. Wittgenstein, *Remarks,* 18e.

21. Michel de Certeau, *The Writing of History,* trans. Tom Conley (New York: Columbia University Press, 1988), 343.

22. Frank R. Ankersmit, *Sublime Historical Experience* (Stanford, CA: Stanford University Press, 2005), 14; Marilyn McCord Adams, *Wrestling for Blessing* (London: Darton, Longman, and Todd, 2005), 17. See also Constantin Fasolt, *The Limits of History* (Chicago: University of Chicago Press, 2004); Joan Wal-

lach Scott, *The Fantasy of Feminist History* (Durham, NC: Duke University Press, 2011).

23. On the "separate sense" and the "limits of consciousness," see Christopher Bollas, *Cracking Up: The Work of Unconscious Experience* (London: Routledge, 1995); D. W. Winnicott, *Playing and Reality* (London: Tavistock / Routledge, 1971), 50, 65–85; Apolito, *Apparitions of the Madonna at Oliveto Citra,* 107, 109–110.

24. I borrow the concept of "routes" from Bollas, *Cracking Up,* 48–70, although I use it in a way that is somewhat different from Bollas's meaning of strands of unconscious thought, "the self traveling thousands of ideational routes, leading not to nowhere, but to otherwhere, to an explosive creation of meanings, which nonetheless meet up with new units of life experience." Then again, maybe not so different. On some days, Father Norris says about the Bronx Lourdes, "it appears as if it is a car wash." Elliott, "Believers Bring Their Aches to Bathe in the City's Water."

25. Religion, or true religion, as a politically potent form of divine madness, appears, among other places, in Reinhold Niebuhr, *Moral Man and Immoral Society: A Study in Ethics and Politics* (1932; repr., New York: Charles Scribner's Sons, 1960), 255. "The secular imagination," Niebuhr writes, is incapable of producing in the political sphere "attitudes of repentance which recognize that the evil in the foe is also in the self" and "impulses of love which claim kinship with all men in spite of social conflict." These require religion's "sublime madness which disregards immediate appearances and emphasizes profound and ultimate unities." This idea echoes in all notions of the holy fool, of divine disobedience, and of the transcendence of the saints. See, for instance, liberation theologian Leonardo Boff's meditation on Saint Francis of Assisi as a model for Pope Francis I, in *Francis of Rome, Francis of Assisi: A New Springtime for the Church?* (Maryknoll, NY: Orbis Books, 2014), 43–46. Boff quotes Saint Francis as yearning to be "a new madman: mad for the poor Christ and *Lady Poverty*" (43). "Divine disobedience" is the title of Francine du Plessix Gray's history of Catholic radicalism, *Divine Disobedience: Profiles in Catholic Radicalism* (New York: Vintage, 1971).

26. Ankersmit, *Sublime Historical Experience,* 125; Harris, *Lourdes,* xiii, xiv–xv.

3. HOLY INTIMACIES

1. Bilinda Straight, *Miracles and Extraordinary Experience in Northern Kenya* (Philadelphia: University of Pennsylvania Press, 2007), 7.

2. Estimations of annual or daily attendance at the shrine vary, although the number 100,000 is fairly common for the former. See James P. Keleher, *Catholic Shrines and Places of Pilgrimage in the United States, Jubilee Edition* (Washington DC: United States Catholic Conference, Inc., 1998), 97; Laura Roxanne Seagraves puts the number of visitors annually at 300,000, in "A Bit about Dirt: Pilgrimage and Popular Religion at El Santuario de Chimayo" (PhD diss., Graduate Theological Union, Berkeley, California, 2002), 1. Ramón A. Gutiérrez calls Chimayo "the most popular shrine in the United States"; see "El Santuario de Chimayo: A Syncretic Shrine in New Mexico," in *Feasts and Celebrations in North American Communities,* ed. Ramón A. Gutiérrez and Geneviève Fabre (Albuquerque: University of New Mexico Press, 1995), 71.

3. The story of Don Bernardo's Good Friday discovery is the one most often heard about the shrine's origins. It is faithfully recounted in publications available at Chimayo, such as Father Julio González, SF, *The Shrine of Our Lord of Esquípulas and the Holy Child: Santuario de Chimayo in New Mexico* (Chimayo, NM: Sons of the Holy Family, 2013). It is also the story most often told in the Catholic press; see, for example, James Martin, SJ, "Holy Dirt," *America* 198, no. 6 (February 25, 2008): 9–12; Ann Hood, "Looking for a Healing in New Mexico," *Catholic Digest* 63 (July 1999): 23–36; Gerard E. Sherry, "The Blessed Earth at Chimayo," *Our Sunday Visitor* 79 (April 21, 1991): 12–13. There are many variations of the founding legend, none of them with much traction among practitioners. Some say a "friar" saw the light rising up from the ground: see Michelle Heather Pollock, "My Miracle at Chimayo," *Catholic Digest* 70 (February 2006): 35–39; that Don Bernardo believed the light was rising from "the fabled Seven Cities of Cibola," in Margaret M. Nava, "The 'Lourdes of America': Chimayo, New Mexico," *Liguorian* 83 (March 1995): 12–15; that the cross was buried there when "rebellious Indians" expelled the friars in 1680: see Neil M. Clark, "They Want No Progress in Chimayo," *Saturday Evening Post,* May 9, 1951, 38–39, 172–175. One version holds that a Guatemalan priest from Esquipulas ("El Padre de Esquipulas") traveled to the site in 1808, where he preached to the local people until he was murdered by "Indians seeking to rid the landscape of Europeans." This unnamed friar was buried at Chimayo, but after several days, the rising Santa Cruz River washed the soil off his body, exposing it and "the large crucifix that never left his side." This is in John B. Wright, "El Santuario de Chimayo: New Mexico's Lourdes," *FOCUS on Geography* 47, no. 2 (Winter 2002): 9–13. There are many other accounts of the shine's origins, although almost all share the details of Don Bernardo and a black crucifix buried in the

earth. Gutiérrez attributes the legend of the miraculous discovery to Don Bernardo's granddaughters, "A Syncretic Shrine," 76. Gutiérrez and Stephan F. de Borhegyi, a distinguished archaeologist, link Chimayo to the much older devotion to Our Lord of Esquipulas that flourished in postconquest Guatemala among the Chorti-speaking Maya Indians, after whose chief, Esquipulas, the village where the devotion first arose was named. Borhegyi associated the figure's black skin with the magical qualities that the native peoples of Middle America and Mexico believed to be linked to the color. The specific site of *el posito* is said to have been the spot where Tewa Indians believed fire had erupted from the earth during the mythical battle of the Warrior Twins, leaving behind a healing hot spring. Gutiérrez says that Don Bernardo, a merchant, had a shrine built to attract travelers to his shops with the hope of making Chimayo a major trading post. See Stephan F. de Borhegyi, "The Cult of Our Lord of Esquípulas in Middle America and New Mexico," *El Palacio* 61, no. 12 (December 1954): 387–401, and Gutiérrez, "A Syncretic Shrine," esp. 74–78.

4. The purchase of the shrine by the Society for the Revival of Spanish Arts and the Society for the Restoration and Preservation of Spanish Missions of New Mexico and its nearly immediate donation to the Archdiocese of Santa Fe is recounted in Patricia Trujillo-Oviedo, *Chimayó* (Charleston, SC: Arcadia Publishing, 2012), 39. In "They Want No Progress in Chimayo," Clark reports, "It was the Santuárió [*sic*] de Chimayo that occupied the thoughts of New Mexican soldiers, so many of whom were on tragic Bataan [as members of the 200th Coast Artillery], when they prayed for rescue. Many of them vowed pilgrimages if allowed to return. Many of them still make such pilgrimages each year" (40). For this period in Mexican American history, see Maggie Rivas-Rodriguez, ed., *Mexican Americans and World War II* (Austin: University of Texas Press, 2005), esp. chapter 4; Lynne Marie Getz, "Lost Momentum: World War II and the Education of Hispanos in New Mexico," 93–113. It is from Getz that I have the information about the 200th Coast Artillery cited above (108). Hood writes of being disappointed to learn that *el posito* was refilled by shrine staff; she believed it "replenished itself in some inexplicable way"; see "Looking for a Healing," 32. The shrine priests do not hide the refilling of the hole. "No, we gather the dirt from a nearby field," a priest at Chimayo told a visitor in 2002, "sift it, bless it, and bring it here." Quoted in Wright, "New Mexico's Lourdes," 13.

5. The detail about the roads at the time of Lizzie's visit is from Hood, "Looking for a Healing," 24.

6. On this figure, see Giles Huckenbeck, OFM, "Santo Niño de Atocha," *Saint Anthony Messenger* 71 (January 1964): 21–23; Alexander M. Frankfurter, "A Gathering of Children: Holy Infants and the Cult of El Santo Niño de Atocha," *El Palacio* 94, no. 1 (Summer / Fall 1988): 31–39. Frankfurter dates the cult of Santo Niño de Atocha in Chimayo to 1857, having made its way there along the active trade route from Mexico (36). During World War II, Santo Niño de Atocha became an intercessor for local men interred in prisoner-of-war camps, which in turn gave new life to the old legend that, during the "Moorish occupation" of Spain, a child in pilgrim's clothing miraculously freed Christians held captive (31).

7. Hood, "Looking for a Healing," 32.

8. Pollock, "My Miracle at Chimayo," 38.

9. Gutiérrez, "A Syncretic Shrine," 77.

10. The technical term for the human consumption of dirt is "geophagy," a practice that goes back to prehistoric times. Humans have eaten dirt for many reasons, in times of great danger or social dislocation. Geophagy has been practiced by pregnant women suffering from mineral deficiencies, individuals during famine, and African slaves on the horrific journey across the Atlantic, who may have believed it was a means to commit suicide. A recent expert opinion maintains that "soil consumption should be considered . . . within the normal range of human behavior." See Peter W. Abrahams, "Human Geophagy: A Review of Its Distribution, Causes, and Implications," in *Geology and Health: Closing the Gap,* ed. H. Catherine Skinner and Anthony R. Berger (New York: Oxford University Press, 2003), 32.

11. Identifying this visionary so insistently as "housewife" was itself already a gendered act of social control. Elaine Tyler May writes that in the context of wartime anxiety about female independence, the identity "housewife" was imposed on women as the safest and most acceptable designation for them. See Elaine Tyler May, *Homeward Bound: American Families in the Cold War,* 20th anniversary ed. (1988; repr., New York: Basic Books, 2008), 60–68. The visionary's words are from "Fatima Rosary, Family Rosary, Block Rosary," distributed by the Block Rosary Lay Apostolate, Detroit, Michigan (in the Archdiocese of Detroit Archives). No date is given. The text is accompanied by a warning from Nicholas J. Schorn—whose role in the history of the Block Rosary Apostolate will become clear later in this chapter—telling readers that the account of the vision has not been "examined and approved by Ecclesiastical Authority." There are Block Rosary societies around the world today unaffiliated with the Detroit

housewife. Because the visions were never officially recognized, a shrouded quality remains about the events in Detroit; this has led to many variations in accounts of it. For example, in "Columbiettes Hear Speaker Describe How Block Rosary Movement Started," *Wave* (Rockaway Beach), September 29, 1955, section 2, p. 2, a man named Robert Froehlich, "director of the Block Rosary Lay Associates," speaking to a group of young women in the local auxiliary of the Knights of Columbus, gives 1943 as the date of the visions, says the visionary was worried about her "sons," and identifies the crisis in the language of Cold War Marian piety as "troubled world conditions due to the absence of prayer."

12. James T. Sparrow, *Warfare State: World War II Americans and the Age of Big Government* (Oxford: Oxford University Press, 2011), 12; "maternalist patriotism," 56; Kate Smith is quoted on 119. So seriously did Americans take the responsibility of buying war bonds, Sparrow says, that they came to resent as unseemly and offensive the crude spirit of hucksterism associated with public war bond campaigns. Neither "strictly ideological appeals" to freedom and democracy nor outright commercialism worked to sell bonds. The most effective pitch "simply confronted audiences with someone with whom they could identify or sympathize, the G. I." (145–146). This was precisely the message Mary subverted.

13. On devotion to the Sacred Heart, see David Morgan, *The Sacred Heart of Jesus: The Visual Evolution of a Devotion* (Amsterdam: Amsterdam University Press, 2008); Jean Bainvel, *Devotion to the Sacred Heart of Jesus,* trans. E. Leahy (New York: Benziger Bros., 1924).

14. Catholic authorities in the Southwest and northern Midwest were not of a single mind vis-à-vis the question of language, although from the 1930s into the 1980s, they shared the fear that Protestant proselytizers were making headway in Mexican communities. The general position among Catholic educators from just before the Second World War seems to have been that while the Spanish language along with some Mexican customs ought to be respected, in order to make lives for themselves in the new country, migrants and especially their children needed to learn English. Much of the support for bilingualism was intended as a step in this direction. See, for example, Lawrence J. Mosqueda, "Twentieth Century Arizona, Hispanics, and the Catholic Church," *U.S. Catholic Historian* 9, nos. 1 and 2 (Winter–Spring 1990): 87–103; "Lo, the Poor Mexican!" *Priest* 12, no. 5 (May 1956): 389–393; Ed Willock, "North of the Border," *Mission Digest* 12 (March 1954): 5–8; "Bishop Deplores Prejudice against Mexican Immigrants," *Interracial Review* 26 (May 1953): 86; John O'Grady,

"New Life Comes from the Bottom," *Catholic Charities Review* 39 (December 1955): 14–16; Kenneth D. Eberhard, CSSR, "Mexican Migrants: A Pastoral Problem," *Priest* 19 (July 1963): 583–586; A Missionary, "Frontier of the Faith—II. Mexicans' Backgrounds and Traits," *Social Justice Review* 45 (April 1952–March 1953): 65–67; A Missionary, "Frontier of the Faith—III. Riches of the Mexican Soul," *Social Justice Review* 45 (July–August 1952): 105–107; Rev. Robert A. Keller, "Instructing Migrant Children," *Catholic School Journal* 59 (June 1959): 53–54; Robert A. Keller, "Hello, My Name Is Pedro," *Catholic School Journal* 63 (June 1963): 42–43. "We have noticed a tendency," the director of the Hispanic apostolate office in Saginaw, Michigan, wrote in the early 1960s, "on the part of agencies, organizations, and the community at large to forget the Spanish-speaking once they have moved out of farm labor to become part of the urban community." Quoted in Moisés Sandoval, "The Organization of a Hispanic Church," in *Hispanic Catholic Culture in the U.S.: Issues and Concerns,* ed. Jay P. Dolan and Allan Figueroa Deck, SJ (South Bend, IN: University of Notre Dame Press, 1994), 135. As class differences within Mexican American Catholic populations became more pronounced in the second half of the twentieth century, a linguistic divide opened between the longer resident and more prosperous, who wanted instruction for their children in English, and the newly arrived and poorer, for whom Spanish remained the primary language. See, for example, Roberto R. Treviño, *The Church in the Barrio: Mexican American Ethno-Catholicism in Houston* (Chapel Hill: University of North Carolina Press, 2006), 124–125. "This heterogeneity," Treviño writes, "resulted in slightly different ethnic identities and religious practices that distinguished Mexican Catholics not only from Anglo Catholics but also, to a degree, from each other" (125). Although he is focused specifically on Houston, Treviño's comments underscore how isolated Natalie was in Arizona from English-speaking Catholics as well as longer-established Mexican Americans. Richard Rodriguez, *Hunger of Memory: The Education of Richard Rodriguez, a Memoir* (New York: Bantam Books, 1982), was helpful to me in thinking about the social experience of bilingualism in the borderlands, among the children and grandchildren of Mexican migrants; see also Kathleen Holscher, *Religious Lessons: Catholic Sisters and the Captured School Crisis in New Mexico* (New York: Oxford University Press: 2012), esp. 64–65, 92–93.

15. It is relevant here that Lizzie was a self-described "biker chick," and although by the time of the incident in the text she had lost most of the physical evidence of this identity, such as her long, dyed-red hair and her leather jackets,

this was still how she thought of and presented herself. Her husband was a tall, rail-thin man who worked in one of the few remaining factories in southern Indiana. His hair reached to the middle of his back and he spoke in a distinctive local working-class drawl. The gap in social class between this couple and the medical professionals they were now so dependent upon could not have been clearer. Keith Wailoo discusses the consequences of discrepant social, racial, and economic status for health care in *Pain: A Political History* (Baltimore: Johns Hopkins University Press, 2014). This paragraph also relies on Arthur Kleinman, *The Illness Narratives: Suffering, Healing, and the Human Condition* (New York: Basic Books, 1988); Cheri Register, *Living with Chronic Illness: Days of Patience and Passion* (New York: Free Press, 1987); Edward Shorter, *Bedside Manners: The Troubled History of Doctors and Patients* (New York: Simon and Schuster, 1985); Edward Shorter, *From Paralysis to Fatigue: A History of Psychosomatic Illness in the Modern Era* (New York: Free Press, 1992); Paul Starr, *The Social Transformation of American Medicine* (New York: Basic Books, 1982); Joanna Bourke, *The Story of Pain: From Prayer to Painkillers* (Oxford: Oxford University Press, 2014); Wendy Cadge, *Paging God: Religion in the Halls of Medicine* (Chicago: University of Chicago Press, 2012); David A. Karp, *Speaking of Sadness: Depression, Disconnection, and the Meanings of Illness* (New York: Oxford University Press, 1996). What I say about the social consequences of Natalie's abuse relies on Jody Messler Davies and Mary Gail Frawley, *Treating the Survivor of Childhood Sexual Abuse: A Psychoanalytic Perspective* (New York: Basic Books, 1994); Elisabeth Young-Bruehl, *Childism: Confronting Prejudice against Children* (New Haven, CT: Yale University Press, 2012); Richard B. Gartner, *Betrayed as Boys: Psychodynamic Treatment of Sexually Abused Men* (New York: Guildford Press, 1999); Ellen Bass and Laura Davis, *The Courage to Heal: A Guide for Women Survivors of Child Sexual Abuse,* 20th anniversary ed. (New York: HarperCollins, 2008); and Leonard Shengold, *Soul Murder: The Effects of Childhood Abuse and Deprivation* (New Haven, CT: Yale University Press, 1989).

16. Hannah Arendt's comments on intersubjectivity are from "On Humanity in Dark Times: Thoughts about Lessing," in *Men in Dark Times* (San Diego: Harcourt Brace Jovanovich, 1983), 12, 10. Alongside Arendt, I read Elisabeth Young-Bruehl's discussion of her life and work, *Hannah Arendt: For Love of the World* (New Haven, CT: Yale University Press, 1982), which deeply informed my understanding of Arendt, as did Jeffrey C. Isaac, *Arendt, Camus, and Modern Rebellion* (New Haven, CT: Yale University Press, 1992).

17. Axel Honneth, *The Struggle for Recognition: The Moral Grammar of Social Conflicts*, trans. Joel Anderson (Cambridge, MA: MIT Press, 1995), 135; but on the subject of recognition, compare with Patchen Markell, *Bound by Recognition* (Princeton, NJ: Princeton University Press, 2003). My understanding of recognition has been informed by what might be called the tradition of the inter-subjective third in psychoanalytic theory, as developed from Winnicott to Jessica Benjamin.

18. Michael Jackson, *The Wherewithal of Life: Ethics, Migration, and the Question of Well-Being* (Berkeley: University of California Press, 2013), 8; Wendell Berry, *A Place on Earth* (Berkeley: Counterpoint, 2001), 189. Psychoanalytic theorist Deborah Anna Luepnitz speaks of the phenomenon of having something "that was not on my mind, although it was present in my words," in Deborah Anna Luepnitz, "Thinking in the Space between Winnicott and Lacan," in *Between Winnicott and Lacan: A Clinical Engagement*, ed. Lewis A. Kirshner (New York: Routledge, 2011), 18. The language of detouring via the other to the self is indebted to Paul Ricoeur, *Oneself as Another*, trans. Kathleen Blamey (Chicago: University of Chicago Press, 1992).

19. On the concept of the "unthought known," see Christopher Bollas, *The Shadow of the Object: Psychoanalysis of the Unthought Known* (New York: Columbia University Press, 1987); Adam Phillips, *Terror and Experts* (Cambridge, MA: Harvard University Press, 1995), 22.

20. Phillips, *Terror and Experts*, 22.

21. Aloysius McDonough, CP, "Block Rosary," *Sign Post* 31 (November 1951): 29–30, the caution about "religious fakirs" is on 29.

22. Ibid., 29; Ruth Oswald, "One-Man Apostolate: The Story behind the Block Rosary Crusade," *Our Lady's Digest* 14 (November 1959): 183–187, comment about "visions or dreams" is on 186.

23. McDonough, "Block Rosary," 30; on Father Peyton and the Rosary Crusade, see Patrick J. Peyton, CSC, *All for Her: The Autobiography of Father Patrick Peyton* (Garden City, NY: Doubleday, 1967); Patrick J. Peyton, *The Ear of God: Prayer Is the Language of Man to God* (Garden City, NY: Doubleday, 1951).

24. The story of Father Peyton's preemptory treatment of the Detroit visionary is from Oswald, "One-Man Apostolate," 185. The Block Rosary Lay Apostolate Committee—not the Detroit housewife's vision—was granted official approval in 1950. Nicholas J. Schorn is cited as "Chairman" of the committee. His takeover was complete by early 1952. See Nicholas J. Schorn, "Why the Block Ro-

sary?" *Our Lady of the Cape: Queen of the Most Holy Rosary* (February 1952): 7–9, 20 (in the Detroit Archdiocesan Archives).

25. McDonough, "Block Rosary," 30.

26. Schorn, "Why the Block Rosary?," 7.

27. On the anti-Communist direction of the postwar Block Rosary, see Joseph P. Chinnici, OFM, "The Catholic Community at Prayer, 1926–1976," in *Habits of Devotion: Catholic Religious Practice in Twentieth-Century America,* ed. James M. O'Toole (Ithaca, NY: Cornell University Press, 2004), 57–58. Chinnici does not mention either the Detroit housewife or the appearance of the Blessed Mother. In the same volume, see also Paula M. Kane, "Marian Devotion since 1940: Continuity or Casualty?," 89–129, on 102. Kane dates the Block Rosary to 1946 and identifies it as "an outgrowth of belief in promises made by Our Lady of Fatima about world peace at her apparition in 1917." Its purpose was to "combat the threat of atomic bomb attack." See also Colleen Doody, "Grappling with Secularism: Anti-Communism and Catholicism in Cold War Detroit," *American Communist History* 10, no. 1 (2011): 53–71. Helpful for this period in Detroit's religious history is Matthew Pehl, "'Apostles of Fascism,' 'Communist Clergy,' and the UAW: Political Ideology and Working-Class Religion in Detroit, 1919–1945," *Journal of American History* 99 (September 2012): 440–465.

28. Susan Sontag, *Illness as Metaphor* (New York: Vintage Books, 1978), 3.

29. This is Ruth Leys's characterization of a dominant contemporary approach to trauma, in *Trauma: A Genealogy* (Chicago: University of Chicago Press, 2000), 249; influential in this hole-in-the-mind school of trauma is Cathy Caruth, *Unclaimed Experience: Trauma, Narrative, and History* (Baltimore: Johns Hopkins University Press, 1996); see also Cathy Caruth, ed., *Trauma: Explorations in Memory* (Baltimore: Johns Hopkins University Press, 1995). The phrases "metaphors of agency" and "media of objectification" are from Elaine Scarry, *The Body in Pain: The Making and Unmaking of the World* (New York: Oxford University Press, 1985). The literatures on pain, suffering, and trauma are extensive. I cite here works I consulted in thinking through the issues at stake in this part of the chapter: Judith Lewis Herman, *Trauma and Recovery* (New York: Basic Books, 1992); François Davoine and Jean-Max Gaudillière, *History beyond Trauma,* trans. Susan Fairfield (New York: Other Press, 2004); Marilyn Charles, *Working with Trauma: Lessons from Bion and Lacan* (Lanham, MD: Jason Aronson, 2012); Jeffrey C. Alexander, *Trauma: A Social Theory* (Cambridge, UK: Polity Press, 2012); Jennifer J. Freyd, *Betrayal Trauma: The Logic of Forgetting Childhood Abuse* (Cambridge, MA: Harvard

University Press, 1996). For further sources of my thinking on questions of pain and suffering, refer to Robert A. Orsi, *Thank You, St. Jude: Women's Devotion to the Patron Saint of Hopeless Causes* (New Haven, CT: Yale University Press, 1996), 142–184.

30. Pollock, "My Miracle at Chimayo," 36; Straight, *Miracles and Extraordinary Experience in Northern Kenya,* 17. Straight also refers to signs that are full of "every little . . . thoughtful and intersubjective experience that brought them into being" as "an act of communion" and talks about experience being "incarnated" in signs (9).

31. Tony Hiss, *The Experience of Place* (New York: Vintage Books, 1990), 3, 9.

32. Clifford Geertz, "Religion as a Cultural System," in *The Interpretation of Cultures* (New York: Basic Books, 1973), 104.

33. Arendt, "On Humanity in Dark Times," 24; on this aspect of Arendt's thought, see Elisabeth Young-Bruehl, *Why Arendt Matters* (New Haven, CT: Yale University Press, 2006), 33–76.

34. Jessica Benjamin, "Two-Way Streets: Recognition of Difference and the Intersubjective Third," *Differences: A Journal of Feminist Cultural Studies* 17, no. 1 (Spring 2006): 116–146.

35. Hannah Arendt, *The Human Condition,* 2nd ed., introduction by Margaret Canovan (Chicago: University of Chicago Press, 1998; first published 1958), 23. "No human life," Arendt writes, "not even the life of the hermit in nature's wilderness, is possible without a world which directly or indirectly testifies to the presence of other human beings" (22).

36. Michael Jackson, *Paths toward a Clearing: Radical Empiricism and Ethnographic Inquiry* (Bloomington: Indiana University Press, 1989), 17, emphasis in the original.

37. Phillips, *Terror and Experts,* 27; Jean-Paul Sartre, *Search for a Method,* trans. Hazel E. Barnes (New York: Vintage Books, 1963), 57.

4. PRINTED PRESENCE

1. "Catholic books in a Protestant world" is from Eamon Duffy, *Marking the Hours: English People and their Prayers, 1240–1570* (New Haven, CT: Yale University Press, 2006), 119.

2. For a sense of the *longue durée* of the Catholic book, compare what I describe in this chapter with the examples of medieval and early modern print culture in Duffy, *Marking the Hours,* and Virginia Reinburg, *French Book of*

Hours: Making an Archive of Prayer, c. 1400–1600 (Cambridge, UK: Cambridge University Press, 2012).

3. Personal correspondence, February 4, 2014, cited with permission.

4. Ann Ball, *Encyclopedia of Catholic Devotions and Practices* (Huntington, IN: Our Sunday Visitor Publishing Division, 2003), 233–237. On the history of holy cards, see Alberto Vecchi, *Il culto della immagini nelle stampe popolari*, Biblioteca di Lares, vol. 26 (Florence: L. S. Olschki, 1968); *Des mondes de papier: L'imagerie populaire de Wissembourg* (Strasbourg, France: Musée de la vielle de Strasbourg, 2010); Barbara Calamari and Sandra DiPasqua, *Holy Cards* (New York: Abrams, 2004); Catherine Rosenbaum-Dondaine, *L'image de piété en France: 1814–1914* (Paris: Musée-galerie de la SEITA, 1984); Giuseppe Cocchiara, *Le immagini devote del popolo siciliano* (Palermo, Italy: Sellerio, 1982); F. Riccobono and A. Sarica, *Immagini devote in Sicilia* (Messina, Italy: Edas, 1982); Pierre Lessard, *Les petites images dévotes: Leur utilization traditionnelle au Québec* (Quebec: Presses de l'Université Laval, 1981); Elisabetta Gulli Grigoni and Vittorio Pranzini, *Santi: Piccole immagini devozionali a stampa e manufatte dal XVII al XX Secolo* (Ravenna, Italy: Edizioni Essegi, 1990); Jean Pirotte, "Les images de dévotion du XVe siècle à nos jours: Introduction à l'étude d'un media," in *Imagiers de paradis: Images de piété populaires du XVe au XXe siècle*, 11–76 (Bastogne, Belgium: Musée en Piconrue, Crédit Communal, 1990). I thank David Morgan for his help in assembling this short bibliography on the subject. Brent Devitt, an expert on collecting and identifying holy cards, sent me instructional materials he had prepared, including photocopies of different kinds of cards, richly annotated by him. This was an invaluable primer in the genre.

5. On religion and visual culture, see David Morgan, *The Embodied Eye: Religious Visual Culture and the Social Life of Feeling* (Berkeley: University of California Press, 2012); Hans Belting, *Likeness and Presence: A History of the Image before the Era of Art,* trans. Edmund Jephcott (Chicago: University of Chicago Press, 1994); David Freedberg, *The Power of Images: Studies in the History and Theory of Response* (Chicago: University of Chicago Press, 1989).

6. This paragraph quotes H. J. Heagney, "The First Prayers," *Catholic Home Journal* 45 (October 1945): 8, 11, "special appeal to the very young" on 8; "kiss the piggies" is from Richard A. Duprey, "Heroes for Children," *Grail* 40 (November 1958): 35–37, quotation on 35; Sister Mary, IHM, "Our Lady and Little Children," *America,* May 13, 1933, 134–135, quotation on 135. It also refers to Mary Zook, "Religious Training for the Younger Set," *Sign* 35 (June 1956): 27–28; Sister Mary Clara, "Religion Learned through Living," *Journal of Religious Instruction*

15 (April 1945): 658–661; H. J. Heagney, "Training the Baby," *Catholic Home Journal* 45 (September 1945): 10; Norah Smaridge, "Taking Little Ones to Church," *Catholic Home Journal* 54 (January 1954): 10–11. Holy cards in the nineteenth century were also printed in a brooding black-and-white chiaroscuro, but there are very few of these in Elsie's collection, cards in color obviously having become more popular and available by this time and more desirable. Death cards, distributed at wakes, tended to be black and white.

7. See Lee Palmer Wandel, *The Eucharist in the Reformation: Incarnation and Liturgy* (Cambridge, UK: Cambridge University Press, 2006), 208–255; R. Po-Chia Hsia, *The World of Catholic Renewal, 1540–1770* (Cambridge, UK: Cambridge University Press, 1998), 172–186; Robert Bireley, *The Refashioning of Catholicism, 1450–1700: Reassessment of the Counter Reformation* (Washington, DC: Catholic University of America Press, 1999), 121–146; Louis Châtellier, *The Europe of the Devout: The Catholic Reformation and the Formation of a New Society*, trans. Jean Birrell (Cambridge, UK: Cambridge University Press, 1989), 67–88, 136–158. For a striking example of the Vatican's efforts to confiscate all copies of a forbidden work, see Sergio Luzzato, *Padre Pio: Miracles and Politics in a Secular Age*, trans. Frederika Randall (New York: Picador, 2010), 160–166. On the modern Vatican's evolving attitude toward archives, see Owen Chadwick, *Catholicism and History: The Opening of the Vatican Archives* (London: Cambridge University Press, 1978). See also Una M. Cadegan, *All Good Books Are Catholic Books: Print Culture, Censorship, and Modernity in Twentieth-Century America*, Cushwa Center Studies of Catholicism in Twentieth-Century America (Ithaca, NY: Cornell University Press, 2013).

8. Po-Chia Hsia writes that "contradictory impulses" of "control and exuberance" are evident in the history of the Catholic book after Trent; see *The World of Catholic Renewal*, 172. This paragraph is indebted to Luzzato, *Padre Pio*, which carefully traces the sometimes hostile, sometimes supportive relations between Padre Pio's devout and the Vatican at various times.

9. The national office of the Confraternity of Christian Doctrine (CCD), which oversaw religious instruction for children outside the parochial school system, was established in 1933 in Washington, DC. A decade later, CCD was at work in 107 dioceses around the country. See also "Confraternity [of] Christian Doctrine: Religious Vacation Schools, Yesterday and Today," *Catholic Action* 25 (June 1943): 14, 21. Although Catholic educators regularly declared that the family was the true agent of religious formation, they complained just as regularly that contemporary parents were failing in this responsibility. Prac-

tically speaking, the religious formation of children and adolescents was the work of teaching sisters, and to a much lesser extent of parish priests and religious brothers. For discussions of family duties and failures in this regard, see, for example, James M. Thompson, "Doctrine for Children," *Clergy Review* 21 (October 1941): 225–231; Alice R. May, "The Child, the Home, the School," *Journal of Religious Instruction* 16 (April 1946): 701–710; M. V. Kelly, OSB, "First Friday and Children's Confessions," *Homiletic and Pastoral Review* 37 (October 1936): 65–67. A later example of the apprehension that parents make poor religion teachers is Sister Marilyn, OSF, "Weekly Instructions in Religion," *Catholic School Journal* 57 (September 1957): 229–232.

10. George Vogt, "En Rapport: Religion and the Boy of Today," *Journal of Religious Instruction* 3 (June 1933): 846–851, quotations on 847; Florence D. Sullivan, SJ, "Teaching Children to Pray," *Catholic School Journal* 30 (June 1930): 197–199, "surging allurements of the senses" on 197.

11. On the periodic juvenile delinquency panics in the United States in the twentieth century, see Steven Mintz, *Huck's Raft: A History of American Childhood* (Cambridge, MA: Belknap Press of Harvard University Press, 2004), 159–162, 291–297. One of the leading Catholic commentators on the problem of young gangs and crime was the sociologist and educator Father Paul Hanly Furfey. His most influential work on the subject was *The Gang Age: A Study of the Preadolescent Boy and His Recreational Needs* (New York: Macmillan, 1926); see also his theological reflection on the issue, *The Mystery of Iniquity* (Milwaukee: Bruce Publishing, 1944).

12. Vera Hinman, "Lucky to Be a Catholic?," *Family Digest* 14 (June 1959): 21–24; "shifting sureties" is on 24. On the professionalization of teaching sisters early in the twentieth century, see Kathleen Sprows Cummings, *New Women of the Old Faith: Gender and American Catholicism in the Progressive Era* (Chapel Hill: University of North Carolina Press, 2009), 130–153; for later in the century, see Mary Oates, "The Professional Preparation of Parochial School Sisters, 1870–1940," *Historical Journal of Massachusetts* 12, no. 1 (1984): 60–72, and Kathleen Holscher, *Religious Lessons: Catholic Sisters and the Captured School Crisis in New Mexico* (New York: Oxford University Press: 2012), in particular chap. 3, "A Space between Walls: Inside the Sister-Taught Public Classrooms of New Mexico," 77–105. On the openness of Catholic educators to new progressive educational theories after the Second World War, see Holscher's discussion of the prominent Catholic educator Reverend Thomas Shields, 90–91; see also Timothy Walch, *Parish School: American Catholic Parochial Education from Colonial*

Times to the Present (New York: Crossroad Publishing, 1996), 119–124, 139–142.

13. "A Curriculum in Religion, Grade I—The Childhood of Christ," *Catholic School Journal* 30 (December 1930): 439–441; "A Curriculum in Religion, Grade II—Preparation for Holy Communion," *Catholic School Journal* 31 (January 1931): 1–7; "A Curriculum in Religion, Grade III—The Public Life of Christ," *Catholic School Journal* 31 (February 1931): 48–51; "A Curriculum in Religion, Grade IV—Old Testament History," *Catholic School Journal* 31 (March 1931): 93–98; "A Curriculum in Religion, Grade V—Church History," *Catholic School Journal* 31 (April 1931): 132–138; "A Curriculum in Religion, Grade VI—The Mass," *Catholic School Journal* 31 (May 1931): 170–176. "A Curriculum in Religion, Grade VII—Christian Doctrine," *Catholic School Journal* 31 (September 1931): 335–339; "A Curriculum in Religion, Grade VIII—Christian Doctrine," *Catholic School Journal* 32 (January 1932): 18–23.

14. Sister Mary Consilia, OP, "The Religious Practices of Children," *Journal of Religious Instruction* 8 (February 1938): 497–512, quotations on 500. But compare M. V. Kelly, CSB, "Memorizing Prayers," *Journal of Religious Instruction* 6 (May 1936): 829.

15. Sister Mary Consilia, "The Religious Practices of Children," 499.

16. Vogt, "En Rapport," 847; Sister M. Evangela, SSND, "The Religion Teacher and Her Problem," *Journal of Religious Instruction* 15 (January 1945): 430–437, the religion teacher's "main objective" and the role of "desire" in achieving it is on 438, emphasis in the original; Sister Mary Marguerite, CSJ, "Telling Religious Stories to Children," *Journal of Religious Instruction* 12 (September 1941): 45–51, quotations on 45, 50. Sister Mary Evangela was the supervisor of the School Sisters of Notre Dame in Pittsburgh, Pennsylvania.

17. Sullivan, "Teaching Children to Pray," "a pest or an enemy" is on 197; Sister M. Felice, FSPA, "Literature for Louis and Louise," *Catholic School Journal* 46 (June 1946): 196. The comment about "thirsty imaginations" is made in the context of the postwar comic book scare.

18. Some examples of prayer books for children are *The Child's Prayerbook: Prayers and Instructions for Catholic Children Compiled from Approved Sources* (Winterberg, NY: John Baptist Steinberner, 1899); *My Little Prayerbook: Instructions and Prayers for Catholic Children* (New York: Benziger Brothers, 1894); Patrick F. Shine, ed., *Come My Jesus: Prayers and Instructions for Children* (New York: Catholic Book Publishing, 1957); Most Rev. Louis Laravoire Morrow, *My Jesus and I* (Kenosha, WI: My Mission House, 1949); *Manual of Prayers for Chil-*

dren in Catholic Grade and High Schools (O'Fallon, MO: Sisters of the Adoration of the Most Precious Blood, 1949); *Remembrance of My First Holy Communion* (New York: William J. Hirten, 1942); Auleen B. Eberhardt, *Small Prayers for Small Children* (St. Benedict, OR: Benedictine Press, 1949); Daniel A. Lord, SJ, *A Child at Prayer* (New York: Devotional Publishing, 1945). The coloring book cited is Daniel A. Lord, SJ, *Angel and Imp at Home Paint Book* (St. Louis: Queen's Work, n.d.), n.p. The American Catholic History Research Center and University Archives at Catholic University, Washington DC, provides online access to the children's comic book *Treasure Chest,* published between 1946 and 1972 by George A. Pflaum, including full-color comics of the lives of the saints; see *Treasure Chest of Fun and Fact,* http://cuislandora.wrlc.org/islandora/object /cuislandora%3A9584. The genre of Catholic children's fiction referenced in (5a) includes such titles as Martin J. Scott, SJ, *A Boy Knight* (New York: P. J. Kenedy and Sons, 1921); Thomas B. Chetwood, SJ, *Tony* (St. Louis: Queen's Work, 1933) (of course!); Sister Mary St. Virginia, BVM, *Peggy's Growing Up (A Fictional Saint)* (St. Louis: Queen's Work, 1940); Thomas B. Chetwood, SJ, *Nicky* (St. Louis: Queen's Work, 1934); Thomas B. Chetwood, SJ, *Frida* (St. Louis: Queen's Work, 1933); and Anthony F. La Bau, SJ, *Saint Bill of New York* (St. Louis: Queen's Work, 1945). For children's books on the sacraments, see, for example, Daniel A. Lord, SJ, *The Seven Sacraments,* illustrated by Katherine Wireman (New York: Devotional Publishing, n.d.). Books written for children and adolescents about individual saints or collections of stories about the saints are too numerous even to cite examples reasonably. Suggestions for religious art that children ought to know comes from "A Curriculum in Religion, Grade III—The Public Life of Christ," 49. The illustrated edition of the *Baltimore Catechism* is Ellamay Horan and James W. O'Brien, *A Catechism of Christian Doctrine: The Illustrated Revised Edition of the Baltimore Catechism, No. 1* (New York: W. H. Sadlier, 1944). Copies of various cutout books published by Daniel Lord can be found in the Daniel Lord Manuscript Collection, Pius XII Memorial Library, St. Louis University. On prayer flashcards, see Rev. P. Henry Sullivan, "Notes on Teaching the 'Our Father' and the 'Hail Mary' to Small Children," *Journal of Religious Instruction* 7 (November 1936): 265–268; another example of tactile pedagogy is Sister Mary Louise, SL, "Cutting Out Theological Paper Dolls," *Journal of Religious Instruction* 15 (March 1954): 639–641; on visual aids in the classroom, see, for example, the series by Jerome F. O'Connor, SJ, and William Hayden, SJ, *Chalk Talks, or, Teaching Catechism Graphically* (St. Louis: Queen's Work, 1928).

19. Sister M. Leo, "Making Little Catholics More Catholic," *Journal of Religious Instruction* 14 (November 1943): 254–259, quotations on 255.

20. This paragraph is informed by Juhani Pallasmaa, *The Thinking Hand: Existential and Embodied Wisdom in Architecture* (West Sussex, UK: John Wiley and Sons, 2009); on the relationship between writing and reality, see Geoffrey Galt Harpham, *The Ascetic Imperative in Culture and Criticism* (Chicago: University of Chicago Press, 1987), esp. 5–17, 114–115; on writing and the formation of the self, either individually or in relation to a greater whole, see Pierre Hadot, *Philosophy as a Way of Life: Spiritual Exercises from Socrates to Foucault,* trans. Michael Chase (Malden, MA: Blackwell Publishing, 1995), 209–211. This chapter also takes inspiration from Walter J. Ong, SJ, *The Presence of the Word: Some Prolegomena for Cultural and Religious History* (New Haven, CT: Yale University Press, 1967).

21. Sister Mary Jarlath, OP, "Active Religion," *Catholic School Interests* 10 (July 1931): 90–95; Sister Cecilia Ann Benson, FCSP, "Teaching Christian Social Principles to Pupils in the First Grade," *Catholic Educational Review* (November 1946): 368–376; Sister Elizabeth Marie, OSF, "To My Guardian Angel," *Catholic School Journal* 47 (October 1947): 294, 24a, quotation on 294; Sister Marilyn, "Weekly Instructions in Religion," hand-tracing exercise on 230.

22. One of the most powerful examples of this Cold War genre is the long comic book, *This Godless Communism,* serialized in *Treasure Chest of Fun and Fact,* beginning on September 28, 1961 (vol. 17, no. 2), 3–8, and continuing in even-numbered issues through no. 20. Reed Leonard Crandall (1917–1982), the comic book's illustrator, was a prolific comic book artist, whose credits included stories in *Tales from the Crypt, The Vault of Horror,* and *Weird Fantasy* (all published by EC Comics), along with issues of *Classics Illustrated. This Godless Communism* deserves a place in the literature of the Cold War generally, the supernatural Cold War in particular. I describe an instance of Cold War devotional practice in Robert A. Orsi, "U.S. Catholics between Memory and Modernity," in *Catholics in the American Century: Recasting Narratives of U.S. History,* ed. R. Scott Appleby and Kathleen Sprows Cummings (Ithaca, NY: Cornell University Press, 2012), 11–42, on 35.

23. Sister Marilyn, "Weekly Instructions in Religion," 230, 231; for Sister Marilyn's well-informed reflections on the plight of religion teachers in the second half of the twentieth century, see "The Paradox of a Religious Teacher," *Cord* 7 (March 1957): 90–91.

24. *Saint Joseph Daily Missal,* ed. Hugo H. Hoever, SO Cist. (New York: Catholic Book Publishing, 1959).

25. All of these examples are drawn from the 1997 conversations, as described in the note on research methods.

26. A School Sister of Notre Dame, "Consider the Lives of the Saints," *Journal of Religious Instruction* 5 (November 1934): 206–211, quotation on 209; Sister Anne Catherine, CSJ, "Teaching the Truth about the Saints," *Journal of Religious Instruction* 12 (March 1942): 586–602, quotations on 600–601.

27. This account of Isaac Jogues's torture is from Neil Boynton, SJ, *Mangled Hands: A Story of the New York Martyrs* (New York: Benziger Brothers, 1926), 39–40. A later devotional book for boys about the New York martyrs (as American Catholics called them; Canadians thought otherwise) is Milton Lomask, *Saint Isaac and the Indians* (New York: Vision Books, 1956). This latter was one of my favorite books as a boy. Brian Moore likewise does not minimize the physical horror of the torture of native converts or of the Jesuits in his novel, *Black Robe* (1985; repr., New York: Plume, 1997). For a recent historical treatment of the subject, see Emma Anderson, *The Death and Afterlife of the North American Martyrs* (Cambridge, MA: Harvard University Press, 2013).

28. A popular account of this figure is Marie Cecilia Buehrle, *Saint Maria Goretti* (Milwaukee: Bruce Publishing, 1950). There is, of course, a very graphic comic book depicting the life of the saint: Mary Fabyan Windeatt, "Saint Maria Goretti: The Blood-Stained Lily," illus. Mart Bailey, *Treasure Chest of Fun and Fact* 6, no. 5 (November 9, 1950): 9–14. See Figures 8–13 in this chapter. On Mart Bailey, see "Mart Bailey," Lambiek Comiclopedia, September 5, 2012, www .lambiek.net/artists/b/bailey_mart.htm.

29. Daniel A. Lord, SJ, *Miniature Stories of the Saints,* bk. 1 (New York: William J. Hirten, 1943), n.p., "Saint Aloysius."

30. Sister M. Brendan, SSND, "Training in Habits of Prayer," *Journal of Religious Instruction* 9 (March 1939): 541–549, quotations on 543, 546; Sister Marita, OSF, "Marshaling Troops for Christ," *Catholic School Journal* 53 (September 1953): 204–205, quotation on 204.

31. My friend Terence McKiernan helped me first to notice and then to think about the mystery of Elsie's two signatures.

32. Mary Coughlin, "Saint Joseph of Cupertino," illus. Malcolm Kildale, *Treasure Chest of Fun and Fact* 2, no. 13 (February 18, 1947): 6–9, quotation on 9; Mary Fabyan Windeatt, "The Boys' Friend: St. John Bosco," illus. Paul Karch, *Treasure Chest of Fun and Fact* 8, no. 9 (January 1, 1953): 12–17; Don Bosco

discusses Grey's heavenly origins on 17. Malcolm Kildale (1913–1970) was a much-sought-after illustrator, whose work appeared in *Private Detective Stories, Centaur Comics, Classics Illustrated, Leading Western,* and *Fighting Western,* in addition to *Treasure Chest of Fun and Fact.* See "Malcolm Kildale," Field Guide to Wild American Pulp Artists, 2013, www.pulpartists.com/Kildale.html.

33. The event is described in David Hajdu, *The Ten-Cent Plague: The Great Comic-Book Scare and How It Changed America* (New York: Farrar, Straus, and Giroux, 2008), 121–127. For some sense of how the Binghamton fire is commonly construed, see Joe Sergi, "1948: The Year that Comics Met Their Match," Comic Book League Defense Fund, June 8, 2012, http://cbldf.org/2012/06/1948-the-year-comics-met-their-match/. There are many other references to the Binghamton fire on the Internet, usually in conjunction with the broader topic of book burning. See, for instance, the relatively recent entry by Daniel Schwartz of CBS News, "Timeline: The Books Have Been Burning—A Timeline of 2,200 Years of Book Burnings, from Ancient China to the Book of Negroes," CBC News, September 10, 2010, www.cbc.ca/news/world/the-books-have-been-burning-1.887172. It is curious that this local and equivocal—if the smiling faces of the children around the fire are taken into account—instance of "book burning" should make it into a two-millennia overview. I begin to think this is not about burning comic books; it is about the scandal of Catholic modernity. The number of comic books burned in Binghamton is from "Catholic Students Burn Up Comic Books," *New York Times,* December 11, 1948, 18; for other coverage of Catholic comic book pyres, see "Pupils Burn Comic Books: Auburn Parochial School Has Bonfire of Crime-Sex Volumes," *New York Times,* December 23, 1948, 22; "Sex and Crime Tales Hit," *New York Times,* December 31, 1949, 10.

34. This is Hajdu's view. See also Bradford W. Wright, *Comic Book Nation: The Transformation of Youth Culture in America* (Baltimore: Johns Hopkins University Press, 2001); Gerard Jones, *Men of Tomorrow: Geeks, Gangsters, and the Birth of the Comic Book* (New York: Basic Books, 2004).

35. A Missionary Sister, "Correspondence: An Antidote for Modern Poison," *Journal of Religious Instruction* 14 (April 1944): 734–736, quotation on 734. For Catholic commentary on comic books, see, for example, Norbert Engels, "Funnies Are Not Funny Anymore," *Ave Maria* 41 (May 18, 1935): 619–621; Sister M. Katherine and Marion W. Smith, "How Many Comic Magazines Does the Child Read and Why?," *Catholic Library World* 13 (May 1942): 275–279; Sister M. Katherine, "Comics Are Crimes against Our Children," *America* 67, no. 9 (June

6, 1942): 234–235; Evelyn B. Coogan, "War and the Comics," *Poise* 5 (1943): 15, 35; Evelyn B. Coogan, "Intellectual Effect of 'Comics,'" *Catholic School Journal* 48 (February 1948): 42; John B. Sheerin, CSP, "Lewd and Brutal Horror—Comics," *Homiletic and Pastoral Review* 55, no. 9 (June 1955): 731–735; Gabriel Lynn, "The 'Comics' Are Not to Be Laughed At," *Extension* 39 (May 1945): 12–13; Harold C. Gardiner, "Comic Books: Cultural Threat?," *America* 91 (June 19, 1954): 319–321; Harold C. Gardiner, "Comic Books: Moral Threat?," *America* 91 (June 26, 1954): 340–342; Theophilus Lewis, "Christian Comic Books," *Interracial Review* 27, no. 12 (December 1954): 211–213; Gabriel Lynn, "A Tragedy Caused by the Comics," *Catholic Digest* 8, no. 11 (September 1944): 22–24; Katherine Burton, "Children and the Comics," *Sign* 22 (September 1942): 91.

36. Wright makes the connection between American Catholics and Nazis in *Comic Book Nation,* 86.

37. A Missionary Sister, "Correspondence," 734.

38. On the Grand Concourse apparitions, see John T. McGreevy, "Bronx Miracle," *American Quarterly* 52, no. 3 (September 2000): 405–443.

39. "Grotesquely pictorial and weirdly impossible" is from Sister Dolorice, "Combating the Comics—One Way," *America* 14 (January 9, 1943): 381–382, on 381. It was to oppose the corrupting influence of "pagan" comics that in 1941 Father Louis A. Gales in St. Paul, Minnesota, began publishing *Timeless Topix* (later shortened to *Topix*) and in 1946 George A. Pflaum, in Dayton, Ohio, introduced the more sophisticated and better-illustrated *Treasure Chest of Fun and Fact.* Calling *Timeless Topix* "a positive means" of "curing an evil," Missionary Sister observes of the new Catholic comic book, "Characters like the gentle Saint Francis of Assisi, the brave Damien of Molokai, the clever Father Chaminade, and above all the humble maid of Lourdes, St. Bernadette, leave a deep impression on the child's mind," in "Correspondence," 735.

40. In a spirit reminiscent of Rudolf Otto's *Das Heilige,* Paulist father John B. Sheerin, a prominent writer and editor in U.S. Catholic publishing in the twentieth century, suggested in 1945 that ghost stories and tales of nautical hauntings offered a "faint glimmer" of the greater truth of Catholic teaching that "the soul continues after death to know, love, and remember." John B. Sheerin, CSP, "Dark before Dawn," *Homiletic and Pastoral Review* 45 (February 1945): 321–326, quotation on 323. The editors of *Ave Maria* specifically commended the decision of the new Comics Magazine Association of America, founded in 1954, to remove "horror and terror books" first from the shelves, in "Horror Comics on the Run?," *Ave Maria* 80 (October 16, 1954): 4–5. In an

article urging Catholic parents to join in the anti-comic-books crusade, *America,* the Jesuit magazine, quoting the leading crusader against comics, Frederic C. Wertham, maintained that juvenile delinquency increased by 20 percent after horror and terror comics began appearing in 1947: see Gardiner, "Comic Books: Moral Threat?," 341. Southard is quoted in Hajdu, *The Ten-Cent Plague,* 81. Hajdu's contempt for Jesuits in particular, and Catholics generally, is striking. Catholics are less a part of his history than they are its rejected alternative. On anti- and philo-Catholicism and American horror fiction, see Edward J. Ingebretsen, *Maps of Heaven, Maps of Hell: Religious Terror as Memory from the Puritans to Stephen King* (Armonk, NY: M. E. Sharpe, 1996).

41. See *Comic Books and Juvenile Delinquency, A Part of the Investigation of Juvenile Delinquency in the United States,* Interim Report of the Subcommittee to Investigate Juvenile Delinquency to the Committee of the Judiciary (Washington, DC: United States Government Printing Office, 1955), 36–38.

42. For the elder Crumb's appreciation of nuns, see Jean-Pierre Mercier, "Who's Afraid of R. Crumb?" (1999), in *R. Crumb: Conversations,* ed. D. K. Holm (Jackson: University Press of Mississippi, 2004), 196; on Crumb's childhood Catholic fanaticism, see Susan Goodrick, "Apex Interview: R. Crumb," in ibid., 84–91, on 87; that Crumb was a "faithful Catholic" until age sixteen is from Alexander Wood, "The History of Crumb," ed. and illus. Robert Crumb, on the Official Crumb Site, www.crumbproducts.com/pages/about/history1.html. In a letter to his friend, artist Marty Pahls, on "St. Patrick's Day, March 17, 1960," written from Dover, Delaware, Crumb recalls a thought that deeply troubled him as a child: "I couldn't see how the saints could be so strong and sincere in their faith, and why couldn't I, if I had free will?" In *Your Vigor for Life Appalls Me: Robert Crumb Letters, 1958–1977,* ed. Ilse Thompson (Seattle: Fantagraphics Books, 1998), 114. On Crumb's role in the revival of comics, see Mark James Estren, *A History of Underground Comics* (1986; repr., Berkeley: Ronin Publisher, 1974).

43. For Catholicism as an "underlying current" and "Catholic brainwashing," see Mercier, "Who's Afraid of R. Crumb?," 195. "It doesn't ever completely go away," Crumb adds. "Twisted and sadistic women" is on 196; on repression leading to sickness and twistedness, see Goodrick, "Apex Interview," 88; on "big giant scary women," see B. N. Duncan, "A Joint Interview with R. Crumb and Aline Kominsky-Crumb" (1980), in Holm, *R. Crumb: Conversations,* 117–132, on 118; on never abandoning his faith (a promise Crumb dates to the fourth grade), see Goodrick, "Apex Interview," 87.

44. Mercier, "Who's Afraid of R. Crumb?," 195; on *The Exorcist* as a Catholic film, see Colleen McDannell, "Catholic Horror: *The Exorcist* (1973)," in *Catholics in the Movies,* ed. Colleen McDannell (New York: Oxford University Press, 2008), see especially the discussion of "real horror," 199–204. On the Iowa exorcism, see Carl Vogt, *Begone, Satan! A Soul Stirring Account of Diabolical Possession in Iowa* (1935; repr., Rockford, IL: TAN Books, 1994). Blatty cites this as one of the stories behind his book, in William Peter Blatty, *If There Were Demons, Then Perhaps There Were Angels: William Peter Blatty's Own Story of the Exorcist* (Suffolk, UK: ScreenPress Books), 22–24. On Blatty's New York Catholic childhood and Jesuit education, see his autobiography, *I'll Tell Them I Remember You* (New York: W. W. Norton, 1973).

45. For the *Paris Review* interview, see Robert Crumb, "The Art of Comics No. 1: Interview with Ted Widmer," *Paris Review,* no. 193 (Summer 2010), www.theparisreview.org/interviews/6017/the-art-of-comics-no-1-r-crumb; Crumb's comment is in response to the interviewer's fourth question. On Crumb's portrayals of women, see Robert Crumb, *Gotta Have 'Em: Portraits of Women* (Los Angeles: Greybull Press, 2003).

46. I have found Arthur C. Danto's writing about these artists inspiring and deeply illuminating. See *Andy Warhol* (New Haven, CT: Yale University Press, 2009); *Playing with the Edge: The Photographic Achievement of Robert Mapplethorpe* (Berkeley: University of California Press, 1996); "Censorship and Subsidy in the Arts," *Bulletin of the American Academy of Arts and Sciences* 47, no. 1 (October 1993): 25–41, esp. 39–40; and *The Transfiguration of the Commonplace: A Philosophy of Art* (Cambridge, MA: Harvard University Press, 1981). On Robert Mapplethorpe (a former altar boy, whose mother dreamed of his becoming a priest), see Patricia Morrisroe, *Mapplethorpe: A Biography* (New York: Da Capo Press, 1995), and Patti Smith, *Just Kids* (New York: Ecco, 2010). Smith writes that Mapplethorpe compared the "thrill and fear blossoming in his stomach" at the beginning of his first acid trip to what he felt as an altar boy "as he stood behind the velvet curtains in his small robe holding the processional cross, readying to march" (21). Among Mapplethorpe's first artworks were miniature devotional shrines. Smith has her own fascination with Catholicism. She recalls keeping a secret stash of treasured things under her bed as a child, such as "winnings from marbles, trading cards, religious artifacts I rescued from Catholic trash bins: old holy cards, worn scapulars, plaster saints with chipped hands and feet" (7).

47. Crumb, "The Art of Comics No. 1," responses to questions nine and ten.

5. THE DEAD IN THE COMPANY OF THE LIVING

1. On the history and practice of the cult of the souls in purgatory, see Diana Walsh Pasulka, *Heaven Can Wait: Purgatory in Catholic Devotional and Popular Culture* (New York: Oxford University Press, 2014).

2. John B. Sheerin, CSP, "Conspiracy against Death," *Homiletic and Pastoral Review* 54, no. 6 (March 1954): 485–488, on 486; Leo J. Trese, "How a Christian Dies," *Ave Maria* 92 (October 1960): 26–29, on 29; Louis G. Miller, "Taking the Sting Out of Death," *Liguorian* (November 1954): 661–665, on 661, 662. Miller is also the source of the comparison between Catholicism and other religions on the subject of death.

3. Children ought to be "encouraged to carry a pair of blessed beads with them wherever they go. This practice has often been the means by which Catholics have been identified as such in the case of accidents, and consequently had the good fortune of having a priest called to minister to them at the hour of death." See A School Sister of Notre Dame, "Devotion to the Queen of the Rosary," *Catholic School Journal* 33 (October 1933): 236. The Cold War generated distinctive martyrologies of its own. Among the most important was the autobiographical trilogy by Tom Dooley, *Dr. Tom Dooley's Three Great Books: Deliver Us from Evil, The Edge of Tomorrow, The Night They Burned the Mountain* (New York: Farrar, Straus and Cudahy, 1956, 1958, 1960). See also Ray Kerrison, *Bishop Walsh of Maryknoll: Prisoner of Red China* (New York: G. P. Putnam's Sons, 1962); John F. Donovan, MM, *The Pagoda and the Cross: The Life of Bishop Ford of Maryknoll* (New York: Charles Scribner's Sons, 1967); Harold W. Rigney, SVD, *Four Years in a Red Hell: The Story of Father Rigney* (Chicago: Henry Regnery Company, 1956); Sister Mary Victoria, *Nun in Red China* (New York: McGraw-Hill, 1953). For further discussion of Cold War martyrdom and the belief among American Catholics that they were suffering on behalf of the United States, see Robert A. Orsi, "U.S. Catholics between Memory and Modernity," in *Catholics in the American Century: Recasting Narratives of U.S. History*, ed. R. Scott Appleby and Kathleen Sprows Cummings (Ithaca, NY: Cornell University Press, 2012), 11–42. A Cold War miracle that brings together several themes of this book was Padre Pio's bilocation into the recently imprisoned Hungarian cardinal József Mindszenty's cell sometime between 1948 and 1956; see Andrea Tornielli, "Quella 'visita' di Padre Pio nella cella del cardinal Mindszenty, *La Stampa* [Vatican insider], July 7, 2014, http://vaticaninsider .lastampa.it/news/dettaglio-articolo/articolo/pio-pietrelcina-35037/. On the prohi-

bition of burying Protestants in Catholic cemeteries, see, for example, "Burial of Non-Catholic in Catholic Cemetery," *Ecclesiastical Review* 83 (November 1930): 535–536; Stanislaus Woywod, OFM, "Sacraments to Unconscious Persons after Life without Religion, Catholic Burial of These Persons," *Homiletic and Pastoral Review* 30 (May 1930): 867–868; Rev. E. J. Mahoney, "Burial of Non-Catholics," *Clergy Review* 20 (January 1941): 84–86.

4. "Fertile missionary field" comes from "A Unique Apostolate," *Ave Maria* 55, no. 3 (January 3, 1942): 5, as does the phrase "with no appearance of Catholicity about it." Blanshard's suspicions may be found in the chapter on "the Church and medicine," in Paul Blanshard, *American Freedom and Catholic Power* (Boston: Beacon Press, 1949), 107–131; "if she is zealous" is on 118. The count of prayer cards distributed is from "Help for the Dying," *Liguorian* 43 (September 1955): 568. The "little card *appears to be nothing more than a collection of prayers,*" the unnamed author of "A Unique Apostolate" writes, whereas in fact the prayers "contain all that is necessary to prepare the soul of such a one for a holy [meaning, a Catholic] death" (emphasis added). On the new "Judeo-Christian" identity of the United States in the mid-twentieth century, see Kevin M. Schultz, *Tri-Faith America: How Catholics and Jews Held Postwar America to Its Protestant Promise* (New York: Oxford University Press, 2011); Wendy L. Wall, *Inventing the "American Way": The Politics of Consensus from the New Deal to the Civil Rights Movement* (New York: Oxford University Press, 2008).

5. Rev. Napoleon J. Gilbert, "The Spiritual Anointing of the Sick," *Hospital Progress* 11 (April 1930): 175–178, on 176. Children were taught what to do as a relative neared death; see, for example, A School Sister of Notre Dame, "Extreme Unction," *Catholic School Journal* 34 (July 1934): 158 (describes a classroom drama project acting out the sacrament). The necessary preparations for the last rites in the home were described (for example) as follows in a 1955 article in a devotional magazine: "There is a marked box in the linen closet, holding the linens, blessed candles, candle holders, instructions, [*sic*] how to set up a bedside altar, and the text for the last rites and prayers for the dying. The crucifix with the indulgence for the hour of death is kept on the chest in the bedroom." This is from Therese Mueller, "Death in Your Home," *Voice of St. Jude* 21 (October 1955): 32. There are many sick call sets for sale on the Internet.

6. A recent critical study of this period in American Catholic history is Joseph P. Laycock, *The Seer of Bayside: Veronica Lueken and the Struggle to Define Catholicism* (New York: Oxford University Press, 2015).

7. For another woman's nearly contemporary account of the death of her three-year-old daughter from leukemia, written in equally unsparing prose, see Julia C. Mahon, "Good-Bye, Dear Betty," *Marriage* 44 (February 1962): 10–15; see also Owenita Sanderlin, "Johnny's Life—and Death," *Family Digest* 19 (November 1963): 31–36. An excruciating example of the genre, by widely published American Catholic author Eugene S. Geissler, is *There Is a Season: A Search for Meaning* (Notre Dame, IN: Ave Maria Press, 1970). On the theology and practice of the victim soul, see Paula M. Kane, *Sister Thorn and Catholic Mysticism in Modern America* (Chapel Hill: University of North Carolina Press, 2013), and Paula M. Kane, "'She Offered Herself Up': The Victim Soul and Victim Spirituality in Catholicism," *Church History* 71, no. 1 (March 2002): 80–119. James R. Kincaid, *Child-Loving: The Erotic Child and Victorian Culture* (New York: Routledge, 1992), informs my understanding of the nineteenth-century Anglo-American fascination with dying children. Kerouac's brother's dying is described in Jack Kerouac, *Visions of Gerard* (1963; repr., New York: Penguin Books, 1991).

8. P. J. Carroll, CSC, "Soft-Pedaling Death," *Ave Maria* 49, no. 20 (May 1939): 628. There is an Act of Resignation for Death for dying Catholics to say; see Agatha D. Brungardt, "Not Afraid of Death," *Family Digest* 11 (July 1956): 27–29.

9. Leo J. Trese, "It Will Happen to You," *Ave Maria* 93, no. 25 (February 1961): 12–14, quotations from 14, emphasis in the original.

10. "Final holocaust" is from Miller, "Taking the Sting Out of Death," 661; "love or hatred" and "intolerably alone" are from "What Death Proves," *Liguorian* 49 (November 1961): 52–53, "supreme payment" is from B. Ehmann, "Christian Death," *North American Liturgical Week* 22 (1961): 83–88, on 85.

11. "Funeral Services for an Unbaptized Infant," *American Ecclesiastical Review* 131 (December 1954): 399–400, on 399; Thomas Kinkead, *Catechism of Christian Doctrine: Prepared and Enjoined by Order of the Third Plenary Council of Baltimore, No. 3* (New York: Benzinger Brothers, 1921), 130.

12. On this topic, see, for example, Joseph A. Breig, "Does Death Make Sense Today?," *Lamp* 61 (November 1963): 12; "Last Sacraments to Apparently Dead Persons," *Ecclesiastical Review* 82 (May 1930): 510–511; Ernest Graf, OSB, "The Exact Moment of Birth and Death," *Homiletic and Pastoral Review* 40, no. 1 (October 1939): 320–321; "Period between Apparent and Real Death," *Ecclesiastical Review* 106 (May 1942): 383–384 (specifically concerned with fighter pilots whose planes crash).

13. "Burial of Non-Catholic in Catholic Cemetery," 535.

14. Another name for what I am talking about here, in relation to urban political machines, is "ward politics and clientelism"; see Reginald Byron, *Irish America,* Oxford Studies in Social and Cultural Anthropology (Oxford: Clarendon Press, 1999), phrase on 165. On "favors" to be done for the dead, see Ernest F. Miller, CSSR, "Merciless Mourners," *Liguorian* 45 (July 1957): 17–21, quotations on 18, 19. On children's prayers for the souls in purgatory, see Gerald T. Brennan, *Angel Food: Little Talks to Little Folks* (Milwaukee: Bruce Publishing, 1939), 110. If you pray faithfully for the souls in purgatory, Father Brennan assures his young readers, then one day, when you need them, these souls, now in heaven as the result of your prayers, will pray for you. The implication is clear: if you do not, they will not.

15. John B. Sheerin, CSP, "Dark before Dawn," *Homiletic and Pastoral Review* 45 (February 1945): 323; A. C. W., "The Day Our Baby Died," *Liguorian* 52 (June 1964): 20–22, "still a member of our family" on 22, "thronged around his body" on 23; Sister M. Rose Patricia, OP, "A Birthday in Heaven," *Catholic School Journal* 64 (February 1964): 65, 68, quotations on 68; relevant here, too, is Alfred C. Rush, CSSR, "Birthday: Death as a New Birth," *Liguorian* 53 (July 1965): 41–43; also, Alfred C. Rush, "The Passing of Susan," *Family Digest* 11 (May 1956): 48–50.

16. Alfred C. Rush, CSSR, "The Rosary and the Christian Wake," *American Ecclesiastical Review* 152 (May 1965): 289–297, "this problem" is on 291. Rush was professor of church history at the Catholic University of America. He goes on in the article to reassure readers (and perhaps also to protect himself against heaven's displeasure) that "there is no attempt to exclude Mary from the wake itself." On concern for non-Catholics being disoriented by the rosary at the bier, see also Gerard P. Weber, "Wakes and Funerals," *Worship* 35 (January 1961): 114–115.

17. John Wright, "Guest Editorial: Wakes and Rosaries," *Liguorian* 52 (August 1964): 60.

18. Sister M. Madeleva, CSC, "Lucy Rehearses Her Funeral," *Catholic Digest* 19 (June 1955): 36–39, on 37; "disguise and camouflage death" is from Miller, "Taking the Sting Out of Death," 661; "conspiracy against death" is the title of the article by Sheerin cited above; the article from *Liguorian* is Miller, "Merciless Mourners," 20.

19. "The art of glamorizing a corpse" is from Mary Whiteford, "Froth on the Bier," *St. Joseph Magazine* 58 (November 1957): 16–17, quotation on 17, as is "pretensions and artifices." The association of corpse and tabernacle is the subject of many articles, but see, for example, Terry F. Brock, "'Simple and Dignified'—The Christian View," *Ave Maria* 96, no. 14 (October 6, 1962): 18.

Also referenced here is K. A. L., "Making a Circus Out of Death," *Information* 73 (November 1959): 60–61.

20. This paragraph relies on David Charles Sloane, *The Last Great Necessity: Cemeteries in American History* (Baltimore: Johns Hopkins University Press, 1991); Richard E. Meyer, ed., *Ethnicity and the American Cemetery* (Bowling Green, OH: Bowling Green State University Popular Press, 1993); Lawrence R. Samuel, *Death, American Style: A Cultural History of Dying in America* (Lanham, MD: Rowman and Littlefield Publishers, 2013). Sloane's observation that even as the first funeral homes began to appear in the 1880s, most Americans resisted moving the wake from the home is on 120. Immigrants were "offended, frightened, and horrified" by the American cemetery, Sloane writes, preferring instead a "closer relationship with dead" and insisting on family responsibility for handling the remains of the deceased (113). He characterizes "ethnic cemeteries" as "stone records of families, communities, and generations" (125). On the rise to prominence of the funeral director, see 201–202. Writing specifically about Italian immigrants and their children and grandchildren, Joseph J. Inguanti calls attention to "the permeability of boundaries among church, cemetery, shrine and home," in "Landscape of Order, Landscape of Memory," in *Italian Folk: Vernacular Culture in Italian-American Lives,* ed. Joseph Sciorra (New York: Fordham University Press, 2011), 87. The comment about the improvement of the new funeral homes over the traditional Catholic wake is from John E. Leonard, "Wasn't It the Grand Wake?" *Priest* 16 (September 1960): 783–785, on 784.

21. Leonard, "Wasn't It the Grand Wake?," 784, 785. The distinction made between mourners who are sincere and those who are not is striking. By the more familiar Catholic logic of practice, such judgments of intention are largely irrelevant. What matters is being there in the presence of the corpse and the company of the grieving. Sincerity has nothing to do with this. On "sincerity" as a key modern virtue, see Adam B. Seligman, Robert P. Weller, Michael J. Puett, and Bennett Simon, *Ritual and Its Consequences: An Essay on the Limits of Sincerity* (New York: Oxford University Press, 2008).

22. Kate Dooley, "Where the Heart Is," *Ave Maria* 86 (December 1957): 25; Robert T. Reilly, "Poteen and Sympathy," *Ave Maria* 91, no. 11 (March 12, 1960): 10–14, "Arabian rug" on 14, the "suit-and-tie décor of American cadavers" on 12; the comments about the absence of children is from Rose Grieco, "The Wake of My Aunt Rose," *Catholic Digest* 17 (June 1953): 17–20, quotations on 18, 20. This article was originally published in *Commonweal* magazine. "Regimented remorse" is from Reilly, "Poteen and Sympathy," 12. For a complaint about chil-

dren misbehaving in funeral homes, confirming Grieco's sense that there was increasingly no place for young people in the company of the dead, see Howard Morin, CSSR, "How to Recognize a Spoiled Child," *Liguorian* 47 (April 1959): 18–22.

23. The observations about companionship and the old wake as the tangible demonstration of the communion of saints are from Reilly, "Poteen and Sympathy," 14; Grieco, "The Wake of My Aunt Rose," 20.

24. The encouragement of children to pray with the dying is from "When We Should Say an Act of Contrition," *Junior Catholic Messenger* 9 (February 24, 1943): 143. Mueller, "Death in Your Home," 32; Geraldine Hertz, "When Death Comes Close, so Also Does God," *Family Digest* 8 (July 1953): 27–28, quotation on 27. Christ will be with the dying person "every step of the way," says Father Sheerin, "Dark before Dawn," 323. The comment about Jesus sweetening death's anxiety is from Valentine Long, OFM, "Death Is a Key," *Friar* 4 (July 1955): 39–44, on 44; "Brother Death" is evoked by Alfred Wilson, CP, "Why Fear Death?," *Ave Maria* 88, no. 3 (July 1958): 12–14, 16, on 14; the death notice is from "The Sacraments of the Sick," *Truth* 34 (November 1930): 38.

25. Bill McClinton, "The Seventh Work of Mercy," *Catholic Digest* 25 (November 1960): 55–57; see also "A Brief History of the Pittsburgh Ladies of Charity," Ladies of Charity, Diocese of Pittsburgh, http://locpittsburgh.org /General/WhoWeAre.aspx.

26. The Spiritual Society for the Unclaimed Dead was founded as a women's auxiliary of the Saint Vincent de Paul Society, but it soon became an organization in its own right, while remaining affiliated with the larger society. Volunteers continue to keep Margaret O'Konski's promise today. Bishop Wright, who appears earlier in this chapter speaking in defense of the practice of saying the rosary at wakes, wrote a special prayer for the Spiritual Society; see McClinton, "The Seventh Work of Mercy," 56.

27. Titus Cranny, SA, "Our Lady of a Happy Death," *Our Lady's Digest* 12 (November 1957): 211–215, the story of the dying woman is on 212; James G. Alexander, SCJ, "A Devotion for Life's Most Important Hour," *Our Lady's Digest* 11, no. 5 (November 1956): 189–193, the observation about the needs of the dying is on 190–191, the story of the old woman's lonely passing is on 192; Alastair Guinan, "Our Lady as Patroness of the Dying, According to the Liturgists of Eighteenth-Century France," *Life of the Spirit* 9 (December 1954): 252–261.

28. Mary's association with death and dying begins, of course, with her presence at the foot of her son's cross, a scene that is commemorated in many ways

in Christian art, especially in images of Mary holding her dead child, just taken from the cross, in her arms. Readers who have come this far will know that it was Catholic practice to imagine scenes from the life of Jesus and Mary in gritty lived detail. Jesus's blood soaks through Mary's garments. The thorns of his crown pierce her skin. The relation between Mary and death was an important theme in Pope John Paul II's theology, which was generally and deeply centered on the Blessed Mother. See, for example, his short essay, "Mary and the Human Drama of Death," first published in *L'Osservatore Romano,* English edition, July 2, 1997, www.ewtn.com/library/papaldoc/jp2bvm53.htm. Mary as the "patroness" of death, as Father Cranny put it, was a trope endlessly elaborated upon in pictures and stories. Her image as the suffering Mother has surely contributed to the constitution of Catholic women's subjectivities as the ones whose role it is to endure pain on behalf of others. At the same time, as I have argued in the first two chapters, such images are not stable and univocal, certainly not in lived experience, as the Detroit housewife's vision shows. For a discussion of Mary's often ambivalent presence in the context of Catholic colonialism and after and its mixed implications and consequences for people's lives, see Linda B. Hall, *Mary, Mother and Warrior: The Virgin in Spain and in the Americas* (Austin: University of Texas Press, 2004). The high demand for rosaries during World War II is from Dorothy Fremont Grant, *War Is My Parish* (Milwaukee: Bruce Publishing, 1944), 21–22; on Our Lady's Knights, see 24.

29. There is an embedded allusion in this paragraph to Richard Sennett and Jonathan Cobb, *The Hidden Injuries of Class* (New York: Random House, 1972). For a fuller discussion of the tensions of this period in American Catholic history, see Robert A. Orsi, *Thank You, St. Jude: Women's Devotion to the Patron Saint of Hopeless Causes* (New Haven, CT: Yale University Press, 1996), 40–69. On the problem of the new sensitivity to non-Catholics' incomprehension of the rosary, see Weber, "Wakes and Funerals," 114–115; also Rush, "The Rosary and the Christian Wake," 290; Gerard P. Weber, "How to Make Wakes More Christian," *Information* 75 (November 1961): 42–46.

30. Harry S. Smith, CSSR, "Funeral Problems—Towards Greater Efficiency," *Priest* 22 (December 1966): 1000–1002, traffic problems discussed on 1000.

31. Ibid., 1000.

32. Ibid., 1001, 1002.

33. "The SHRINE—Modern Concept in Catholic Cemeteries," *Catholic Property Administration* 23 (November–December 1959): 63–66, 173, quotations on 64, 66. The unnamed author (or authors) of this article maintains that the

shrine model of cemetery organization was first introduced in 1951 at Chicago's Queen of Heaven Cemetery. Also on this important cemetery, see "Roman Church Will Dedicate New Cemetery," *Chicago Sunday Tribune,* September 7, 1947, pt. 3, p. 13; "Catholics Plan Grass Program for Cemeteries," *Chicago Daily Tribune,* April 10, 1950, pt. 1, p. 8. There is no history of Catholic cemeteries in the United States, unfortunately. In preparing this section of the chapter, I consulted a number of different sources, including Cornelius Michael Power, *The Blessing of Cemeteries: An Historical Synopsis and Commentary,* a dissertation submitted to the Faculty of the School of Canon Law of the Catholic University of America (Washington, DC: Catholic University of America Press, 1943), a highly technical review of canon law; "Defense of Cemeteries," *Ave Maria* 74, no. 29 (September 1951): 388; Joseph F. Kelley, "Holy Cross Cemetery in Cleveland," *Catholic Property Administration* 17, no. 3 (May–June 1953); Arthur L. H. Street, "Cemetery Rules as to Vaults Was Void," *Catholic Property Administration* 18, no. 1 (January–February 1954): 62–64 (on the rights of consumers versus the authority of cemetery managers in determining details of burial); "New Cemetery Buildings Dedicated," *Church Property Administration* 19, no. 1 (January–February 1955): 50–52, 200 (on North Side Catholic Cemetery, Pittsburgh, Pennsylvania); Erle O. Blair, "Location of Cemetery Structures," *Catholic Property Administration* 17, no. 2 (March–April 1955): 64, 108 (on landscaping); Arthur L. H. Street, "Cemeteries as Unwelcome Neighbors," *Catholic Property Administration* 19, no. 4 (July–August 1955): 80–83; Thomas J. Tobin, "Parish Funeral Services," *Worship* 30, no. 5 (April 1956): 342–343; J. B. Lux, "The Artistic and the Devotional," *Extension* 51 (May 1957): 31–32 (describes the struggles of a Vermont Catholic, Ezra White, to find a satisfactory way of fixing actual rosaries to headstones so that they would not deteriorate in weather conditions over time); "A Milestone in Mausoleum Architecture," *Catholic Property Administration* 22, no. 1 (January–February 1958): 39–45 (on Chicago's Queen of Heaven Cemetery Mausoleum); "Regulations of Concern to Catholic Cemeteries," *Catholic Property Administration* 24 (May–June 1960): 140–145, 158–167; Wilfred Sheed and Shirley Feltmann, "The Funeral Business," *Jubilee* 8 (November 1960): 30–35; Daniel D. Donovan, "God's Acres," *Catholic Digest* 25 (January 1961): 82–84 (on New York City's Calvary Cemetery); "National Catholic Cemetery Conference," *Social Justice Review* 55, no. 7 (November 1962): 239; Ida Kosciesza, "Surveying the Catholic Funeral," *New City,* September 15, 1964, 12–13; John J. McMahon, *The Catholic Cemetery: A Vision for the Millennium* (Des Plaines, IL: National Catholic Cemetery Conference, 1997).

34. "Better control" is from "The SHRINE," 63; the worry that younger Catholics are turning away from Catholic teaching about death and the afterlife is expressed in, for example, John J. McMahon, "Catholic Students Look at Death," *Commonweal* 87, no. 16 (January 26, 1968): 491–494. McMahon taught philosophy at Marquette; his conclusions are based on the students in his classes. See also James DiGiacomo and Edward Wakin, *We Were Never Their Age (A Guide for Christian Parents)* (New York: Holt, Reinhart and Winston, 1972), especially "The Faith of Our Children," 109–126.

35. A. G. Leystan, "The Revised Funeral Rite," *Priest* 26 (November 1970): 52–56, the judgment that the new funeral rite is on balance "an improvement on the old" is on 56; the shift from black to white is discussed in O. Battista, "The Mourners Wore White," *Family Digest* 25 (November 1969): 33–37, on 34 and 37; the description of the new Paschal candle is from Rev. Laurence Brett, "The Revised Funeral Rites: A Source of Catechesis," *Living Light* 7 (Spring 1970): 71–83, on 76; "amended or eliminated" is from A. T., "The New Funeral Rites," *Worship* 40, no. 10 (December 1966): 658–661, on 658. In addition to being a liturgist, Brett was also a "notorious child abuser," protected by fellow priests and the local hierarchy in Bridgeport, Connecticut, where he was a parish priest, until the 1990s, when he fled the United States to avoid prosecution. See Daniel Tepfer, "Two Priests Disciplined in Shielding Sex Abuser, Both Knew Caribbean Location, Never Told [Bishop William E.] Lori," *Connecticut Post* (Bridgeport), September 1, 2002. According to a report in the *Stamford Advocate,* Brett used a small crucifix as a pointer to indicate on the corpus of a larger crucifix to a ten-year-old boy how taut the crucified Christ's stomach was, promising to teach the boy how to develop such muscles himself. He demanded the boy exercise in front of him while wearing only silk underpants, in imitation of Christ's crucifixion garb. See "Angela Carella: Little Resolved by Priest's Final Fall," StamfordAdvocate.com, January 10, 2011, www.stamfordadvocate.com/local/article/Angela-Carella-Little-resolved-by-priest-s-final-948400.php.

36. Brett, "The Revised Funeral Rites," 71; also see Laurence Brett, "Planning Public Acceptance of New Burial Plan," *Catholic Property Administration* 25 (October 1961): 118, 120–122.

37. Sheerin warns against gruesome evocations of the horrors of dying, which he sets in the context of the changed reality of modern death, arguing that "physical death is not usually an agony; it comes quietly in most cases and without much pain," "Dark before Dawn," 322. "In sermons on death or the Judgment, special care must be taken not to disturb the peace of mind of the devout" (325).

The comment about "pre-kerygmatic days" is from McMahon, "Catholic Students Look at Death," 494.

38. Gary Wills, *Bare Ruined Choirs: Doubt, Prophecy, and Radical Religion* (Garden City, NY: Doubleday, 1972), 37; Brett, "The Revised Funeral Rites," 73; Curtis B. Schmidt, SJ, *Too Late Is Forever* (St. Louis: Queen's Work, 1959), 20–21.

39. Brett, "The Revised Funeral Rites," 73.

40. Ibid., 77, 78; the image of people wailing with green faces is from Kerouac, *Visions of Gerard*, 111.

41. I take the phrase "ambient dead" from Todd Ramón Ochoa, *Society of the Dead: Quita Manaquita and Palo Praise in Cuba* (Berkeley: University of California Press, 2010), 37. Ochoa refers to the men and women among whom he worked and studied as "people who live with the dead in the materiality of their lives everyday" (46). Sometimes he refers to the dead so present as "the responsive dead" (47). Sloane argues that "the rise of science as an important social idea" in the latter half of the nineteenth century contributed to strengthening the boundary between the living and the dead, as it changed the meaning of death itself. See Sloane, *The Last Great Necessity*, 145.

42. This paragraph and the next, on Audrey Santo, rely on Kane, " 'She Offered Herself Up,' " 80–119; Matthew N. Schmalz, "The Silent Body of Audrey Santo," *History of Religions* 42 (2002): 116–142; Matthew N. Schmalz, "Performing the Miraculous in Central Massachusetts," in *Practicing Catholic: Ritual, Body, and Contestation in Catholic Faith,* ed. Bruce T. Morrill, Joanna E. Ziegler, and Susan Rodgers (New York: Palgrave Macmillan, 2006), 139–241 (this latter is accompanied by a number of stunning photographs taken by the author). I also consulted the website of the Little Audrey Santo Foundation, www.littleaudreysantofoundation.org.

6. THE HAPPINESS OF HEAVEN

1. The catechetical questions about heaven come from Ellamay Horan and James W. O'Brien, *Revised Edition of the Baltimore Catechism, No. 2* (Patterson, NJ: St. Anthony Guild Press, 1941), 1, 36.

2. One of the most influential statements of the fragility of social meanings and subjective identities, and the role of religion in underwriting them, especially in the context of death or pain, is Peter Berger, *The Sacred Canopy: Elements of a Sociological Theory of Religion* (New York: Doubleday, 1967).

3. This appears in Ellamay Horan and James W. O'Brien, *A Catechism of Christian Doctrine: The Illustrated Revised Edition of the Baltimore Catechism, No. 1* (New York: W. H. Sadlier, 1944), 3–4, emphasis in the original.

4. Sister Mary of Grace, CDP, "Apparitions of Lourdes—Playlet for December 8," *Catholic School Journal* 34 (December 1934): 287–289, on 288. The various Catholic educational journals I have cited in earlier chapters published scores of these playlets over the years, on the lives of the saints, holy days, Bible stories, morality tales, and so on, all intended to be performed in the classroom by children of different ages. But I have yet to meet a Catholic of any generation who actually appeared in one.

5. Father Romano Guardini reflects on the book of Revelation in the last chapters of his major work, *The Lord*, trans. Elinor Castendyk Briefs (Chicago: Henry Regnery, 1954), quotations from 530–531. All verse translations in the text are taken from Guardini, who appears to translate the biblical texts himself.

6. Ellen Badone, *The Appointed Hour: Death, Worldview and Social Change in Brittany* (Berkeley: University of California Press, 1989), 230.

7. "Holding" is a central idea of Winnicott's and may be found throughout his work. Cited in the text is D. W. Winnicott, *The Maturational Processes and the Facilitating Environment: Studies in the Theory of Emotional Development* (New York: International Universities Press, 1965), 113, 49, 44. "We cannot exist without addressing" is from Judith Butler, *Giving an Account of Oneself* (New York: Fordham University Press, 2005), 33; also helpful here is Adriana Cavarero, *Relating Narratives: Storytelling and Selfhood*, trans. Paul A. Kottman (New York: Routledge, 2000).

7. EVENTS OF ABUNDANT EVIL

1. Benedict XVI, "Year for Priests," general audience, Saint Peter's Square, June 24, 2009, http://w2.vatican.va/content/benedict-xvi/en/audiences/2009 /documents/hf_ben-xvi_aud_20090624.html; Patrick F. Shine, ed., *Come My Jesus: Prayers and Instructions for Children* (New York: Catholic Book Publishing, 1954), 46, 48. A collection of Pope Benedict's thoughts about priests and the priesthood is Benedict XVI, *The Priest: A Bridge to God,* edited and selected by Christopher Bailey (Huntington, IN: Our Sunday Visitor Publishing Division, 2012). This little volume, conveniently sized to fit into the pocket of a soutane, was explicitly assembled in order to provide "inspiration and encouragement for priests and seminarians" in the context of the global clerical sexual

abuse scandal. At the start of the section titled "Dealing with Scandal," the editor poses a question for readers' reflection: "To think about: How can I convey the greatness of the priesthood to a world that seems to be interested in nothing but scandal?" (109)

2. On the twentieth-century American Catholic parish as a social world, see, for example, Joseph H. Fichter, *Dynamics of a City Church* (Chicago: University of Chicago Press, 1951); Jay P. Dolan, *The American Catholic Parish: A History from 1850 to the Present*, 2 vols. (New York: Paulist Press, 1987); John T. McGreevy, *Parish Boundaries: The Catholic Encounter with Race in the Twentieth-Century Urban North* (Chicago: University of Chicago Press, 1996); Andrew Greeley, *Confessions of a Parish Priest: An Autobiography* (New York: Simon and Schuster, 1986); Gary Wray McDonogh, *Black and Catholic in Savannah, Georgia* (Knoxville: University of Tennessee Press, 1993); Thomas J. Shelley, *Greenwich Village Catholics: St. Joseph's Church and the Evolution of an Urban Faith Community, 1829–2002* (Washington, DC: Catholic University of America Press, 2003); Jerome P. Baggett, *Sense of the Faithful: How American Catholics Live Their Faith* (New York: Oxford University Press, 2008); John C. Seitz, *No Closure: Catholic Practice and Boston's Parish Shutdowns* (Cambridge, MA: Harvard University Press, 2011); and the wonderful novel by Francis W. Nielsen, *The Witness of St. Ansgar's: A Novel* (Hanover, NH: Steerforth Press, 2006), which was written in 1985.

3. On American Catholic Mass attendance, see Margaret M. McGuinness, "Let's Go to the Altar: American Catholics and the Eucharist, 1926–1976," in *Habits of Devotion: Catholic Religious Practice in Twentieth-Century America,* ed. James M. O'Toole, 187–235; see also James M. O'Toole, *The Faithful: A History of Catholics in America* (Cambridge, MA: Belknap Press of Harvard University Press, 2008), 214–216, 303–304.

4. The examples in this paragraph are drawn from my fieldwork with survivors, as well as from Grand Jury Report, CPL § 190.85(1)(C), Suffolk County Supreme Court, Special Grand Jury, May 6, 2002, dated January 17, 2003; for "another way of receiving communion," see Elizabeth Hamilton and Eric Rich, "A Predator Blessed with Charm," *Hartford Courant,* September 15, 2002, http://articles.courant.com/2002-09-15/news/0209151546_1_church-officials-charm-priest. This is about Father Laurence Brett, who appears in Chapter 5 as an advocate of the new post-Conciliar funeral ritual. The major source for documentation of the clerical sexual abuse crisis in the Catholic Church, in the United States and around the world, is the online archive, www.bishopaccountability.org.

5. The phrase "absence of words" is from Jody Messler Davies and Mary Gail Frawley, *Treating the Adult Survivor of Childhood Sexual Abuse: A Psychoanalytic Perspective* (New York: Basic Books, 1994), 55.

6. Jonathan Z. Smith, *Imagining Religion: From Babylon to Jonestown* (Chicago: University of Chicago Press, 1982), 54.

7. For a history of the Linkup (or simply "Linkup"), see Brian J. Clites, "Breaking the Silence: The Catholic Sexual Abuse Survivor Movement in Chicago" (PhD diss., Northwestern University, Department of Religious Studies, 2015).

8. Davies and Frawley, *Treating the Adult Survivor of Childhood Sexual Abuse,* 50; D. W. Winnicott, *Playing and Reality* (London: Tavistock / Routledge, 1971), 2, 64.

9. On the dilemma of the unsayable, which was experienced by many of the men and women who have appeared in the pages of this book, see Annie Rogers, *The Unsayable: The Hidden Language of Trauma* (New York: Random House, 2006).

10. Leon J. Podles, *Sacrilege: Sexual Abuse in the Catholic Church* (Baltimore: Crossland Press, 2008), on Gilbert Gauthe, see 80–88, on James R. Porter, see 113–127.

11. There is as yet no single historical study of how American priests experienced these times of change, but see Tim Unsworth, *The Last Priests in America: Conversations with Remarkable Men* (New York: Crossroad, 1991); Donald B. Cozzens, *The Changing Face of the Priesthood* (Collegeville, MN: Liturgical Press, 2000); Paul E. Dinter, *The Other Side of the Altar: One Man's Life in the Catholic Priesthood* (New York: Farrar, Straus and Giroux, 2003); John L'Heureux, *Picnic in Babylon: A Jesuit Priest's Journal, 1963–1967* (New York: Macmillan, 1967); James Kavanagh, *A Modern Priest Looks at His Outdated Church,* 25th anniversary. ed. (Highland Park, IL: Steven J. Nash Publishing, 1992); Paul Lakeland, *The Liberation of the Laity: In Search of an Accountable Church* (New York: Continuum, 2003); Joseph M. White, *The Diocesan Seminary in the United States: A History from the 1780s to the Present* (Notre Dame, IN: University of Notre Dame Press, 1989); John Tracy Ellis, ed., *The Catholic Priest in the United States: Historical Investigations* (Collegeville, MN: Saint John's University Press, 1971). The best book on the lives of American priests over time, although this is not its main subject, is Leslie Woodcock Tentler, *Seasons of Grace: A History of the Archdiocese of Detroit* (Detroit: Wayne State University Press, 1990).

12. Joseph M. Champlin, *The New Yet Old Mass* (Notre Dame, IN: Ave Maria Press, 1977), 12 (Champlin is quoting the council's *Constitution on the Sacred Liturgy* here), 13.

13. Massimo Faggioli, *True Reform: Liturgy and Ecclesiology in* Sacrosanctum Concilium (Collegeville, MN: Liturgical Press, 2012).

14. O'Toole, *The Faithful,* 264.

15. The literature on the clergy sex abuse crisis is extensive and growing. Here is a personal and brief list of works I have found useful: Jason Berry, *Lead Us Not Into Temptation: Catholic Priests and the Sexual Abuse of Children* (Urbana: University of Illinois Press, 1992); Podles, *Sacrilege*; David France, *Our Fathers: The Secret Life of the Catholic Church in an Age of Scandal* (New York: Broadway Books, 2004); Karol Jackowski, *The Silence We Keep: A Nun's View of the Catholic Priest Scandal* (New York: Harmony Books, 2004); Mary Gail Frawley-O'Dea, *Perversion of Power: Sexual Abuse in the Catholic Church* (Nashville: Vanderbilt University Press, 2007); Carmine Galasso, *Crosses: Portraits of Clergy Abuse* (London: Trolley, 2007); Nicholas P. Cafardi, *Before Dallas: The U.S. Bishops' Response to Clergy Sexual Abuse of Children* (Mahwah, NJ: Paulist Press, 2008). Among survivor memoirs, I consulted the following: Yvonne Maes, with Bonita Slunder, *The Cannibal's Wife: A Memoir* (New York: Herodias, 1999); Virginia Tranel, *Benita: Prey for Him* (Fairfield, IA: First World Publishing, 2010); Hilary Stiles, *Assault on Innocence* (Albuquerque: B&K Publishers, 1987). Especially important to my understanding of the religious consequences of clerical sexual abuse is T. Pitt Green, *Restoring Sanctuary* (Indianapolis: Dog Ear Publishing, 2010).

16. Jessica Benjamin, *The Bonds of Love: Psychoanalysis, Feminism, and the Problem of Domination* (New York: Pantheon Books, 1988), 73.

17. Jessica Benjamin, "Two-Way Streets: Recognition of Difference and the Intersubjective Third," *Differences: A Journal of Feminist Cultural Studies* 17, no. 1 (Spring 2006): 116–146, on 118; also in this context, see Jessica Benjamin, "Beyond Doer and Done To: An Intersubjective View of Thirdness," *Psychoanalytic Quarterly* 73 (2004): 5–46.

18. On the history and social life of twelve-step programs in the United States, see Robert Wuthnow, *Sharing the Journey: Support Groups and America's New Quest for Community* (New York: Free Press, 1994).

19. Benjamin, "Two-Way Streets," 116, 117.

EPILOGUE

1. This program was sponsored by the Open Society Institute, Higher Education Support Program under the Regional Seminar for Excellence in Teaching (ReSet) program; its codirectors were Ketevan Khutsishvili (Tbilisi State University); Maria Louw (Aarhus University), and John Schoeberlein (Harvard University). My friend Besarion Kitsmarishvili accompanied me on the visit to the monastery, providing commentary and translations.

BIBLIOGRAPHY

PRIMARY SOURCES

Acosta, José de. *Natural and Moral History of the Indies.* Edited by Jane E. Mangan, translated by Frances López-Morillas. 1590. Durham, NC: Duke University Press, 2002.

A. C. W. "The Day Our Baby Died." *Liguorian* 52 (June 1964): 20–24.

Alexander, James G., SCJ. "A Devotion for Life's Most Important Hour." *Our Lady's Digest* 11, no. 5 (November 1956): 189–193.

A. T. "The New Funeral Rites." *Worship* 40, no. 10 (December 1966): 658–661.

Battista, O. "The Mourners Wore White." *Family Digest* 25 (November 1969): 33–37.

Benedict XVI. *The Priest: A Bridge to God.* Edited and selected by Christopher Bailey. Huntington, IN: Our Sunday Visitor Publishing Division, 2012.

———. "Year for Priests." General audience, Saint Peter's Square, June 24, 2009. http://w2.vatican.va/content/benedict-xvi/en/audiences/2009/docu ments/hf_ben-xvi_aud_20090624.html.

"Bishop Deplores Prejudice against Mexican Immigrants." *Interracial Review* 26 (May 1953): 88.

Blair, Erle O. "Location of Cemetery Structures." *Catholic Property Administration* 17, no. 2 (March–April 1955): 64, 108.

Blanshard, Paul. *American Freedom and Catholic Power.* Boston: Beacon Press, 1949.

Boynton, Neil, SJ. *Mangled Hands: A Story of the New York Martyrs.* New York: Benziger Brothers, 1926.

Breig, Joseph A. "Aunt Annie Is Dead, Lady-Like as Always." *Ave Maria* 88 (September 27, 1958): 19.

———. "Does Death Make Sense Today?" *Lamp* 61 (November 1963): 12–13, 28.

Brennan, Gerald T. *Angel Food: Little Talks to Little Folks.* Milwaukee: Bruce Publishing, 1939.

Brett, Rev. Laurence. "Planning Public Acceptance of New Burial Plan." *Catholic Property Administration* 25 (October 1961).

———. "The Revised Funeral Rites: A Source of Catechesis." *Living Light* 7 (Spring 1970): 71–83.

Brock, Terry F. "'Simple and Dignified'—The Christian View." *Ave Maria* 96, no. 14 (October 6, 1962): 18.

Brother Edward, FSC. "Leveling the Mountains." *Journal of Religious Instruction* 17 (February 1947): 512–515.

Brungardt, Agatha D. "Not Afraid of Death." *Family Digest* 11 (July 1956): 27–29.

Buehrle, Marie Cecilia. *Saint Maria Goretti.* Milwaukee: Bruce Publishing, 1950.

Bulletin of the Catholic Laymen's Association of Georgia. "Georgetown Names Law Regent." November 10, 1928.

"Burial of Non-Catholic in Catholic Cemetery." *Ecclesiastical Review* 83 (November 1930): 535–536.

Burton, Katherine. "Children and the Comics." *Sign* 22 (September 1942): 91.

Carroll, P. J., CSC. "Soft-Pedaling Death." *Ave Maria* 49, no. 20 (May 1939): 628.

The Catholic Cemetery: A Vision for the Millennium. Des Plaines, IL: National Catholic Cemetery Conference, 1997.

Champlin, Joseph M. *The New Yet Old Mass.* Notre Dame, IN: Ave Maria Press, 1977.

Chetwood, Thomas B., SJ. *Frida.* St. Louis: Queen's Work, 1933.

———. *God's Law of Obedience: A Course of Seven Lenten Sermons.* New York: Joseph F. Wagner, 1938.

———. *Handbook of Newman.* New York: Schwartz, Kirwin and Fauss, 1927.

———. *Nicky.* St. Louis: Queen's Work, 1934.

———. *Priest of a Doubting Flock.* St. Louis: Queen's Work, 1933.

———. *Tony.* St. Louis: Queen's Work, 1933.

Chicago Daily Tribune. "Catholics Plan Grass Program for Cemeteries." April 10, 1950.

Chicago Sunday Tribune. "Roman Church Will Dedicate New Cemetery." September 7, 1947.

The Child's Prayerbook: Prayers and Instructions for Catholic Children Compiled from Approved Sources. Winterberg, NY: John Baptist Steinberner, 1899.

Clark, Neil M. "They Want No Progress in Chimayo." *Saturday Evening Post,* May 9, 1951, 38–39, 172–175.

Collins, Joseph. "Death Is a Celebration." *Messenger of the Sacred Heart* 93 (November 1958): 27–29, 64.

Comic Books and Juvenile Delinquency: A Part of the Investigation of Juvenile Delinquency in the United States. Interim Report of the Subcommittee to Investigate Juvenile Delinquency to the Committee of the Judiciary. Washington, DC: United States Government Printing Office, 1955.

"Confraternity [of] Christian Doctrine: Religious Vacation Schools, Yesterday and Today." *Catholic Action* 25 (June 1943): 14, 21.

Coogan, Evelyn B. "Intellectual Effect of 'Comics.'" *Catholic School Journal* 48 (February 1948): 42.

———. "War and the Comics." *Poise* 5 (1943): 15, 35.

Coughlin, Mary, and Malcolm Kildale (illus.). "Saint Joseph of Cupertino." *Treasure Chest of Fun and Fact* 2, no. 13 (February 18, 1947): 6–9.

Cox, Ignatius, SJ. *Birth Control, Birth Controllers and Perversion of Logic.* New York: Paulist Press, 1936.

———. *Birth Control Is Wrong!* New York: America Press, 1930.

Crandall, Reed Leonard (illus.). *This Godless Communism.* Serialized in *Treasure Chest of Fun and Fact,* beginning on September 28, 1961 (vol. 17, no. 2).

Cranny, Titus, SA. "Our Lady of a Happy Death." *Our Lady's Digest* 12 (November 1957): 211–215.

Cunningham, Rev. Daniel F. "Teaching Children the Mass." *Catholic School Journal* 30 (September 1930): 316–319.

"A Curriculum in Religion, Grade I—The Childhood of Christ." *Catholic School Journal* 30 (December 1930): 439–441.

"A Curriculum in Religion, Grade II—Preparation for Holy Communion." *Catholic School Journal* 31 (January 1931): 1–7.

"A Curriculum in Religion, Grade III—The Public Life of Christ." *Catholic School Journal* 31 (February 1931): 48–51.

"A Curriculum in Religion, Grade IV—Old Testament History." *Catholic School Journal* 31 (March 1931): 93–98.

"A Curriculum in Religion, Grade V—Church History." *Catholic School Journal* 31 (April 1931): 132–138.

"A Curriculum in Religion, Grade VI—The Mass." *Catholic School Journal* 31 (May 1931): 170–176.

"A Curriculum in Religion, Grade VII—Christian Doctrine." *Catholic School Journal* 31 (September 1931): 335–339.

"A Curriculum in Religion, Grade VIII—Christian Doctrine." *Catholic School Journal* 32 (January 1932): 18–23.

"Defense of Cemeteries." *Ave Maria* 74, no. 29 (September 1951): 388.

DiGiacomo, James, and Edward Wakin. *We Were Never Their Age (A Guide for Christian Parents)*. New York: Holt, Reinhart and Winston, 1972.

Donovan, Daniel D. "God's Acres." *Catholic Digest* 25 (January 1961): 82–84.

Donovan, John F., MM. *The Pagoda and the Cross: The Life of Bishop Ford of Maryknoll*. New York: Charles Scribner's Sons, 1967.

Dooley, Kate. "Funerals Could Be More Christian." *Ave Maria* 86 (November 30, 1957): 25.

———. "Neither Aesthetic nor Yet Pleasant." *Ave Maria* 86 (December 7, 1957): 25.

———. "To Comfort the Sorrowful." *Ave Maria* 86 (December 14, 1957): 25.

———. "Where the Heart Is." *Ave Maria* 86 (December 1957).

Dooley, Tom. *Dr. Tom Dooley's Three Great Books: Deliver Us from Evil, The Edge of Tomorrow, The Night They Burned the Mountain*. New York: Farrar, Straus and Cudahy, 1956, 1958, 1960.

Duprey, Richard A. "Heroes for Children." *Grail* 40 (November 1958): 35–37.

Eberhard, Kenneth D., CSSR. "Mexican Migrants: A Pastoral Problem." *Priest* 19 (July 1963): 583–586.

Eberhardt, Auleen B. "God Makes No Mistakes." *Ave Maria* 77 (January 24, 1953): 119–120.

———. *Small Prayers for Small Children*. St. Benedict, OR: Benedictine Press, 1949.

Ehmann, B. "Christian Death." *North American Liturgical Week* 22 (1961): 83–88.

Engels, Norbert. "Funnies Are Not Funny Anymore." *Ave Maria* 41 (May 18, 1935): 619–620.

"Family Lot in a Cemetery of Another Parish." *Ecclesiastical Review* 84 (March 1931): 299–301.

"Fatima Rosary, Family Rosary, Block Rosary." Distributed by the Block Rosary Lay Apostolate, Detroit, Michigan. Archdiocese of Detroit Archives. No date.

"Funeral Services for an Unbaptized Infant." *American Ecclesiastical Review* 131 (December 1954): 399–400.

Furfey, Paul Hanly. *The Gang Age: A Study of the Preadolescent Boy and His Recreational Needs*. New York: Macmillan, 1926.

———. *The Mystery of Iniquity*. Milwaukee: Bruce Publishing, Inc. 1944.

Gardiner, Harold C. "Comic Books: Cultural Threat?" *America* 91 (June 19, 1954): 319–321.

———. "Comic Books: Moral Threat?" *America* 91 (June 26, 1954): 340–342.

Geissler, Eugene S. "Annie of Happy Memory." *Marriage* 42 (February 1960): 43–50.

———. *There Is a Season: A Search for Meaning*. Notre Dame, IN: Ave Maria Press, 1970.

Gibbons, James, M. Orsini, Henry Formby, John Francis Hogan, and John Gilmary Shea. *Fathers, Martyrs and Queen of the Holy Rosary*. New York: Thomas Kelly, 1880.

Gilbert, Rev. Napoleon J. "The Spiritual Anointing of the Sick." *Hospital Progress* 11 (April 1930): 175–178.

Graf, Ernest, OSB. "The Exact Moment of Birth and Death." *Homiletic and Pastoral Review* 40, no. 1 (October 1939: 320–321.

Grant, Dorothy Fremont. *War Is My Parish*. Milwaukee: Bruce Publishing, 1944.

Green, T. Pitt. *Restoring Sanctuary*. Indianapolis: Dog Ear Publishing, 2010.

Grieco, Rose. "The Wake of My Aunt Rose." *Catholic Digest* 17 (June 1953): 17–20.

Guinan, Alastair. "Our Lady as Patroness of the Dying, According to the Liturgists of Eighteenth-Century France." *Life of the Spirit* 9 (December 1954): 252–261.

Heagney, H. J. "The First Prayers." *Catholic Home Journal* 45 (October 1945): 8, 11.

———. "Training the Baby." *Catholic Home Journal* 45 (September 1945): 10.

"Help for the Dying." *Liguorian* 43 (September 1955): 568.

Hertz, Geraldine. "When Death Comes Close, so Also Does God." *Family Digest* 8 (July 1953): 27–28.

Hinman, Vera. "Lucky to Be a Catholic?" *Family Digest* 14 (June 1959): 21–24.

Hoever, Hugo H., SO Cist., ed. *Saint Joseph Daily Missal*. New York: Catholic Book Publishing, 1959.

Holleran, J. J. "Christian Death." *Orate Fratres* 14 (November 2, 1941): 529–533.

Hood, Ann. "Looking for a Healing in New Mexico." *Catholic Digest* 63 (July 1999): 22–37.

Horan, Ellamay, and James W. O'Brien. *A Catechism of Christian Doctrine: The Illustrated Revised Edition of the Baltimore Catechism, No. 1.* New York: W. H. Sadlier, 1944.

————. *Revised Edition of the Baltimore Catechism, No. 2.* Patterson, NJ: St. Anthony Guild Press, 1941.

"Horror Comics on the Run?" *Ave Maria* 80 (October 16, 1954): 4–5.

Hume, David. *The Natural History of Religion. 1757.* Stanford, CA: Stanford University Press, 1956.

"Infant's Funeral." *American Ecclesiastical Review* 129 (September 1953): 199–200.

John Paul II. "Mary and the Human Drama of Death." *L'Osservatore Romano,* English edition, July 2, 1997. www.ewtn.com/library/papaldoc/jp2bvm53.htm.

Judermanns, Rev. N. "The Sacraments of the Sick." *Truth* 34 (November 1930): 38.

K. A. L. "Making a Circus Out of Death." *Information* 73 (November 1959): 61.

Kavanaugh, James. *A Modern Priest Looks at His Outdated Church.* 25th Anniversary Edition. Highland Park, IL: Steven J. Nash Publishing, 1992.

Kearney, James F., SJ. "The Chaplain Looks at Death." *America* 43 (October 4, 1930): 612–614.

Keller Rev. Robert. A. "Hello, My Name Is Pedro." *Catholic School Journal* 59 (June 1959).

————. "Instructing Migrant Children." *Catholic School Journal* 59 (June 1959): 53–54.

Kelley, Joseph F. "Holy Cross Cemetery in Cleveland." *Catholic Property Administration* 17, no. 3 (May–June 1953): 84–85, 144–146.

Kelly, M. V., OSB. "First Friday and Children's Confessions." *Homiletic and Pastoral Review* 37 (October 1936): 65–67.

————. "Memorizing Prayers." *Journal of Religious Instruction* 6 (May 1936): 829.

Kerouac, Jack. *Visions of Gerard.* 1963. New York: Penguin Books, 1991.

Kerrison, Ray. *Bishop Walsh of Maryknoll: Prisoner of Red China.* New York: G. P. Putnam's Sons, 1962.

Kinkead, Thomas. *Catechism of Christian Doctrine: Prepared and Enjoined by Order of the Third Plenary Council of Baltimore, No. 3.* New York: Benzinger Brothers, 1921.

Kosciesza, Ida. "Surveying the Catholic Funeral." *New City.* September 15, 1964, 12–13.

La Bau, Anthony F., SJ. *Saint Bill of New York.* St. Louis: Queen's Work, 1945.

"Last Sacraments to Apparently Dead Persons." *Ecclesiastical Review* 82 (May 1930): 510–511.

Leonard, John E. "Wasn't It the Grand Wake?" *Priest* 16 (September 1960): 783–785.

Lewis, Theophilus. "Christian Comic Books." *Interracial Review* 27, no. 12 (December 1954): 211–212.

Leystan, A. G. "The Revised Funeral Rite." *Priest* 26 (November 1970): 52–56.

L'Heureux, John. *Picnic in Babylon: A Jesuit Priest's Journal, 1963–1967.* New York: Macmillan, 1967.

Little Audrey Santo Foundation Website. www.littleaudreysantofoundation.org.

Lomask, Milton. *Saint Isaac and the Indians.* New York: Vision Books, 1956.

Long, Valentine, OFM. "Death Is a Key." *Friar* 4 (July 1955): 39–44.

Lord, Daniel A., SJ. *Angel and Imp at Home Paint Book.* St. Louis: Queen's Work, n.d.

———. *A Child at Prayer.* New York: Devotional Publishing, 1945.

———. *Miniature Stories of the Saints.* Bk. 1. New York: William J. Hirten, 1943.

———. *Speaking of Birth Control.* St. Louis: Queen's Work, 1930.

———. *What Birth Control Is Doing to the United States.* St. Louis: Queen's Work, 1936.

———. *What of Lawful Birth Control?* St. Louis: Queen's Work, 1935.

"Lo, the Poor Mexican!" *Priest* 12, no. 5 (May 1956): 389–393.

Lux, J. B. "The Artistic and the Devotional." *Extension* 51 (May 1957): 31–32.

Lynch, Dan. "The Amazing Truth of Our Lady of Guadalupe." Catholic Education, December 2002. www.catholiceducation.org/en/culture/catholic-contributions/the-amazing-truth-of-our-lady-of-guadalupe.html.

Lynn, Gabriel. "The 'Comics' Are Not to Be Laughed At." *Extension* 39 (May 1945): 12–13, 39.

———. "A Tragedy Caused by the Comics." *Catholic Digest* 8, no. 11 (September 1944): 22–24.

Maes, Yvonne, with Bonita Slunder. *The Cannibal's Wife: A Memoir.* New York: Herodias, 1999.

Mahoney, Rev. E. J. "Burial of Non-Catholics." *Clergy Review* 20 (January 1941): 84–86.

———. "Funeral Customs." *Clergy Review* 20 (February 1941): 177–178.

Mahon, Julia C. "Good-Bye, Dear Betty." *Marriage* 44 (February 1962): 10–15.

Manual of Prayers for Children in Catholic Grade and High Schools. O'Fallon, MO: Sisters of the Adoration of the Most Precious Blood, 1949.

Martin, James, SJ. "Holy Dirt." *America* 198, no. 6 (February 25, 2008): 9–12.

May, Alice R. "The Child, the Home, the School." *Journal of Religious Instruction* 16 (April 1946): 701–710.

McClinton, Bill. "The Seventh Work of Mercy." *Catholic Digest* 25 (November 1960): 55–57.

McDonough, Aloysius, CP. "Block Rosary." *Sign Post* 31 (November 1951): 29–30.

McMahon, John J. "Catholic Students Look at Death." *Commonweal* 87 (January 26, 1968): 491–494.

The Michigan Catholic. "The Story of Our Lady Guadalupe." November 27, 2013. http://themichigancatholic.com/2013/11/the-story-of-our-lady-of-guadalupe/.

Mihanovich, Clement S. *Whither Birth Control? The Death of a Nation.* St. Louis: Queen's Work, 1947.

"A Milestone in Mausoleum Architecture." *Catholic Property Administration* 22, no. 1 (January–February 1958): 39–45.

Miller, Ed Mack. *And Baby Makes Seven: A Father Looks at Birth Control.* St. Louis: Queen's Work, 1954.

Miller, Ernest F., CSSR. "Merciless Mourners." *Liguorian* 45 (July 1957): 17–21.

Miller, Louis G. "Taking the Sting Out of Death." *Liguorian* 42 (November 1954): 661–665.

A Missionary Sister. "Correspondence: An Antidote for Modern Poison." *Journal of Religious Instruction* 14 (April 1944): 734–736.

Morin, Howard, CSSR. "How to Recognize a Spoiled Child." *Liguorian* 47 (April 1959): 18–22.

Morrow, Most Rev. Louis Laravoire. *My Jesus and I.* Kenosha, WI: My Mission House, 1949.

Mueller, Therese. "Death in Your Home." *Voice of St. Jude* 21 (October 1955): 32.

Mullaney, Thomas U., OP. "The Rosary, Our Secret Weapon." *Ave Maria* 88 (October 4, 1958): 5–7, 23.

My Little Prayerbook: Instructions and Prayers for Catholic Children. New York: Benziger Brothers, 1894.

Nagle, Joan C. "Billy: The Death of a Ten-Year Old." *Queen's Work* 55 (April 1963): 9–11, 21.

"National Catholic Cemetery Conference." *Social Justice Review* 55, no. 7 (November 1962): 239–240.

"Negroes Enact the Way of the Cross." *New World* (March 13, 1942).

"New Cemetery Buildings Dedicated." *Church Property Administration* 19, no. 1 (January–February 1955): 50–52, 200.

New York Daily News. "He without Sin?" April 12, 1998.

New York Times. "Catholic Students Burn Up Comic Books." December 11, 1948.

———. "Priests Save Host from Church Fire." December 23, 1923, 15.

———. "Pupils Burn Comic Books: Auburn Parochial School Has Bonfire of Crime-Sex Volumes." December 23, 1948.

———. "Sex and Crime Tales Hit." December 31, 1949.

Nowell, Alexander, and William Day. *The True Report of the Disputation, or Rather Private Conference Had in the Tower of London, with Ed. Campion, Jesuit, the Last of August 1581.* London: Christopher Barker, 1583. https://drive .google.com/file/d/oB9Gzqjp_hcXIOGtTLTJ4dk5YcXM/view.

O'Connor, Jerome F., SJ, and William Hayden, SJ. *Chalk Talks, or, Teaching Catechism Graphically.* St. Louis: Queen's Work, 1928.

The Official Catholic Directory. New York: P. J. Kenedy and Sons, 1921.

O'Grady, John. "New Life Comes from the Bottom." *Catholic Charities Review* 39 (December 1955): 14–16.

O'Nan, Jill. "Waking the Dead." *Commonweal* 49 (August 18, 1944): 442–443.

Orsini, M. *The Queen of Angels, or, Life of the Blessed Virgin, with a Universal History of the Catholic Church.* New York: Gay Brothers and Co., 1881.

Oswald, Ruth. "One-Man Apostolate: The Story behind the Block Rosary Crusade." *Our Lady's Digest* 14 (November 1959): 183–187.

"Period between Apparent and Real Death." *Ecclesiastical Review* 106 (May 1942): 383–384.

Peyton, Patrick J., CSC. *All for Her: The Autobiography of Father Patrick Peyton.* Garden City, NY: Doubleday, 1967.

———. *The Ear of God: Prayer Is the Language of Man to God.* Garden City, NY: Doubleday, 1951.

"Planning Public Acceptance of New Burial Plan." *Catholic Property Administration* 25 (October 1961): 118, 120–122.

Pollock, Michelle Heather. "My Miracle at Chimayo." *Catholic Digest* 70 (February 2006): 34–38.

"Prayers at Funerals." *Ecclesiastical Review* 105 (July 1941): 51.

Quirk, Josephine. "The Rosary . . . A Weapon against Communism." *Extension* 46 (October 1951): 30–31.

"Regulations of Concern to Catholic Cemeteries." *Catholic Property Administration* 24 (May–June 1960): 140–145, 158–167.

Reilly, Robert T. "Poteen and Sympathy." *Ave Maria* 91 (March 12, 1960): 10–14.

Remembrance of My First Holy Communion. New York: William J. Hirten, 1942.

"Right to Choose Church of Funeral and Place of Burial." *Ecclesiastical Review* 84 (June 1931): 629–630.

Rigney, Harold W., SVD. *Four Years in a Red Hell: The Story of Father Rigney.* Chicago: Henry Regnery, 1956.

Riker, Charles, and Audrey Riker. "Parents, Children, and Death." *Marriage* 43 (November 1961): 12–17.

Rush, Alfred C., CSSR. "Birthday: Death as a New Birth." *Liguorian* 53 (July 1965): 41–42.

———. "Cemetery: Sign of Faith and Sleep of Peace." *Liguorian* 52 (August 1964): 44–46.

———. "The Passing of Susan." *Family Digest* 11 (May 1956): 48–50.

———. "The Rosary and the Christian Wake." *American Ecclesiastical Review* 152 (May 1965): 289–295.

Sanderlin, Owenita. "Johnny's Life—and Death." *Family Digest* 19 (November 1963): 31–36.

Schmidt, Curtis B., SJ. *Too Late Is Forever.* St. Louis: Queen's Work, 1959.

A School Sister of Notre Dame. "Consider the Lives of the Saints." *Journal of Religious Instruction* 5 (November 1934): 206–211.

———. "Devotion to the Queen of the Rosary." *Catholic School Journal* 33 (October 1933): 234–238.

———. "Extreme Unction." *Catholic School Journal* 34 (July 1934): 158.

———. "Teaching the Mass to Children." *Catholic School Journal* 33 (September 1933): 205–209.

Schorn, Nicholas J. "Why the Block Rosary?" *Our Lady of the Cape: Queen of the Most Holy Rosary* (February 1952).

Scott, Martin J., SJ. *A Boy Knight.* New York: P. J. Kenedy and Sons, 1921.

"Sentimentality at the Deathbed." *America* 88 (November 15, 1952): 169.

Sheed, Wilfred, and Shirley Feltmann. "The Funeral Business." *Jubilee* 8 (November 1960): 30–35.

Sheerin, John B., CSP. "Conspiracy against Death." *Homiletic and Pastoral Review* 54, no. 6 (March 1954): 485–488.

———. "Dark before Dawn." *Homiletic and Pastoral Review* 45 (February 1945): 321–326.

———. "Lewd and Brutal Horror—Comics." *Homiletic and Pastoral Review* 55, no. 9 (June 1955): 731–735.

Shine, Patrick F., ed. *Come My Jesus: Prayers and Instructions for Children.* New York: Catholic Book Publishing, 1954.

"The SHRINE—Modern Concept in Catholic Cemeteries." *Catholic Property Administration* 23 (November–December 1959): 63–66, 172–173.

Shroyer, Gail. "Rosary Under Mortar Fire." *Catholic Digest* 15 (October 1951): 30–35.

Sister Anne Catherine, CSJ. "Teaching the Truth about the Saints." *Journal of Religious Instruction* 12 (March 1942): 586–602.

Sister Cecilia Ann Benson, FCSP. "Teaching Christian Social Principles to Pupils in the First Grade." *Catholic Educational Review* 48 (November 1946): 368–376.

Sister Dolorice. "Combating the Comics—One Way." *America* 14 (January 9, 1943): 381–382.

Sister Elizabeth Marie, OSF. "To My Guardian Angel." *Catholic School Journal* 47 (October 1947): 294, 29a.

Sister Jean Marie. "Hello, My Name Is Pedro," *Catholic School Journal* 63 (June 1963): 42–43.

Sister M. Amatora, OSF. "Mary's Weapon—The R-Bomb." *Catholic Educator* 21 (October 1950): 99, 101.

———. "Molding Youth in Sanctity and Sanity." *Catholic Educational Review* 51 (December 1953): 649–659.

Sister Marilyn, OSF. "The Paradox of a Religious Teacher." *Cord* 7 (March 1957): 90–91.

———. "Weekly Instructions in Religion." *Catholic School Journal* 57 (September 1957): 229–232.

Sister Marita, OSF. "Marshaling Troops for Christ." *Catholic School Journal* 53 (September 1953): 204–205.

Sister Mary. "Our Lady and Little Children." *America,* May 13, 1933: 134–135.

Sister Mary Clara. "Religion Learned through Living." *Journal of Religious Instruction* 15 (April 1945): 658–659.

Sister Mary Consilia, OP. "The Religious Practices of Children." *Journal of Religious Instruction* 8 (February 1938): 497–512.

Sister Mary, IHM. "Our Lady and Little Children." *America,* May 13, 1933, 134–135.

Sister Mary Imelda, OP. "The Kindergarten Child and the Liturgy." *Journal of Religious Instruction* 13 (January 1943): 351–356.

Sister Mary Jarlath, OP. "Active Religion." *Catholic School Interests* 10 (July 1931): 90–92.

Sister Mary Louise, SL. "Cutting Out Theological Paper Dolls." *Journal of Religious Instruction* 15 (March 1954): 639–641.

Sister Mary Marguerite, CSJ. "Telling Religious Stories to Children." *Journal of Religious Instruction* 12 (September 1941): 45–51.

Sister Mary M. Brendan, SSND. "Training in Habits of Prayer." *Journal of Religious Instruction* 9 (March 1939): 541–549.

Sister Mary of Grace, CDP. "Apparitions of Lourdes—Playlet for December 8." *Catholic School Journal* 34 (December 1934): 287–289.

Sister Mary St. Virginia, BVM. *Peggy's Growing Up (A Fictional Saint)*. St. Louis: Queen's Work, 1940.

Sister Mary Vera, SND. "The Primary Curriculum." *Journal of Religious Instruction* 1 (June 1931): 458–459.

Sister Mary Victoria. *Nun in Red China*. New York: McGraw-Hill, 1953.

Sister M. Brendan. "Training in the Habits of Prayer." *Journal of Religious Instruction* 9 (March 1939): 54–59.

Sister M. Evangela, SSND. "The Religion Teacher and Her Problem." *Journal of Religious Instruction* 15 (January 1945): 430–437.

Sister M. Felice, FSPA. "Literature for Louis and Louise." *Catholic School Journal* 46 (June 1946): 196.

Sister M. Katherine. "Comics Are Crimes against Our Children." *America* 67, no. 9 (June 6, 1942): 234–235.

Sister M. Katherine and Marion W. Smith. "How Many Comic Magazines Does the Child Read and Why?" *Catholic Library World* 13 (May 1942): 275–279, 286.

Sister M. Leo. "Making Little Catholics More Catholic." *Journal of Religious Instruction* 14 (November 1943): 254–259.

Sister M. Madeleva, CSC. "Lucy Rehearses Her Funeral." *Catholic Digest* 19 (June 1955): 36–39.

Sister M. Paul, OSF. "Catholic Action in the Grades." *Catholic School Journal* 59 (January 1959).

Sister M. Pierre. "Our Atom Bomb, the Rosary." *Catholic School Journal* 48 (May 1948): 165–166.

Sister M. Rose Patricia, OP. "A Birthday in Heaven." *Catholic School Journal* 64 (February 1964): 65, 68.

Smaridge, Norah. "Taking Little Ones to Church." *Catholic Home Journal* 54 (January 1954): 10–11.

Smith, Harry S., CSSR. "Funeral Problems—Towards Greater Efficiency." *Priest* 22 (December 1966): 1000–1002.

StamfordAdvocate.com. "Angela Carella: Little Resolved by Priest's Final Fall." January 10, 2011. www.stamfordadvocate.com/local/article/Angela-Carella -Little-resolved-by-priest-s-final-948400.php.

Stiles, Hilary. *Assault on Innocence.* Albuquerque: B&K Publishers, 1987.

Stitzenberger, Virginia. "Our Children Learn the Facts of Death." *Family Digest* 9 (May 1954): 49–52.

Street, Arthur L. H. "Cemeteries as Unwelcome Neighbors." *Catholic Property Administration* 19, no. 4 (July–August 1955): 80–83.

———. "Cemetery Rules as to Vaults Was Void." *Catholic Property Administration* 18, no. 1 (January–February 1954): 62, 64.

Sullivan, Florence D., SJ. "Teaching Children to Pray." *Catholic School Journal* 30 (June 1930): 197–199.

Sullivan, Rev. P. Henry. "Instructing Little Children: Some Notes on 'Morning and Night Prayers' and 'Prayers before Meals." *Journal of Religious Instruction* 7 (April 1937).

———. "Notes on Teaching the 'Our Father' and the 'Hail Mary' to Small Children." *Journal of Religious Instruction* 7 (November 1936).

"Ten Commandments for Catholic Cemeteries." *Catholic Property Administration* 28 (January 1964): 36–37, 48–51.

Thompson, James M. "Doctrine for Children." *Clergy Review* 21 (October 1941): 225–231.

Tobin, Thomas J. "Parish Funeral Services." *Worship* 30 (April 1956): 342–343.

Tranel, Virginia. *Benita: Prey for Him.* Fairfield, IA: First World Publishing, 2010.

Treasure Chest of Fun and Fact. Dayton, OH: George A. Pflaum, 1946–1972. www.aladino.wrlc.org/gsdl/collect/treasure/treasure.shtml.

Trese, Leo J. "Bringing Up Saints." *Marriage* 43 (December 1961): 7–13.

———. "How a Christian Dies." *Ave Maria* 92 (October 1960): 26–29.

———. "It Will Happen to You." *Ave Maria* 93, no. 25 (February 1961): 12–14.

"A Unique Apostolate." *Ave Maria* 55, no. 3 (January 3, 1942): 5.

Unsworth, Tim. *The Last Priests in America: Conversations with Remarkable Men.* New York: Crossroad, 1991.

USA Today. "Believers Flock to Virgin Mary Statue 'Crying' Red Tears." November 27, 2005. http://usatoday30.usatoday.com/news/religion/2005-11-27 -marystatue_x.htm.

Vogt, George. "En Rapport: Religion and the Boy of Today." *Journal of Religious Instruction* 3 (June 1933): 846–851.

Wave (Rockaway Beach). "Columbiettes Hear Speaker Describe How Block Rosary Movement Started." September 29, 1955.

Weber, Gerard P. "How to Make Wakes More Christian." *Information* 75 (November 1961): 42–46.

———. "Wakes and Funerals." *Worship* 35 (January 1961): 114–115.

"What Death Proves." *Liguorian* 49 (November 1961).

"When We Should Say an Act of Contrition." *Junior Catholic Messenger* 9 (February 24, 1943): 143.

Whiteford, Mary. "Froth on the Bier." *St. Joseph Magazine* 58 (November 1957): 16–17.

Wilson, Alfred, CP. "Why Fear Death?" *Ave Maria* 88, no. 3 (July 19, 1958): 12–14, 26.

Windeatt, Mary Fabyan, and Mart Bailey (illus.). "Saint Maria Goretti: The Blood-Stained Lily." *Treasure Chest of Fun and Fact* 6, no. 5 (November 9, 1950): 9–14.

Windeatt, Mary Fabyan, and Paul Karch (illus.). "The Boys' Friend: St. John Bosco." *Treasure Chest of Fun and Fact* 8, no. 9 (January 1, 1953): 12–17.

Woywod, Stanislaus, OFM. "Sacraments to Unconscious Persons after Life without Religion, Catholic Burial of These Persons." *Homiletic and Pastoral Review* 30 (May 1930): 867–868.

Wright, John. "Guest Editorial: Wakes and Rosaries." *Liguorian* 52 (August 1964): 60.

Wuerl, Donald. "Our Lady of Guadalupe, the Star of the New Evangelization." *Cardinal's Blog,* December 12, 2013. http://cardinalsblog.adw.org/2013/12/our-lady-of-guadalupe-the-star-of-the-new-evangelization/.

Zook, Mary. "Religious Training for the Younger Set." *Sign* 35 (June 1956): 27–28.

SECONDARY SOURCES

Abrahams, Peter W. "Human Geophagy: A Review of Its Distribution, Causes, and Implications." In *Geology and Health: Closing the Gap,* ed. H. Catherine Skinner and Anthony R. Berger, 31–35. New York: Oxford University Press, 2003.

Ackerman, Robert. *The Myth and Ritual School: J. G. Frazer and the Cambridge Ritualists.* New York: Garland Publishing, 1991.

Adams, Marilyn McCord. *Wrestling for Blessing.* London: Darton, Longman, and Todd, 2005.

Alexander, Jeffrey C. *Trauma: A Social Theory.* Cambridge, UK: Polity Press, 2012.

Allen, Irving Lewis. *The City in Slang: New York Life and Popular Speech.* New York: Oxford University Press, 1993.

Allman, Jean, and John Parker. *Tongnaab: The History of a West African God.* Bloomington: Indiana University Press, 2005.

Almond, Philip C. *The British Discovery of Buddhism.* Cambridge, UK: Cambridge University Press, 1988.

Anderson, Emma. *The Death and Afterlife of the North American Martyrs.* Cambridge, MA: Harvard University Press, 2013.

Ankersmit, Frank R. *Sublime Historical Experience.* Stanford, CA: Stanford University Press, 2005.

Apolito, Paolo. *Apparitions of the Madonna at Oliveto Citra: Local Visions and Cosmic Drama.* Translated by William A. Christian Jr. University Park: Pennsylvania State University Press, 1998.

———. *The Internet and the Madonna: Religious Visionary Experience on the Web.* Translated by Antony Shugaar. Chicago: University of Chicago Press, 2005.

Arditti, Michael. *Easter.* London: Arcadia Books, 2000.

Arendt, Hannah. *The Human Condition.* 2nd ed. Introduction by Margaret Canovan. Chicago: University of Chicago Press, 1998. First published 1958.

———. *Men in Dark Times.* San Diego: Harcourt Brace Jovanovich, 1983.

Asad, Talal. *Genealogies of Religion: Discipline and Reasons of Power in Christianity and Islam.* Baltimore: Johns Hopkins University Press, 1993.

Ashforth, Adam. *Witchcraft, Violence and Democracy in South Africa.* Chicago: University of Chicago Press, 2005.

Badone, Ellen. *The Appointed Hour: Death, Worldview and Social Change in Brittany.* Berkeley: University of California Press, 1989.

Baggett, Jerome P. *Sense of the Faithful: How American Catholics Live Their Faith.* New York: Oxford University Press, 2008.

Bainvel, Jean. *Devotion to the Sacred Heart of Jesus.* Translated by E. Leahy. New York: Benziger Bros., 1924.

Ball, Ann. *Encyclopedia of Catholic Devotions and Practices.* Huntington, IN: Our Sunday Visitor Publishing Division, 2003.

Barkan, Elazar, and Ronald Busch, eds. *Prehistories of the Future: The Primitivist Project and the Culture of Modernism.* Stanford, CA: Stanford University Press, 1995.

Bartlett, Robert. *The Making of Europe: Conquest, Colonization, and Cultural Change, 950–1350.* Princeton, NJ: Princeton University Press, 1993.

Bass, Ellen, and Laura Davis. *The Courage to Heal: A Guide for Women Survivors of Child Sexual Abuse.* 20th anniversary ed. New York: HarperCollins, 2008.

Bastin, Rohan. *The Domain of Constant Excess: Plural Worship at the Munnesvaram Temples in Sri Lanka.* New York: Berghahn Books, 2002.

Bayly, C. A. *The Birth of the Modern World, 1780–1914: Global Connections and Comparisons*. Malden, MA: Blackwell, 2004.

Beard, Mary. "Frazer, Leach, and Virgil: The Popularity (and Unpopularity) of *The Golden Bough.*" *Comparative Studies in Society and History* 34, no. 2 (April 1992): 203–224.

Behrend, Heike. *Resurrecting Cannibals: The Catholic Church, Witch-Hunts, and the Production of Pagans in Western Uganda*. Suffolk, UK: James Currey, 2011.

Belting, Hans. *Likeness and Presence: A History of the Image before the Era of Art*. Translated by Edmund Jephcott. Chicago: University of Chicago Press, 1994.

Benjamin, Jessica. "Beyond Doer and Done To: An Intersubjective View of Thirdness." *Psychoanalytic Quarterly* 73 (2004): 5–46.

———. *The Bonds of Love: Psychoanalysis, Feminism, and the Problem of Domination*. New York: Pantheon Books, 1988.

———. "Two-Way Streets: Recognition of Difference and the Intersubjective Third." *Differences: A Journal of Feminist Cultural Studies* 17, no. 1 (Spring 2006): 116–146.

Bennett, Jeffrey S. *When the Sun Danced: Myth, Miracles, and Modernity in Early Twentieth-Century Portugal*. Charlottesville: University of Virginia Press, 2012.

Berger, Peter. *The Sacred Canopy: Elements of a Sociological Theory of Religion*. New York: Doubleday, 1967.

Bernanos, Georges. *The Diary of a Country Priest*. 1937. Translated by Pamela Morris. New York: Fount, 1977.

Berry, Jason. *Lead Us Not into Temptation: Catholic Priests and the Sexual Abuse of Children*. Urbana: University of Illinois Press, 1992.

Berry, Wendell. *A Place on Earth*. Berkeley: Counterpoint, 2001.

Bireley, Robert. *The Refashioning of Catholicism, 1450–1700: Reassessment of the Counter Reformation*. Washington, DC: Catholic University of America Press, 1999.

Bishop Accountability. "Who We Are." 2004. www.bishop-accountability.org /WhoWeAre/.

Blackbourn, David. *Marpingen: Apparitions of the Virgin Mary in Bismarckian Germany*. New York: Alfred A. Knopf, 1994.

Black, Timuel D., Jr. *Bridges of Memory: Chicago's Second Generation of Black Migration*. Evanston, IL: Northwestern University Press, 2007.

Blatty, William Peter. *If There Were Demons, Then Perhaps There Were Angels: William Peter Blatty's Own Story of the Exorcist*. Suffolk, UK: ScreenPress Books, 1999.

————. *I'll Tell Them I Remember You.* New York: W. W. Norton, 1973.

Boff, Leonardo. *Francis of Rome, Francis of Assisi: A New Springtime for the Church?* Maryknoll, NY: Orbis Books, 2014.

Bollas, Christopher. *Cracking Up: The Work of Unconscious Experience.* London: Routledge, 1995.

————. *The Shadow of the Object: Psychoanalysis of the Unthought Known.* New York: Columbia University Press, 1987.

Borhegyi, Stephan F. de. "The Cult of Our Lord of Esquípulas in Middle America and New Mexico." *El Palacio* 61, no. 12 (December 1954): 387–401.

Bourke, Joanna. *The Story of Pain: From Prayer to Painkillers.* Oxford: Oxford University Press, 2014.

Brading, D. A. *Mexican Phoenix, Our Lady of Guadalupe: Image and Tradition across Five Centuries.* Cambridge, UK: Cambridge University Press, 2001.

Bradshaw, Brendan, and Dàire Keogh, eds. *Christianity in Ireland: Revisiting the Story.* Dublin: Columba Press, 2002.

Brickman, Celia. *Aboriginal Populations in the Mind: Race and Primitivity in Psychoanalysis.* New York: Columbia University Press, 2003.

Brown, Karen McCarthy. *Mama Lola: A Vodou Priestess in Brooklyn.* Berkeley: University of California Press, 1991.

Brown, Kate. *A Biography of No Place: From Ethnic Borderland to Soviet Heartland.* Cambridge, MA: Harvard University Press, 2004.

Brown, Peter. *The Cult of the Saints: Its Rise and Function in Latin Christianity.* Chicago: University of Chicago Press, 1981.

————. *The Rise of Western Christendom: Triumph and Diversity, A.D. 200–1000.* 10th anniversary rev. ed. West Sussex, UK: Wiley-Blackwell, 2013. First published 1996.

Bulman, Raymond F., and Frederick J. Parrella, eds. *From Trent to Vatican II: Historical and Theological Investigations.* New York: Oxford University Press, 2006.

Burris, John P. *Exhibiting Religion: Colonialism and Spectacle at International Exhibitions, 1851–1893.* Charlottesville: University Press of Virginia, 2001.

Burrus, Virginia. *Saving Shame: Martyrs, Saints, and Other Abject Subjects.* Philadelphia: University of Pennsylvania Press, 2008.

Bushman, Richard Lyman. *Joseph Smith: Rough Stone Rolling.* New York: Alfred A. Knopf, 2005.

Butler, Dom Cuthbert. *The Vatican Council, 1869–1870: Based on Bishop Ulathorne's Letters.* Westminster, MD: Newman Press, 1962.

Butler, Jon. *Awash in a Sea of Faith: Christianizing the American People.* Cambridge, MA: Harvard University Press, 1990.

Butler, Judith. *Giving an Account of Oneself.* New York: Fordham University Press, 2005.

Bynum, Caroline Walker. *Christian Materiality: An Essay on Religion in Late Medieval Europe.* New York: Zone Books, 2011.

———. *The Resurrection of the Body in Western Christianity, 200–1336.* New York: Columbia University Press, 1995.

Byron, Reginald. *Irish America.* Oxford Studies in Social and Cultural Anthropology. Oxford: Clarendon Press, 1999.

Cadegan, Una M. *All Good Books Are Catholic Books: Print Culture, Censorship, and Modernity in Twentieth-Century America.* Cushwa Center Studies of Catholicism in Twentieth-Century America. Ithaca, NY: Cornell University Press, 2013.

———. "The Queen of Peace in the Shadow of War: Fatima and U.S. Catholic Anti-Communism." *U.S. Catholic Historian* 22, no. 4 (Fall 2004): 1–15.

Cadge, Wendy. *Paging God: Religion in the Halls of Medicine.* Chicago: University of Chicago Press, 2012.

Cafardi, Nicholas P. *Before Dallas: The U.S. Bishops' Response to Clergy Sexual Abuse of Children.* Mahwah, NJ: Paulist Press, 2008.

Calamari, Barbara, and Sandra DiPasqua. *Holy Cards.* New York: Abrams, 2004.

Calasso, Roberto. *Literature and the Gods.* Translated by Tim Parks. New York: Knopf, distributed by Random House, 2001.

Cañizares-Esguerra, Jorge. *Puritan Conquistadores: Iberianizing the Atlantic, 1550–1700.* Stanford, CA: Stanford University Press, 2006.

Cannell, Fenella. *Power and Intimacy in the Christian Philippines.* Cambridge, UK: Cambridge University Press, 1999.

Carey, Patrick W. *Orestes A. Brownson: American Religious Weathervane.* Grand Rapids, MI: William B. Eerdmans Publishing, 2004.

Carroll, Michael P. *The Cult of the Virgin Mary: Psychological Origins.* Princeton, NJ: Princeton University Press, 1986.

———. *Madonnas That Maim: Popular Catholicism in Italy since the Fifteenth Century.* Baltimore: Johns Hopkins University Press, 1992.

Caruth, Cathy. ed. *Trauma: Explorations in Memory.* Baltimore: Johns Hopkins University Press, 1995.

———. *Unclaimed Experience: Trauma, Narrative, and History.* Baltimore: Johns Hopkins University Press, 1996.

Castro, Daniel. *Another Face of Empire: Bartolomé de Las Casas, Indigenous Rights, and Ecclesiastical Imperialism.* Durham, NC: Duke University Press, 2007.

Cavarero, Adriana. *Relating Narratives: Storytelling and Selfhood.* Translated by Paul A. Kottman. New York: Routledge, 2000.

Certeau, Michel de. *The Writing of History.* Translated by Tom Conley. New York: Columbia University Press, 1988.

Chadwick, Owen. *Catholicism and History: The Opening of the Vatican Archives.* London: Cambridge University Press, 1978.

———. *The Secularization of the European Mind in the Nineteenth Century.* Cambridge, UK: Cambridge University Press, 1977.

Chakrabarty, Dipesh. *Provincializing Europe: Postcolonial Thought and Historical Difference.* Princeton, NJ: Princeton University Press, 2000.

Charles, Marilyn. *Working with Trauma: Lessons from Bion and Lacan.* Lanham, MD: Jason Aronson, 2012.

Châtellier, Louis. *The Europe of the Devout: The Catholic Reformation and the Formation of a New Society.* Translated by Jean Birrell. Cambridge, UK: Cambridge University Press, 1989.

———. *The Religion of the Poor: Rural Missions in Europe and the Formation of Modern Catholicism, c. 1500–1800.* Translated by Brian Pearce. Cambridge, UK: Cambridge University Press, 1997.

Chau, Adam Yuet. *Miraculous Response: Doing Popular Religion in Contemporary China.* Stanford, CA: Stanford University Press, 2006.

Chidester, David. *Empire of Religion: Imperialism and Comparative Religion.* Chicago: University of Chicago Press, 2014.

———. *Savage Systems: Colonialism and Comparative Religion in Southern Africa.* Charlottesville: University Press of Virginia, 1996.

Chinnici, Joseph P., OFM. "The Catholic Community at Prayer, 1926–1976." In *Habits of Devotion: Catholic Religious Practice in Twentieth-Century America,* ed. James M. O'Toole, 9–87. Ithaca, NY: Cornell University Press, 2004.

Christian, William A., Jr. *Visionaries: The Spanish Republic and the Reign of Christ.* Berkeley: University of California Press, 1996.

Clites, Brian J. "Breaking the Silence: The Catholic Sexual Abuse Survivor Movement in Chicago." PhD diss., Northwestern University, Department of Religious Studies, 2015.

Cocchiara, Giuseppe. *Le immagini devote del popolo siciliano.* Palermo, Italy: Sellerio, 1982.

Cohen, David William. *The Combing of History.* Chicago: University of Chicago Press, 1994.

Coman, Brian J. "Frazer, Wittgenstein, and the Savage Mind." *Quadrant* 48 (June 2004): 14–19.

Connell, Janice T. *The Visions of the Children: The Apparitions of the Blessed Mother at Medjugorje.* 1992. New York: St. Martin's Griffin, 2007.

Coppa, Frank J. *Controversial Concordats: The Vatican's Relations with Napoleon, Mussolini, and Hitler.* Washington, DC: Catholic University of America Press, 1999.

Cornwell, John. *The Pope in Winter: The Dark Face of John Paul II's Papacy.* New York: Viking, 2004.

Cozzens, Donald B. *The Changing Face of the Priesthood.* Collegeville, MN: Liturgical Press, 2000.

Craig, Mary. *Spark from Heaven: The Mystery of the Madonna of Medjugorje.* Notre Dame, IN: Ave Maria Press, 1988.

Cross, Whitney R. *The Burned-Over District: The Social and Intellectual History of Enthusiastic Religion in Western New York, 1800–1850.* 1950. Ithaca, NY: Cornell University Press, 1981.

Crumb, Robert. "The Art of Comics No. 1: Interview with Ted Widmer." *Paris Review,* no. 193 (Summer 2010). www.theparisreview.org/interviews/6017/the-art-of-comics-no-1-r-crumb.

———. *Gotta Have 'Em: Portraits of Women.* Los Angeles: Greybull Press, 2003.

———. *Your Vigor for Life Appalls Me: Robert Crumb Letters, 1958–1977.* Edited by Ilse Thompson. Seattle: Fantagraphics Books, 1998.

Cummings, Kathleen Sprows. *New Women of the Old Faith: Gender and American Catholicism in the Progressive Era.* Chapel Hill: University of North Carolina Press, 2009.

Cuneo, Michael. *The Smoke of Satan: Conservative and Traditionalist Dissent in Contemporary American Catholicism.* Baltimore: Johns Hopkins University Press, 1999.

Danto, Arthur C. *Andy Warhol.* New Haven, CT: Yale University Press, 2009.

———. "Censorship and Subsidy in the Arts." *Bulletin of the American Academy of Arts and Sciences* 47, no. 1 (October 1993): 25–41.

———. *Playing with the Edge: The Photographic Achievement of Robert Mapplethorpe.* Berkeley: University of California Press, 1996.

———. *The Transfiguration of the Commonplace: A Philosophy of Art.* Cambridge, MA: Harvard University Press, 1981.

Davies, Jody Messler, and Mary Gail Frawley. *Treating the Adult Survivor of Childhood Sexual Abuse: A Psychoanalytic Perspective.* New York: Basic Books, 1994.

Davis, Natalie Zemon. *Society and Culture in Early Modern France: Eight Essays.* 1965. Stanford, CA: Stanford University Press, 1975.

Davoine, François, and Jean-Max Gaudillière. *History beyond Trauma.* Translated by Susan Fairfield. New York: Other Press, 2004.

Delumeau, Jean. *Catholicism between Luther and Voltaire: A New View of the Counter-Reformation.* Translated by Jeremy Moiser. London: Burns and Oates, 1977.

Des mondes de papier: L'imagerie populaire de Wissenbourg. Strasbourg, France: Musée de la vielle de Strasbourg, 2010.

Diefendorf, Barbara B. *Beneath the Cross: Catholics and Huguenots in Sixteenth-Century Paris.* New York: Oxford University Press, 1991.

Dinter, Paul E. *The Other Side of the Altar: One Man's Life in the Catholic Priesthood.* New York: Farrar, Straus and Giroux, 2003.

Dolan, Jay P. *The American Catholic Experience: A History from Colonial Times to the Present.* Garden City, NY: Doubleday, 1985.

———, ed. *The American Catholic Parish: A History from 1850 to the Present.* 2 vols. New York: Paulist Press, 1987.

Doody, Colleen. "Grappling with Secularism: Anti-Communism and Catholicism in Cold War Detroit." *American Communist History* 10, no. 1 (2011): 53–71.

Duffy, Eamon. *Marking the Hours: English People and Their Prayers, 1240–1570.* New Haven, CT: Yale University Press, 2006.

The Economist. "Tears in Sacramento." January 5, 2006. www.economist.com/node/5364759.

Elliott, Andrea. "Believers Bring Their Aches to Bathe in the City's Water." *New York Times,* October 3, 2004. www.nytimes.com/2004/10/03/nyregion/03journal.html?_r=0.

Ellis, John Tracy, ed. *The Catholic Priest in the United States: Historical Investigations.* Collegeville, MN: Saint John's University Press, 1971.

Estren, Mark James. *A History of Underground Comics.* 1974. Berkeley: Ronin Publisher, 1986.

Evans, Curtis J. *The Burden of Black Religion.* New York: Oxford University Press, 2008.

Fabian, Johannes. *Time and the Other: How Anthropology Makes Its Object.* 1983. New York: Columbia University Press, 2002.

Fabre-Vassas, Claudine. *The Singular Beast: Jews, Christians, and the Pig.* Translated by Carol Volk. New York: Columbia University Press, 1997.

Faggioli, Massimo. *True Reform: Liturgy and Ecclesiology in* Sacrosanctum Concilium. Collegeville, MN: Liturgical Press, 2012.

Fasolt, Constantin. *The Limits of History.* Chicago: University of Chicago Press, 2004.

Fichter, Joseph H. *Dynamics of a City Church.* Chicago: University of Chicago Press, 1951.

Findlay, Jean. *Chasing Lost Time: The Life of C. K. Scott Moncrieff, Soldier, Spy, and Translator.* New York: Farrar, Strauss, and Giroux, 2014.

Foucault, Michel. *Madness and Civilization: A History of Insanity in the Age of Reason.* Translated by Richard Howard. New York: Vintage Books, 1965.

———. *Religion and Culture.* Edited by Jeremy R. Carrette. New York: Routledge, 1999.

France, David. *Our Fathers: The Secret Life of the Catholic Church in an Age of Scandal.* New York: Broadway Books, 2004.

Franchot, Jenny. *Roads to Rome: The Antebellum Protestant Encounter with Catholicism.* Berkeley: University of California Press, 1994.

Frankfurter, Alexander M. "A Gathering of Children: Holy Infants and the Cult of El Santo Niño de Atocha." *El Palacio* 94, no. 1 (Summer / Fall 1988): 31–39.

Fraser, Robert. *The Making of* The Golden Bough: *The Origins and Growth of an Argument.* New York: St. Martin's Press, 1990.

Frawley-O'Dea, Mary Gail. *Perversion of Power: Sexual Abuse in the Catholic Church.* Nashville: Vanderbilt University Press, 2007.

Freedberg, David. *The Power of Images: Studies in the History and Theory of Response.* Chicago: University of Chicago Press, 1989.

Freeman, Charles. *Holy Bones, Holy Dust: How Relics Shaped the History of Medieval Europe.* New Haven, CT: Yale University Press, 2011.

Frend, W. H. C. *Martyrdom and Persecution in the Early Church: A Study of a Conflict from the Maccabees to Donatus.* Oxford: Basil Blackwell, 1965.

Freyd, Jennifer J. *Betrayal Trauma: The Logic of Forgetting Childhood Abuse.* Cambridge, MA: Harvard University Press, 1996.

Fuller, C. J. *The Renewal of the Priesthood: Modernity and Traditionalism in a South Indian Temple.* Princeton, NJ: Princeton University Press, 2003.

Galasso, Carmine. *Crosses: Portraits of Clergy Abuse.* London: Trolley, 2007.

Garrard-Burnett, Virginia. *Terror in the Land of the Holy Spirit: Guatemala under General Efraín Ríos Montt, 1982–1983.* New York: Oxford University Press, 2010.

Gartner, Richard B. *Betrayed as Boys: Psychodynamic Treatment of Sexually Abused Men.* New York: Guildford Press, 1999.

Geertz, Clifford. "Religion as a Cultural System." In *The Interpretation of Cultures,* 87–125. New York: Basic Books, 1973.

Getz, Lynne Marie. "Lost Momentum: World War II and the Education of Hispanos in New Mexico." In *Mexican Americans and World War II,* ed. Maggie Rivas-Rodriguez, 93–113. Austin: University of Texas Press, 2005.

Gilman, Richard. *Faith, Sex, Mystery: A Memoir.* New York: Simon and Schuster, 1986.

Ginsberg, Allen. *Howl and Other Poems.* 1956. San Francisco: City Lights, 1980.

Giradot, Norman J. *The Victorian Translation of China: James Legge's Oriental Pilgrimage.* Berkeley: University of California Press, 2002.

Gleason, Philip. *Contending with Modernity: Catholic Higher Education in the Twentieth Century.* New York: Oxford University Press, 1995.

González, Julio, SF. *The Shrine of Our Lord of Esquípulas and the Holy Child: Santuario de Chimayo in New Mexico.* Chimayo, NM: Sons of the Holy Family, 2013.

Goodrick, Susan. "Apex Interview: R. Crumb." In *R. Crumb: Conversations,* ed. D. K. Holm, 84–91. Jackson: University Press of Mississippi, 2004.

Gray, Francine du Plessix. *Divine Disobedience: Profiles in Catholic Radicalism.* New York: Vintage, 1971.

Greeley, Andrew. *Confessions of a Parish Priest: An Autobiography.* New York: Simon and Schuster, 1986.

Greenblatt, Stephen. *Marvelous Possessions: The Wonder of the New World.* Chicago: University of Chicago Press, 1991.

Grigoni, Elisabetta Gulli, and Vittorio Pranzini. *Santi: Piccole immagini devozionali a stampa e manufatte dal XVII al XX Secolo.* Ravenna, Italy: Edizioni Essegi, 1990.

Gross, David. *Lost Time: On Remembering and Forgetting in Late Modern Culture.* Amherst: University of Massachusetts Press, 2000.

———. *The Past in Ruins: Tradition and Critique of Modernity.* Amherst: University of Massachusetts Press, 1992.

Guardini, Romano. *The Lord.* Translated by Elinor Castendyk Briefs. Chicago: Henry Regnery, 1954.

Gutiérrez, Ramón A. "El Santuario de Chimayo: A Syncretic Shrine in New Mexico." In *Feasts and Celebrations in North American Communities,* ed. Ramón A. Gutiérrez and Geneviève Fabre, 71–86. Albuquerque: University of New Mexico Press, 1995.

Gutiérrez, Ramón A., and Geneviève Fabre, eds. *Feasts and Celebrations in North American Communities.* Albuquerque: University of New Mexico Press, 1995.

Haberman, David L. *River of Love in an Age of Pollution: The Yamuna River of Northern India.* Berkeley: University of California Press, 2006.

Hadot, Pierre. *Philosophy as a Way of Life: Spiritual Exercises from Socrates to Foucault.* Translated by Michael Chase. Malden, MA: Blackwell Publishing, 1995.

Hajdu, David. *The Ten-Cent Plague: The Great Comic-Book Scare and How It Changed America.* New York: Farrar, Straus, and Giroux, 2008.

Hales, E. E. Y. *Pio Nono: A Study in European Politics and Religion in the Nineteenth Century.* London: Eyre and Spottiswoode, 1954.

Hall, Linda B. *Mary, Mother and Warrior: The Virgin in Spain and in the Americas.* Austin: University of Texas Press, 2004.

Hamdy, Sherine. *Our Bodies Belong to God: Organ Transplants, Islam, and the Struggle for Human Dignity in Egypt.* Berkeley: University of California Press, 2012.

Hamilton, Elizabeth, and Eric Rich. "A Predator Blessed with Charm." *Hartford Courant,* September 15, 2002. http://articles.courant.com/2002-09-15 /news/0209151546_1_church-officials-charm-priest.

Hanson, Ellis. *Decadence and Catholicism.* Cambridge, MA: Harvard University Press, 1997.

Harpham, Geoffrey Galt. *The Ascetic Imperative in Culture and Criticism.* Chicago: University of Chicago Press, 1987.

Harrell, David Edwin, Jr. *All Things Are Possible: The Healing and Charismatic Revivals in Modern America.* Bloomington: Indiana University Press, 1975.

———. *Oral Roberts: An American Life.* San Francisco: HarperCollins, 1987.

Harris, Ruth. *Lourdes: Body and Spirit in the Secular Age.* New York: Viking, 1999.

Hatch, Nathan O. *The Democratization of American Christianity.* New Haven, CT: Yale University Press, 1989.

Hennesey, James J., SJ. *American Catholics: A History of the Roman Catholic Community in the United States.* New York: Oxford University Press, 1981.

———. *The First Council of the Vatican: The American Experience.* New York: Herder and Herder, 1963.

Herman, Judith Lewis. *Trauma and Recovery.* New York: Basic Books, 1992.

Hillman, David, and Carla Mazzio, eds. *The Body in Parts: Fantasies of Corporeality in Early Modern Europe.* New York: Routledge, 1997.

Hiss, Tony. *The Experience of Place.* New York: Vintage Books, 1990.

Hitchcock, James. *The Decline and Fall of Radical Catholicism.* New York: Herder and Herder, 1971.

Holscher, Kathleen. *Religious Lessons: Catholic Sisters and the Captured School Crisis in New Mexico.* New York: Oxford University Press: 2012.

Holt, Mack P. *The French Wars of Religion, 1562–1629.* Cambridge, UK: Cambridge University Press, 1995.

Honneth, Axel. *The Struggle for Recognition: The Moral Grammar of Social Conflicts.* Translated by Joel Anderson. Cambridge, MA: MIT Press, 1995.

Hsia, R. Po-Chia. *The World of Catholic Renewal, 1540–1770.* Cambridge, UK: Cambridge University Press, 1998.

Huckenbeck, Giles, OFM. "Santo Niño de Atocha." *Saint Anthony Messenger* 71 (January 1964): 21–23.

Huggins, Nathan Irvin. *Harlem Renaissance.* New York: Oxford University Press, 1971.

Hynes, Eugene. *Knock: The Virgin's Apparition in Nineteenth-Century Ireland.* Cork, Ireland: Cork University Press, 2008.

Inden, Ronald B. *Imagining India.* Bloomington: Indiana University Press, 1990.

Ingebretsen, Edward J. *Maps of Heaven, Maps of Hell: Religious Terror as Memory from the Puritans to Stephen King.* Armonk, NY: M. E. Sharpe, 1996.

Inguanti, Joseph J. "Landscape of Order, Landscape of Memory." In *Italian Folk: Vernacular Culture in Italian-American Lives,* ed. Joseph Sciorra, 83–106. New York: Fordham University Press, 2011.

Isaac, Jeffrey C. *Arendt, Camus, and Modern Rebellion.* New Haven, CT: Yale University Press, 1992.

Jackowski, Karol. *The Silence We Keep: A Nun's View of the Catholic Priest Scandal.* New York: Harmony Books, 2004.

Jackson, Michael. *Minima Ethnographica: Intersubjectivity and the Anthropological Project.* Chicago: University of Chicago Press, 1998.

———. *Paths toward a Clearing: Radical Empiricism and Ethnographic Inquiry.* Bloomington: Indiana University Press, 1989.

———. *The Wherewithal of Life: Ethics, Migration, and the Question of Well-Being.* Berkeley: University of California Press, 2013.

Jay, Martin. *Songs of Experience: Modern American and European Variations on a Universal Theme.* Berkeley: University of California Press, 2005.

Joas, Hans. *Do We Need Religion? On the Experience of Self-Transcendence.* Translated by Alex Skinner. Boulder, CO: Paradigm Publishers, 2008.

Johnson, Sylvester A. *African American Religions, 1500–2000: Colonialism, Democracy, and Freedom.* Cambridge, UK: Cambridge University Press, 2015.

Jones, Gerard. *Men of Tomorrow: Geeks, Gangsters, and the Birth of the Comic Book.* New York: Basic Books, 2004.

Jouanna, Arlette. *The Saint Bartholomew's Day Massacre: The Mysteries of a Crime of State.* Translated by Joseph Bergin. Manchester: Manchester University Press, 2013.

Jungmann, Joseph A., SJ. *The Mass of the Roman Rite.* Vol. 1, *Its Origins and Development,* translated by Francis A. Brunner, CSSR. New York: Benziger Brothers, 1951.

Kane, Paula M. "Marian Devotion since 1940: Continuity or Casualty?" In *Habits of Devotion: Catholic Religious Practice in Twentieth-Century America,* ed. James M. O'Toole, 89–129. Ithaca, NY: Cornell University Press, 2004.

———. "'She Offered Herself Up': The Victim Soul and Victim Spirituality in Catholicism." *Church History* 71, no. 1 (March 2002): 80–119.

———. *Sister Thorn and Catholic Mysticism in Modern America.* Chapel Hill: University of North Carolina Press, 2013.

Karp, David A. *Speaking of Sadness: Depression, Disconnection, and the Meanings of Illness.* New York: Oxford University Press, 1996.

Kaufman, Suzanne K. *Consuming Visions: Mass Culture and the Lourdes Shrine.* Ithaca, NY: Cornell University Press, 2005.

Keane, Webb. *Christian Moderns: Freedom and Fetish in the Mission Encounter.* Berkeley: University of California Press, 2007.

Keleher, James P., ed. *Catholic Shrines and Places of Pilgrimage in the United States, Jubilee Edition.* Washington, DC: United States Catholic Conference, 2000.

Khalid, Adeeb. *Islam after Communism: Religion and Politics in Central Asia.* Berkeley: University of California Press, 2007.

Kincaid, James R. *Child-Loving: The Erotic Child and Victorian Culture.* New York: Routledge, 1992.

King, Richard. *Orientalism and Religion: Postcolonial Theory, India, and the "Mystic East."* New York: Routledge, 1999.

Kirkland, Russell. *Taoism: The Enduring Tradition.* New York: Routledge, 2004.

Kirshner, Lewis A., ed. *Between Winnicott and Lacan: A Clinical Engagement.* New York: Routledge, 2011.

Kleinman, Arthur. *The Illness Narratives: Suffering, Healing, and the Human Condition.* New York: Basic Books, 1988.

Knox, Ronald A. *Enthusiasm: A Chapter in the History of Religion, with Special Reference to the XVII and XVIII Centuries.* New York: Oxford University Press, 1950.

Kramnick, Isaac, ed. *The Portable Enlightenment Reader.* London: Penguin Books, 1995.

Kselman, Thomas A., and Steven Avella. "Marian Piety and the Cold War in the United States." *Catholic Historical Review* 72, no. 3 (July 1986): 403–424.

Küng, Hans. *Memoirs.* Vol. 1, *My Struggle for Freedom,* translated by John Bowden. Grand Rapids, MI: William B. Eerdmans Publishing, 2003.

LaCapra, Dominick. *Writing History, Writing Trauma.* Baltimore: Johns Hopkins University Press, 2001.

Lakeland, Paul. *The Liberation of the Laity: In Search of an Accountable Church.* New York: Continuum, 2003.

Lambek, Michael J. *The Weight of the Past: Living with History in Mahajanga, Madagascar.* New York: Palgrave Macmillan, 2002.

Larsen, Timothy. *The Slain God: Anthropologists and the Christian Faith.* Oxford: Oxford University Press, 2014.

Laycock, Joseph P. *The Seer of Bayside: Veronica Lueken and the Struggle to Define Catholicism.* New York: Oxford University Press, 2015.

Lessard, Pierre. *Les petites images dévotes: Leur utilisation traditionnelle au Québec.* Quebec: Presses de l'Université Laval, 1981.

Levine, Daniel H. *Popular Voices in Latin American Catholicism.* Princeton, NJ: Princeton University Press, 1992.

Leys, Ruth. *Trauma: A Genealogy.* Chicago: University of Chicago Press, 2000.

Lomnitz, Claudio. *Death and the Idea of Mexico.* New York: Zone Books, 2005.

Lopez, Donald S., Jr., ed. *Curators of the Buddha: The Study of Buddhism under Colonialism.* Chicago: University of Chicago Press, 1995.

———. *From Stone to Flesh: A Short History of the Buddha.* Chicago: University of Chicago Press, 2013.

Lord, Daniel A. *The Seven Sacraments.* Illustrated by Katherine Wireman. New York: Devotional Publishing, n.d.

Luepnitz, Deborah Anna. "Thinking in the Space between Winnicott and Lacan." In Kirshner, *Between Winnicott and Lacan,* 1–28.

Luther, Martin. *Luther's Works: American Edition.* Vol. 37. Edited by Robert H. Fischer and Helmut T. Lehmann. Minneapolis: Fortress Press, 1961.

Luzzatto, Sergio. *Padre Pio: Miracles and Politics in a Secular Age.* Translated by Frederika Randall. New York: Picador, 2010.

MacDougall, Hugh A. *The Acton-Newman Relations: The Dilemma of Christian Liberalism.* New York: Fordham University Press, 1962.

Macy, Gary. *Treasures from the Storeroom: Medieval Religion and the Eucharist.* Collegeville, MN: Liturgical Press, 1999.

Markell, Patchen. *Bound by Recognition.* Princeton, NJ: Princeton University Press, 2003.

Matovina, Timothy. *Guadalupe and Her Faithful: Latino Catholics in San Antonio, from Colonial Origins to the Present.* Baltimore: Johns Hopkins University Press, 2005.

May, Elaine Tyler. *Homeward Bound: American Families in the Cold War.* 20th anniversary ed. 1988. New York: Basic Books, 2008.

McAvoy, Thomas T., CSC. *The Americanist Heresy in Roman Catholicism, 1895–1900.* Notre Dame, IN: University of Notre Dame Press, 1963.

McCoog, Thomas M. *"And Touching Our Society": Fashioning Jesuit Identity in Elizabethan England.* Toronto: Pontifical Institute of Medieval Studies, 2013.

McDannell, Colleen. "Catholic Horror: *The Exorcist* (1973)." In *Catholics in the Movies,* ed. Colleen McDannell, 197–225. New York: Oxford University Press, 2008.

McDonogh, Gary Wray. *Black and Catholic in Savannah, Georgia.* Knoxville: University of Tennessee Press, 1993.

McGreevy, John T. "Bronx Miracle." *American Quarterly* 52, no. 3 (September 2000): 405–443.

———. *Parish Boundaries: The Catholic Encounter with Race in the Twentieth-Century Urban North.* Chicago: University of Chicago Press, 1996.

McGuinness, Margaret M. "Let's Go to the Altar: American Catholics and the Eucharist, 1926–1976." In *Habits of Devotion: Catholic Religious Practice in Twentieth-Century America,* ed. James M. O'Toole, 187–235. Ithaca, NY: Cornell University Press, 2004.

Mercier, Jean-Pierre. "Who's Afraid of R. Crumb?" (1999). In Holm, *R. Crumb: Conversations,* 191–222.

Meyer, Birgit. "Mediation and the Genesis of Presence: Towards a Material Approach to Religion." Lecture from October 19, 2012, University of Utrecht. www2.hum.uu.nl/onderzoek/lezingenreeks/pdf/Meyer_Birgit_oratie.pdf.

Meyer, Richard E., ed. *Ethnicity and the American Cemetery.* Bowling Green, OH: Bowling Green State University Popular Press, 1993.

Mintz, Steven. *Huck's Raft: A History of American Childhood*. Cambridge, MA: Belknap Press of Harvard University Press, 2004.

Mishra, Pankaj. *The Romantics: A Novel*. New York: Random House, 2000.

A Missionary. "Frontier of the Faith—II. Mexicans' Backgrounds and Traits." *Social Justice Review* 45 (April 1952–March 1953): 65–67.

———. "Frontier of the Faith—III. Riches of the Mexican Soul." *Social Justice Review* 45 (July–August 1952): 105–107.

———. "Frontier of the Faith—IV. Living Conditions in the Southwest." *Social Justice Review* 45 (September 1952): 133–135.

Mitchell, Nathan, OSB. *Cult and Controversy: The Worship of the Eucharist Outside Mass*. New York: Pueblo Publishing, 1982.

Mitchell, W. J. T. *What Do Pictures Want? The Lives and Loves of Images*. Chicago: University of Chicago Press, 2005.

Moore, Brian. *Black Robe*. 1985. New York: Plume, 1997.

Morgan, David. *The Embodied Eye: Religious Visual Culture and the Social Life of Feeling*. Berkeley: University of California Press, 2012.

———, ed. *Icons of Protestantism: The Art of Warner Sallman*. New Haven, CT: Yale University Press, 1996.

———. *The Sacred Heart of Jesus: The Visual Evolution of a Devotion*. Amsterdam: Amsterdam University Press, 2008.

Morris, Charles R. *American Catholic: The Saints and Sinners Who Built America's Most Powerful Church*. New York: Times Books / Random House, 1997.

Morrisroe, Patricia. *Mapplethorpe: A Biography*. New York: Da Capo Press, 1995.

Mosqueda, Lawrence J. "Twentieth Century Arizona, Hispanics, and the Catholic Church." *U.S. Catholic Historian* 9, nos. 1 and 2 (Winter–Spring 1990): 87–103.

Moss, Candida R. *Ancient Christian Martyrdom: Diverse Practices, Theologies, and Traditions*. New Haven, CT: Yale University Press, 2012.

Nandy, Ashis. *Time Warps: Silent and Evasive Pasts in Indian Politics and Religion*. New Brunswick, NJ: Rutgers University Press, 2002.

Nava, Margaret M. "The 'Lourdes of America': Chimayo, New Mexico." *Liguorian* 83 (March 1995): 12–17.

Niebuhr, Reinhold. *Moral Man and Immoral Society: A Study in Ethics and Politics*. 1932. New York: Charles Scribner's Sons, 1960.

Nielsen, Francis W. *The Witness of St. Ansgar's: A Novel*. Hanover, NH: Steerforth Press, 2006.

Oates, Mary. "The Professional Preparation of Parochial School Sisters, 1870–1940." *Historical Journal of Massachusetts* 12, no. 1 (1984): 60–72.

O'Brien, David J. *Isaac Hecker: An American Catholic.* New York: Paulist Press, 1992.

Ochoa, Todd Ramón. *Society of the Dead: Quita Manaquita and Palo Praise in Cuba.* Berkeley: University of California Press, 2010.

O'Connell, Marvin R. *The Counter-Reformation, 1559–1610.* New York: Harper Torchbooks, 1974.

O'Connor, Flannery. *The Habit of Being: Letters of Flannery O'Connor.* Edited by Sally Fitzgerald. New York: Farrar, Straus, Giroux, 1979.

O'Malley, John, SJ. *Trent and All That: Renaming Catholicism in the Early Modern Era.* Cambridge, MA: Harvard University Press, 2000.

———. *The World of Catholic Renewal, 1540–1770.* Cambridge, UK: Cambridge University Press, 1998.

Ong, Walter J., SJ. *The Presence of the Word: Some Prolegomena for Cultural and Religious History.* New Haven, CT: Yale University Press, 1967.

Orsi, Robert A. *Between Heaven and Earth: The Religious Worlds People Make and the Scholars Who Study Them.* Princeton, NJ: Princeton University Press, 2005.

———. " 'The Infant of Prague's Nightie': The Devotional Origins of Contemporary Catholic Memory." *U.S. Catholic Historian* 21, no. 2 (Spring 2003): 1–18.

———. *The Madonna of 115th Street: Faith and Community in Italian Harlem, 1880–1950.* 3rd ed. New Haven, CT: Yale University Press, 2010. First published 1985.

———. *Thank You, St. Jude: Women's Devotion to the Patron Saint of Hopeless Causes.* New Haven, CT: Yale University Press, 1996.

———. "U.S. Catholics between Memory and Modernity." In *Catholics in the American Century: Recasting Narratives of U.S. History,* ed. R. Scott Appleby and Kathleen Sprows Cummings, 11–42. Ithaca, NY: Cornell University Press, 2012.

Ossa-Richardson, Anthony. "From Servius to Frazer: The Golden Bough and Its Transformations." *International Journal of the Classical Tradition* 15, no. 3 (September 2008): 339–368.

O'Toole, James M. *The Faithful: A History of Catholics in America.* Cambridge, MA: Belknap Press of Harvard University Press, 2008.

———, ed. *Habits of Devotion: Catholic Religious Practice in Twentieth-Century America.* Ithaca, NY: Cornell University Press, 2004.

Pagden, Anthony. *European Encounters with the New World: From Renaissance to Romanticism.* New Haven, CT: Yale University Press, 1993.

————. *The Fall of Natural Man: The American Indian and the Origins of Comparative Ethnology*. Cambridge, UK: Cambridge University Press, 1982.

Pallasmaa, Juhani. *The Thinking Hand: Existential and Embodied Wisdom in Architecture*. West Sussex, UK: John Wiley and Sons, 2009.

Pangilinan, Christian. "A Laboratory for Legal Education: The Graduate Program at Georgetown Law." Washington, DC: Georgetown University Law Center Office of Graduate Programs, 2012.

Pasulka, Diana Walsh. *Heaven Can Wait: Purgatory in Catholic Devotional and Popular Culture*. New York: Oxford University Press, 2014.

Pehl, Matthew. "'Apostles of Fascism,' 'Communist Clergy,' and the UAW: Political Ideology and Working-Class Religion in Detroit, 1919–1945." *Journal of American History* 99 (September 2012): 440–465.

Pelikan, Jaroslav. *The Christian Tradition: A History of the Development of Doctrine*. Vol. 3, *The Growth of Medieval Theology (600–1300)*. Chicago: University of Chicago Press, 1978.

Perry, Nicholas, and Loreto Echeverría. *Under the Heel of Mary*. New York: Routledge, 1988.

Phillips, Adam. *Terror and Experts*. Cambridge, MA: Harvard University Press, 1995.

————. *Winnicott*. Cambridge, MA: Harvard University Press, 1988.

Pietz, William. "The Problem of the Fetish, I." *RES: Anthropology and Aesthetics* 9 (Spring 1985): 5–17.

————. "The Problem of the Fetish, II: The Origin of the Fetish." *RES: Anthropology and Aesthetics* 13 (Spring 1987): 23–45.

————. "The Problem of the Fetish, IIIa: Bosman's Guinea and the Enlightenment Theory of Fetishism." *RES: Anthropology and Aesthetics* 16 (Autumn 1988): 105–122.

Pirotte, Jean. "Les images de dévotion du XVe siècle à nos jours: Introduction à l'étude d'un media." In *Imagiers de paradis: Images de piété populaires du XVe au XXe siècle*, 11–76. Bastogne, Belgium: Musée en Piconrue, Crédit Communal, 1990.

Podles, Leon J. *Sacrilege: Sexual Abuse in the Catholic Church*. Baltimore: Crossland Press, 2008.

Polner, Murray, and Jim O'Grady. *Disarmed and Dangerous: The Radical Lives and Times of Daniel and Philip Berrigan, Brothers in Religious Faith and Civil Disobedience*. New York: Basic Books, 1997.

Porter, Roy. *Mind-Forg'd Manacles: A History of Madness from the Restoration to the Regency.* Cambridge, MA: Harvard University Press, 1987.

Potter, G. R. *Zwingli.* Cambridge, UK: Cambridge University Press, 1976.

Poust, Mary Ann. "It Was 'Wrong.'" *Catholic New York,* April 9, 1998. http://cny.org/stories/It-Was-Wrong,2636?content_source=&category_id= &search_filter=&event_mode=&event_ts_from=&list_type=&order _by=&order_sort=&content_class=&sub_type=stories&town_id=%20 But%20of%20course%20it%20happens%20every%20day%20without%20 any%20onotoriety.

Power, Cornelius Michael. *The Blessing of Cemeteries: An Historical Synopsis and Commentary.* Washington, DC: Catholic University of America Press, 1943.

Preus, J. Samuel. *Explaining Religion: Criticism and Theory from Bodin to Freud.* New Haven, CT: Yale University Press, 1987.

Register, Cheri. *Living with Chronic Illness: Days of Patience and Passion.* New York: Free Press, 1987.

Reinburg, Virginia. *French Book of Hours: Making an Archive of Prayer, c. 1400–1600.* Cambridge, UK: Cambridge University Press, 2012.

Riccobono, F., and A. Sarica. *Immagini devote in Sicilia.* Messina, Italy: Edas, 1982.

Ricoeur, Paul. *Oneself as Another.* Translated by Kathleen Blamey. Chicago: University of Chicago Press, 1992.

Rivas-Rodriguez, Maggie, ed. *Mexican Americans and World War II.* Austin: University of Texas Press, 2005.

Roberts, Oral. *Expect a Miracle: My Life and Ministry.* Nashville: Thomas Nelson, 1995.

Rodriguez, Richard. *Hunger of Memory: The Education of Richard Rodriguez, a Memoir.* New York: Bantam Books, 1982.

Rogers, Annie. *The Unsayable: The Hidden Language of Trauma.* New York: Random House, 2006.

Rosenbaum-Dondaine, Catherine. *L'image de piété en France: 1814–1914.* Paris: Musée-galerie de la SEITA, 1984.

Rubin, Miri. *Corpus Christi: The Eucharist in Late Medieval Culture.* Cambridge, UK: Cambridge University Press, 1991.

———. *Gentile Tales: The Narrative Assault on Late Medieval Jews.* New Haven, CT: Yale University Press, 1999.

Sachs, Lynne. *Investigation of a Flame: A Documentary Portrait of the Catonsville 9.* Directed, produced, and edited by Lynne Sachs. First Run / Icarus Films, 2001.

Salisbury, Joyce E. *The Blood of Martyrs: Unintended Consequences of Ancient Violence*. New York: Routledge, 2004.

Samuel, Lawrence R. *Death, American Style: A Cultural History of Dying in America*. Lanham, MD: Rowman and Littlefield Publishers, 2013.

Sandoval, Moisés. "The Organization of a Hispanic Church." In *Hispanic Catholic Culture in the U.S.: Issues and Concerns*, ed. Jay P. Dolan and Allan Figueroa Deck, SJ, 131–165. South Bend, IN: University of Notre Dame Press, 1994.

Sartre, Jean-Paul. *Search for a Method*. Translated by Hazel E. Barnes. New York: Vintage Books, 1963.

Sawday, Jonathan. *The Body Emblazoned: Dissection and the Human Body in Renaissance Culture*. New York: Routledge, 1995.

Scarry, Elaine. *The Body in Pain: The Making and Unmaking of the World*. New York: Oxford University Press, 1985.

Scheper Hughes, Jennifer. *Biography of a Mexican Crucifix: Lived Religion and Local Faith from the Conquest to the Present*. New York: Oxford University Press, 2010.

Schloesser, Stephen, SJ. *Jazz Age Catholicism: Mystic Modernity in Postwar Paris, 1919–1933*. Toronto: University of Toronto Press, 2005.

Schmalz, Matthew N. "Performing the Miraculous in Central Massachusetts." In *Practicing Catholic: Ritual, Body, and Contestation in Catholic Faith*, ed. Bruce T. Morrill, Joanna E. Ziegler, and Susan Rodgers, 139–241. New York: Palgrave Macmillan, 2006.

———. "The Silent Body of Audrey Santo." *History of Religions* 42 (2002): 116–142.

Schmidt, Leigh Eric. *Hearing Things: Religion, Illusion, and the American Enlightenment*. Cambridge, MA: Harvard University Press, 2000.

Schmitt, Karl M., ed. *The Roman Catholic Church in Modern Latin America*. New York: Alfred A. Knopf, 1972.

Schroth, Raymond A., SJ. *The American Jesuits: A History*. New York: New York University Press, 2007.

Schultz, Kevin M. *Tri-Faith America: How Catholics and Jews Held Postwar America to Its Protestant Promise*. New York: Oxford University Press, 2011.

Schwaller, John Frederick. *The History of the Church in Latin America: From Conquest to Revolution and Beyond*. New York: New York University Press, 2011.

Schwartz, Daniel. "Timeline: The Books Have Been Burning—A Timeline of 2,200 Years of Book Burnings, from Ancient China to the Book of Negroes."

CBC News, September 10, 2010. www.cbc.ca/news/world/the-books-have -been-burning-1.887172.

Scott, Joan Wallach. *The Fantasy of Feminist History.* Durham, NC: Duke University Press, 2011.

Scull, Andrew, Charlotte MacKenzie, and Nicholas Hervey. *Masters of Bedlam: The Transformation of the Mad-Doctoring Trade.* Princeton, NJ: Princeton University Press, 1996.

Seagraves, Laura Roxanne. "A Bit about Dirt: Pilgrimage and Popular Religion at El Santuario Chimayo." PhD diss., Graduate Theological Union, Berkeley, California, 2002.

Sedensky, Matt. "Neighborhood Report: Bronxdale; Solace, Pilgrims, and Maybe a Cure, at a Grotto in the Bronx." *New York Times,* October 28, 2001. www.nytimes.com/2001/10/28/nyregion/neighborhood-report-bro nxdale-solace-pilgrims-maybe-cure-grotto-bronx.html.

Segundo, Juan Luis. "The Shift within Latin American Theology." *Journal of Theology for Southern Africa* 52 (1985): 17–29.

Seitz, John C. *No Closure: Catholic Practice and Boston's Parish Shutdowns.* Cambridge, MA: Harvard University Press, 2011.

Seligman, Adam B., Robert P. Weller, Michael J. Puett, and Bennett Simon. *Ritual and Its Consequences: An Essay on the Limits of Sincerity.* New York: Oxford University Press, 2008.

Sennett, Richard, and Jonathan Cobb. *The Hidden Injuries of Class.* New York: Random House, 1972.

Sergi, Joe. "1948: The Year that Comics Met Their Match." Comic Book League Defense Fund, June 8, 2012. http://cbldf.org/2012/06/1948-the-year-comics -met-their-match/.

Sharf, Robert H. "Experience." In Taylor, *Critical Terms for Religious Studies,* 94–116.

Sharpe, Eric J. *Comparative Religion: A History.* 1975. La Salle, IL: Open Court, 1986.

Shelley, Thomas J. *Greenwich Village Catholics: St. Joseph's Church and the Evolution of an Urban Faith Community, 1829–2002.* Washington, DC: Catholic University of America Press, 2003.

Shengold, Leonard. *Soul Murder: The Effects of Childhood Abuse and Deprivation.* New Haven, CT: Yale University Press, 1989.

Sherry, Gerard E. "The Blessed Earth at Chimayo." *Our Sunday Visitor* 79 (April 21, 1991): 12–13.

Shorter, Edward. *Bedside Manners: The Troubled History of Doctors and Patients.* New York: Simon and Schuster, 1985.

———. *From Paralysis to Fatigue: A History of Psychosomatic Illness in the Modern Era.* New York: Free Press, 1992.

Silber, Joan. *The Art of Time in Fiction: As Long as It Takes.* Minneapolis: Graywolf Press, 2009.

Simpson, Richard. *Edmund Campion: A Biography.* London: John Hodges, 1896.

Sister Mary Ann Walsh, RSM. *From Pope John Paul II to Benedict XVI: An Inside Look at the End of an Era, the Beginning of a New One, and the Future of the Church.* Lanham, MD: Sheed and Ward / Rowman and Littlefield Publishers, 2005.

Skinner, H. Catherine, and Anthony R. Berger, eds. *Geology and Health: Closing the Gap.* New York: Oxford University Press, 2003.

Sloane, David Charles. *The Last Great Necessity: Cemeteries in American History.* Baltimore: Johns Hopkins University Press, 1991.

Smith, Jonathan Z. *Imagining Religion: From Babylon to Jonestown.* Chicago: University of Chicago Press, 1982.

———. *Map Is Not Territory: Studies in the History of Religions.* Leiden, Netherlands: E. J. Brill, 1978.

———. "A Twice-Told Tale: The History of the History of Religion's History." In *Relating Religion: Essays in the Study of Religion,* 362–374. Chicago: University of Chicago Press, 2004.

Smith, Patti. *Just Kids.* New York: Ecco, 2010.

Sontag, Susan. *Illness as Metaphor.* New York: Vintage Books, 1978.

Sparrow, James T. *Warfare State: World War II Americans and the Age of Big Government.* Oxford: Oxford University Press, 2011.

Starr, Paul. *The Social Transformation of American Medicine.* New York: Basic Books, 1982.

Steiner, George. *Real Presences.* Chicago: University of Chicago Press, 1989.

Stocking, George W., Jr., ed. *Objects and Others: Essays on Museums and Material Culture.* Vol. 3 of *History of Anthropology.* Madison: University of Wisconsin Press, 1985.

———. *Victorian Anthropology.* New York: Free Press, 1987.

Straight, Bilinda. *Miracles and Extraordinary Experience in Northern Kenya.* Philadelphia: University of Pennsylvania Press, 2007.

Strenski, Ivan. *Thinking about Religion: An Historical Introduction to Theories of Religion.* Oxford: Blackwell Publishing, 2006.

Stroumsa, Guy G. *A New Science: The Discovery of Religion in the Age of Reason.* Cambridge, MA: Harvard University Press, 2010.

Taves, Ann. *Fits, Trances, and Visions: Experiencing Religion and Explaining Experience from Wesley to James.* Princeton, NJ: Princeton University Press, 1999.

Taylor, Charles. *A Secular Age.* Cambridge, MA: Belknap Press of Harvard University Press, 2007.

Taylor, Lawrence J. *Occasions of Faith: An Anthropology of Irish Catholics.* Philadelphia: University of Pennsylvania Press, 1995.

Taylor, Mark C., ed. *Critical Terms for Religious Studies.* Chicago: University of Chicago Press, 1998.

Tentler, Leslie Woodcock. *Catholics and Contraception: An American History.* Ithaca, NY: Cornell University Press, 2004.

———. *Seasons of Grace: A History of the Archdiocese of Detroit.* Detroit: Wayne State University Press, 1990.

Tepfer, Daniel. "Two Priests Disciplined in Shielding Sex Abuser, Both Knew Caribbean Location, Never Told [Bishop William E.] Lori." *Connecticut Post* (Bridgeport), September 1, 2002.

Theisen, Reinhold. *Mass Liturgy and the Council of Trent.* Collegeville, MN: St. John's University Press, 1965.

Thiemann, Ronald F. "Sacramental Realism: Martin Luther at the Dawn of Modernity." In *Lutherrenaissance: Past and Present,* ed. Christine Helmer and Bo Kristian Holm, 156–173. Forschungen zur Kirchen- und Dogmengeschichte 106. Göttingen, Germany: Vandenhoeck and Ruprecht, 2015.

Thurston, Herbert, SJ. *The Physical Phenomena of Mysticism.* Edited by J. H. Crehan, SJ. London: Burns Oates, 1952.

Tiele, C. P. *Elements of the Science of Religion,* pt. 1, *Morphological;* pt. 2, *Ontological.* Edinburgh: William Blackwood and Sons, 1897.

Todorov, Tzvetan. *The Conquest of America: The Question of the Other.* New York: Harper and Row, 1984.

Torgovnick, Marianna. *Gone Primitive: Savage Intellects, Modern Lives.* Chicago: University of Chicago Press, 1990.

———. *Primitive Passions: Men, Women, and the Quest for Ecstasy.* Chicago: University of Chicago Press, 1996.

Tornielli, Andrea. "Quella 'visita' di Padre Pio nella cella del cardinal Mindszenty." *La Stampa* [Vatican insider], July 2, 2014. http://vaticaninsider.lastampa.it/news/dettaglio-articolo/articolo/pio-pietrelcina-35037/.

Treviño, Roberto R. *The Church in the Barrio: Mexican American Ethno-Catholicism in Houston.* Chapel Hill: University of North Carolina Press, 2006.

Trouillot, Michel-Rolph. *Silencing the Past: Power and the Production of History.* Boston: Beacon Press, 1995.

Trujillo-Oviedo, Patricia. *Chimayó.* Charleston, SC: Arcadia Publishing, 2012.

Turner, Edith L. "Our Lady of Knock: Reflections of a Believing Anthropologist." *New Hibernia Review* 15 (Summer 2011): 121–125.

Tylor, Edward Burnett. *Religion in Primitive Culture.* 1871. Gloucester, MA: Peter Smith, 1970.

Unsworth, Tim. *The Last Priests in America: Conversations with Remarkable Men.* New York: Crossroad, 1991.

Vance, William L. *America's Rome.* Vol. 1, *Classical Rome;* Vol. 2, *Catholic and Contemporary Rome.* New Haven, CT: Yale University Press, 1989.

Van der Veer, Peter. *Imperial Encounters: Religion and Modernity in India and Britain.* Princeton, NJ: Princeton University Press, 2001.

Vecchi, Alberto. *Il culto della immagini nelle stampe popolari.* Biblioteca di Lares, vol. 26. Florence: L. S. Olschki, 1968.

Ventresca, Robert A. *Soldier of Christ: The Life of Pope Pius XII.* New Haven, CT: Yale University Press, 2013.

Vidal, Fernando. "Miracles, Science, and Testimony in Post-Tridentine Saint-Making." *Science in Context* 20, vol. 3 (2007): 481–508.

Vogt, Carl. *Begone, Satan! A Soul Stirring Account of Diabolical Possession in Iowa.* 1936. Rockford, IL: TAN Books, 1994.

Vovelle, Michel. *The Revolution against the Church: From Reason to the Supreme Being.* Translated by Alan José. Columbus: Ohio State University Press, 1991.

Wailoo, Keith. *Pain: A Political History.* Baltimore: Johns Hopkins University Press, 2014.

Walch, Timothy. *Parish School: American Catholic Parochial Education from Colonial Times to the Present.* New York: Crossroad Publishing, 1996.

Wall, Wendy L. *Inventing the "American Way": The Politics of Consensus from the New Deal to the Civil Rights Movement.* New York: Oxford University Press, 2008.

Walsh, Michael. *The Apparition at Knock: A Survey of Facts and Evidence.* Naas, Ireland: Leinster Leader, 1955.

Wandel, Lee Palmer. "The Body of Christ at Marburg, 1529." Unpublished paper.

———. *The Eucharist in the Reformation: Incarnation and Liturgy.* Cambridge, UK: Cambridge University Press, 2006.

Waugh, Evelyn. *Edmund Campion: A Life.* 1935. San Francisco: Ignatius Press, 2005.

Weaver, Mary Jo, and R. Scott Appleby, eds. *Being Right: Conservative Catholics in America.* Bloomington: Indiana University Press, 1995.

Weigel, George. *Witness to Hope: The Biography of Pope John Paul II.* New York: Cliff Street Books, 1999.

White, Joseph M. *The Diocesan Seminary in the United States: A History from the 1780s to the Present.* Notre Dame, IN: University of Notre Dame Press, 1989.

Willock, Ed. "North of the Border." *Mission Digest* 12 (March 1954): 5–8.

Wills, Gary. *Bare Ruined Choirs: Doubt, Prophecy, and Radical Religion.* Garden City, NY: Doubleday, 1972.

Wilson, Stephen. *The Magical Universe: Everyday Ritual and Magic in Pre-Modern Europe.* London: Hambleton and London, 2000.

Wiman, Christian. *My Bright Abyss: Meditation of a Modern Believer.* New York: Farrar, Straus and Giroux, 2013.

Winnicott, D. W. *The Maturational Process and the Facilitating Environment: Studies in the Theory of Emotional Development.* New York: International Universities Press, 1965.

———. *Playing and Reality.* London: Tavistock / Routledge, 1971.

Wittgenstein, Ludwig. *Remarks on Frazer's* Golden Bough. 1979. Translated by A. C. Miles, revised and edited by Rush Rhees. Atlantic Highlands, NJ: Humanities Press International, 1991.

Wolf, Hubert. *The Nuns of Sant'Ambrogio: The True Story of a Convent in Scandal.* Translated by Ruth Martin. New York: Alfred A. Knopf, 2015.

Wood, Alexander. "The History of Crumb." Edited and illustrated by Robert Crumb. The Official Crumb Site. www.crumbproducts.com/pages/about /history1.html.

Wright, Bradford W. *Comic Book Nation: The Transformation of Youth Culture in America.* Baltimore: Johns Hopkins University Press, 2001.

Wright, John B. "El Santuario de Chimayo: New Mexico's Lourdes." *FOCUS on Geography* 47, no. 2 (Winter 2002): 9–13.

Wright-Rios, Edward. *Revolutions in Mexican Catholicism: Reform and Revelation in Oaxaca, 1887–1934.* Durham, NC: Duke University Press, 2009.

Wuthnow, Robert. *Sharing the Journey: Support Groups and America's New Quest for Community.* New York: Free Press, 1994.

Young-Bruehl, Elisabeth. *Childism: Confronting Prejudice against Children.* New Haven, CT: Yale University Press, 2012.

————. *Hannah Arendt: For Love of the World.* New Haven, CT: Yale University Press, 1982.

————. *Why Arendt Matters.* New Haven, CT: Yale University Press, 2006.

Zimdars-Swartz, Sandra L. *Encountering Mary: From La Salette to Medjugorje.* Princeton, NJ: Princeton University Press, 1991.

ACKNOWLEDGMENTS

I am indebted to Harvard University and Northwestern University for providing me with essential research support, and to the efficient and long-suffering interlibrary loan offices at both institutions, without which this book truly would not have been possible.

I thank in particular the Duda family, who endowed the Grace Craddock Nagle chair in Catholic Studies at Northwestern, which I now occupy. Research funds associated with the chair supported much of the later research for the book. A grant from the Social Science Research Council, under the auspices of its New Directions in the Study of Prayer project in which it was my privilege to participate, underwrote research for the final chapter. The first steps in this project were taken over dinner with Sharmila Sen of Harvard University Press, at Casablanca, in Cambridge. As Rick says to Captain Louis Renault at the end of the eponymous movie, I had the feeling this was the beginning of a beautiful friendship, and so it was. Sharmila is a brilliant editor, with an unerring eye for where arguments fail, prose stumbles, and coherence falls away. I have benefited enormously from her critical acumen, wisdom, and warmth. Liza Debevec, Roger Ferlo, Anna-Karina Hermkens, Willy Jansen, Adam R. Nelson, Catrien Notermans, John L. Rudolph, and Samuli Schielke offered me the opportunity to publish sections of this work, in embryonic form, in volumes they were editing. Randall J. Stephens and Donald A. Yerxa, former editors of the wonderfully provocative but now sadly defunct *Historically Speaking,* and Robert Wilson of the *American Scholar* gave me space in their respective journals to test drive my inchoate ideas about abundant historiography at a very early stage. My old friend Rich Remsberg, a great photographer and photo-researching genius, located the book's most compelling images. That is, with the sole exception of the picture of the Sacred Heart of Jesus, which was David Morgan's contribution, together with his infallible guidance in identifying and dating holy cards and his rich work on Catholic material and visual culture. The late Marilyn McCord Adams, Constance Furey, and Don Yerxa read the penultimate version of the manuscript and provided timely comments. Lee Palmer Wandel responded graciously to a fellow historian's SOS, which reached her in Augsburg of all places, and at very short notice read over my discussion of the sixteenth- and seventeenth-century debates about the nature of the divine presence in the Host. Having noted Lee's extraordinary generosity, I must state especially clearly that any remaining errors of interpretation on this subject are mine. I have been blessed once again in my graduate research assistants, first Brian J. Clites and Matthew J. Cressler, and more recently, T. R. Noddings and the indefatigable Stephanie N. Brehm.

During the time of the writing of this book, I lost two of my dearest friends, John McRae and Anthony Stellato. In the words of the Catholic funeral rite, my friendships with both men did not end with their deaths; they changed. I wish I could fully believe this, as I sometimes tell an image of Tony that sits on the bookshelf in front of my desk, but he reminds me that belief has nothing to do with it. On what turned out to be his last day but one on earth, Tony told me that what he most regretted about dying was that there were so many books still to read. I grieve that he and John are not here to read this one. Although I cannot mention their names, I am indebted to the men and women I came to know in several fieldwork contexts over the years, who trusted me with their memories of growing up Catholic; talked to me about and often invited me to join them in their devotional practices; dragged out old boxes filled with holy cards, parochial school religion practice sheets, rosaries, missals, and more; and hosted and fed me. Most recently I have been working among men and women who were abused as children by priests. I am deeply grateful to them for their courage, and their patience, in helping me to understand the often-lifelong religious consequences of the violence done to them as children by God's special representatives on earth.

A circle of good friends accompanied me all the way through the researching, mulling, fretting, writing, fretting, mulling . . . right up to the finish line(s). I thank in particular Jason and Nina Bivins, Jeremy and Christine Bloomfield, John Efron, Elliott Gorn, Teresa Pitt Green, Ed Hoke and the late Jennifer Locascio, Jeff Keller, Terence McKiernan, and especially Jeff Isaac and Bill Reese. My family's love is the most sustaining presence of all in my life, surrounding me every day: my older son, Clarence, who has long been my most cherished conversation partner and whose own writing is an inspiration to me; his partner, Abigail Brackins; my younger son, Anthony, whose crazy sense of humor, many passions, keen intelligence, and ebullient joy have for a decade been a bottomless wellspring of delight in my life; my brother Francis, his wife, Cathy, and my niece, Jessica; and my father, Mario, who is not only a deep reservoir of Catholic devotional objects but a great storyteller, too. My beloved wife, Christine Helmer, who fortunately for me is a distinguished scholar of religion as well as my dear partner, read (more than one time) and commented on every line of this text, giving me the tremendous benefit of her deep learning, insight, and intellectual rigor, all shot through with love, which is her greatest gift to me. The book is dedicated to her.

Chapter 6 is a slightly revised version of "The Happiness of Heaven," a chapter I contributed to *Heaven,* edited by Roger Ferlo and published by Seabury Books in 2007. I thank Seabury Books for their permission to republish the text here.

INDEX

Death *(continued)*
  299n5; relationship between
  Mary and, 180–182, 303–304n28
De Certeau, Michel, 64
Demonic mimesis of Catholic
  sacraments, accusations of by
  early modern Catholic mission-
  aries, 33–34
"Detroit housewife," 83–86, 89–92,
  93–100, 101, 107, 280–281n11
Devotional eroticism, 217
Devotionalism, 21–22, 27–28, 149;
  Marian, 52–57
Devotional relationships, 66–67
Devotional visualization, 138–139
Dirt: from el Santuario de Chimayo,
  76–77, 81, 82, 92–93, 102, 108;
  consumption of, 280n10
Dooley, Kate, 176
Double directionality, in relations
  between humans and the divine,
  107, 240–241
Doubt, religious 210–213
Dramas, of sacred stories, for
  children, 135

EBay, 116
Ejaculations, pious (spontaneous
  prayer), 127
El posito, 78, 81, 103, 105, 279nn3,4
Enchantment, pre-modern, 37
Eroticism, devotional, 217
Eucharist: and access to presence,
  1–2; debate regarding, 2–4,
  16–20; internecine controversy
  regarding nature of, 9; and
  meaning of real presence, 9;

internal criticism of "superstition" and purity of, 27; coloring
  books of, 131; rosary and, 173;
  those present at, 215; priest and,
  216; as social event, 216–217;
  sexual abuse victims' attachment to, 227–228; sexual abuse
  victims' alienation from, 224–225;
  as not safe for survivors of
  clerical sexual abuse, 221–222;
  renewal of, 234; returning
  to, 245
Eucharistic Congress, 28th International (1926), in Chicago,
  14–15
Evangelical Protestant reformers,
  22–23
Exorcist, The, 159
Extreme unction, sacrament of,
  113, 170
Extreme unction crucifix, 165–166

Faggioli, Massimo, 234
Family Rosary Crusade, 99–101
Fetiços, 34–35
Fetish, 34–36, 82, 268n39
First Communion: preparation for,
  125–126, 154; certificates com-
  memorating, 134
Flash cards, 133–134
Frawley, Mary Gail, 225
Frazer, Sir James George, 63–64,
  267–268n36, 276n19
Funeral directors, 175–176
Funeral homes, American Catholic
  ambivalence toward, 175–177,
  184, 185, 302n20

Norris, Robert, Rev., pastor of Saint
Lucy's, Bronx, New York, 52
Nuestra Señora de Guadalupe, 31, 55

O'Connor, Cardinal John, 1–2, 46
O'Connor, Flannery, 44–45, 46
O'Konski, Margaret, 180
O'Toole, James, 235
Our Lady of Fatima, 50, 55–56, 101
Our Lady of Guadalupe, 31, 55,
266n31
Our Lady of Lourdes, 52–54, 56–57,
60, 112
Our Lady of Medjugorje, 50

Paganism, American Catholic
accusations of modernity as,
33–37, 115, 124, 130
Paul IV, Pope, 120
Paul VI, Pope, 120
Penmanship, and children's religious
formation, 135–136
Peoples of presence, approach of, to
works of culture, 149–151
Peyton, Patrick, Father, 99–100
Phillips, Adam, 97, 98, 110
Picture books, for Catholic children,
131–132
Pietz, William, 34–35, 268n39
Pilgrims: to Marian shrines, 49–50,
54; to Lourdes, 52, 70; to El
Santuario de Chimayo, 75,
77–79, 82, 102–105; to home of
Audrey Santo, 195–196; to shrine
for dead monk, 251–252
Pio of Pietrelcina, Santo, holy cards
of, 120–122

Playing, in D. W. Winnicott's
understanding, 225–226
Pontifical Association of the Holy
Childhood, 133
Potter, G. R., 23
Prayer: as dialogic, 97; of pilgrims to
El Santuario de Chimayo,
103–104; aspiratory, 142; for
souls in purgatory, 171–172, 195,
301n14; of sexual abuse victims,
223–224; angry, 232; difficulty
of, 247
Prayer books, cards, and pamphlets,
for children, 131
"Prayer Cards for Dying Non-
Catholics," 165
"Prayer Service for a Christian
Wake," following Vatican II, 184
Presence: Church efforts to control,
2; debates over Christ's real, 2–4,
249; as norm of human existence, 6–7; versus real presence,
8–10; divergent conceptions of,
9; conflict over meaning of,
16–18; doctrine of, in sixteenth
century and afterward, 18–22;
longing for, 43–44
Priest: A Bridge to God, The (Benedict XVI), 308–309n1
Priesthood, Protestant reformers'
rejection of Catholic doctrine
of, 216
Priest(s): power and authority of,
216; sexual abuse and intimacies with, 217–220; decline in
status of, 233–234. See also
Sexual abuse